Chinese Cinema

Crossings: Asian Cinema and Media Culture

Editors: Po-Shek Fu (University of Illinois, Urbana-Champaign) and Man-Fung Yip
(University of Oklahoma)

The series "Crossings" publishes books in English and Chinese that investigate Asian cinema and media from cross-disciplinary and cross-methodological perspectives. It situates Asian cinema and media within a global or regional framework and explores different dimensions of transnationality in relation to production, distribution, and reception. It also entails trans-medial interrogations of past and present media culture, looking into the complex interactions of media forms and how they have shaped aesthetic and social practices. Wide-ranging in scope and method, the series places special emphasis on cutting-edge scholarship that draws on careful archival research or derives from vigorous, insightful theoretical study.

Books in the series:

Chinese Cinema: Identity, Power, and Globalization
Edited by Jeff Kyong-McClain, Russell Meeuf, and Jing Jing Chang

Malaysian Cinema in the New Millennium: Transcendence beyond Multiculturalism
Adrian Yuen Beng Lee

Remapping the Sinophone: The Cultural Production of Chinese-Language Cinema in Singapore and Malaya before and during the Cold War
Wai-Siam Hee

Screening Communities: Negotiating Narratives of Empire, Nation, and the Cold War in Hong Kong Cinema
Jing Jing Chang

Chinese Cinema

Identity, Power, and Globalization

Edited by Jeff Kyong-McClain, Russell Meeuf,
and Jing Jing Chang

Hong Kong University Press
The University of Hong Kong
Pokfulam Road
Hong Kong
https://hkupress.hku.hk

© 2022 Hong Kong University Press

ISBN 978-988-8528-53-0 (*Hardback*)

British Library Cataloguing-in-Publication Data
A catalogue record for this book is available from the British Library.

10 9 8 7 6 5 4 3 2 1

Printed and bound by J&S Printing Co., Ltd. in Hong Kong, China

Contents

Acknowledgments

The chapters here were initially presented at a conference on the global contexts informing Chinese cinema held at the University of Idaho in the spring of 2019. Funding for the conference was provided by the College of Letters, Arts and Social Sciences, the Confucius Institute, and the Division of Strategic Enrollment Management at the University of Idaho. We would like to thank the following University of Idaho faculty and staff who helped make the conference possible: Mikayla Frey, Dale Graden, Robin Johnson, Dean Kahler, Sean Quinlan, and Hexian Xue. Additionally, many thanks are due to the participants whose wonderful contributions to the conference do not appear in this collection: Nikki J. Y. Lee, Erich Schwartzel, Julian Stringer, Liying Sun, Kristof Van den Troost, and Min Hui Yeo. Po-Shek Fu and Stanley Rosen not only brought their experience and knowledge to the initial conference but have provided a thoughtful epilogue here, and have provided advice and encouragement as we have brought this collection to print. Finally, we very much appreciate the editorial and production work of the staff at Hong Kong University Press, especially that of Kenneth Yung.

Introduction

Jeff Kyong-McClain, Russell Meeuf, and Jing Jing Chang

As this volume took shape, film industry analysts were busy declaring China the largest film market in the world, since box office receipts in the People's Republic of China would soon overtake those in the US.[1] This one metric, of course, cannot tell a nuanced story about the ascendant Chinese film industry in the early twenty-first century, but it certainly fed a popular narrative in the Western press about the increasing power and global reach of the Chinese film industry and China more broadly. The need for Hollywood blockbusters to make money in the growing Chinese market, alongside the increase in Chinese investment in US film production, tells a story in which the Chinese film industry is steadily encroaching upon Hollywood's long-held position as the dominant player in the global film industry.

This narrative, however, simplifies the complex cultural and economic relationships of the global film industry, pitting two monolithic visions of seemingly "national" cinemas ("China" versus "Hollywood") against each other in an epic battle worthy of contemporary global blockbusters. But just as Hollywood is a complex, global industry, in reality the Chinese film industry is multifaceted and diverse, has a long history of engagement with global film industries, and has been influenced by other world cinemas such as Hollywood as much as it has influenced them. Moreover, its recent successes have only come through a long period of negotiation with global market forces as it navigates its identity comprising both semi-private and state-sponsored production companies. To understand the role of China in global cinema today, one must extend a nationalistic lens to tell the nuanced stories of both the Chinese film industry and the interconnected nature of global, commercial filmmaking.

It is worth keeping in mind that the global reach of the contemporary Chinese film industry is part of a much longer history of Chinese engagement with the world. Although Marx and Engels wrote of the European bourgeoisie's necessary role in "batter[ing] down all Chinese walls," suggesting a China hopelessly closed off from the rest of the world, in fact, the argument can be made that such apparent closure (be it late Qing or Maoist) is more an aberration than the norm.[2] Indeed, in the case of cinema, residents in Shanghai and Beijing were watching films almost as soon as they first appeared in France, and in no time at all a whole movie-going culture consuming both Chinese and foreign-made films emerged—this oft-noted fact suggests tight connectivity between China and the world.[3] Though Mao's "lean to one side" policy did largely cut off mainland China from global (though not Soviet) cinema, Sinophone cinema still flourished in places like Hong Kong and Taiwan, and Deng Xiaoping's 1978 policy of "reform and opening up" restored global engagement as the norm in the People's Republic. At the beginning of the twenty-first century, the exact place of China in the world seems somewhat in doubt, due in no small part to the rise of nationalist enthusiasm in all quarters of the globe. Political scientists debate the extent to which Beijing will want to engage the world in the near future, but the apparent ongoing commitment to a global capitalist order, even an American-led one, suggests that one can reasonably expect a continuation of China in the World and the World in China for the foreseeable future.[4] In light of China's long history of going global, it is imperative to investigate all aspects of the engagement, including the ways in which Chinese cinema engages global cinema.

This collection, then, explores the many entanglements of Chinese filmmaking with a variety of global influences, forces, and historical contexts. Exploring aesthetics, identities, audiences, industry, and politics, the essays here unpack the multifaceted ways that Chinese filmmaking has been interwoven with a host of local, national, and global histories and contexts. Although we are by no means the first group of scholars to explore the relationship between globalization and Chinese cinema, the essays in this book represent a fresh set of voices and perspectives on these questions. The research presented here, moreover, analyzes a diverse and innovative range of films and phenomena—from the possibilities of an emergent Chinese "ecocinema" and the transnational sampling of historical Chinese documentaries to the uses of language dialects in international coproductions, to name a few examples. In this way, this collection hopes to extend existing debates around Chinese cinema and globalization to new films, filmmakers, industry structures, and transnational influences.

Rethinking Chinese Cinema Historiography

This volume is indebted to the English-language scholarship on Chinese cinema since the pre-1980s.[5] These works explored the contours of Chinese cinema, asking questions like, What is Chinese cinema? How does Chinese cinema relate to different forms of cultural identities as Chinese or otherwise? How does Chinese cinema interact with other film industries? And how is Chinese cinema impacted by local, national, and global politics such as the Cultural Revolution, the Hong Kong handover, globalization, the Cold War, and other forces during various historical periods?[6]

Early on, the answers to these questions relied on the concept of national cinemas and were informed by Andrew Higson's seminal work.[7] From this perspective, films from various Chinese production centers were seen as representative of a unified national identity, and particular attention was paid to the cinemas of Greater China, including mainland China, Taiwan, and Hong Kong.[8] These foundational works introduced Western audiences and many Western scholars to the works of auteurs like Zhang Yimou, Chen Kaige, and Tian Zhuangzhuang from the Fifth Generation, as well as film movements such as Taiwan New Cinema and the Hong Kong New Wave. This approach tended to view the directors and products of Chinese cinema against the backdrop of Chinese nation-state politics. The national cinema model, in other words, presented at times a homogenous vision of Chinese identity while neglecting the contribution of Chinese language filmmaking in places such as Singapore, Malaya, and others during and after the Cold War.[9]

Since the 1990s, scholars of Chinese cinema (in both English and Chinese) have employed a broader array of methodologies that built on, revised, and at times moved beyond the national cinema paradigm. These methodologies have not only changed the ways that scholars have studied Chinese cinema, but have opened up new ways of understanding what constitutes Chinese cinema itself. Song Hwee Lim, for instance, identifies six different conceptions of Chinese cinemas used by scholars to understand its scope over the past thirty years.[10] The first three concepts use a Chinese national cinema model to demarcate different forms of Chinese cinema: (1) Chinese cinema(s), which focus on mainland China, Taiwan, and Hong Kong as well as the Chinese diaspora; (2) Taiwan cinema under Japanese colonial rule; and (3) Hong Kong cinema before and after the 1997 handover. The additional three concepts, however, acknowledge the complex array of cinematic practices that cross or transcend national borders. The fourth model includes transnational Chinese cinemas and Chinese-language cinema, taking into account the border-crossing processes of production, distribution, and reception.[11] This model includes the production and reception of films made in the Chinese language within Greater China and beyond, incorporating the production and reception of films of the Chinese diaspora as well as transnational collaborations: for instance, this conception would include films by Singapore director Eric Khoo. The fifth model focuses exclusively on diasporic cinema, including Chinese film productions distributed for overseas Chinese consumption or films made within the Chinese diaspora.[12] And the sixth model is Sinophone cinema, which includes all Chinese-language films produced outside of China.[13] These overlapping models illustrate the complexity informing the very definition of "Chinese cinema" as a concept and practice.[14]

As these different models suggest, scholars' understanding of Chinese cinema since the late 1990s has been most influenced by theories of transnational cinema and a transnational understanding of Sinophone cinema.[15] Sheldon Lu's groundbreaking 1997 publication *Transnational Chinese Cinemas*, for example, has massively influenced the field of Chinese cinema studies.[16] The transnational turn has yielded studies that move the site of production, distribution, and reception beyond Greater China, situating the study of Chinese "cinemas" in the plural form within the contexts of East Asian and Asian cinema, women's cinema, action stars and directors, affect and embodiment studies, and Asian and Asian American identities, among many others.[17]

Of course, by positioning Chinese cinema in a global or transnational context, such approaches must often reckon with the relationship between Chinese cinema and Hollywood as one of the other globally dominant film industries. In various anthologies addressing global cinema, for example, there is a tendency to pit Hollywood (seen as mainstream) against non-Hollywood (other national cinemas that have "adopted a different aesthetic model of filmmaking from Hollywood").[18] While attempting to grapple with the complex realities of transnational cinema production, this "Hollywood versus the world" approach to understanding trans-national cinema may in turn perpetuate its own monolithic narratives, deploying Hollywood as a singular, global force against which all other cinemas are measured.

Within Chinese film studies, despite an emphasis on the cross-cultural and transnational connections between Chinese cinema and diasporic communities, global film culture is often still seen as synonymous with Hollywood.[19] So while the turn toward a transnational understanding of Chinese cinema has attempted to de-center a homogenous perspective of Greater China and its culture, these approaches must also grapple with the tendency to see Hollywood as the "center" of global film culture against which all other global cinemas are measured, in addition to the tendency to condense a variety of Chinese cultures, languages, and identities into a seemingly unified national identity.[20]

Scholars of Chinese cinema have thus sought to redefine what constitutes the transnational and its relation to the local, national, and global, affirming Mette Hjort's call for a more nuanced understanding of transnationalism as a "scalar concept allowing for the recognition of strong or weak forms of transnational-ity."[21] Such work disavows a dichotomous connection between West and East in favor of polylocal, polycentric, relational, and multidirectional perspectives. For example, inspired by Ella Shohat and Robert Stam's concept of "polycentric mul-ticulturalism," the polycentric approach presented by Lucia Nagib, Chris Perriam, and Rajinder Dudrah seeks to challenge and present an alternative "third way" to the "dual model" pitting American Hollywood cinema as mainstream and the rest of world's film traditions as the periphery.[22] Similarly, Yingjin Zhang notes that in the age of "globalizing China," Chinese cinema is both "polylocal and translocal at different scales," from local to national and global across production, distribution, exhibition, and reception.[23] Zhang writes that "all localities across scale must be coordinated in an efficient way, and all disparate elements must weave together into a seamless screen product. It is a truism to declare that 'no film is an island.'"[24]

These nuanced approaches to transnationalism have engendered a more rela-tional perspective that challenges Hollywood's position as the homogenizing center against which Chinese cinema must always be measured. Cindy Hing-Yuk Wong's research on global film culture, for instance, de-centers Euro-American film festivals as arbiters of Chinese cinema. Western audiences certainly came to know of Fifth Generation film directors like Zhang Yimou and Chen Kaige, as well as new Taiwan filmmakers Edward Yang and Hou Hsiao-hsien, after their films either won European film festival awards or were nominated at the Oscars. However, Wong reminds us that such filmmakers and other examples of Sinophone cinema also participated in a variety of international festivals that helped spread the influence of Chinese language filmmakers.[25]

Moreover, in works by Michael Curtin, Wendy Su, and Aynne Kokas, Hollywood is no longer defined as the sole juggernaut of global media.[26] In Michael Curtin's *Playing to the World's Biggest Audience*, he presents "alternative accounts of global media" and refutes the idea that "Hollywood hegemony is forever."[27] In looking at how multinational media companies conduct their operations to reach the global Chinese audience, Curtin decenters Hollywood as a representative of global culture and global markets. Indeed, the history of Chinese cinema shows that the media center shifts and has not been tied solely to production location, but is transnational and very much connected with transborder processes of production, distribution, circulation, reception, and consumption. Similarly, Su and Kokas look at the encounter between China and Hollywood within the global media market not as one of American cultural imperialism but one where both China and Hollywood engage in negotiation, collaboration, and competition, vying for the hegemon position.[28] These studies engage with the relational connections between Chinese theory and Western theory, different media forms, cosmopolitanism, and the links between Chinese cinema and global issues like environmental change.[29]

Of course, despite these efforts to expand on the national cinema perspective and contend with the transcultural impact of globalization and various film movements, award-winning and even blockbuster films by Zhang Yimou, Ang Lee, or films that have crossed over to Hollywood through the endorsements of gatekeepers such as Quentin Tarantino have become oversaturated within Chinese film studies.[30] Studies that focus on films from the "periphery as a relational and shifting concept" or that "uncover the multiplicity of interactions that take place around and beyond the centers of power"—not only within the Chinese state but also the very academic disciplines of Chinese studies and Chinese film historiography—have been few and far in between.[31] Indeed, more emphasis certainly needs to be placed on Chinese independent documentary films or "sub-state" cinemas, including those made by ethnic minorities.[32]

This volume, therefore, moves beyond the singular focus on a particular period, genre, film studio, film auteur, film, political moment, or film movement, seeking out interconnections between Chinese cinema and larger global contexts. In doing so, we have two primary goals.

First, this book revisits the meaning of the global and what constitutes "Chineseness" in and beyond Chinese film culture. We agree with Jeroen de Kloet that "the 'Chineseness' of Chinese cinema is not just located in the text or its auteur, but also in both cinematic production and reception."[33] In particular, we focus on identity politics, global reception, and transnational influences on aesthetics and iconography from the past and present. As noted by Laikwan Pang, the problematization of Chinese national cinema did not always yield a rethinking of Chinese cinema as a field of study. Rather, Pang suggests, the critical positions challenging the paradigm of national Chinese cinema, ironically, only secured the place of such scholarship, institutionalizing Chinese cinema as a "coherent and legitimate academic discipline."[34] On the 10th anniversary of the publication of the *Journal of Chinese Cinemas*, therefore, Christopher K. Tong selected "scale" as his keyword to revisit the historiography and future trends of Chinese cinema studies, suggesting the need for more nuanced and less nationalistic perspectives on Chinese cinema: "Scale sheds light on the stakes of contemporary life by calling attention to the standards by which we judge an entity to be significant or meaningful."[35]

The second objective, therefore, is to explore the different scales and diverse patterns of transnationalism in relation to Chinese cinema in all its pluralities. However, instead of invoking Chinese "cinemas," this volume retains the singular form. This is because Chinese cinema is not seen merely as the sum of all instances of Chinese film productions in various production and exhibition sites (e.g., mainland China, Hong Kong, Taiwan, Chinese diaspora). Rather, this study situates Chinese cinema within a shifting and transmedial global context that takes into consideration the films' production, circulation, and reception milieus. This volume looks at the local and national in the global, and vice-versa, in all aspects of Chinese cinema as art and aesthetics, social practice and cultural imagination, politics and activism, industry and market—both in Chinese films and as "cited" in world cinema.[36]

The Chapters

To achieve these goals, this book explores the complex global relationships of Chinese cinema through four primary lenses, although each lens often spills over and informs the others: (1) politics and dissent in global contexts, (2) transnational reception, (3) globalization and Chinese identities, and (4) film markets and financial reform. These lenses allow a more scalar approach to the transnational influences that have yielded a variety of cinematic practices and economic structures in Chinese cinema over time. There is not a single set of global forces that have structured Chinese cinema over the years nor a monolithic vision of "Chinese cinema" itself; rather, there is a diverse set of influences and shifting global structures impacting local, national, and global contexts. The four lenses we deploy here attempt to approach the multifaceted and dynamic concept of Chinese cinema from different angles and perspectives, drawing out a series of complex scales of global influence. From these different perspectives, the essays in this book illustrate the multifaceted ways that Chinese cinematic practices straddle the intersections of local, national, and global influences.

The first section explores a series of transnational circuits and influences underpinning cinema and political critique of China and the Chinese government. Contrasted with the tightly regulated and controlled mainland Chinese film industry, these essays explore moments of cinematic critique and dissent in which transnational filmmaking, art, and activism intersect with Chinese cinema and politics. In its exploration of a transnational sampling of historical Chinese documentaries, underground films about Hong Kong activism, to coproduced, and environmentally conscious Chinese art cinema, this section interrogates the transnational dynamics of political critique in cinematic practices at the margins of Chinese cinema.

Chapter 1, "Seeing (through) the Struggle Sessions: Cinema, Recycling, and Transnational Circulation," explores the intersections between cinema and *pidouhui*: sessions of mass denunciation in which those labeled as class enemies were accused and tormented in public. Analyzing the cinematic nature of such political theater along with the global circulation of images of *pidouhui*, Belinda Qian He tracks a variety of *pidouhui* images—both fictional and recycled, "found" footage images—within Chinese media and across national borders. These mediated references to *pidouhui* engage a variety of audiences in debates around historical memory and politics, according to He. From depictions of *pidouhui* in the 2018 Chinese film *Forever Young* (*Wuwen xi dong*, dir. Li Fangfang), to a parody of *pidouhui* in the 1974 French comedy *Chinese in Paris* (*Les Chinois à Paris*, dir. Jean Yanne), to the recycling of historical *pidouhui* footage across a range of documentaries, this chapter interrogates the global sampling and recycling of *pidouhui* imagery in disparate ideological contexts, showing how these cinematic allusions tell us more about their deployment and their audiences than they actually document the history and politics of Mao's China.

Joseph Tse-Hei Lee continues this discussion of cinema and dissent in Chapter 2, "Screening Politics in Hong Kong," by analyzing a series of international films focused on the youthful rebellion of the Umbrella Movement in Hong Kong in the 2010s. From low-budget, independent Hong Kong films such as *Ten Years* (*Shi nian*, dir. Kwok Zune, Fei-Pang Wong, Jevons Au, Kwun-Wai Chow, and Ka-Leung Ng, 2015) to internationally produced documentaries *Lesson in Dissent* (dir. Matthew Torne, 2014) and *Joshua: Teenager vs. Superpower* (dir. Joe Piscatella, 2017), this chapter demonstrates the power of cinema to articulate not only political critiques of Chinese authoritarianism in Hong Kong but also an emerging vision of Hong Kong identity that is caught between global, national, and local politics. These cinematic texts and the subjects they depict, Lee argues, have shaped a compelling model of local identity and civic engagement for young people in Hong Kong grappling with the city's colonial past, tumultuous present, and uncertain future.

Chapter 3 also situates critical Chinese cinema practices within a global network of art and activism, in this case Zhao Liang's 2015 film *Behemoth* (*Beixi moshou*) and its relationship to the aesthetics of global "ecocinema." In this final chapter of Part I, "'All of Us Are Part of the Monster': Toxic Sublimity and Ethical Reflexivity in Zhao Liang's *Behemoth*," Man-Fung Yip explores the aesthetic and affective functions of *Behemoth*, a documentary that eschews a traditional documentary format to present lyrical, beautifully crafted images of environmental destruction and decay without commentary or extensive narration. Yip offers a detailed analysis of the film's visual imagery and narrative arc that embeds *Behemoth* within a set of global artistic movements and cultural referents, from its use of the "toxic sublime" to its invocation of Dante's *Divine Comedy*, to articulate the film's political critique. For this French-funded Chinese film that was intended primarily for audiences on the international film festival circuit, its critiques of Chinese and global environmental destruction are entwined in a larger global framework of activist artistic practices.

In the next main section, the book turns its attention to the critical reception of Chinese film and the ways that audiences engage with transnational cinema. The essays in this section explore how various Chinese films exist alongside global cinema and global genres, with a particular emphasis on reception and aesthetics. How have audiences and critics understood Chinese cinema in relation to transnational cinema practices and global film styles?

Chapter 4, "From *Gone with the Wind* to *The Spring River Flows East*: Melodrama and Historical Imagination in Postwar Chinese Cinema," explores the global contexts of melodrama as a transnational storytelling tradition. Analyzing the 1947 film *The Spring River Flows East* (*Yi jiang chun shui xiang dong liu*, dir. Cai Chusheng and Zheng Junli), Kenny Ng compares the critical reception of local, Chinese melodrama with the Chinese reception of *Gone with the Wind* (dir. Victor Fleming, 1939). In this way, Ng shows how Chinese cinema in this period negotiated the leftist dictates of film critics as well as the popular appeal of big-budget, Western, sentimental romances such as *Gone with the Wind*. *The Spring River Flows East*, Ng argues, uses the melodramatic mode to navigate issues of gender, family, and national identity in conversation with Hollywood melodramas. This transnational encounter between Chinese and Hollywood melodramas reveals the inherently cosmopolitan culture of pre-1950 Chinese cinema. Through this encounter, local melodramas such as *The Spring River Flows East* reveal the complex global currents informing Chinese film production and national identity in this period.

Chapter 5 similarly positions Chinese cinema against globally popular film, exploring the sensory reception of transnational cinema rather than its textual or ideological significance. Xi W. Liu's essay, "Spatial Perception: The Aesthetics of *Yijing* in Transnational Kung Fu Films," provocatively asks if there are particular feelings or sensations associated with either national or transnational cinema spectatorship and, if so, how can an analysis of feeling help us understand the global flows of culture? Interrogating the concept of *yijing*—a kind of pre-cognitive, emotional response that transcends the iconography that may have evoked it—Xi W. Liu analyzes key visual moments from the globally popular Chinese kung fu film *The Grandmaster* (*Yidai zongshi*, dir. Wong Kar-wai, 2013) and the US animated film series *Kung Fu Panda* (dir. Mark Osborne and John Stevenson, 2008), coproduced by DreamWorks and its Chinese branch, Oriental DreamWorks, now Pearl Studio. Exploring how these sequences evoke the feeling of *yijing*, this chapter shows how this feeling vacillates between a form of authentic Chinese aesthetics and a globally disseminated, culturally vague distillation of "Chineseness" for international audiences. Ultimately, this chapter asks us to consider how the sensations of cinema navigate our understanding of transnational culture and aesthetics.

Chapter 6, then, turns its attention to the public reception of international coproductions—which are often critical and commercial failures—by asking what makes for a successful coproduction. Analyzing the Sino-French coproduction *Wolf Totem* (*Lang tuteng*, dir. Jean-Jacques Annaud, 2015), Wendy Su's essay, "Global Network, Ecocinema, and Chinese Contexts: *Wolf Totem* as a Successful Model of Transnational Coproduction," shows how this film achieved success across national borders by appealing to global environmental themes that would resonate in transnational contexts, all while telling a culturally specific story about China during the Cultural Revolution. The film's exploration of human-wolf relationships on the steppe of Mongolia in the 1960s provided a compelling ecological framework for the story that engages with the international environmental movement but is not controversial or critical enough to risk the ire of the Chinese government. Additionally, Su points to the internationally diverse crew overseen by French director Jean-Jacques Annaud and the support given to the film by state authorities in order to bolster its commercial viability. These factors combined to make the massive, eight-year-long production of *Wolf Totem* a financially and culturally successful venture for the partner nations.

Building off these discussions of transnational reception, the third section of the book explores issues of identity and globalization, from the representation of "Chineseness" in global film culture to the production of a global Sinophone culture spanning China, Taiwan, and Singapore and the construction of gender identity in relation to global genre filmmaking.

Chapter 7 initiates this discussion by analyzing cosmopolitanism in 1990s, Shanghai-set, international coproductions. In "The Sound of Chinese Urban Cinema: Multilingualism and the Re-globalization of Shanghai in the 1990s," Lin Feng traces the representation of urban spaces as sites of ideological contamination in Chinese cinema, with an emphasis on spoken language and the disparagement of regional dialects since the 1960s. In several 1990s Chinese–Hong Kong coproductions set in Shanghai, however, the films attempt to depict Shanghai's urban regeneration through the nuanced co-existence of different languages and dialects. Feng analyzes the linguistic diversity in these urban films to explore the construction of Shanghai as a site of increased global trade and cosmopolitanism in the 1990s. By detailing the relationships between language, space, and the shifting relationships between Shanghai and Hong Kong in that period, this chapter reveals the struggles between the local, the national, and the global.

These negotiations are also evoked through language and song in the Chinese-language, Singapore filmmaking of Royston Tan. Exploring Tan's work in Chapter 8, Alison M. Groppe's essay, "Sound, Allusion, and the 'Wandering Songstress' in Royston Tan's Films," analyzes the persistent references to the figure of the songstress across Tan's films, evoking nostalgia for a popular cultural trope in 1940s and 1950s Chinese film and music. The often-tragic figure of the wistful songstress represented a dominant and internationally popular screen icon emanating from Shanghai and Hong Kong cinema in the 1940s and 1950s, producing transnational stars such as Grace Chang (Ge Lan) in the process. Throughout his body of work, Singapore filmmaker Royston Tan references the songs, styles, and narrative tropes from this period of Chinese filmmaking, illustrating the transnational flows that link culture in Singapore, Hong Kong, and China more broadly. Drawing out the nuanced allusions to the songstress figure in Tan's film, Groppe shows how these transnational cultural references help illustrate the dynamics of local cultural politics in Singapore, in the process illuminating the construction of identity via language and dialect in Sinophone Asia.

Issues of gender, of course, are central to these dynamics, and the intersections of gender and global film culture form the background to Chapter 9. In "Implicit Sexuality: The Representation of the Femme Fatale Figure in *Black Coal, Thin Ice*," Yushi Hou takes up the global figure of the "femme fatale"—gleaned from Hollywood film noir but utilized across international filmmaking traditions—to interrogate representations of gender and sexuality in the Chinese neo-noir *Black Coal, Thin Ice* (*Bairi yanhuo*, dir. Diao Yi'nan, 2014). Situating the femme fatale from the film within a Chinese post-socialist cultural context, Hou argues that Chinese neo-noir expresses the powerlessness of the femme fatale—as well as the anti-hero—within contemporary political systems. In particular, by contrasting the Chinese femme fatale's sexuality with the representation of sexuality and power in classical Hollywood and other global film noir, this essay shows how Chinese neo-noir modifies the noir tradition to explore gender and politics within the government-sponsored vision of the "Chinese Dream."

The final section of the book examines the financial transformations in the Chinese film industry that have opened up many of the global influences and transnational complexities of the previous chapters. These chapters explore how various government-led financial reforms in the film industry over the past several decades have impacted industry structures, global collaboration and commercialization, and even the place of cinema in the government's promotion of Chinese interests abroad.

Examining the business practices of the contemporary Chinese film industry, Chapter 10, "The China Film Co., Ltd. and the Stock Market: Financialization with Chinese Characteristics," analyzes the relationships between globalization, national identity, and politics with a focus on the financial operations of the industry. In this chapter, Shiying Liu explores the complex history of the China Film Company, Ltd. (CFC), a subsidiary company created by the massive, state-owned China Film Group Corporation (CFGC) in 2010 and publicly traded since 2016. As the Chinese film industry attempted to transition from a propaganda enterprise to a commercially viable entity (one that still reflects the politics and ideology of the state), several failed attempts at an IPO by the state-owned China Film Group Corporation led to a new venture: the China Film Company, Ltd., an enterprise that would assume some of the commercial dealings of the CFGC, facilitate the further influx of foreign investment into the expanding Chinese film industry, and operate alongside private commercial media companies such as the Huayi Brothers Media Corporation. Exploring this history leading up to the creation of the CFC in 2010—along with the CFC's initial struggles to work toward an IPO—Liu illustrates the financial and cultural tensions between the state-owned Chinese film industry and the commercial pressures of globalization, as new cinema ventures must be both globally appealing (especially in competition with Hollywood blockbusters) as well as ideologically appropriate for the Chinese government.

These pressures are also at the heart of Chapter 11. Qi Ai's essay, *"Big Shot's Funeral*: Sino-foreign Collaboration and Industrial Commercialization," draws out the self-reflexive commentary about the commercialization of the Chinese film industry embedded in Feng Xiaogang's 2001 film *Big Shot's Funeral* (*Dawan*), a coproduction between Huayi Brothers Media and Columbia Pictures. The film itself is a product of the rapidly shifting economic climate for Chinese cinema throughout the 1990s as the Chinese government sought a variety of approaches to commercialize the industry while maintaining some degree of ideological control and cultural specificity. According to Ai, within the narrative and imagery in the film, Feng Xiaogang layers a series of references to the economics and working conditions of Chinese film personnel as they grapple with the turmoil of international cooperation. Through the film and its negotiation of artistic vision and new market imperatives, Ai explores how commercialization and coproduction impact Chinese cinema.

Financial changes to the Chinese film industry, however, are also part of a larger strategy of international diplomacy in which Chinese cinema helps sell the "Chinese Dream" to domestic and international audiences. Katherine Chu's essay, "Sticks, Not Carrots: The Discourse of Soft Power in Popular Chinese Cinema," looks to Chinese geopolitics to contextualize contemporary Chinese film production. Chu analyzes the Chinese government's attempts to leverage various forms of "soft power" through globally popular Chinese films such as *Wolf Warrior 2* (*Zhan lang 2*, dir. Wu Jing, 2017). Outlining the history of soft power in Chinese media policy and the key strategies in place to project positive images of China around the world, this chapter explores how the commercialization of the Chinese film industry must also be understood alongside the Chinese government's promotion of itself and the nation.

Finally, in the epilogue, Po-Shek Fu and Stanley Rosen grapple with two key issues that can be traced through all the chapters of this book: (1) the global negotiations around Chinese and Sinophone identity, and (2) the place of cinema in the projection of Chinese power both domestically and around the world, especially through coproductions and other financial reforms. Linking together the different arguments and examples from across the book, Fu and Rosen synthesize the key contributions of the scholars presented here while pointing the way forward for future research.

Notes

1. For instance, Paul Bond, "China Film Market to Eclipse U.S. Next Year: Study," *Hollywood Reporter*, June 5, 2019, accessed January 23, 2020, https://www.hollywoodreporter.com/news/china-film-market-eclipse-us-next-year-study-1215348.

2. *The Marx-Engels Reader*, 2nd ed. (New York: W. W. Norton, 1978), 477. Cf., for instance, Andre Gunder Frank, *ReOrient: Global Economy in the Asian Age* (Berkeley: University of California Press, 1998) on China as a center of world history and economy, or Wang Gungwu, *The Chinese Overseas: From Earthbound China to the Quest for Autonomy* (Cambridge, MA: Harvard University Press, 2000) on the movement of Chinese peoples and cultures around the world through the centuries.

3. On that culture in Shanghai, see Leo Ou-fan Lee, *Shanghai Modern: The Flowering of a New Urban Culture in China, 1930–1945* (Cambridge, MA: Harvard University Press, 1999).

4. David Shambaugh, *China Goes Global: The Partial Power* (Oxford: Oxford University Press, 2013); Ho-fung Hung, *The China Boom: Why China Will Not Rule the World* (New York: Columbia University Press, 2016).

5. The two earliest works on Chinese cinema include Jay Leyda, *Dianying: An Account of Films and the Film Audience in China* (Cambridge, MA: MIT Press, 1972), and Ian Jarvie, *Window on Hong Kong: A Sociological Study of the Hong Kong Film Industry* (Hong Kong: Centre of Asian Studies, University of Hong Kong, 1977).

6. At the forefront of these trends is the *Journal of Chinese Cinemas*, which has published various issues specializing in such topics as transnational cinema and sound, among others, since its inauguration in 2006.

7. Andrew Higson, "The Concept of National Cinema," *Screen* 30, no. 4 (1989): 36–47.

8. See, for instance, Paul Clark, *Chinese Cinemas: Culture and Politics Since 1949* (Cambridge: Cambridge University Press, 1987), and Chris Berry, ed., *Perspectives on Chinese Cinema* (London: BFI, 1991).

9. See Wai-Siam Hee, *Remapping the Sinophone: The Cultural Production of Chinese-Language Cinema in Singapore and Malaya before and during the Cold War* (Hong Kong: Hong Kong University Press, 2019).

10. Song Hwee Lim, "Six Chinese Cinemas in Search of a Historiography," in *The Chinese Cinema Book*, ed. Song Hwee Lim and Julian Ward (London: BFI, 2011), 35–43.

11. Sheldon Hsiao-peng Lu, ed., *Transnational Chinese Cinemas: Identity, Nationhood, Gender* (Honolulu: University of Hawaiʻi Press, 1997); Sheldon H. Lu and Emile Yueh-yu Yeh, eds., *Chinese-Language Film: Historiography, Poetics, Politics* (Honolulu: University of Hawaiʻi Press, 2005).

12. Po-Shek Fu, ed., *China Forever: The Shaw Brothers and Diasporic Cinema* (Urbana: University of Illinois Press, 2008).

13. Shu-mei Shih, *Visuality and Identity: Sinophone Articulations Across the Pacific* (Berkeley: University of California Press, 2007); Lim, "Six Chinese Cinemas in Search of a Historiography," 26.

14. For a discussion of the debate of the discourses of centrifugal and centripetal Chinese-language cinema and a review of the historiography of Sinophone cinema, see Hee, introduction to *Remapping the Sinophone*.

15. See Audrey Yue and Olivia Khoo, eds., *Sinophone Cinemas* (New York: Palgrave Macmillan, 2014), and Zoran Lee Pecic, *New Queer Sinophone Cinema: Local Histories, Transnational Connections* (London: Palgrave Macmillan, 2016).

16. Lu, ed., *Transnational Chinese Cinemas*.

17. Examples include Leon Hunt and Leung Wing-fai, eds., *East Asian Cinemas: Exploring Transnational Connections on Film* (London: I. B. Tauris, 2008); Joseph Tse-Hei Lee and Satish Kolluri, eds., *Hong Kong and Bollywood: Globalization of Asian Cinemas* (New York: Palgrave Macmillan, 2016); Lingzhen Wang, ed., *Chinese Women's Cinema: Transnational Contexts* (New York: Columbia University Press, 2011); Lisa Funnell, *Warrior Women: Gender, Race, and the Transnational Chinese Action Star* (Albany: State University of New York Press, 2014); Kin-Yan Szeto, *The Martial Arts Cinema of the Chinese Diaspora: Ang Lee, John Woo, and Jackie Chan in Hollywood* (Carbondale: Southern Illinois University Press, 2011); Brian Bergen-Aurand, Mary Mazzilli, and Hee Wai-Siam, eds., *Transnational Chinese Cinema: Corporeality, Desire, and the Ethics of Failure* (Los Angeles: Bridge21 Publications, 2014); and Philippa Gates and Lisa Funnell, eds., *Transnational Asian Identities in Pan-Pacific Cinemas: The Reel Asian Exchange* (New York: Routledge, 2012).

18. John Hill and Pamela Church Gibson, eds., *World Cinema: Critical Approaches* (Oxford: Oxford University Press, 2000), xiv.

19. Tan See-Kam, Peter X Feng, and Gina Marchetti, eds., *Chinese Connections: Critical Perspectives on Film, Identity, and Diaspora* (Philadelphia: Temple University Press, 2009), 2.

20. For an example of scholarship that encourages a more nuanced understanding of global cinema and transnational film culture, see Jeremy E. Taylor's: *Rethinking Transnational Chinese Cinemas: The Amoy-Dialect Film Industry in Cold War Asia* (London: Routledge, 2011). On the tendency to replace the essentialism of national cinemas with a form of "lingua-centrism," see Lim, "Six Chinese Cinemas in Search of a Historiography," 38. For an example of how scholars reimagine the transnational in relation to Chinese cinema, see Song Hwee Lim, "Speaking in Tongues: Ang Lee, Accented Cinema, Hollywood," in *Theorizing World Cinema*, ed. Lucia Nagib, Chris Perriam, and Rajinder Dudrah (London: I. B. Tauris, 2012), 129–44. Song's analysis of Ang Lee expands Hamid Naficy's definition of accented cinema—which accounted for movements between third and first world as hierarchical—and provincializes Hollywood by arguing that the work

of Ang Lee illustrates the porous borders of what constitutes "Chinese cinema" and the transnational cultural and economic flows that inform Chinese cinema's engagement with the broader international film industry.

21. Mette Hjort, "On the Plurality of Cinematic Transnationalism," in *World Cinemas, Transnational Perspectives*, ed. Nataša Ďurovičová and Kathleen Newan (New York: Routledge, 2010), 13; see also Song Hwee Lim, "Concepts of Transnational Cinema Revisited," *Transnational Screens* 10, no. 1 (2019): 1–12. Lim discusses the cinematic trends of slow cinema, ecocinema, and poor cinema from the Global South.

22. Ella Shohat and Robert Stam, *Unthinking Eurocentrism: Multiculturalism and the Media* (New York: Routledge, 1994); Lucia Nagib, Chris Perriam, and Rajinder Dudrah, eds., *Theorizing World Cinema* (London: I. B. Tauris, 2012), xxii.

23. Yingjin Zhang, *Cinema, Space, and Polylocality in a Globalizing China* (Honolulu: University of Hawaii Press, 2010), 1, 10.

24. Y. Zhang, *Cinema, Space, and Polylocality in a Globlalizing China*, 19.

25. Cindy Hing-Yuk Wong, *Film Festivals: Culture, People, and Power on the Global Screen* (New Brunswick: Rutgers University Press, 2011), 4.

26. Michael Curtin, *Playing to the World's Biggest Audience: The Globalization of Chinese Film and TV* (Berkeley: University of California Press, 2007); Wendy Su, *China's Encounter with Global Hollywood: Cultural Policy and the Film Industry, 1994–2013* (Lexington: University Press of Kentucky, 2016); Aynne Kokas, *Hollywood Made in China* (Oakland: University of California Press, 2017).

27. Curtin, *Playing to the World's Biggest Audience*, 4.

28. Su, *China's Encounter With Global Hollywood*; Kokas, *Hollywood Made in China*.

29. Victor Fan, *Cinema Approaching Reality: Locating Chinese Film Theory* (Minneapolis: University of Minnesota Press, 2015); Ling Zhang, "Rhythmic Movement, Metaphoric Sound, and Transcultural Transmediality: Liu Na'ou and *The Man Who Has a Camera* (1933)," in *Early Film Culture in Hong Kong, Taiwan, and Republic China: Kaleidoscopic Histories*, ed. Emilie Yueh-yu Yeh (Ann Arbor: University of Michigan Press, 2018), 277–301; Brian Hu, *Worldly Desires: Cosmopolitanism and Cinema in Hong Kong and Taiwan* (Edinburgh: Edinburgh University Press, 2018); Sheldon H. Lu and Jiayan Mi, eds., *Chinese Ecocinema in the Age of Environmental Challenge* (Hong Kong: Hong Kong University Press, 2009).

30. Gary D. Rawnsley and Ming-Yeh T. Rawnsley, eds., *Global Chinese Cinema: The Culture and Politics of* Hero (London: Routledge, 2010); Leon Hunt, "Asiaphilia, Asianisation, and the Gatekeeper Auteur: Quentin Tarantino and Luc Besson," in *East Asian Cinemas*, ed. Hunt and Leung, 220–36.

31. Dina Iordanova, David Martin-Jones, and Belén Vidal, eds., *Cinema at the Periphery* (Detroit: Wayne State University Press, 2010), 9.

32. Paul G. Pickowicz and Yingjin Zhang, eds., *From Underground to Independent: Alternative Film Culture in Contemporary China* (Lanham: Rowman & Littlefield, 2006); Paul Pickowicz and Yingjin Zhang, eds., *Filming Everyday: Independent Documentaries in Twenty-First-Century China* (Lanham: Rowman & Littlefield, 2017); Stephen Crofts, "Concepts of National Cinema," in *World Cinema: Critical Approaches*, ed. John Hill and Pamela Church Gibson (Oxford: Oxford University Press, 2000), 6.

33. Jeroen de Kloet, "Crossing the Threshold: Chinese Cinema Studies in the Twenty-First Century," *Journal of Chinese Cinemas* 1, no. 1 (2006): 67.

34. Laikwan Pang, "The Institutionalization of 'Chinese' Cinema as an Academic Discipline," *Journal of Chinese Cinemas* 1, no. 1 (2006): 59.

35. Christopher K. Tong, "Scale," *Journal of Chinese Cinemas* 10, no. 1 (2016): 26.

36. See Gina Marchetti, *Citing China: Politics, Postmodernism, and World Cinema* (Honolulu: University of Hawaii Press, 2018).

Part I

Politics and Dissent in Global Contexts

1

Seeing (through) the Struggle Sessions

Cinema, Recycling, and Transnational Circulation

Belinda Q. He

A scene in the classic epic *Farewell, My Concubine* (*Bawang bie ji*, dir. Chen Kaige, 1993) exemplifies one of the most iconic forms of spectacular violence in social-ist China. A set of highly visible formal elements marks the familiar moment for many Chinese people: gesticulating and slogan-shouting masses, the objects of struggle hanging their heads or kneeling (sometimes also wearing dunce caps or holding their arms in a humiliating and painful position called the jet-plane style), and big signboards with denunciatory labels written on them and with the person's name crossed out. The scene is called *pidou* (literally, "denouncing and struggling") or *pidouhui* ("struggle session"): mass gatherings in which those labelled as class enemies (or "the enemies of the people") were accused, shamed, and tormented in public. As shown in the film, such struggle scenes frame an open spot that demar-cates the people as the enclosure and their enemies as the center. Comparable to Soviet phenomena ranging from shop-floor scapegoating to agitation trials, Chinese struggle sessions incorporated theatrical elements and seemingly judicial or semi-judicial procedures, such as interrogation, trial, torture, and punishment.[1] While the literary term *pidou*, coined by the Chinese Communist Party (CCP), was most used during the heyday of Chinese socialism, the technical form—a large set of gatherings and meetings—had been likened and applied before the founding of the People's Republic of China in 1949. The pervasive *pidou* form, without being named literally as such, was a visual landmark of the land revolution and land reform that forever transformed tradition-bound rural China. It then developed into a con-stellation of practices that caused ordinary people to commit bodily, linguistic, or symbolic violence in the name of the people's justice through the following decades.

The struggle session is well known as a landmark of a bygone era and a politi-cally verboten image. And yet it has proliferated as a web of reused and recreated images that are scattered in recycled folk materials, autobiographical accounts, and marketplaces of unofficial archives.[2] This chapter looks at how the knowledge of struggle sessions has been produced in images being lost and found though border-crossing film and media practices, which has shaped the need for us to rethink the question of recycling and circulation as central to intersecting histories of socialist imagery and global cinema. I propose that we must read found images/footage as integral to a "history of cinema without names," widely acknowledged but rarely treated as history.[3] As Catherine Russell notes, "archiveology" is a mode of critical thinking derived from Walter Benjamin's work that provides valuable tools for grasping the implications of the practice of recycling, remixing, and reconfiguring the image bank.[4] Acknowledging the crucial role of the found image/footage in transnational visual economies and historiographic inquiries enables access to a new past and calls into question the old cinematic medium itself. With a focus on the discovery of the struggle session and its espitomological remaking enabled by circulation, this chapter is an attempt to present a way of thinking about moving images beyond both the national-cinema paradigm and the familiar terrain of the film and art historiography—considering auteurs, masterpieces, major studios, aesthetic trends, and movements.

In what follows, I briefly introduce the historical construction of struggle sessions in Chinese revolution. I then describe the limited and changing visibility of the struggle session in contemporary Chinese films and mediascapes through the two sections: struggle sessions as images lost and found and as visual knowledge. Furthermore, I take a look at the enduring reproduction and border-crossing circulation of images of the struggle session, which connect and mediate the past and the present in a global context. Exploring cases of the struggle session as live shows and as found scenes/footage, the chapter also elucidates how, paradoxically, such images have been integral to both the making and unmaking of justice, as they were and are circulated, recycled, appropriated, and deployed in the transnational context at various moments. I argue that the struggle sesson (or rather, the *pidou* form) has been, in and of itself, an image-making machine across border, time, and genre, as well as a regime of visibility not necessarily coded in "class." This chapter intends to keep the visual economies alive as I examine the images in their recycled narratives side by side with their archival versions. Such a methodology considers images as both primary and secondary sources, and as the central frame of reference—and then, it works outward. It serves to critically question the oversimplified discourses of socialist visual culture as state propaganda, or *pidou*, as one-sided spectacle bound up with the Chinese Great Cultural Revolution (1966–1976), and to reflect on what has been concealed and misrepresented in dominant narratives.

Struggle Session as History

To understand the struggle session, it is necessary to trace the history of the Chinese revolution led by the Chinese Communist Party, which was a struggle communicated in the language of class. At the heart of socialist class struggle, identifying who was part of the proletarian masses was a matter of violent urgency and intense publicity. The first sentences on the first page of the first volume of the canonical *Selected Works of Mao Zedong* served to define the parameters of this framework by asking, "Who are our enemies? Who are our friends? This is a question of the first importance for the revolution."[5] Originally written in 1926, the questions set up the conceptual basis of a police force prior to the invention of the socialist state and described the motor of the CCP's campaign-style politics: defending the Party's power by policing the line between friend and enemy.[6] Mao's questions reappeared in the August 1966 publication of Mao Zedong's "Mother of All Mass Movements" but with a notable addition: "Who are our enemies? Who are our friends? This is a question of the first importance for the revolution, as well as a question of the first importance for the Great Cultural Revolution."[7] Wang Xiaojue observes that this claim has to be understood within the Cold War framework that had been deeply ingrained in Chinese politics, society, and culture since the late 1940s.[8] The framework provided a key foundation for the entire sets of claims, concepts, and cultural representations in China's socialist era. Popular practices of unmasking, accusing, and expelling class enemies functioned as a guarantee of the continued purity and transparency on which China's communist revolution and its "continuous revolution" depended.[9] I describe the preoccupation with such historical-specific practices in China as class(ist) exorcism—a working concept inspired by what Barend J. ter Haar calls a "demonological paradigm," Peter Baehr's notion of unmasking, and other works concerning exorcism.[10] The penetration of class exorcism into Chinese people's everyday life took the form of violence that was driven and enacted by a singular and overarching system of partitioning coded in class. On the one hand, class exorcism appeared to be practiced as widespread corporeal, linguistic, and symbolic violence in divergent forms such as shame penalties, sanctions, and executions on the spot. On the other hand, class exorcism was embedded in cultural production and perceptual encounters of incrimination (through mass media, with a trial-like setting) that endorsed "class justice" for and of the people.

The violence of class exorcism in China was a rich network of gatherings that went by a variety of names with different connotations—denunciation rallies, struggle meetings, public shaming rituals, and so forth. Apart from the most familiar ways of naming *pidou* or *pipan dahui* ("mass struggle meetings"), there were many other struggle sessions, either old practices in a new form with changing faces, or perhaps similar practices being named differently across periods and/or in various campaigns of the same period.[11] Whether material or mediated, those encounters were driven by the enduring logic whereby the social imaginary of justice was achievable and perceivable only via the appearance of class enemies and the visibility of the people-enemy demarcation. Although those gatherings varied in form and scope, their overall look and essential act remained the same throughout time; they embodied and performed the establishment of certain binary (class) categories and hierarchies that would justify the structure of power and violence. Hence, by distinguishing it from the struggle session, namely, an assemblage of practices that must not be understood in isolation from one another, I define the *pidou form* as the shared visual and spatial mechanism of those practices, which is portable and even transhistorical.

Struggle Session as Images Lost and Found

The violence of Chinese socialist revolution is well known, but the (audio)visual form of its cruelty as exemplified in struggle sessions remains understudied. The struggle session somehow survives as a history of "the missing pictures."[12] To put it differently, the violence of Chinese class struggle was and is visible in limited ways, mostly documented in a chronicle, without living images, of eventful practices involving certain individuals as targets. This problem of documentation echoes the need to problematize classic issues, often raised by the fields of genocide studies and critical violence studies. The term "without living images" could be interpreted on two levels that do not necessarily contradict each other. First, the actual perfor-mance of the most violent aspects of the struggle session seemed to have largely escaped movie cameras or remained almost invisible due to the concealment and closure of audiovisual archival materials. Second, no footage whatsoever readily succeeded in depicting struggle sessions properly other than the oversimplified spectacle of bodily violence, as scholars have questioned whether any image can adequately represent or reenact violence.[13] Thus, found footage offers a methodo-logical possibility to recognize and approach the struggle session as living images. It serves to note that the image of the struggle session could be fully produced, named, and understood only through an ongoing process of its dynamic and even belated circulation, recycling, and recirculation. Without such recycling and reproduction across temporal divides, the moving images of struggle sessions would have all but disappeared and perhaps never have become available for viewers and scholars today.

The struggle session has been accessible with varying degrees of recycling and restricted circulation across time. Due to lack of mainstream accessibility, Chinese people would recognize the struggle session visually via unofficial sources and unauthorized films, most of which revolve around the Chinese Cultural Revolution. Apart from *Farewell, My Concubine*, examples include a set of films marked as "the underground": banned features such as *Hibiscus Town* (*Furong zhen*, dir. Xie Jin, 1986), *The Blue Kite* (*Lan fengzheng*, dir. Tian Zhuangzhuang, 1993), and *To Live* (*Huozhe*, dir. Zhang Yimou, 1994); independent documentaries like *1966, My Time in the Red Guards* (*Yijiu liuliu wo de Hongweibing shidai*, dir. Wu Wenguang, 1993), *Searching for Lin Zhao's Soul* (*Xunzhao Lin Zhao de linghun*, dir. Hu Jie, 2004), and *Though I Am Gone* (*Wo sui siqu*, dir. Hu Jie, 2006); and artists' personal testimo-nial artifacts, such as Wang Shui-bo's *Sunrise Over Tiananmen Square* (1998), Liu Dahong's *Childhood* series (2013), and Zhang Xiaotao's *The Spring of Huangjueping*

(*Huangjueping zhi chun*, 2016). Non-PRC-based audiences are readily allowed to visualize struggle sessions through various sites: within a history classroom, across archives and libraries, through popular prints, or on the screen. A visual economy of struggle sessions is shaped through overseas pedagogical materials about Chinese revolution and global Maoism; mass-mediated archival images, including newsreel footage and amateur photographs produced in the socialist period; and non-PRC epic film productions, such as *The Last Emperor* (dir. Bernardo Bertolucci, 1987), *The Red Violin* (*Le violon rouge*, dir. François Girard, 1998), and *Mao's Last Dancer* (dir. Bruce Beresford, 2009), among others.[14]

The changing visibility of the struggle session proves to be a testing ground of people's access to archival materials of the socialist era. New and diverse forms of unofficial memories (or what people call "popular memories") have appeared over the last decade in print and online publications, on film, and among personal collectors and amateur historians.[15] The image of struggle sessions has become even more visible and materially accessible with the all-pervasive use of digital media: an increasing body of historical images (mostly undated or unauthored, from untraceable sources) has appeared on media websites, in WeChat public accounts, and in digital flea markets, particularly among the stock photos of e-commerce platforms like Kongfuzi or 7788. One of the most eye-catching examples from overseas Chinese websites is a set of undated photos depicting the "Anti-Party Element Xi Zhongxun" being paraded through the streets by Red Guards.[16] Another domestically circulated case is one among a list of photos (without traceable sources of individual ones) from *Sohu*, with the sensational title "Shameful Struggle Sessions in the Cultural Revolution."[17] The struggle session became a visual cue of how accessible and mentionable the socialist past could be for both popular cultural consumers and historians. It not only becomes a recurring label for memorabilia items that capitalize on nostalgia within the postsocialist mediascape, but also tests the boundary of public knowledge production amid increasing restrictions in the official archives and textbooks.

Scholars have noted the (post-)socialist period's popular cultural fascination with struggle sessions on different occasions, but rarely as the primary concept of historical analysis, hardly as art history or a broader (audio)visual media culture of its own, and never in terms of the interrelated sociocultural and judicious functions so often assigned to it. Few scholars have addressed struggle sessions directly as a historical category beyond the violence of the Cultural Revolution and even fewer have made it a specific subject of research inquiry.[18] Susie Linfield is an exception whose work sheds light on visual representations of the struggle session. While Linfield turns to the newly released photographic records of struggle sessions, she considers those merely as "the calling card of the Cultural Revolution," namely, a legitimized lawless encounter during a specific decade-long period—a kind of public humiliation marked by mob rule in opposition to legal punishment.[19]

Struggle Session as Visual Knowledge

While the image of the struggle session seems to be largely bound up with the Chinese Cultural Revolution, another image, derived from a recent Chinese film that sparked extensive debate, reveals the suspicious bloodline between *pidou* discourses and the Cultural Revolution. Completed in 2012 for Tsinghua's hundredth anniversary celebration in 2011, *Forever Young* (*Wuwen xi dong*, dir. Li Fangfang, 2018) was blocked by censors until January 2018. The film became a box-office hit when it was finally released. What is stunning is that neither its over-the-top craft and sensationalist approaches nor its multiperspective, intertwined storylines about four generations of Tsinghua graduates (played by an all-star cast)—based on real cases spanning a hundred years of modern Chinese history—attracted an extremely polarized reaction. Rather, the polarization revolved around one episode that traces the life of a young woman whose accidental mistakes led to political persecution and resulted in humiliation, social ostracism, and, eventually, another woman's suicide. One of the most controversial moments in this film is a scene of the young woman being cruelly shamed in public. Through the formal details of the scene, viewers could easily identify it as a struggle sesson that is meant to be a politically sensitive image and previously unachievable in a film permitted for public release in China. The film sparked debates that engaged a few questions: Is it really a reference to the Cultural Revolution considering the scene that seems to be a struggle session is moved up about five years, to 1962, in the film?[20] Is the scene historically authentic or not?[21] Is such a representation either a form of historical nihilism due to the general lack of factual rigor, intellectual sophistication, and critical reflection—or is it a filmmaker's bold decision to toy with the censorship policy and make the sensitive subject matter somewhat explicit? Is it merely a byproduct of the negotiations between the filmmakers and censors during the long wait for its release? While those questions remain unsolved, they show the interpretive space within which the film might (or at least was imagined to) have developed cinematic techniques and styles that are at once subtle and satirical, to go beyond the political restrictions and to defend its makers against the critique of the regime. Some of the debates were expanded to the pattern of the struggle session in other comparable films, historical photographs, and vernacular printed illustrations. According to a person's first response to and interpretation of the struggle session scene (whether it is *pidou* or not) in *Forever Young*, people discussed the political stance others might take and evaluated their attitudes toward Chinese socialism.[22]

Whether or not one can recognize the *pidou* form as integral to a wider history of images, *Forever Young* makes the struggle session an image-of-images rather than just a single kind of socialist visual icon in its own right. The image endorsed in the scene from *Forever Young* shows both a reflection and refraction of the struggle session at the same time. In either case, it is less about the actual practice of struggle sessions than about how it was experienced and is remembered by people, and how its images have been archived, circulated, and remade. As such, the *Forever Young* debate is built up through the contradiction between two versions of the struggle session: one as the conventionally perceptible and the other as unimagined beyond the Cultural Revolution discourses. Further, the twin images remind us of a possible parallax history of the struggle session as visual knowledge beyond the Cultural Revolution paradigm. It is not my intention to provide any essentialist response to the *Forever Young* debates by correcting the authentic image of the struggle session or restoring a more valid version of historical and film textual analysis. My aim is rather to show how a global perspective on the intertwining of the struggle session and cinema helps us to free the notion of *pidou* from the confines within which the prevailing historiographies and representations have imprisoned it.

Struggle Session as a Live Show

The struggle session has been a recurring, found scene in cinematic work—primarily fiction—that represents, distorts, or reduces the Chinese Cultural Revolution. The dramatized images of the struggle session shape the most recognizable aspect of socialist class struggle and are readily assumed to be more a performative copy than an appropriate record or recreation. Misrepresentation and inauthenticity are the keywords that describe the major ethical concerns, yet we need to take a more careful look at such "fake" images of the struggle session, particularly those produced and circulated in the capitalist Western bloc. One example that deserves discussion is a French case which, unlike its cinematic contemporaries, offers an iconic reference of how the *pidou* form originally worked in China. A scene of televisual struggle session appears in Jean Yanne's comedy *Chinese in Paris* (*Les Chinois à Paris*, 1974), based on a novel by Robert Beauvais. As part of the pervasive cultural influence of Maoism in the global 1960s and a wave of popular interest in China among French intellectual Maoists and students, Yanne's film imagines an alternative, parodical picture of Paris occupied by the Chinese People's Liberation Army (PLA) as a kind of global colonial threat.[23]

In the film, the imaginary Parisian television program *Le Pilori Televise* puts the purported capitalist enemies on TV as a way of naming and shaming in public (see Figure 1.1). Through a close-up of the target—an evil old man on display—a mugshot effect is generated. The screening and viewing of such scenes in the family living room become a performative communal event in which people eat, talk, laugh together, and partake in the shaming of a distant Other seemingly from within their home. Yanne creates a playful moment of the struggle session by mixing elements from the visual layout of a European guillotine and Chinese cangue punishment (*jiaxing*).[24] Originally adopted for detaining prisoners, the cangue had been used in China with varying regulations for its size; it was primarily arranged for public humiliation, as the supplementary punishment to accompany sentences and as a form of torture to aid in judicial interrogation.[25] The televisual struggle session in

Figure 1.1: A family viewing a televisual struggle session in *Chinese in Paris* (1974).

Chinese in Paris brings up multiple histories at the same time: one of the French Revolution with the guillotine as a primary symbol of the Reign of Terror, one of the wartime shame during the Nazi Occupation, and that of Chinese penal violence and public execution. In the process, Yanne renders the scene that seems too fancy to be "true" as an unexpectedly faithful echo to the actual televisual struggle session practices in socialist China.

Struggle sessions were staged on TV in China even before the 1970s, when television became the fastest-growing medium nationwide. For instance, in 1968, Zhang Chunqiao designated a form of televisual struggle session for the case of the accused musician He Lüting in Shanghai.[26] The famous writer Ba Jin was another target to be struggled against on television. Various booklets that covered the transcripts, on-site photos, pictures, and post-struggle session debates were published as special issues about the televisual struggle session of Ba Jin.[27] Indeed, in China, the struggle session was primarily shaped as a profilmic event. Usually staged in front of the camera in order to be photographed or filmed as it occurred, this mode of the struggle session was a doubly theatrical event by nature. One example is shown in the work of Li Zhensheng, who worked as a photojournalist for the party newspaper *Heilongjiang Daily* and was allowed to appear on various occasions to take photos that served political agendas.[28] Many of Li's photos depicted scenes of the struggle session in Northeast China, which made both the masses attending a struggle session and the "class enemy" highly visible and equally important. Since their deferred release, those images have appeared and reappeared within exhibitionary spaces, in classrooms, and across the old and new media.

One case in point is one of Li's photographs showing a large-scale struggle session in 1966 Harbin, within which, at the top right, a movie camera is set up in a stationary position with a cinematographer at work. What is stunning is that as Li's camera freezes the moment, the movie camera points toward the masses in the background and does not focalize the target, Ren Zhongyi, who is forced to bow at the waist in humiliation. As Li Zhensheng describes in his memoir essay about the shooting of the struggle session, as a political duty, the Heilongjiang TV cinematographer who held the movie camera in the photo was trying to record and 'broadcast' the large-scale struggle session for Ren Zhongyi, while she knew it would never be accessible to the public as live television show.[29] The struggle session was filmed, and yet neither broadcasted nor shown afterward. In this sense, the *Le Pilori Televise* scene in *Chinese in Paris*, perhaps without being recognized as a struggle session, served as an unmotivated response to two mass-mediated encounters: the 1966 shooting event in Harbin and the 1968 televisual "trial" in Shanghai. The struggle session is recycled in a way that unexpectedly unsettles a binary, ideological antagonism. Yanne's film seems to be a surrealist and satirical construction and recasting of Maoism, filled with politically incorrect and racist humor. Many elements such as exaggerated gestures, modified Red-Guard-style uniforms, and *Carmen* as a revolutionary ballet are depicted as "Maoist" and offensively adopted in the film.[30]

Yanne's televisual struggle session stands out as a portrayal of how the most recognizable socialist mass spectacle could be remade in Paris. However, distinct from the Chinese material practice of struggle sessions, the French counterpart takes the form of a TV show and turns into a solo performance without the masses present but with a virtual crowd across households. The struggle session is not fully replicated in terms of staging; however, it is recycled through its enactment, which essentially motivates and entertains the viewing participants. The viewers within the film's diegesis, both those in the living room and those offscreen in the television audience as a shadow public in PLA-occupied France, embodies the film audience's surrogates as well as a large crowd of conformists.

Overall, the micro-allegorical scene of the struggle session helps to identify the complicated dynamic surrounding *Chinese in Paris*. Yanne's film was produced in a context in which the French Left and the French Right were radically ambivalent and confused. The central target of the film was French leftism as well as the collaborationist ideology that emerged in the aftermath of WWII.[31] While playing with a set of French perceptions of China and Chinese people, the film is neither about engaging the penetrating power of global Maoism at the time of the Chinese Cultural Revolution, nor for the purpose of ridiculing the depicted conquering Chinese. Rather, the film is more a question than an answer, concerning the confusion, complicity, and cowardice of the occupied French who learn to live with their conquerors on a daily basis. The film's audiences are asked to identify with the character Régis Forneret (played by Yanne himself), whose cynical collaboration rather than resistance to the PLA occupation is contested. By drawing an unlikely and speculative parallel between the Chinese socialist revolution and the French Resistance during the Nazi occupation with the televisual struggle session as one of the most compelling tropes, the film attempts to dismiss the idea of revolution in the official Gaullist discourses derived in the postwar periods.[32] The struggle session as a live show points to the essence of a revolutionary era in its double sense: the so-called Long Sixties, an age of radical revolution and global leftist politics, as well as an age of media revolution in which people increasingly found themselves watching instant history unfold live on air. The televisual medium becomes a scaffold per se, where a trial and an execution have no difference but the shared ontological quality of being a live event. Justice needs to be seen and mediated to be done. The emphasis on liveness in Yanne's case of seeing the struggle session as Chinese ready-made and recycling it in a fictionalized French context brings the history in the moment to critical attention.

Yanne's treatment of the struggle session recalls the method Sunil Manghani names "image critique"—a double procedure of both critiquing images and engaging them for new critical purposes.[33] Not fully removed from the Chinese context, the image of the *pidou* form is a self-reflexive echo of the ongoing performative and mass-mediated components of Mao's continuous revolution (a "permanent revolution" essentially shaped by various images), as well as its French double placed in a new, not-so-unfamiliar future history. Through both journalistic and historical references, scholars have contextualized the deep connections between two seemingly disparate events at that time: Georges Pompidou's 1973 presidential visit to the PRC, and the filming and release of *Chinese in Paris* in 1974. As Catherine Clark argues, both events produced flawed visions of Franco-Chinese relations and suggested the complexities of the period.[34] In this sense, the transnational reproduction and circulation of the struggle session in *Chinese in Paris* is never about faking an image of a struggle session and of China under Mao, but is far beyond the issue of either fact or fiction. The misplaced struggle session reveals itself as part of a corpus of hybrid cultural stereotypes to mock both French *résistants* and collaborators, which complicates the conceptual and ideological construction of Maoism as global knowledge. Yanne's approach to performing the *pidou* form in the film at once benefits from and is limited to a perspective that blurs the borderline between what is on TV/stage and what is off TV/stage, between news and history, and between play and reality.

Struggle Session as Found Footage

The struggle session was always found and rediscovered through human encounters with images in motion. One of the most recent examples is from the English-language documentary *Mao in Colour: A Study in Tyranny* (Big Ape Media, 2015), released through the Discovery HD World channel.[35] The documentary contains rare footage of a struggle session against the landlords. However, people are hesitant to literally name what is shown in the scene as *pidou*.[36] The authenticity of a cinematic record of an actual struggle session is called into question and put on trial through *Mao in Colour*. It is neither the film scene nor the viewer's knowledge of struggle sessions that needs to be tested. Rather, it is the boundary of the dominant definition and reception of the struggle session aligned to its conventionally assumed look being questioned and contested. The hidden artificiality of documentary filmmaking in the dual temporalities (one as the profilmic in the socialist past and the other, in the present, as the making of *Mao in Colour* without actual filming) and potential behind-the-scene dynamics across time also need to be brought to the testing ground. The contestation was assigned to the visual literacy of people in search of the historical facts of socialist class struggle through struggle sessions. Ambivalently, the footage seemed to be both a familiar and a defamiliarized image of struggling against the landlords (*doudizhu*). As shown in the textual information of the onscreen banner, the filmed event is a "struggle meeting for liberating peasants." Meanwhile, elements ranging from shot angle, costume, gesture, and overacted facial expressions of the masses to the mobility of their structured formation and deformation point to the performative nature of both the depicted event and the shooting itself. Among the scholars who have emphasized the theatricality of the Chinese revolution and socialist political campaigns, Wang Tuo specifically regards the struggle session as one of the many ways in which the masses lived out the revolutionary "scripts."[37] For Wang, the struggle session was integral to "the overacting phenomenon," the internal mechanism that mobilized Chinese people's revolutionary acts and contributed to their eagerness to keep performing ideal socialist subjects. The ambivalent image of the struggle session in *Mao in Colour*, at once the true and the fake, exposes what Wang notes as the paradox between the fundamentally performative nature of *overacting* and the necessity for revolutionary performers not to appear to be acting.[38]

A number of questions thus need to find their way into the historical exploration of the struggle session and related methodological concerns. What can we learn from such questionable footage about the struggle session? How do scholars who flock to flea markets and roam in moving image archives develop relationships to their sources in circulation? With these in mind, I examine archival materials and their recycled forms across border and genre, which reveal both the hybrid looks and the common visual mechanisms (including framing strategies, spatial order, figure placement, etc.) of struggle sessions. The comparative analysis of a handful of images and scenes renders the struggle session even more visible, technically and intellectually. The Soviet documentary *The New China* (dir. Sergei Gerasimov, 1950) contains a scene that resonates with the struggle session in *Mao in Colour*. While other parts of the two scenes are different, both share certain aspects of *mise-en-scène* and are perhaps based on the same struggle-session event shot from different angles. One would be able to capture at least one screenshot of each with almost the same look.

As such, a few more findings need to be noted. The documentary *Great Land Reform* (*Weida de tudi gaige*, dir. Jiang Yunchuan and Ye Hua, 1953), produced in China, and *A Night over China* (*Noch nad Kitaem*, 1971), a Soviet documentary by Aleksandr Medvedkin, share some scenes depicting the struggle session, which is recognizable through the same object of the struggle: the landowner, with a small cap, tied up on a stage and surrounded by the masses. Most likely, Medvedkin and his crew were able to access the footage from a Chinese documentary film and reused it in a different context. Produced after the Sino-Soviet split, *A Night over China* generally offers a critical engagement with the militarization and aggressive foreign policy of China. A variety of images of struggle sessions featured from time to time in the Soviet film served a purpose fully opposite that of the source film in 1950s' China.

Further, images of struggle sessions travel across mediums. One of the most famous photos depicting the struggle session in the form of "struggling against the landlords" during the land reform in China was shot by photographer Qi Guanshan in 1950: *A Landlord Is Publicly Criticized*. The man being struggled against across multiple scenes of *The New China* resembles the landlord figure in Qi's photo and in *Mao in Colour*. Additionally, through a comparative close reading of the visual details, one can discover that one of the male peasants (noticeable throughout a close-up shot) in *Mao in Colour* appears to be the same one photographed by Qi Guanshan.

Likewise, another landlord being struggled against in *Mao in Colour* appeared and reappeared across a series of films: the Chinese feature film *Blood Monument* (*Xue bei*, dir. Gao Heng, 1964); a Japanese TV documentary made by Nagisa Oshima, *Mao Tsetung and the Cultural Revolution* (*Mo-taku-to to bunka daika-kumei*, 1969); and again, the Soviet documentary *A Night over China* (1971). Yet the limited access and lack of archival evidence prevented scholars from investigating a set of key questions: which individuals or group(s) of people originally filmed the footage? Who set up the filming event, how did they do it, and for what purposes? What enabled the transnational flow of the footage—was there a footage database not merely sharable between China and its Soviet brother, but also accessible in countries beyond the Communist bloc—for example, Japan? How did it work? Did the depicted struggle session scenes across those different films really refer to the same event(s)? Was the footage staged specifically for the camera, and if so, how? Were there multiple cameras at work at the time the event happened? If so, what role did the Chinese cameramen, filmmakers, crew members, and those who were non-Chinese play, and how did they work both individually and together? Although the original source of the footage or the specific context and actual process of its production, reproduction, and circulation across borders are unknown and yet to be clarified, seeing the struggle session *through* and *as* found footage enables us to continue this line of inquiry and develop "recycling" as an analytical notion.[39]

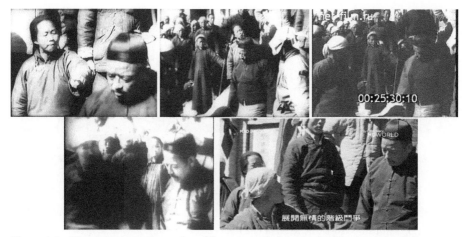

Figure 1.2: The struggle session as found footage, with the same landlord, in *Blood Monument* (1964, China, left and center), *A Night over China* (1971, USSR, right), *Mao Tsetung and the Cultural Revolution* (1969, Japan, left on the bottom) and *Mao in Colour* (2015, USA/UK, right on the bottom).

Recycling breaks down the separation of old and new and instead stresses a dialectic, dynamic relationship between the two. Through various modes of recycling, archival images and footage thus stay in constant flux among use, storage, reuse, and rediscovery. Recycled images are moving to shape "a laboratory of gazes dedicated to the idea that it is possible to rework buried fragments, to fill the gap between distant acts of seeing and a more recent eagerness to know.[40] Recycling describes and theoretically frames a primary mode of material and cultural production and circulation that came to characterize filmmaking in or about the socialist lifeworld, historical research on Chinese socialism, and even the potential that cinematic medium holds for the global leftist imaginary.

In late September 2019, the Rossiya TV channel of the All-Russia State Television and Radio Broadcasting Company (VGTRK) aired a six-episode documentary called *The Rebirth of China* (*Vtoroe roždenie Podnebesnoj*, 2019), dedicated to both the seventieth birthday of the PRC and the seventieth anniversary of the establishment of Sino-Russia diplomatic relations.[41] The rare color footage of the PRC's founding featured in the documentary was released for the first time and was originally shot by a group of Soviet documentary cameramen sent to China in 1949. For several months, the Soviet group was making a documentary about the victory of the Chinese people under the CCP's leadership in the war with the Kuomintang (KMT) government. Some of the footage constituted the documentary *The Victory of the Chinese People* (*Pobeda kitayskogo naroda*, 1950), known as a Sino-Soviet co-produced film. Large-scale reenactments of four key battles in the Chinese civil war were the centerpieces of the film, while a few months earlier Chinese filmmakers

Figure 1.3: Film stills from *The Rebirth of China* (2019, Russia).

had shot actual footage of these battles in real time.[42] In other words, the Russian televisual documentary *The Rebirth of China* recycles footage that is both new and old from the 1950s. The recycled parts include at least sequences of two different eventful struggle sessions. A few Chinese internet users celebrated the release by initiating discussions about related historical issues and producing a variety of media byproducts via social media. Some who were Russian speakers volunteered free Chinese subtitle translations for each episode and posted the video link for public views and downloads.

Many online comments regarding Episode 5 specifically resonated in the *Forever Young* film debate, as discussed earlier. Some comments show people's concerns about justice that linked the past and the present: the footage is so rare and valuable that it allows us to see "how to put Old China on trial (*shenpan jiu zhongguo*)" in color, with the actual soundtrack of that time; "Isn't [the scene] just a *pidou*? It must be earlier than the chaotic time depicted in *Farewell, My Concubine*"; "I know little about the Cultural Revolution but I would read this [*pidou*] as the archetype of what happened later then"; "Why don't we do a struggle session nowadays to struggle against those rich real estate developers and seek justice?"; "It resembles the public trial of corrupted officials in Henan Province."[43] The Chinese viewers gave different meanings to the footage depending on how much they (did not) recognize with respect to other images of the struggle session, like canonized pictures in award-winning films, historical textbooks and monographs, or non-iconic ones such as family photos. Paradoxically, for those who encounter the struggle session primarily in its literary afterlives, mostly through the term *pidou*, the less they know about the iconography of the Cultural Revolution—and perhaps the more they recognize the struggle session in Episode 5 of *The Rebirth of China* as integral to a much longer history of images than assumed. The struggle session thus turns into a form of sensible, mass-produced knowledge of (in)justice that not merely migrates across genre and media platforms but also mediates the coexistence of multiple historical temporalities and different sociocultural times.

Thus the reception of found footage is a matter of recycling and (re)making. Found footage cannot simply be understood in reference to widely discussed avant-garde and experimental cinema practices; it must be considered in light of the everyday engagement with media fragments.[44] People make use of such found footage for their social commentary, repurposing a variety of, in Yomi Braester's terms, "images made for occasion other than the ones in which it is used."[45] Diverse and even historically ignorant understandings of the footage help to create alternative spaces to redefine what a struggle session is about and to break the monopoly of both state-sponsored socialist historiographies and dominant interpretations of *pidou* at play either under the Cultural Revolution paradigm (*"pidou* has to do with the Chinese Cultural Revolution") or within the larger Cold War framework of ideological antagonism.

Although the struggle session remains a mystery to many people, it turns into more of a mental construct and sensorial category than a still or moving picture. Both filmmakers and viewers deal with problems of the present by (re)collecting and recycling material and symbolic elements of the struggle session as hybrid pasts in order to gain and maintain some control over the ongoing transformation. As a fluid archive that points to the multilayered signification of the struggle-session images, Chinese viewers' discussions and cinephiliac quotations related to films like *The Rebirth of China* perform "an auteurial agency behind the use of readymade images."[46] Due to the pervasiveness of digital reproduction, repositioning, and redistribution, found footage is a central facet of the mediascape from which my self-reflection on methodologies of both archival work and filmmaking emerge. It enlightens the ways spectators could partake in the making and recycling of archival materials as committed to historical detection and social engagement.

Ways of Seeing (through) *Pidou*?

This chapter suggests a shared critical engagement with how the struggle session is being unseen and seen, defined and redefined, tested and contested, in the paratextual world of films. Above all, the mechanisms of the struggle session as live shows and as found footage help to theorize a body of cinematic and mediated encounters in which multiple selves and others are involved and negotiated beyond the conventional, binary viewer-screen relationship. Understanding the struggle session through recycling relies on a combination of archival materials and their remade forms as a way of creating heterogeneous texts that oscillate in their relationship to the present and the past, made and found. Recycling promises a journey during which meanings are rediscovered and remade through the negotiation between the new and the old. An image of the struggle session turns into an archive when it is excised from its original documentary form and narrative origins. In other words, recycling is necessary. If previously filmed material about the struggle session is lost by being either hidden, overlooked, or underexamined, it is found as soon as the temporality in which it partakes is shifted.

I conclude with my own experiences of recycling images of the struggle session to demonstrate how found footage can be understood as a kind of human encounter with moving images, or rather as one's relationship to the archives, which defines and mediates itself in the intertwined act of recycling and circulation. The struggle session served as found footage by traveling from the archival collection to the image bank for my presentational and pedagogical experiments. In a visual anthropology workshop with the Cambodian filmmaker Rithy Panh, I recycled some problem footage about the struggle session in conjunction with clips from other source films to make a videographic essay called *Cinema as Show Trial*. I juxtaposed two sets of footage and played them with a split screen and audiovisual dissonance. For instance, the footage about the struggle session from *Mao in Colour* was set parallel to footage from the Chinese documentary *Great Land Reform* (1953), which was replayed and repackaged via the Nostalgia Theater channel of the Chinese Central Television Station (CCTV) in recent years. I see both pieces of the recycled archival footage as mutually resonant in the aftermath of their ideologically antagonistic production. The two were shot more or less in the same period—supposedly from two fully oppositional perspectives within the Cold War context, yet with highly similar compositional details and emotionally charged human expressions. In many ways, the two pieces of footage speak to and testify to each other as two possible versions of what the struggle session looks like.

Cinema as Show Trial is more a thought experiment than a found footage film. A co-product of self-theorizing is at play for the potential viewers and myself. I hoped its screening would be a live show as well as a rhetorical trial through which the mode of spectatorship could be ethically tested. Contemporary viewers who encounter the video do not judge either the films or the footage concerning the struggle session recycled by me. Rather, it is those films and images concerning

Figure 1.4: Two versions of the struggle session in parallel: still from the video essay, *Cinema as Show Trial* (2017).

the struggle session that judge them and put their reaction on trial to see how they might or might not be able to watch, recognize, and understand the struggle session without being trapped in the Cold-War mentality and ideological framework.

Seeing through the struggle session helps to remind us of the power of the archivable, the recyclable, and the circulatable, which potentially enables us to cross-examine the past and the present in the courtroom of history. What we can learn from the Chinese moving images and global cinema in this case is also to turn the *dispositif* notion—which, in past decades, has been widely explored—into an actual analytical tool and a mode of critical rethinking. This chapter hopes for further steps in that direction.

Notes

1. See Elizabeth A Wood, *Performing Justice: Agitation Trials in Early Soviet Russia* (Ithaca: Cornell University Press, 2005). There are various ways of naming such similar historical phenomena as accusatory practices, mass denunciation, and so forth. See Sheila Fitzpatrick and Robert Gellately, eds., *Accusatory Practices: Denunciation in Modern European History, 1789–1989* (Chicago: University of Chicago Press, 1997) and Sheila Fitzpatrick, *Tear off the Masks: Identity and Imposture in Twentieth-Century Russia* (Princeton: Princeton University Press, 2005).

2. See Sebastian Veg, *Popular Memories of the Mao Era from Critical Debate to Reassessing History* (Hong Kong: Hong Kong University Press, 2019).

3. See Diego Cavalotti, Federico Giordano, and Leonardo Quaresima, eds., *A History of Cinema without Names: A Research Project* (Milan: Mimesis, 2016).

4. See Catherine Russell, *Archiveology: Walter Benjamin and Archival Film Practices* (Durham: Duke University Press, 2018).

5. This sentence is from Mao's article originally published in 1926. For the English translation, see Mao Zedong, "Analysis of the Classes in Chinese Society (March 1926)," in *Selected Works of Mao Zedong, Volume 1* (Beijing: Foreign Languages Press, 1967; 1977), 13.

6. See Michael Robert Dutton, *Policing Chinese Politics: A History* (Durham: Duke University Press, 2005).

7. The English translation is from Michael Schoenhals, ed., *China's Cultural Revolution, 1966–1969: Not a Dinner Party* (Armonk: M. E. Sharpe, 1996), 33–43. About Mao's claims about the people-enemy dichotomy, see Mao Zedong, "On the Correct Handling of Contradictions among the People," in *Mao Zedong xuanji diwujuan* [Selected works of Mao Zedong, vol. 5] (Beijing: People's Press, 1977).

8. Xiaojue Wang, *Modernity with a Cold War Face: Reimagining the Nation in Chinese Literature Across the 1949 Divide* (Cambridge: Harvard University Asia Center, 2013), 4–5.

9. The idea of "continuous revolution" implies that the Chinese Communist Party was not merely to lead the Communist Revolution and achieve political power, but also has to maintain a continuous process of class struggle and development after the founding of the People's Republic of China in 1949. About the "continuous revolution" in theory

and in practice, see Stuart R. Schram, "Mao Tse-tung and the Theory of the Permanent Revolution, 1958–69," *The China Quarterly* (London) 46, no. 46 (1971): 221–44; Lowell Dittmer, *China's Continuous Revolution: The Post-liberation Epoch, 1949–1981* (Berkeley: University of California Press, 1987); Timothy Cheek, "Introduction: Comrade, Chairman, Helmsman—The Continuous Revolutions of Mao Zedong," in *Mao Zedong and China's Revolutions: A Brief History with Documents* (Boston: Bedford/St. Martin's, 2002), 1–36.

10. See Barend J. ter Haar, "China's Inner Demons: The Political Impact of the Demonological Paradigm," *China Information* 11, nos. 2–3 (1996): 54–85; Peter Baehr and Daniel Gordon, "Unmasking and Disclosure as Sociological Practices: Contrasting Modes for Understanding Religious and Other Beliefs," *Journal of Sociology* 48, no. 4 (2012): 380–96; and Mary Douglas, *Purity and Danger: An Analysis of the Concepts of Pollution and Taboo* (London: Ark Paperbacks, 1984). I am also indebted to what Haiyan Lee regards as "class racism" that served as a principle of exclusion and closure in socialist China. See Lee, *The Stranger and the Chinese Moral Imagination* (Stanford: Stanford University Press, 2014), 202–10.

11. Those related forms included *doudizhu* ("struggling against landlords") or other forms called *shuolihui* ("reasoning-out meetings"); *minzhu pipinghui* ("democratic criticism meetings"); *qingsuanhui* ("settling-account meetings"); *tongzhi shenpan hui* ("comrades' trial"); *qunzhong fating* ("people's court"); *kongsu hui* ("public accusation meeting"); *gongpan/gongshen dahui* ("public sentencing/trial"); and *youjie* ("shame parade"), among many others. Those were mostly characterized by the discursive currency of terms like "exposing," "unmasking" (*baolu, jielou, chuochua*, etc.), or "tear off the mask" (*sikai huapi*).

12. I borrow the phrase "missing picture" from Rithy Panh's autobiographic animated documentary *The Missing Picture* (2013) concerning the violence of Khmer Rouge–ruled Cambodia.

13. Similar issues around images and violence have been raised in media and historical scholarship. See Leshu Torchin, "Since We Forgot: Remembrance and Recognition of the Armenian Genocide in Virtual Archives," in *The Image and the Witness: Trauma, Memory and Visual Culture*, ed. Frances Guerin and Roger Hallas (London: Wallflower Press, 2010), 82–97; Vicente Sánchez-Biosca, "Non-Author Footage, Fertile Re-Appropriations. On Atrocity Images from Cambodia's Genocide," in *A History of Cinema without Names*, ed. Cavallotti, Giordano, and Quaresima (Milan: Mimesis, 2015), 137–45; and Lior Zylberman and Vicente Sánchez-Biosca, "Reflections on the Significance of Images in Genocide Studies: Some Methodological Considerations," *Genocide Studies and Prevention: An International Journal* 12, no. 2 (2018): 1–17.

14. For examples, documentaries such as *Morning Sun* (*Bajiu dian zhong de taiyang*, dir. Carma Hinton, Richard Gordon, Geremie Barmé, 2003) that include actual scenes of the struggle session have been distributed outside of PRC, while those are hardly accessible in China. Related feature films made by non-Chinese filmmakers have been accessible in China mostly through online film piracy.

15. The phrase "amateur historians" refers to people without formal academic training in history—some of whom conduct independent investigative research, oral history, or testimonial filmmaking projects (often among family members or local communities).

16. "Wenge Pidou Changjing Xi Jinping zhi Fu Xi Zhongxun youjie" [Scenes of Cultural Revolution denunciation: 11 photos of Xi Jinping's father Xi Zhongxun, etc. being paraded through the streets], *Boxun News*, January 11, 2012, http://boxun.com/news/gb/z_special/2012/01/201201110210.shtml.

17. See "Wenge zhong Jianta renge de pidou baren tuijin wanrenkeng dou" [Shameful struggle sessions in the Cultural Revolution: Pushing and struggling against people into the mass grave], *Sohu Culture Channel*, April 25, 2013, http://cul.sohu.com/20130425/n373885613_6.shtml.

18. Most of the scholarly attention paid to the struggle session touches on its components and associated practices, usually within the field of Cultural Revolution studies: on criticism and "self-criticism," see Lowell Dittmer, "The Structural Evolution of 'Criticism and Self-Criticism,'" *The China Quarterly* 53 (1973): 708–29; Ji Fengyuan, "The Public Criticism Meeting: Discourse, Ritual, and Formulae," in *Linguistic Engineering: Language and Politics in Mao's China* (Honolulu: University of Hawai'i Press, 2004), 161–72; for rituals and symbolic practices, see Daniel Leese, *Mao Cult: Rhetoric and Ritual in the Cultural Revolution* (Cambridge: Cambridge University Press, 2011); and Tuo Wang, *The Cultural Revolution and Overacting: Dynamics between Politics and Performance* (Lanham: Lexington Books, 2014), 103–26; among others.

19. See Susie Linfield, "From Malraux's Dignity to the Red Guards' Shame," in *The Cruel Radiance: Photography and Political Violence* (Chicago: University of Chicago, 2010), 101–23. Victoria Gao is another exceptional scholar who writes about a single photograph of the struggle session (by the same photographer, Li Zhensheng, whose work appears in Linfield's discussion). See Victoria Gao, "Chinese Political Persecution, Red Square, Harbin, 1966," in *Getting the Picture: The Visual Culture of the News*, ed. Jason E. Hill and Vanessa R. Schwartz (London: Bloomsbury Academic, 2015), 88–90.

20. While this episode of the film is set in 1962, before the Cultural Revolution, there have been noticeable misunderstandings and misrecognitions, such as "*Forever Young* straight-forwardly depicts innocent people falsely accused of spying being beaten to death by an angry mob during the Cultural Revolution." See Wei Xi, "Nostalgia and Willingness to Tackle Sensitive Subjects Helps Chinese Director Li Fangfang Find an Audience," *Global Times*, January 18, 2018, http://www.globaltimes.cn/content/1085539.shtml.

21. Most debates took place online, such as this question on the Zhihu platform: "Is that true or not: The *pidou* in which a person could be tortured to death happened in 1962?" Zhihu, accessed August 15, 2018, https://www.zhihu.com/question/266219355.

22. During my fieldwork and oral historical project in China, more than five interviewees immediately asked my opinion about *Forever Young* or shared their and their friends' various reactions to the *pidou*-like scene after they noticed struggle sessions shaped the key concern in my research.

23. See Julian Bourg, "Principally Contradiction: The Flourishing of French Maoism," in *Mao's Little Red Book: A Global History*, ed. Alexander C. Cook (Cambridge: Cambridge University Press, 2012), 225–44.

24. For the cultural history of the guillotine, see Ludmilla Jordanova, "Medical Mediations: Mind, Body and the Guillotine," *History Workshop Journal* 28, no. 1 (1989): 39–52; Daniel C. Gerould, *Guillotine: Its Legend and Lore* (New York: Blast Books, 1992); and

Deborah Kennedy, "Spectacle of the Guillotine: Helen Maria Williams and the Reign of Terror," *Philological Quarterly* 73, no. 1 (1994): 95–113.

25. See Nancy Park, "Imperial Chinese Justice and the Law of Torture." *Late Imperial China* 29, no. 2 (December 2008): 40.

26. Xiao Ding and Xu Ying, "Ying gutou yinyuejia He Lüting" [The hard-bone musician He Lüting], in *Dang he renmin de hao er'nü* [The good son and daughter of the party and the people] (Beijing: Qunzhong chubanshe, 1979), 204–13; and Liang Maochun et al., *Zhongguo yinyue lun bian* [Debates over Chinese music] (Nanchang: Baihuazhou wenyi chubanshe, 2007), 370–73. The struggle session as a television show deserves more discussion, yet it is beyond the scope of this chapter. I discuss the genre in greater detail elsewhere in my in-progress book project *Expose and Punish*, which explores how moving images enacted and were, in turn, shaped by shaming punishment in socialist China.

27. "Ba Jin dianshi pidou dahui zhuanji: chedi pidou chou wuchanjieji zhuanzheng de sidi Ba Jin" [Special issue on the televisual struggle session of Ba Jin: Fundamentally struggle against the deadly enemy of the proletariat dictatorshi, Ba Jin], *Shanghai Workers' Literature and Art Team*, June 1968.

28. Li Zhensheng risked a lot to hide and preserve 20,000 original negatives for nearly forty years. Then Li was able to turn thosesurviving negatives into a rare visual record of the Chinese Cultural Revoluiton with rare. See Zhensheng Li, *Red-Color News Soldier: A Chinese Photographer's Odyssey through the Cultural Revolution* (London: Phaidon, 2003).

29. For various accounts of Li Zhensheng's recollection of the same struggle session event and how he took the photo of Ren Zhongyi, see Zhensheng Li, "Lishi beiju de zhenshi jilu" [The true record of the historical tragedy], *Dangshi Zongheng* [Over the party history] no. 3 (1996): 42–45; Zhensheng Li, "Wo suo paishe de wenge jishi zhaopian zhurengong" [The main character in the documentary photo about the Chinese Cultural Revolution that I took], *Yanhuang Chunqiu* [China through the ages] no. 6 (1998): 44–48.

30. For the intertextual connection between the ballet scene and the Chinese classic revolutionary ballet *The Red Detachment of Women* (1964), see Nan Ma, "Les Chinois a Paris: *The Red Detachment of Women* and French Maoism in the Mid-1970s," *China Perspectives*, no. 1 (2020): 43–51.

31. For more discussion of this film as a comedy and Yanne's other work, see Dalton Krauss, "Can Comedy Change the World? Jean Yanne and French Comic Cinema of the 1970's," *Esprit Créateur* 51, no. 3 (2011): 104–17.

32. For the film's connection to the Nazi occupation, see Flora Lewis, "A Film Fascinates the French by Focusing on Nazi Occupation," *New York Times*, March 10, 1974, https://www.nytimes.com/1974/03/10/archives/a-film-fascinates-the-french-by-focusing-on-nazi-occupation.html.

33. Sunil Manghani, *Image Critique and the Fall of the Berlin Wall* (Bristol: Intellect, 2008), 31.

34. For more detailed contexts of the two events, see Catherine E. Clark, "When Paris Was 'à L'Heure Chinoise' or Georges Pompidou in China and Jean Yanne's *Les Chinois a Paris* (1974)," *French Politics, Culture and Society*, 37, no. 2 (2019): 56–86.

35. *Mao in Colour*, with official Chinese subtitles available, was easily accessible on YouTube and attracted more Chinese-speaking audiences to view and leave various conflicting comments.

36. For example, when a colleague introduced the film to me, she emphasized the film as "a piece of unusual material with rare color footage of an interesting crowd scene." I read her description as stimulating in terms of vocabulary. She said, "It looks like *pidou*, but different from those during the Cultural Revolution. It is too 'real' to be *true*. Maybe because it's in color, quite unprecedented at that time. Or because I never saw this kind of footage before. Part of the documentary was claimed to be from the newly released CIA archives and I wonder if it was a *real pidou*."

37. For detailed discussions of the performative nature of Chinese revolution, see Xiaomei Chen, *Acting the Right Part: Political Theater and Popular Drama in Contemporary China* (Honolulu: University of Hawai'i Press, 2002); Leese, *Mao Cult*; and Brian James De Mare, *Mao's Cultural Army: Drama Troupes in China's Rural Revolution* (Cambridge: Cambridge University Press, 2015).

38. Wang, 105–8. According to Wang, overacting means acting in an effort to "compensate for the existential gap between performer and character with more action," which shuts down any space for spectators' imaginations and interpretations (97).

39. Other works concerning recycling that I have benefited from include Helen Siu, "Recycling Rituals," in *Unofficial China: Popular Culture and Thought in the People's Republic*, ed. Perry Link, Richard Madsen, and Paul Pickowicz (Boulder: Westview Press, 1989), 132–34; Ravi Sundaram, "Recycling Modernity: Pirate Electronic Cultures in India," *Third Text* 13, no. 47 (1999): 59–65; Madeleine Yue Dong, *Republican Beijing: The City and Its Histories* (Berkeley: University of California Press, 2003); and Sarah Hill, "Recycling History and the Never-Ending Life of Cuban Things," *Anthropology Now* 3, no. 1 (2011): 1–12.

40. Marco Bertozzi, "The Poetics of Reuse: Festivals, Archives and Cinematic Recycling in Italian Documentary," *Studies in Documentary Film* V, no. 2–3 (2011): 99.

41. In some media reports, the title is translated as *The Second Birth of the Celestial Empire*. In China, the film is also called *Zhongguo de Chongsheng*. See Xu Fan, "Restored Version of Soviet-Made Documentary on China Screened in Beijing," *China Daily*, September 23, 2019, https://www.chinadaily.com.cn/a/201909/23/WS5d8872a8a310cf3e3556cf1a.html; and Alexander Balitsky, Mikhail Artyukhin, and Inna Kazantseva, "Communist China Rediscovered with Lost Soviet Footage! Classified Scenes Seen for First Time!" *Vesti* (Russian TV news program), October 23, 2019, https://www.vesti.ru/doc.html?id=3202479&cid=4441.

42. For a case study, see Qian Ying, "Crossing the Same River Twice: Documentary Re-enactment and the Founding of PRC Documentary Cinema," in *The Oxford Handbook of Chinese Cinemas*, ed. Carlos Rojas and Eileen Cheng-Yin-Chow (Oxford: Oxford University Press, 2013), 590–609.

43. One of the examples is from a microblog post with threads of discussions and comments on Chinese social media. See A'Tai, "A Rare View: Episode 5 of *The Rebirth of China*, the scene of a struggle session against the landlords during the Land Reform with the original soundtrack," *Sina weibo*, September 25, 2019, https://m.weibo.cn/status/4420760988287985.

44. For more discussions about spectatorship and popular cinephilia as found footage practices in contemporary China, see Belinda He, "Animating Herstory? Stillness/Motion, Popular Cinephilia and the Economy of the Instants in the Post-Cinema Age," *Journal of Chinese Cinemas* 11, no. 3 (2017): 243–58.
45. Yomi Braester, "The City as Found Footage: The Reassemblage of Chinese Urban Space," in *Global Cinematic Cities: New Landscapes of Film and Media*, ed. Johan Andersson and Lawrence Webb (New York: Wallflower Press, 2016), 157.
46. Braester, 158–59.

2

Screening Politics in Hong Kong

Joseph Tse-Hei Lee

This chapter explores the cinematic representations of Hong Kong's political change in the post-1997 era. Through a closer look at *Ten Years* (*Shi nian*, dir. Kwok Zune, Fei-Pang Wong, Jevons Au, Kwun-Wai Chow, Ka-Leung Ng, 2015) and independent documentaries on young Umbrella protesters such as *Lesson in Dissent* (dir. Matthew Torne, 2014), *Joshua: Teenager vs. Superpower* (dir. Joe Piscatella, 2017) and *Lost in the Fumes* (*Dihou tiangao*, dir. Nora Lam, 2017), this study argues that these films reframe social and political upheavals and youth activism in historical perspective and bend various genres aesthetically. *Ten Years* and *Lost in the Fumes* were produced by local independent filmmakers who have attracted much attention for their creative works after 1997. *Lesson in Dissent* and *Joshua: Teenager vs Superpower* were made by international filmmakers who have contextualized the new generation of youth activists as part of the emerging sphere of global social media activism. All the films were made after the months-long peaceful sit-in street protests in late 2014, often referred to as the "Umbrella Movement."[1] Carving out their niche audience at community screening events and international film festivals, both local and foreign filmmakers employ cinema as a powerful tool of political critique, re-evaluating the different forms of Chinese dominance over the postcolonial city.

Hong Kong used to be, and may still be, a first-world metropolis, even though it was intertwined with the formation of two rival Chinese polities—Beijing and Taipei—during the Cold War. The configuration of a local cinematic identity was contingent upon the triangular relationship among the British colonialists, the Chinese motherland, both real and imagined, and Hong Kong itself.[2] For years, Hong Kong cinema has operated as "a cinema without a nation, a local cinema with transnational appeal"[3] or "a national cinema in the absence of a nation-state (however small), and, more importantly, without the aspiration for a nation-state."[4] However, any attempt to construct "national cinema as coherent, unified,

homogenous is to lend support to erasure of difference."[5] The conventional definition of a national cinema no longer holds water for this postcolonial society.

Reflecting Cold War politics on local soil, there was a separate Hong Kong
identity with growing demands for social and political participation. Even though
the majority of Hong Kong residents were the descendants of Chinese migrants,
the concept of a unique identity under the British was associated with specific lifestyles and an entrepreneurial ethos. As the British empire declined after the Second
World War, local filmmakers were keen to assert themselves. Po-Shek Fu highlights
Hong Kong's role as the capital of Mandarin-language cinema during the 1960s
and 1970s, when the Shaw Brothers hired Japanese directors and technicians to
produce martial arts pictures. Overlooking divisive Chinese politics and satisfy-
ing commercial audiences, the martial arts films "exhibited an ideological subtext
similar to that of *huangmeidiao* drama: a setting in an imagined China of an unspe-
cific past and cherishing the idealized traditional virtues of loyalty, filial piety, and
self-suppression for the collective good."[6] This border-crossing presaged the trans-
Pacific flow of talent between Hong Kong and Hollywood in the 1990s, and the rise
of China–Hong Kong film co-productions since 2003.

In the years leading up to 1997, Hong Kong filmmakers characterized the
city as "a victim of an uncontrollable destiny"[7] and its belonging as differentiated
from, yet linked to, China.[8] The anxiety about the incremental disappearance of
local ways of life, as well as the perceived failures of the Beijing-appointed executive leadership, led to an "indigenous turn" in politics.[9] Post-1997 youth activists,
such as Joshua Wong, Edward Leung and Agnes Chow, have been confronted with
the pending deadline of 2047, when the "one country, two systems" model expires.
Rejecting their parents' pragmatism, they have put down their roots, fostering a
vibrant civic identity.[10] Their localist sentiment has arisen from their involvement
in postcolonial protests.

Equally significant is the advent of digital cameras, mobile video and social
media at the turn of the 2000s. This virtual public sphere has nurtured a distinct
cinematic culture with its own imagined communities.[11] Benedict Anderson con-
ceptualizes such communities as groups of people whose solidarity is "created
through shared interests and forged through identification rather than face-to-face
communication in everyday life."[12] In this vein, this chapter uses the term "Hong
Kongers" as a generic analytical category to encompass a wide array of identities,
orientations and behaviors that have been shaped by unique historical conditions
from the British era to the present. Capturing the diverse concerns of the post-
1997 generation, what Mirana M. Szeto and Yun-Chung Chen call the "Hong Kong
SAR (Special Administrative Region) New Wave" has responded to the challenges
of Mainlandization by taking on local subjects with a critical awareness of intra-
and inter-cultural flow.[13] Beyond rejecting the "chauvinist and xenophobic petit-
grandiose Hong Kongism typical of the pre-1997 Hong Kong colonial inferiority
complex," the filmmakers under study have gone so far as to champion a vision of

grassroots activism that provides people with hope for change during trying times.[14] Such cinematic initiatives contribute to our understanding of Sinophone cinema on two levels.

The first is Sinophone cinema's capacity to circumvent, bypass, and resist state censorship. The practice of film censorship dates back to the British colonial era. Becoming a regional hub of the film and entertainment business among Chinese diasporas in Asia in the 1950s, Hong Kong's cultural industry became a British colonial bulwark against the spread of Communism, and a key battleground between the Communists on the Mainland and the Nationalists in Taiwan. According to Jing Jing Chang, the British deployed censorship policies to "contain and silence competing political views" amidst the Cold War, thereby setting off "the process of depoliticizing culture and creating an apolitical community."[15] Fearful of the spillover effects of geopolitical conflicts, the British performed a delicate balancing act, permitting the US certain autonomy without provoking major disorders on China's doorstep.[16] Meanwhile, the British banned the entry of films from China and other Communist countries to avoid ideological conflicts. Another censorial practice was to promote an Orientalist understanding of China in mass media, inhibiting any discussion of Chinese politics by pro-Beijing and pro-Taiwan filmmakers. Local filmmakers adjusted and adapted to the censorship. Some producers partnered with the British to normalize colonialism.[17] Some directors made *kung-fu* films to celebrate Confucian precepts, and others turned to the folktales of ghosts and spirits as allegories to project human fears and desires.[18]

This history sets the stage for understanding the state-business nexus between the post-1997 government and filmmakers. Since the 2000s, China has deployed business mechanisms, luring local and Hollywood filmmakers to the vast Mainland market. This policy of co-option remains effective when the Chinese state monopolizes the networks of film distribution and exhibition. Yet, "these relative positions of censored China and Hong Kong free expression began to alter," partly because of the pressure for integration into the Mainland and partly because of the Chinese financial influence and censorship demand upon local filmmaking.[19] One notable example is the genre of undercover cop movies. Benefiting from cross-border co-productions, Johnnie To has not only appropriated nominal Chinese nationalism but also acknowledged localist sensitivity within a larger Sinophone cinema.[20] There is now a *de facto* framework of "one cinema, two systems" in which Hong Kong filmmakers outwit Chinese censors to access the lucrative market, and in which a handful of independent filmmakers learn from their Chinese counterparts to produce online films for limited audiences and profits.[21] This chapter reveals a new, vibrant cinematic culture in which social media technologies and innovative distribution networks permit the wider circulation of unsanctioned films. Because the Communist control of information has become increasingly hegemonic in Hong Kong ever since the implementation of a draconian national security law in July 2020, the growth of grassroots activism around independent movies has potential to "challenge repressive surveillance—particularly through material agencies beyond representational contents as well as participatory activities and the very multimedia forms."[22]

The second level is the continuity of political cinema in Hong Kong. Movies and street protests have served as alternative modes of political expression. Under the British, local discontented sectors rioted against the authorities, and urban business leaders and rural powerholders contested the ruling power through negotiation and cooperation with the colonialists. Since 1997, previous anti-colonial movements have been repurposed against external political intervention, and local activists have formed new civic organizations and parties to claim influence from Beijing.[23] While permitting limited autonomy for the local government to handle the escalating popular discontents, Beijing "is anxious to find a solution for Hong Kong, failing to see herself as the problem."[24] Thus, the Umbrella protests and the confrontations with riot police since June 2019 bear resemblance to numerous examples of popular resistance that are "enshrined in local culture through many fictional scenes of civic protest and other motifs of lateral surveillance" within Hong Kong cinema.[25] These struggles have laid the groundwork for local filmmakers' search for what Stefano Harney calls "a habitable text of identity" against the Chinese discourse of nationalism.[26] The producers of *Ten Years* have spun the fear of censorship into a commercial success. Without relying on conventional business distribution and exhibition networks, they have turned to alternative channels such as community screening events, independent film festivals, and social media platforms.[27] Community-based spectatorship is nothing new in the Chinese world. Open-air Chaozhou or Chiuchow traditional Chinese opera performances are held in Hong Kong every summer. Praising Confucian ethics such as loyalty, respect, and familial piety, the shows are predicated on social harmony. The difference is that post-1997 independent films problematize the sustainability of such virtues, rejecting the authoritarian institutions that underpin the semblance of political unity and social cohesion. The public screening events involve the viewers and stage lived encounters. These innovative formats permit a democratic form of filmmaking, liberating the distribution and exhibition platform from the grip of institutional and commercial networks. In the hands of critically minded artists, independent films become the new weapons of the weak.

Ten Years (2015)

Produced on a modest budget of US$64,000 that was raised by a local Christian media organization and some independent filmmakers, *Ten Years* (*Shi nian*, dir. Kwok Zune, Fei-Pang Wong, Jevons Au, Kwun-Wai Chow, Ka-Leung Ng, 2015) features five short movies that talk about the political present, aimed at the political future.[28] The film broke local box office records upon its initial release, earning more revenue than *Star Wars* and winning "best film" at the 35th Hong Kong Film

Awards in April 2016, although the ceremony was censored in the Chinese media. Against the backdrop of significant political upheavals in post-1997 Hong Kong, the film stood out in "the vicious cycle of direct competition with the dominant China–Hong Kong film co-productions for the limited time and space of local theatrical release."[29] Despite its commercial success, the theatrical release of *Ten Years* was suspended, allegedly because of the local exhibitors' self-censorship. Ironically, this obstacle gave the film a second life. Turning the censorship into a publicity campaign, the tech-savvy producers organized over 200 free screenings at universities, schools, churches, community halls and public squares, and participated in more than thirty film festivals worldwide. Building on the momentum of grassroots activism, *Ten Years* not only broke away from the curse of relying on the conventional framework of China–Hong Kong film co-productions for survival, but also provided a template for "alternatively liberatory and exploitative possibilities for participatory media."[30]

The first of the five stories, *Extras* (dir. Zune Kwok), is a thriller about China's frequent interference with Hong Kong's domestic affairs. During the May 1st Labor Day celebrations, local politicians attend a community event where Chinese government officials and the Hong Kong police chief stage an assassination attempt to provoke mass panic in order to rally support for the legislation of a controversial national security law. They plan the plot behind closed doors and recruit two triad members to carry out the assassination: Long Hair, a middle-aged, unemployed, low-skilled worker from China; and Peter, who comes from a South Asian migrant family. Trapped in the desperation of the underground ecnomy, both Long Hair and Peter are reluctant to harm the targets but feel compelled to do it for survival. When they debate who should fire the shots, the representative of Beijing's liaison office decides that the leaders of both Hong Kong political parties should be wounded to provoke greater fear among the public. Long Hair and Peter assume that they can get away after the plot, but are sadly killed by the police. The Hong Kong authorities immediately condemn the assassins as terrorists and propose to pass a national security law. By blurring the boundary between triad and state, *Extras* reveals the excessive use of fear and intimation as a means to keep people subservient to the political establishment. The deliberate choice of black and white highlights the harsh reality of dirty politics that exploits ordinary people and corrupts the system for narrow ends. The subtext of power abuses resonates with many Hong Kongers who became the targets of police survelliance and harassment during the anti-China extradition bill campaign in 2019.

The second segment, *Season of the End* (dir. Fei-Pang Wong), is the most aesthetic work, exploring the vulnerability of human obsession in a vanishing world. A young couple takes specimens of items from demolished buildings and neighborhoods by day, dreaming of a vast urban wasteland at night. The rustic aura of a rundown city is similar to their tiny apartment where they interact quietly, walk around decrepit hallways, and work on specimen preservation. They eventually lose the resolve to carry on, and the husband decides to turn himself into the last speci-men. The idea of clinging to the past exhibits deep meaning in life, and the couple's determination to hold onto an ideational past is a powerful image. The random cutscenes of galaxies and lizards carry the narrative forward. Towards the end, the husband eats a soft purple clay-like mass before his death, with the background music intensifying, and the wife marks the floor next to a lifeless male body. Unlike the other four shorts, this film never mentions Communism or China. Without using any establishing shots or visual representations that capture the Hong Kong narrative, this work displays "a vaguely post-apocalyptical atmosphere" when the couple strives to preserve all the fragments of human existence in what used to be "a desolate urban landscape" in ruins.[31]

The third segment, *Dialect* (dir. Jevons Au), is a story of linguistic genocide; the gradual decline and eventual extinction of Cantonese as a living language. It addresses the future prospect of linguistic colonialism, in which Mandarin Chinese replaces Cantonese as the official spoken language, and Hong Kong's majority Cantonese population become marginalized in their native city. In the segment, a Cantonese taxi driver is both confused and frustrated when everyone around him speaks Mandarin. Struggling to keep up as a breadwinner, he is about to lose his livelihood because of his inability to understand and speak Mandarin. His wife scolds him for talking to his son in their mother tongue, even though the son only replies in Mandarin. Worse still, the local government requires all Cantonese taxi drivers to acquire Mandarin proficiency as a precondition of keeping their licenses. One can envision a two-tier taxi licensing system that discriminates against non-Mandarin-speakers; Mandarin-speaking drivers can pick up wealthy passengers from the airport, cruise terminal, train station and downtown financial center, while non-Mandarin speakers are prohibited from doing so. The segment ends with a passenger being fired for her failure to communicate with a Mandarin client. This final scene hints at the silent solidarity of the oppressed Cantonese—and that of other marginalized dialect groups such as Wenzhouese, Chaozhouese and Shanghainese—in a Mandarin-dominated nation.

The fourth segment, *Self-Immolator* (dir. Kwun-Wai Chow) begins with an activist who adheres to the Gandhian principles of truth and nonviolence and who becomes Hong Kong's first political prisoner to die during a hunger strike. This activist, along with his university peers, including a Cantonese-speaking girl of South Asian descent, pursue civil disobedience, campaign for Hong Kong's inde-pendence, and appeal to Britain to uphold the Sino-British Joint Declaration (1984) over the unfulfilled promise of autonomous governance. Another group of activists, who are disheartened by police abuse and brutality, resort to violence and set fire to Beijing's liaison office. The fire gives the Communist leaders a pretext to send in the People's Liberation Army to suppress peaceful protesters and impose martial law. In a flashback that reminds people of Beijing's Tiananmen Incident on June 4, 1989, the Umbrella Movement, and the months-long popular resistance against police violence in 2019, a grandmother witnesses demonstrators being tear-gassed, assaulted, and arrested by the riot police. In the thick smoke of tear gas, she and other civilians do not know how to react when the officers attack people with batons indiscriminately. Representing the silent majority, the grandmother looks defiant and disdainful of the violent regime. She never utters a word, but her deep gaze shows her strength and determination. The story ends with this elderly woman walking with an umbrella to immolate herself outside the British Consulate-General. The final image of her burning umbrella shows that she chooses to live by Jack London's credo:

> I would rather be ashes than dust! I would rather that my spark should burn out in a brilliant blaze than it should be stifled by dry-rot. I would rather be a superb meteor, every atom of me in magnificent glow, than a sleepy and permanent planet.[32]

Inspired by the acts of self-immolation among Tibetans and in Tunisia, this short draws a parallel among discontented masses everywhere.

The final segment, *Local Egg* (dir. Ka-Leung Ng), draws attention to struggling shopkeepers in a working-class neighborhood. A grocer and a bookseller confront a gang of indoctrinated school children called Young Pioneers, a local equivalent of Hilter's Brown Shirts or Mao Zedong's Red Guards, who police neighborhood stores for banned words and books that favor localism. On one occasion, the Young Pioneers throw eggs at a bookstore that sells politically incorrect materials. The grocer's son is a mole in the Young Pioneers who has helped the bookseller to remove censored titles before an inspection. The boy and the bookseller pursue a subtle form of resistance, symbolizing the weapons of the weak in a politicized environment. The film segment concludes with a biblical verse from Amos 5:13–14: "It is an evil time. Seek good, and not evil, that you may live," and this is immediately followed by an additional quote, "Already too late," which changes to "Not too late." This hopeful message reminds audiences that integrity is vital to the fabric of Hong Kong.

In *Ten Years*, the color and lighting seems to get brighter as each sgement progresses. The use of black and white in *Extras* offers a blunt critique of political corruption. *Season of the End*, which is shown in muted colors, conveys a sense of sadness and loss. Both *Dialect* and *Local Egg* are filmed mostly in daylight, capturing the changing father-son relations in diverse settings. *Self-Immolator* displays the most striking use of color and light. When the elderly woman sets herself on fire, the camera shifts between her Buddha-like sitting posture and the burning umbrella from multiple angles.

Thematically, the producers acknowledge that a new governing culture has been normalized in the political status quo, with systematic restrictions ranging from propagandistic rhetoric to violations of personal autonomy and bodily integrity. The increase of external pressure that the films project reflects the elites' obsession with stability and order. *Extras*, *Dialect* and *Self-Immolator* present a gloomy picture of human inviolability—Hong Kongers can never overthrow this violent system, and society appears to be moving toward apocalyptic destruction. Paying attention to local sensitivities, *Season of the End* and *Local Egg* construct a vision of popular resistance against an alien rule. At a time when authoritarian film censorship is no longer confined to the Chinese world, *Ten Years* advances the "diffusionary nature of participatory media and media citizenship" as a mode of resistance.[33] Its easily translatable template has crossed geographical and cultural boundaries to become a global cinematic icon, inspiring filmmakers worldwide to address a host of domestic crises. Some of the *Ten Years* producers have shifted their attention elsewhere, focusing on a "*Ten Years* International Project." They are entering new ground and working with independent directors in Japan, South Korea, Thailand, and Taiwan, utilizing similar narratives to discuss structural changes facing their respective nations in ten years' time. *Ten Years Japan* addresses the aging population, digital surveillance, "Big Data," nuclear disasters, and rising militarism, and *Ten Years Taiwan* explores nuclear waste and pollution, migrant workers from Southeast Asia, industrial collapse, low birth rates, and insomnia. Losing access to the profitable Chinese market turned out to be blessing in disguise because some of these Hong Kong directors have discovered a larger media landscape through collaborations with like-minded Asian artists who are not intimidated by China's growing clout.

Lesson in Dissent (2014) and *Joshua: Teenager vs. Superpower* (2017)

Coinciding with the release of *Ten Years* were the exhibition of several independent documentaries on major political upheavals in post-1997 Hong Kong on overseas commercial media platforms, such as Amazon and Netflix, and in regional and local independent film festivals. Produced by foreign directors, these two documentaries tell the story of real political actors, especially Joshua Wong, born in 1996, and reveal the changing patterns of nonviolent activism in a series of single-issue protests leading up to the Umbrella Movement of 2014. *Lesson in Dissent* (dir. Matthew Torne, 2014) is composed of seven lessons, which trace the visions, concerns, and strategies of Hong Kong's postcolonial generation of civil rights activists. It compares the journeys of Joshua Wong, an articulate and media-savvy political operator, and Ma Wan-Kei, a quiet and dedicated member of the League of Social Democrats, a radical leftwing party.

Joshua Wong came to the spotlight at age fifteen when he organized Scholarism, a high school activist group, to oppose the Beijing-initiated national education curriculum as mandatory in mid-2012. In July and August 2012, Joshua and his comrades organized a successful occupation protest outside the Hong Kong Government Headquarters, attracting around 120,000 supporters and widespread media support. They eventually forced the local authorities to abandon the mandatory patriotic learning program. Wong's campaign provided a vital moment of clarity as he took on the ruling authorities and rejected the propagandistic nature of the patriotic education. By comparison, Ma Wan-Kei is a community organizer, assisting the League of Social Democrats in electoral campaigns and public protests. He is more willing than Joshua to challenge riot police during demonstrations. Spontaneous and quick learning, the two young men adapt and adjust to different crises as they come along. The cinematic discourse of youthful idealism explains why so many college and high school students braved tear gas and rubber bullets fighting for their civil rights in 2014 and 2019.

Joshua: Teenager vs. Superpower (2017) is director Joe Piscatella's second film about politically engaged teenagers, following his *#chicagoGirl: The Social Network Takes on a Dictator* (2013), an account of Ala'a Basatneh, a Syrian American activist who used social media to support the Syrian revolution. After hearing about the unlawful arrest of fifteen students in Daraa in 2011, Ala'a coordinated her first public protest in Chicago, calling for the end of martial law in Syria. She later used Facebook to coordinate more rallies inside Syria, assisting local activists on the ground, and distributing the rare digital footage to US cable channels. Striving to relate the story of Joshua Wong to the growth of social media activism around the globe, Piscatella places him in a binary struggle against the mighty Chinese Communist state, following in the footsteps of Ala'a Basatneh and offering a messianic hope for Hong Kong. Piscatella traces the rise of Joshua Wong to his breathtaking stand against the top-down proposal to launch a citywide patriotic learning program. After founding Scholarism, Joshua recruited supporters via peer and online networks and circulated protest leaflets, culminating in the weeks-long occupation outside the headquarters of the Hong Kong government. This single-issue campaign grew into a mass movement, and people came to the public square after being inspired by Joshua's charisma and oratory eloquency. Piscatella captures the scene when Joshua confronted Hong Kong's Chief Executive Chun-Ying Leung over the patriotic curriculum. Joshua's crusade eventually forced the Leung administration to suspend the program.

Having won the patriotic education controversy, Joshua's Scholarism shifted its focus from educational affairs to city politics. In partnership with other civic groups, Scholarism opposed Beijing's intervention in district and legislative council elections, even endorsing its own candidates. As these battles intensified, Joshua and his teammates were coming of age. In the Umbrella Movement, they repeated the same occupation tactic to put pressure on the Leung administration but eventually failed to accomplish the political objective. They were in disagreement with other opposition groups over the resistance's direction and were harassed by police and thugs in the streets. The film ends with Joshua facing a trial for his protests.

Both Torne and Piscatella draw on rare footage to show the life of a young activist in the social media age. The mass rallies organized by Joshua witness a significant transition from vertical to horizontal leadership in political mobilization. No longer relying on the moral leadership of a few charismatic figures, Joshua masters the skills of democratic electioneering among teenagers, and forms new coalitions with progressive church groups, civic organizations, and opposition parties to resist Beijing. Both documentaries highlight the formation of Joshua as an effective political organizer through the lens of his devout Christian background. According to Torne, Joshua Wong's Chinese name, "Chi-Fung," literally meant "of sharp," is rooted in a biblical reference to God who stroke down King David's enemies in the Psalms. This seems to have made Joshua a destined leader, willing to fight the good fight for the public good.[34] His religious upbringing has taught him how to socialize with strangers, develop organizational and oratory skills, question many conventional values and norms, and continue to engage in electoral politics. Seeing Christianity as a matter of personal conscience rather than an instrumental tool with which to appeal to other people yearning for comfort in an uncertain time, Wong has said, "Christianity motivates me to care about politics and society. But I am not saying that I am pushing for self-determination because God or Jesus gave me a signal. I don't want religion to become the instrument for me to gain some support and social capital."[35] His reflections are more drawn from the Bible than from neoliberalism and Chinese patriotism.[36] A closer look at his Christian upbringing in both films reveals the compatibility between spiritual piety and civic engagement in an increasingly authoritarian society.

Joshua Wong's journey toward faith-based activism marks a clear break from the culture of political apathy and fear so pervasive in the Chinese Church. This apathetic mindset originates from contentious church-state conflicts in modern China and a transplantation of conservative theology from the West.[37] The Hong Kong governance crisis reflects the longstanding debate about the extension of Christian spiritual sovereignty in the civil sphere. Since the early twentieth century, Chinese Christians and foreign missionaries have debated about whether Christianity should be a motivating force against injustice and corruption, or a principle of personal conscience. The period of the 1910s and 1920s saw a serious discussion about the privatization of religion, an idea thought to benefit church growth, urging Christians to abstain from politics in the name of spiritual purity. At that time, Christians thought that in the Republican era, without a state religion or a centralized ideology, there would be an autonomous space for Christianity to thrive. Yet, the emphasis on the privatization of the religious sphere backfired during the revolutionary upheavals of the mid-1920s, when radical activists and progressive mission school students criticized this otherworldly Christianity for lacking political and social significance. The Soviet-supported Nationalists and Communists launched a series of anti-Christian campaigns in coastal China to cultivate a sense of national unity against Western imperialism. Taking up revolutionary activities represented a significant change among some progressive Christians, who dropped their long-held distaste for politics and considered activism compatible with their sacred calling to serve God and country. The outcome of the socialist revolution was different from what progressive Christians had initially expected. Maoism displayed many of the trappings of a religion, with a well-developed theology, demanding absolute loyalty from citizens. As a result, many missionaries and church leaders fled China for Hong Kong, Taiwan, and Southeast Asia, re-establishing their ministries abroad. These refugees made up the majority of the Hong Kong church membership in the mid-twentieth century. The connection with the colonialists made the Christians less critical of structural injustice. Nonetheless, since 1997 new realities have forced young Christians like Joshua Wong to reassess their relationship with the Chinese state.

Lost in the Fumes (2017)

Much attention has been given to the bravery of Joshua Wong, but independent filmmakers have explored the role of other actors in the Umbrella Movement. *Lost in the Fumes* (*Dihou tiangao*, dir. Nora Lam, 2017) narrates the rise and fall of another political star, Edward Leung, born in 1991 and former spokesperson of the Hong Kong Indigenous, a populist radical party known for its stance on democratic localism. Both Joshua Wong and Edward Leung signify the gradual growth of local consciousness among the post-1997 generation. Frustrated with Hong Kong's "subordinate relationship with China," Leung calls on people of Hong Kong "to fight on our [*sic*] own" rather than dreaming of an institutional transformation "thousands of miles away" on the mainland. His activism contributes to "a further temporal, intergenerational division" between the 1989 generation of China's prodemocracy activists and the post-1997 youth.[38] Unlike the two aforementioned documentaries on Joshua Wong's heroic courage, first-time director Nora Lam has produced an antihero documentary. "People have put a lot of labels on him—radical, rioter, troublemaker, anti-China—while others hold him up as a hero," says Lam, "but as I got to know him better, I realized he was a lot like us."[39]

The film characterizes Leung as an accidental activist or a reluctant hero in postcolonial Hong Kong. His political journey began at the University of Hong Kong, where, thanks to residential dorm and campus activities, Leung and his comrades learned to see themselves as unique individuals with a calling to serve the public. During the Umbrella Movement in 2014 and the massive protests against the China extradition bill in 2019, the university dorms provided students of all ideological and socioeconomic stripes an interactive space to debate and explore what democratic governance truly meant to Hong Kongers. What makes Leung a tragic figure is the fact that he has become one of the first postcolonial political prisoners. Like Joshua Wong, Leung worries about the propsect of authoritarian rule in Hong Kong: "The elderly generation escaped to Hong Kong from China. We don't want to hand over the next generation to the Chinese Communists and let them suffer like the last generation." He experimented with electoral politics for the 2016 Legislative Election.[40] Caring about personal integrity more than party loyalty, Leung champions the marginalized and hates seeing himself end up as "the type of politicians he despises." Unfortunately, his dream has never materialized because the government disenfranchised him from the electoral process.

Lam portrays Leung as a thoughtful and charismatic orator, not as a shrewd political operator. As a philosophy major in college and a deep thinker, Leung finds in political engagement an antidote to severe bouts of depression. He calls himself a "loser," whose pleasures include smoking, eating, and playing guitar, even though his public speeches electrify young people with hope and courage. Out of desperation, he left Hong Kong for the United States in 2017. In early 2018, he returned home to face charges. On June 11, 2018, less than a week after the 29th anniversary of the Tiananmen Incident, he was given a six-year sentence for inciting violence against police officers during the "fishball revolution" of 2015, a series of street clashes that broke out in Mong Kok over gentrification and the displacement of unlicensed food vendors on Chinese Lunar New Year's Day. Even though Leung was convicted of rioting under a colonial statute, the verdict sends a clear message that prison is the only place for radical revolutionaries. By making himself a political martyr, Leung has turned into Hong Kong's Wei Jingsheng or Nelson Mandela, inspiring disillusioned young people to continue the prodemocracy struggle. His eloquent speeches in support of Hong Kong's self-determination, and his TV interviews became popular downloadable items during the youth-driven protests of 2019.

Aesthetically, Lam utilizes unique camera angles to display Leung's vulnerability. Showing his tears and gaze at the camera through close-ups and medium shots, Lam humanizes her subject and reduces distance from the audience. This technique of cinematic gaze—who watches whom—enables viewers to identify with Leung's dilemma, seeing their own fear mirrored in this young man. She documents the frequent harassments of Leung by pro-Beijing agents, and of his followers' clashes with riot police. As the ending credits roll, we hear a song composed by Leung: "Many rotten souls reside in this earth. I don't want to be among them. Pretend there are no boundaries between good and evil. Let this song be with me in all weathers [sic]." Despite all the political pressure that he has faced, he holds onto his sense of human decency and integrity.

Cinematic Critiques of Hong Kong

Three worrying political trends can be discerned in these cinematic narratives. The first trend concerns the marginalization of Hong Kong, in which the constitutional framework of "one country, two systems" has changed from within. The cinematic characterization of Hong Kong as a vanishing landscape points to the reproduction of certain colonial norms and regulatory restrictions that have undermined social bonds, and precluded any possibility of collective action.[41] Because the scope of the new national security law continues to evolve, it is difficult to be politically neutral. The public fear that today's definition of politics focuses narrowly on any opinion and action that could be perceived as a security threat. Many entrepreneurs, civil servants, educators and students deleted Facebook and Twitter posts that showed support for the protests. The need to compromise under pressure has shaped everyday life and artistic practices on the ground.

The second political trend is a sense of collective vulnerability in the post-1997 era. Mutual distrust prohibits solidarity among the subaltern people. Living in fear, the subalterns internalize the reign of terror as desirable. This gloomy feeling of the state of exception underlines *Ten Years* and *Lost in the Fumes*. The deaths in *Self-Immolators* symbolize a perpetual state of terror that Hong Kongers witnessed during the Communists' crackdown on pro-democracy activists in Beijing's Tiananmen Square on June 4, 1989, and the Hong Kong police's brutal assaults on Umbrella protesters in late 2014 and on demonstrators today. *Extras, Season of the End, Dialect* and *Self-Immolator* dramatize a feeling of powerlessness and estrangement from fellow citizens. *Local Egg* refers to Haruki Murakami's characterization of a fragile egg against a high wall, offering a sense of hope and empowerment against state-imposed amnesia.

In reality, a combination of conservative elitism, a weak culture of civic engagement, and external pressure have obstructed Hong Kong's transition toward effective governance.[42] To reorganize the governing structure of Hong Kong, China has introduced significant electoral changes that enabled political supporters to dominate the legislature in late 2021.[43] This took place against the backdrop of the detention of prominent youth protest leaders and the disqualification of previously elected lawmakers. Furthermore, policing in Hong Kong has become intertwined with the operation of stability maintenance (*weiwen*). The police have moved beyond the colonial tradition of bureaucratic neutrality to become guardians of national security.[44] In the light of incomplete political transformation, the documentaries on Joshua Wong and Edward Leung express a glimpse of hope. This hope is the rebuilding of mutual bonds among citizens of all stripes. The best way to fight injustice is to isolate the status quo so that citizens can search for an alternative mode of governance. When the subalterns engage in what Jeremy Brecher and Tim Costello call "globalization from below," this collectivism will bypass the surveillance of nation-states and ensure victory in their resistance efforts.[45] Both *Self-Immolator* and *Local Egg* point to a deeper commitment to democratic localism. Frustrated with China's autocratic rule, the protagonists—such as student activists, storeowners and school children—want to do something about the futureless society that they see around them. Such widespread grievances have generated new activist energy among like-minded citizens, and their informal bonds enable them to connect and share information without being censored.

The third trend of authoritarian governance is reflected in the anxiety over an uncertain future in 2047. Faced with the aimless society they see around them, the directors portray the postcolonial city as a unique cinematic entity that speaks for and by itself, and that resists pressures for further integration into the Chinese motherland. *Self-Immolator* and *Local Egg* characterize Hong Kong as an unique society with its own sense of historical, political, and socio-cultural consciousness. Such collective awareness is reflexive, inspiring the people to stand up for their rights. The cinematic subtext captures a qualitative change from vertical to horizontal leadership in Hong Kong's political mobilization. Ever since the Umbrella protests, activists have drawn on a repertoire of innovative tactics, appealing slogans, motivating scripts, and elaborate rituals to win sympathy and support for their cause.

Striving to cope with the constantly shifting political climate, these local and foreign filmmakers reject the conventional practice of "one cinema, two systems." They push the envelope when representing the ways in which their protagonists navigate, confront, and cope with endless crises. They display a city fraught with severe tension and conflict, which the local ruling elites have tried to contain and cover up through appeals to economic growth. Yet, Hong Kong still faces the problem of constitutional governance, for coinciding with its steady growth through integration with China is the awakening of its citizens, and with it, the rise of organized activism on an unprecedented level. From the Umbrella movement to the anti-China extradition protests, each upheaval is a lesson for future mobilization.[46] The progressive youth express a variety of aspirations, ranging from democracy and freedom, to the protection of their civil rights. As the battle for a better future is being fought in the public and virtual spheres, the meaning of "one system, two systems" is being contested by the post-1997 generation.

Conclusion

In this age of extreme nationalism amid COVID pandemic, a new cinematic trend of identity formation in Chinese-ruled Hong Kong reveals the confluence of concerns about distinct cultural and religious expressions, political identification, and collective survival. It is in this dynamic process that a variety of cosmopolitan Hong Kong identities have gradually emerged, juxtaposing tradition and modernity, local and global forces, and religious heritage and secular lifestyles.[47] By asserting their agency to reinvent a new sense of belonging to their respective groupings, these foreign and local filmmakers have transmitted their political concerns to viewers at home and abroad. One major difference is that the former can circulate their documentary films through global media companies and social media platforms, bypassing the control of Chinese and local censors, and the latter has to count on grassroots mobilization and international artists' activism to share their works. All these independent films are now popular downloadable items on platforms for contemporary Hong Kong movies.

With Chinese power expanding and Western support fading, there has been little media attention to Hong Kong's marginalized groups. The cinematic realism embraced by *Ten Years* and the critical documentary portrayals of Joshua Wong and Edward Leung represent a conscientious attempt to enmesh moral integrity in a discourse of contentious politics. Behind these endeavors is a hope for the future—to shift the old socio-cultural and political boundaries and facilitate progressive change. The foreign and local filmmakers' determination to explore controversial topics and use new distributive platforms reveals new possibilities for combining grassroots and artists' activism. The effective way to exercise individual agency is to carve out little cinematic space without subverting the hegemonic order.

Although multiple layers of cinematic politics intersect in a display of new opportunities for these directors and their supporters, harsh realities can still trouble them. Nevertheless, cinematic innovations in any crisis situation always instill some elements of dissent. The scope of agency for foreign directors may be broader than that for Hong Kong filmmakers because of an unfavorable set of circumstances. But the latter's efforts to reinvent themselves and rework their situations reveal limited agency in challenging the Chinese hegemon, and seeking better cinematic futures for empowerment.

Notes

1. Francis L. F. Lee and Joseph M. Chan, *Media and Protest Logics in the Digital Era: The Umbrella Movement in Hong Kong* (New York: Oxford University Press, 2018).
2. Yingchi Chu, *Hong Kong Cinema: Coloniser, Motherland and Self* (New York: Routledge, 2003), 117–18; Victor Fan, *Extraterritoriality: Locating Hong Kong Cinema and Media* (Edinburgh: Edinburgh University Press, 2019).
3. Po-Shek Fu and David Desser, eds., *The Cinema of Hong Kong: History, Arts, Identity* (Cambridge: Cambridge University Press, 2002), 5.
4. Ackbar Abbas, "Hong Kong," in *The Cinema of Small Nations*, ed. Mette Hjort and Duncan Petrie (Edinburgh: Edinburgh University Press, 2007), 113.
5. Mette Hjort and Scott Mackenzie, eds., *Cinema and Nation* (New York: Routledge, 2000), 4.
6. Po-Shek Fu, "Cold War Politics and Hong Kong Mandarin Cinema," in *The Oxford Handbook of Chinese Cinemas*, ed. Carlos Rojas and Eileen Cheng-Yin Chow (Oxford: Oxford University Press, 2013), 127–28.
7. Chu, *Hong Kong Cinema*, 132.
8. Chu, *Hong Kong Cinema*, 114.
9. Leo K. Shin, "The 'National Question' and the Stories of Hong Kong," in *Hong Kong Culture and Society in the New Millennium: Hong Kong as Method*, ed. Yiu-Wai Chu (Singapore: Springer, 2017), 135–36.
10. Shin, "The 'National Question' and the Stories of Hong Kong," 143.
11. Amir Husak, "Exercising Radical Democracy: The Crisis of Representation and Interactive Documentary as an Agent of Change," *Alphaville: Journal of Film and Screen Media*, no. 15 (2018): 16–32.
12. Benedict Anderson, *Imagined Communities: Reflections on the Origin and Spread of Nationalism* (London: Verso, 1991), 6–7.
13. Mirana M. Szeto and Yun-Chung Chen, "Mainlandization or Sinophone Translocality? Challenges for Hong Kong SAR New Wave Cinema," *Journal of Chinese Cinema* 6, no. 2 (2012): 115–34.

14. Ibid., 122. See also Mirana M. Szeto, "Sinophone Libidinal Economy in the Age of Neoliberalization and Mainlandization: Masculinities in Hong Kong SAR New Wave Cinema," in *Sinophone Cinemas*, ed. Audrey Yue and Olivia Khoo (New York: Palgrave Macmillan, 2014), 120–46.

15. Jing Jing Chang, *Screening Communities: Negotiating Narratives of Empire, Nation, and the Cold War in Hong Kong Cinema* (Hong Kong: Hong Kong University Press, 2019), 41.

16. Priscilla Roberts, "Cold War Hong Kong: Juggling Opposing Forces and Identities," in *Hong Kong in the Cold War*, ed. Priscilla Roberts and John M. Carroll (Hong Kong: Hong Kong University Press, 2016), 35 and 42.

17. Chang, *Screening Communities*, 59–62.

18. Kenny K. K. Ng, "Censorship at Work: Cold War Paranoia and Purgation of Chinese Ghost Stories," in *Hong Kong Culture and Society in the New Millennium: Hong Kong as Method*, ed. Yiu-Wai Chu (Singapore: Springer, 2017), 124.

19. Karen Fang, "Cinema Censorship and Media Citizenship in the Hong Kong Film *Ten Years*" *Surveillance and Society* 16, no. 2 (2018): 142.

20. Karen Fang, *Arresting Cinema: Surveillance in Hong Kong Film* (Stanford: Stanford University Press, 2017), 147.

21. Paola Voci, "Online Small-Screen Cinema: The Cinema of Attractions and the Emancipated Spectator," in *The Oxford Handbook of Chinese Cinemas*, ed. Carlos Rojas and Eileen Cheng-Yin Chow (Oxford: Oxford University Press, 2013), 377–97.

22. Fang, "Cinema Censorship," 150.

23. Tak-Wing Ngo, ed., *Hong Kong's History: State and Society Under Colonial Rule* (New York: Routledge, 1999); Ray Yep, "Confrontation, State Repression, and the Autonomy of Metropolitan Hong Kong: The Umbrella Movement and the 1967 Riots Compared," in *The Routledge Handbook of Contemporary Hong Kong*, ed. Tai-Lok Lui, Stephen W. K. Chiu and Ray Yep (New York: Routledge, 2019), 227–44.

24. Yep, "Confrontation, State Repression, and the Autonomy," 242.

25. Yep, "Confrontation, State Repression, and the Autonomy," 159.

26. Stefano Harney, *Nationalism and Identity: Culture and the Imagination in a Caribbean Diaspora* (Kingston, Jamaica: University of the West Indies Press, 2006).

27. Ruby Cheung, "Ten Years: An Unexpected Watershed of Twenty-first-century Hong Kong Film Industry," *Frames Cinema Journal* 15 (2019): 12. https://framescinemajournal.com/article/ten-years-an-unexpected-watershed-of-twenty-first-century-hong-kong-film-industry/.

28. Satish Kolluri and Joseph Tse-Hei Lee, "Representing Crisis and Crisis of Representation: Screening Postcolonial Hong Kong in *Ten Years* (2015)," *Cine-East: Journal of East Asian Cinemas* 1, no. 1 (2018): 31–44.

29. Cheung, "Ten Years: An Unexpected Watershed," 12.

30. Fang, "Cinema Censorship and Media Citizenship," 145.

31. Fang, "Cinema Censorship and Media Citizenship,"148.

32. Irving Shepard, *Jack London's Tales of Adventure* (New York: Doubleday, 1956), vii.

33. Fang, "Cinema Censorship and Media Citizenship," 147.

34. Matthew Torne, *Lesson in Dissent* (Witney, Oxon, UK: Torne Films Ltd., 2014), 00:06:27.

35. Ben Bland, *Generation HK: Seeking Identity in China's Shadow* (New York: Penguin, 2017), 33.

36. Daniel H. Bays and Grant Wacker, eds., *The Foreign Missionary Enterprise at Home: Explorations in North American Cultural History* (Tuscaloosa: University of Alabama Press, 2003), 9.

37. Christie Chui-Shan Chow and Joseph Tse-Hei Lee, "Almost Democratic: Christian Activism and the Umbrella Movement in Hong Kong," *Exchange: Journal of Missiological and Ecumenical Research* 45, no. 3 (2016): 252–68.

38. Luke Cooper, "'You Have To Fight On Your Own': Self-Alienation and the *New* Hong Kong Nationalism," in *Citizenship, Identity and Social Movements in Hong Kong: Localism after the Umbrella Movement*, ed. Wai-Man Lam and Luke Cooper (New York: Routledge, 2018), 106.

39. Rachel Cheung, "How Documentary on Hong Kong Localist Politician Edward Leung, *Lost in the Fumes*, Came to be Made," *South China Morning Post* (January 17, 2018). https://www.scmp.com/culture/film-tv/article/2128623/how-documentary-hong-kong-localist-politician-edward-leung-lost.

40. Antony Dapiran, *City of Protest: A Recent History of Dissent in Hong Kong* (New York: Penguin, 2017).

41. Derek Gregory and Allan Pred, eds., *Violent Geographies: Fear, Terror, and Political Violence* (New York: Routledge, 2007), 22.

42. Ralf Horelmann, *Hong Kong's Transition to Chinese Rule: The Limits of Autonomy* (New York: Routledge Cruzon, 2003), 21–23.

43. Shin, "The 'National Question' and the Stories of Hong Kong."

44. Joseph Tse-Hei Lee, "Hong Kong's Fishball Revolution," *Taipei Times* (February 16, 2016), 8.

45. Jeremy Brecher and Tim Costello, *Global Village or Global Pillage: Economic Reconstruction from the Bottom Up* (Cambridge, MA: South End Press, 1988).

46. Yongshun Cai, *The Occupy Movement in Hong Kong: Sustaining Decentralized Protest* (New York: Routledge, 2017); Ho-Fung Hung, "Hong Kong's Resistance," August 19, 2019, https://www.versobooks.com/blogs/4413-hong-kong-s-resistance.

47. Shin, "The 'National Question' and the Stories of Hong Kong," 144.

3

"All of Us Are Part of the Monster"

Toxic Sublimity and Ethical Reflexivity in Zhao Liang's
Behemoth

Man-Fung Yip

Named *Time* magazine's Person of the Year for 2019, Swedish climate activist Greta Thunberg is emblematic of the mainstream recognition bestowed on a burgeoning international movement that seeks to combat the increasingly dire consequences of climate change and other environmental challenges through raising consciousness, influencing policy debates, and triggering political action. In this current age of environmental/climate crisis and activism, films with an ecological or anthropogenic focus have also become a rapidly growing phenomenon worldwide. Miyazaki Hayao's *Princess Mononoke* (1997) and *Spirited Away* (2001), Davis Guggenheim's *An Inconvenient Truth* (2006), Lucien Castaing-Taylor and Véréna Paravel's *Leviathan* (2012), and Bong Joon-ho's *Snowpiercer* (2013)—these are but a few examples from the past two decades or so, ones that encompass both fictional features and documentaries, live action and animation, mainstream and experimental films.[1] Chinese cinema, too, has added significantly to this trend. One can point to a growing number of films that exemplify what Sheldon Lu calls "Chinese ecocinema,"[2] including Jia Zhangke's *Still Life* (*Sanxia haoren*, 2006), a fiction film about the impact of the Three Gorges Dam project, and Wang Jiuliang's *Beijing Besieged by Waste* (*Laji weicheng*, 2011) and *Plastic China* (*Suliao wangguo*, 2014), both of which are documentaries centered on victims of industrial contamination.

A recent example of the Chinese ecocinema trend is Zhao Liang's *Behemoth* (*Beixi moshou*, 2015), an experimental documentary about the ecological and human ravages of coal-mining and iron and steel industries in Inner Mongolia. While the subject matter of the film may not break new ground, its aesthetic approach is anything but conventional: eschewing a clear narrative and traditional documentary devices such as expository voiceover or talking head interviews, the film conveys its meanings primarily through images—notably pictorial shots, at once stunningly beautiful and deeply unnerving, of boundless mining pits, grasslands covered in soot and dust, flaming ironworks, and a pristine but empty ghost city.

There is no question that *Behemoth* is visually spectacular and gorgeous. In an interview, Zhao described his approach as making the ugly beautiful; an approach, it is worth noting, that can already be observed in the director's earlier photographic series *Beijing Green* (*Beijing lü*, 2004–2007) and *Water* (*Shui*, 2004–2008).[3] As Paolo Magagnoli points out, what makes these photographic series so fascinating and unique is their aestheticization of pollution: the ways in which they document the environmental degradation in China in strangely beautiful images meshing the natural and artificial together, while making allusions to the important, long-standing Chinese tradition of *shanshui* ("mountain and river") and flower-and-bird paintings.[4] However, this aestheticized approach, in the photographic series as well as in *Behemoth*, is not without detractors; their main point of criticism has to do with what is seen as willful indifference to, or even mitigation of, the devastating issues portrayed in the photographs and in the film. On the photographic series, for instance, Michael Hatch offers a fierce critique of their "aestheticized quietude" that purportedly undercuts the urgency and seriousness of the ecological calamity experienced by China.[5] Similarly, while many critics are captivated by the gorgeous cinematography and the sheer beauty of the images in *Behemoth*, some of them also express a certain uneasiness over the paradoxical juxtaposition of the beautiful and the depressing ("The longer the film lasted, the less I could enjoy the gorgeous pictures [the director] has captured")[6] as well as over what is perceived as "unnecessary poetic flourishes" in the film.[7]

Such criticisms, I should add, are not specific to Zhao Liang's works and resonate with a rather widespread view that sees aestheticization and representation of the miserable and the terrifying (pain, grief, poverty, catastrophe, etc.) as inherently incompatible with one another. As Susan Sontag points out perceptively with specific reference to photographs:

> Transforming is what art does, but photography that bears witness to the calamitous and the reprehensible is much criticized if it seems "aesthetic"; that is, too much like art. The dual powers of photography—to generate documents and to create works of visual art—have produced some remarkable exaggerations about what photographers ought and ought not to do. Lately, the most common exaggeration is one that regards these powers as opposites. Photographs that depict suffering shouldn't be beautiful. . . . In this view, a beautiful photograph drains attention from the sobering subject and turns it toward the medium itself, thereby compromising the picture's status as a document. The photograph gives mixed signals. Stop this, it urges. But it also exclaims, What a spectacle![8]

According to Sontag, the propensity toward adding aura and beauty to images of suffering and devastation is on the wane. Rather, it is the opposite tendency of "uglifying," a more modern operation that seeks to show "something at its worst," that is regarded as less manipulative and thus more authentic.[9] Sontag's observations about the shifting standards are generally correct, but has this suspicion of the beautiful gone too far? Does aestheticization necessarily bleach out a moral response to what is shown? And how would this dynamic between aesthetics and ethics be changed if we move beyond photography to an audiovisual and time-based medium such as the cinema?

In this chapter, I focus on the film *Behemoth* and try to rethink these (and other) questions in the context of global ecocinema and environmentally engaged art practices. Specifically, the chapter is divided into two major sections. The first is devoted to presenting a theory of toxic sublimity that informs not only *Behemoth* but also a number of cinematic and photographic works, including some of the documentaries of Werner Herzog and the large-scale landscape photographs of Edward Burtynsky. What these creations share in common, I argue, is in part their aestheticized yet tension-ridden visual rhetoric, which creates a kind of disturbance in the viewer's imaginative and cognitive faculty, drawing the viewer into affective, and ultimately ethical, contemplations of ecological devastation. The second part extends the analysis by focusing on the aural and especially structural-narrative aspects of *Behemoth*, which serve in many ways to "anchor" the potential ambiguities of the film's aestheticized images and to render more overt its eco-critical stance. This is the case, for instance, in the way the film borrows the structure of Dante's *Divine Comedy* (i.e., the journey through Inferno, Purgatory, and Paradise), and quotes and adapts the epic poem for its sparse but powerfully haunting voiceover narration. Significantly, as borne out by these allusions to *Divine Comedy*—and by the biblical reference of the film's eponymous beast as well as the visual strategies it shares with Herzog's and Burtynsky's works noted earlier—*Behemoth* evinces a global perspective and propensity that points to its own conditions of possibility, namely those of a low-budget independent documentary funded mainly by French sources and targeted by and large at the international film festival and art-house circuits. Despite its focus on local environmental issues in China, then, the film seeks to speak to a larger international community by situating itself not only in relation to a set of global canonical texts, but also as part of a growing trend in which filmmakers and artists around the world are trying to find new ways to intervene in, and foster dialogue about, the global ecological crisis.

The Toxic Sublime

Born in Dandong in northeastern China, Zhao Liang graduated from the LuXun Academy of Fine Arts in 1992. Since then, he has been working as an independent documentary filmmaker as well as a multimedia artist in photography and video art. As part of China's burgeoning "New Documentary Movement,"[10] Zhao's first documentaries offer, in the words of Li Jie, "penetrating observations of state-society relations in contemporary China, showing both their human and dehumanizing aspects."[11] *Crime and Punishment* (*Zui yu fa*, 2007), for instance, explores abusive law enforcement in China by documenting the everyday operations of a police station in a small town in Liaoning, whereas *Petition* (*Shangfang*, 2009), shot over the course of twelve years, chronicles a community of disgruntled petitioners who come to the capital from all over China to appeal injustices by local officials, but find themselves up against a corrupt judicial system and suffer from all kinds of intimidation and coercion. While continuing this propensity toward acute reflections on social problems and conditions, *Behemoth* represents a major stylistic departure from the director's earlier documentaries. In Bill Nichols' scheme of classification, the change involves a shift away from the observational (the unobtrusive observation of what is in front of the camera) and participatory (an emphasis on the interaction between filmmaker and subject through interviews and other patterns of collaboration or confrontation) modes to the poetic mode, which "stresses visual and acoustic rhythms, patterns, and the overall form of the film."[12] As the director himself admits,

> I find the conventional documentary filmmaking and its linear form limiting. It doesn't satisfy what I crave in filmmaking anymore. When people watch a documentary, they tend to have certain expectations. It is constraining. When I work on a video installation for a gallery space, it is relaxing and I feel more at liberty with the material. I wanted to combine the two. So it means experimentation of some kind in the film, and introducing some aesthetic interest from contemporary art, in terms of perception and understanding of art. I do find contemporary art nourishing in this respect. I don't want to limit myself to the documentary perspective.[13]

Given that the aestheticized rendition of pollution and environmental degradation in *Behemoth*, as noted earlier, can be traced to Zhao's earlier photographic series *Beijing Green* and *Water*, the stylistic departure of the film may precisely be seen as the result of a conscious attempt to incorporate elements of contemporary art into his documentary practice. More importantly, just as the visually appealing images do not make the photographic series less an instance of eco-activist art, neither does the stunning pictorial beauty of the film undercut its central eco-critical message. Quite the contrary, indeed, for it can be argued that the beautifying tendency is integral to the critical perspective of both the photographic series and the film, even though a point of distinction has to be made in terms of how this link between aestheticization and reflection/criticism works in each case. For Magagnoli, it is "irony" that expresses the critical stance of the photographic series:

> [T]he purpose of Zhao's self-consciously composed images was to direct the attention of audiences towards the utter neglect and destruction of Beijing's environment. What defines the edge of Zhao's ironic pictures is . . . the *inappropriateness* of the artist's visual language. . . . Zhao's images deploy a set of conventions borrowed from the context of fine art to depict a significant issue, Beijing's pollution, that would have demanded a more sober and didactic approach. The cynical detachment of *Water* and *Beijing Green* . . . was symptomatic of the purposeful intention to stir and even offend the viewer. . . . Zhao's peculiar brand of irony . . . is less the

symptom of passive acceptance of ecological destruction than a means by which
the artist aims to address them; it is less about *defusing*, than of *engaging* the anger
caused by the massive environmental destruction of Beijing.[14]

Magagnoli goes on to link this ironic mode to the specific timing—that is, a few
months before the Beijing Olympics in 2008—by which the photographic series
were exhibited. During that time, the Chinese government launched a campaign
designed to promote the image of China globally, and one prominent discourse
associated with this attempt involved the utopian vision of forging an environmentally sustainable and economically prosperous China through a return to traditional
Chinese values. With this particular historical context, the ironic mode of Zhao's
photographic series comes into sharp relief: in using the conventions of traditional
Chinese paintings to beautify pollution and thus presenting himself as a model
citizen abiding by the propagandistic discourse conflating environmentalism with
Chinese tradition and nationalism, Zhao ironically exposed Beijing's environmental decay by camouflaging it.[15]

In *Behemoth*, however, this ironic perspective does not figure as prominently
and gives way to a different framework in which the sublime register of the beautiful is highlighted. As formulated by Edmund Burke and Immanuel Kant, among
others,[16] the sublime entails not a form of benign beauty marked by a sense of calm-
ness and balanced order, but rather a darker, more complex experience comprising both pleasure and displeasure. To be specific, sublimity is typically associated
with a realm of extreme magnitude, power, and/or intensity—what Kant calls the
"Mathematically Sublime" and the "Dynamically Sublime"[17]—that defies the capacity of our mind to organize and make sense of it. Due to its propensity to undermine the faculties of imagination and understanding, the experience of the sublime
often evokes fear and anxiety. Yet it also, ultimately, brings about satisfaction or
even joy by leading us inward to reflection, self-knowledge, and a renewed sense
of inner purposiveness—in other words, an overcoming of sensible constraint (the
finitude of the imagination; a sense of existential powerlessness) by reason, thereby
revealing the supersensible vocation of the mind. According to Robert Doran, this
rational transcendence or elevation of the mind above sensible determination that
is integral to the sublime experience is precisely what constitutes the intellectual
realm of freedom and, by extension, a morally purposeful disposition based upon
the practical—as opposed to the purely theoretical or speculative—use of reason.[18]

This kind of sublime experience is frequently found in nature—in overwhelming storms, massive earthquakes, or immense waterfalls, for instance—but it has also
characterized many works of art, including the landscape paintings of Caspar David
Friedrich and the photographic oeuvre of Sebastião Salgado. In cinema, numerous films by Werner Herzog, his documentaries in particular, may be understood
in terms of the concept of the sublime as well. Consider, for instance, *Lessons of
Darkness* (1992), which documents the ecological ravages of the set-ablaze oil fields

in Kuwait in the aftermath of the Persian Gulf War. From the opening epigraph that reads "The collapse of the stellar universe will occur—like creation—in grandiose splendor,"[19] it is already clear that a defining feature of the film is its simultaneous quest for the apocalyptic, the elegiac, and the spectacularly beautiful. Haunting, fearfully awe-inspiring, and yet, in the words of a critic, "obscenely beautiful images" of the calamitous circumstance[20]—endless aerial traveling shots of burning oil fields, lakes and forests covered with oil, and structures reduced to rubble and wreckage; uncanny and hypnotic pictures of firefighters working against massive fields of fire—dominate the film. To those critics reprimanding the film for its aestheticization of horror, Herzog responded bluntly that he was merely following the leads of Dante, Francisco Goya, Pieter Brueghel, and Hieronymus Bosch.[21] What this retort reminds us is that Western art has a long tradition of spectacularizing (i.e., aestheticizing) a terrible or pitiful reality, whether it be a gory battle, a devastated landscape, or, in a more imaginary realm, tortures in hell. To be sure, there are different kinds of beauty, and what we experience in *Lessons of Darkness*—and in the images of horror and grief by the artists invoked by Herzog—is not something associated with grace, refinement, or a balanced, harmonious form preadapted to our judgement. Rather, the beauty is of a more challenging kind, one that leads to a state of sublimity and is capable of disturbing and even disrupting our habitual sensibility and imagination. The recuperation that follows, via a kind of internal probing and reorientation, helps form a new moral consciousness and thus opens up possible ethical interventions.

To further explore this complex intertwining of aesthetics and ethics (and therefore politics), I turn to idea of the "toxic sublime" proposed by Jennifer Peeples. Focusing on the work of Canadian landscape photographer Edward Burtynsky, which evinces a penchant for creating stunning images of polluted and contaminated environments, Peeples argues that the aesthetic—or aestheticized—choices of Burtynsky "capture/create the sublime in the toxic," which manifests itself first and foremost in "the tensions that arise from recognizing the toxicity of a place, object, or situation, while simultaneously appreciating its mystery, magnificence and ability to inspire awe."[22] For Peeples, Burtynsky's photographic work, through its use of massive industrial projects as subject matter, its limited descriptions of what is shown, and its choice of framing, camera distance and angle, and image size, is permeated with precisely the kind of tensions underlining the toxic sublime—tensions between beauty and repulsiveness, magnitude and insignificance, known and unknown, inhabitation and desolation, and security and risk. In the photograph *Nickel Tailings #34*, for instance, the visual beauty of the neon-red river cutting through banks of black earth is held in paradoxical tension with the fact that the vibrant red color is actually the result of pollution (nickel tailings), and the lack of explanatory text adds to the sense of unknown danger.[23] *Silver Lake Operations #1*, on the other hand, provides a long-distance bird-eye's view of a mine in Western Australia, where all forms of human activity are reduced to tiny, irrelevant dots.[24]

These tension-ridden images, in bringing out the complexity, ambiguity, and irrationality of the devastated landscapes, are seen as eliciting in the viewers a sublime response—a response marked by conflicting feelings of marvel, amazement, alienation, and horror—that opens up spaces for ethical reflection and attitude change by bringing about the active contemplation of the self in relation to the destruction one witnesses.

The tensions and dissonances noted by Peeples in Burtynsky's work are no less evident in *Behemoth*. For instance, like the photograph of the Australian mine discussed earlier, the film frequently foregrounds the tension between magnitude and insignificance by using panoramic shots that juxtapose immense mine pits (whose seemingly endless boundaries are highlighted by the use of slow, continuous pans) with trucks and individuals that are reduced to indistinguishable dots. The sheer magnitude of the mine pits is mind-boggling and creates a sense of awe as well as alienation and fear—as if we had landed on an alien planet where our habitual ways of thinking and understanding no longer worked.

There are also many images that conjure beauty while evoking repulsiveness and even terror at the same time. Near the beginning of the film, we see a shot of mountain ranges bathed in early morning light and shrouded with fog-like haze. While the image is visually appealing, the viewers realize that it has a darker aspect in that the smoky haze, its atmospheric and "auratic" quality notwithstanding, is in reality caused by massive controlled explosions that shred mountains into pieces and release invisible toxins into the air.

Figure 3.1: Human insignificance against the immensity of the mine pit in *Behemoth* (2015).

Figure 3.2: An auratic landscape with shredded mountains and invisible toxins in *Behemoth* (2015).

Similarly, the red/orange smoke and halos embellishing the mine at nighttime make for an arrestingly beautiful image, but the alluring visual surface also reveals a depressing truth: the around-the-clock operation of the mining plant and, by extension, the uninterrupted destruction of the environment.

There are other examples. On the one hand, we see quite a few occasions in which the film brilliantly juxtaposes two opposing worlds—the natural and contaminated environments—together in stunning single shots. In one instance, a kind of internal montage divides the frame between the lush green grassland on which a nomadic family and its herd of sheep depend for their continued existence, and the ugly grey mass brought about by open-cast mining, thereby powerfully capturing the clashes between industrial growth and preservation of nature as well as a pastoral way of life. The use of a telephoto lens, which has the effect of flattening the space and thus bringing the mine, the female shepherd, and her sheep alarmingly close to one another, further heightens the conflicts.

On the other hand, it is worth noting the powerful sequence that depicts work in an iron foundry, where the visual pleasure of the images (the scarlet red dominating the screen, the flying sparks and flames from the blast furnace) is countered by the horrifying sight of the workers being engulfed in the searing heat (and noise). As this last example demonstrates, the tensions and contradictions between beauty and repulsiveness that haunt the film are not limited exclusively to the altered natural environments, but can be observed in man-made, manufactured landscapes.

Figure 3.3: The uncanny juxtaposition of natural and contaminated environments in *Behemoth* (2015).

Figure 3.4: Beauty and repulsiveness in iron smelting in *Behemoth* (2015).

Figure 3.5: A "ghost city": The broken dream of China's "economic miracle" in *Behemoth* (2015).

The closing part of the film, which focuses on one of those "ghost cities" symptomatic of the illusory nature of China's "economic miracle," offers another case in point. I return to this broken utopian dream later in this chapter; for now, it suffices to highlight the sense of utter uncanniness and even fear in watching this perfect, clean, but utterly empty and lifeless city—pristine but also unreal, like an apocalypse-themed movie set.

There is no question that *Behemoth* is visually striking, locating a kind of pictorial beauty in the otherwise dreadful and abhorrent landscapes, but this does not disguise or mitigate the ugliness of the subject matter that the film is trying to confront. Rather, the viewers of the film find themselves, time and again, in a conflicted state of awe and alienation, marvel and fear, both riveted and frightened by the sublime images of the contaminated and manufactured environments. These conflicting experiences, I argue, give the film a force that is not available to works that focus simply on scientific descriptions or take a more directly polemical approach. As with *Lessons of Darkness* and the oversized photographs of Burtynsky, *Behemoth* opens up new perceptual and reflective consciousness that disturbs our complacency, induces thought and contemplation, and may even force an internal reckoning that raises questions of complicity and choice in our relationship to the fossil-fuel economy and, more broadly, to our insatiable desire to consume.

Soundscape, Storytelling, and Symbolism

My analysis has so far concentrated on the distinctive visual rhetoric of *Behemoth*. However, insofar as *Behemoth* is a film rather than a work of photography, the focus cannot be on the compositional choices in the images alone; it must expand to include other elements that inform cinema as a medium. Sound is a good case in point: despite being eclipsed to some extent by the stunning visuals, the soundscape of *Behemoth* adds to the impact of the film in important ways. For instance, the eerie tones of Mongolian/Tuvan throat singing—sounding like ghosts from a different era or realm—heighten the mythological undercurrents of the film, which not only draws on the Bible in its invocation of the titular monster but also, as we will see shortly, takes inspiration from Dante's vivid imagining of the afterlife in the *Divine Comedy*. Also worth mentioning is the sequence set in the iron foundry, where an electro-acoustic, heavily percussive soundtrack gradually builds up in intensity and mixes—imperceptibly—with the noises of roaring flame and heavy machinery, and is eventually displaced by them. The blurred distinction between nondiegetic music and diegetic sound echoes the complex interplay between beauty and repulsiveness noted earlier.

An even more important element arises from the time-based nature of the cinematic medium and pertains to the structural-narrative aspect of the film. It is true that, as I pointed out at the beginning of this chapter, *Behemoth* does not have a clear or apparent narrative. Yet this does not mean the absence of a certain narrative structure or trajectory in the film. In fact, a major reference for *Behemoth* is Dante's *Divine Comedy*, which provides not just the film's only spoken words (i.e., the voiceover quotations adapted from the epic poem scattered throughout the movie) but, more importantly, the Inferno-Purgatory-Paradise schema central to the structural framework of the film.

Throughout art history, the landscape of hell is characteristically imagined and depicted as barren and blackened, filled with smoke, fire, and agonizing heat. In *Behemoth*, inferno is represented in a similar way by the fire of scorching iron-works and the black/grey scars that mark the massive mine pits. The descent deeper and deeper into the seemingly bottomless mine shafts—captured by an amazing 100-second continuous shot—parallels the movement down the pit of Hell, level by level. Purgatory manifests itself in the episodes that portray the miners and iron smelters struggling with and dying of pneumoconiosis, otherwise known as black lung disease, while Paradise, ironically, is represented by the "ghost city" of Kangbashi in the prefecture-level municipality aptly named Ordos, which in Mongolian means "palaces in heaven."[25] As Christian Sorace points out, the Ordos government intended to build Kangbashi as a new administrative capital after a natural resource boom that began in 2004, but this newly constructed city failed to attract residents and was thus left empty and desolate of life for many years—a perfect symbol for the bursting of the real estate bubble brought about by unbridled development in China.[26] Drawing on Dante's vision of the afterlife and reimagining it within the reality of ecological devastation and blind economic growth in present-day Inner Mongolia, the (allegorical) journey through Inferno, Purgatory, and Paradise in *Behemoth* not only offers the film a structural framework but also provides the viewers with a certain direction in interpreting the otherwise ambiguous, tension-ridden images.

Another way to conceive of the film's narrative trajectory is to see it as following, in Zhao Liang's own words, the "supply chain" (*chanyelian*) of urban construction: a chain of activities involving the extraction of coal (the first part of the film); the manufacture of steel using coal as the main source of fuel (the second part, set in the iron foundry); and ultimately, urban construction as the culmination of the entire process (the "ghost city" in the last part).[27] Seen along with the Inferno-Purgatory-Paradise framework, this "supply chain" narrative—or its rupture, to be precise, as evidenced by the eerie, utterly mind-boggling sight of the "ghost city" in the haunting last sequences—makes clear the critical stance of the film. The portrayal of the "capitalist dream" as a mere mirage, a hollow illusion, confronts the viewers with their lifestyle choices and how those choices help bring about the horrendous inferno and illusory paradise seen in the film. As the director himself puts it:

> The film's title, *Behemoth*, symbolizes the growth of an enormous evil energy. Just like after the opening of Pandora's box, the devil grows recklessly. It is the totality of humankind's desire and greed. Each and every one of us is a part of the devil. All of us are its accomplices. We all have seen the catastrophic consequences of fuel politics. As some of us are enjoying a more and more luxurious lifestyle, shouldn't we reflect on that way of life? We all are consumers of natural resources, so we are all accomplices of that evil that's hurting the environment. All of us are part of the monster.[28]

The temporality of cinema also allows Zhao Liang to draw attention to what a landscape photographer such as Burtynsky can only hint at: the detail of human lives.[29] Early in the film, we see some lovely pastoral sequences—a horseman riding free on the steppe, sheep grazing lazily on the verdant green plain, a lone baby boy running around in the meadow—that show the unspoiled natural environment and the idyllic life of the nomadic community. These calm and blissful scenes, however, are few and brief, and quickly surpassed by the destructive reality of heavy coal mining: mountains are reduced to rubble; grass fields are turned into ashen pits; and—as poignantly indicated in a shot that juxtaposes the same baby boy mentioned earlier sitting and playing on a shrinking grassland with a blackened, smoke-filled grey mass (that used to be green mountains) in the horizon—the fate of the nomadic community is very much called into question. Despite not being clearly stated in words, the inevitable loss of pastureland and the displacement of the nomadic community are implied through images.

Later on, the film shifts its focus to the workers who toil in the mines and in the iron foundry. *Behemoth* eschews the traditional documentary method in its refusal to use talking-head interviews or to provide biographical information about the miners and iron smelters—and members of the nomadic community, for that matter—who appear in the film. What we find instead is an adamantly visual approach. The film simply observes, in a quietly understated way, its subjects and their daily work: miners risking their lives to work in the depths of a mine shaft, miner-scavengers shoveling coal dust endlessly through the night, and iron smelters enduring the scorching heat in front of the red-hot furnace. There are also scenes that show the workers living in basic, dilapidated rooms with few signs of material wealth, while long, lingering looks are directed at pneumoconiosis patients (presumably workers affected by coal or iron dust) who, with weary faces and vacuous eyes, lie tethered to oxygen tanks in their sickbeds and struggle to breathe. But all this time, no one speaks. For some, this refusal to give the workers a voice seems to further their exploitation by robbing them of their opportunity to speak for themselves—the reduction of the powerless to their powerlessness. Such a view, however, underestimates the power and eloquence of the images to evoke, and illuminate, the stories of these workers. It also misses the larger point that the film is trying to make: the lack of biographical details or any kind of individual storytelling serves to emphasize the workers not so much as individualized beings but as a group—in other words, exploited migrant workers who nonetheless serve as the pivotal laborers of China's modernization process. This "abstraction" is further accentuated by the formal treatment of the workers' bodies, which are often depicted as some kind of damaged matter, just like the devastated landscapes. Whether it is the drawn-out

Figure 3.6: The human body as damaged matter in *Behemoth* (2015).

close-ups on the workers' battered faces, the extended sequence in which we see a woman scrubbing away the dirt and dust caked on the body of her husband, or the labored breathing of frail, bedridden workers suffering from black lung disease, the human bodies become a character—a storyteller, if you will—in their own right.

Zhao Liang describes his approach in this way:

> I don't have to introduce the background of each person specifically. All we know is that this is a group of people who've been tossed about on earth and in the end they didn't get anything. Their bodies are worn out and the environment is damaged. That's all.[30]

Just as the landscape—shredded mountains, grasslands buried beneath ash, air filled with coal dust and other toxins—serves as a testimony of the ecological devastation brought about by heavy mining and, more broadly, by the fossil-fuel economy, the damaged bodies of the workers bear (mute) witness to their "expendability" as well as their "precarity and serial interchangeability,"[31] evoking a harrowing experience that defies words.

Last but not least, it is important not to overlook the poetic use of symbolism in the film. A good case in point is the recurrent figure of a naked body, often—but not always—shown in an embryonically curled position amid the damaged landscape. With its allusion to a fetus and thus to the origin of life, this naked figure is emblematic of humanity in its purest and most unadulterated form, one that is associated more with the natural order than with the modern technologized culture that has come to define our world today. But just as the natural order has become increasingly vulnerable and sick, this symbol of purity, of originary affinity with nature,

Figure 3.7: A naked, fetus-like figure in a warped reality in *Behemoth* (2015).

Figure 3.8: "We are the miner and the miner is us," from *Behemoth* (2015).

also conjures up fragility and helplessness. That the destiny of the two is inextricably linked is clearly suggested by the fact that the naked figure almost always appears in a warped reality, in a fractured natural landscape that has lost its wholeness. Ironically, as humanity seeks to fulfill its boundless desire and succumbs to the ideology of incessant production and consumption, it is destroying not only its natural Other but also, ultimately, itself.

Another important and recurrent symbolic figure is the guide with a mirror on his back. On one level, this almost surreal figure alludes to the poet Virgil in the *Divine Comedy*, who leads Dante through the underworld and heaven. Yet the mirror on the guide's back is a new idea—a symbol of self-reflection that compels viewers to contemplate their complicity in today's eco-crisis. This symbolic point is made most clearly at the end of the film, when the guide is walking along an empty street in the ghost city of Ordo. For the first time in the film, we see in the mirror the reflection of an actual human being—a coal miner holding a potted green plant. Yet the fact that the camera is following the guide directly from behind gives the impression that we are looking at the mirror image of ourselves. The implication here is stark: we are the miner and the miner is us; both are victims in the fake "miracle" of China's blind and unfettered development, with the plant being a poignant reminder of nature under siege.

Yet this moment of reflexive recognition is brief and fleeting; with a shift of the mirror, the reflection of the miner and the plant disappears without a trace. The camera then comes to a halt, even though the guide continues on into the distance before the film cuts to black and ends. In a way, the guide is no longer needed as the journey—one that leads the viewers through the devastation of the natural environment, the plight of the laborers, and the rupture of the supply or capital chain—is over. Through this journey, the film has opened up possibilities for introspection and self-reflection that, while not guaranteed, could lead to changes in attitude and ethical responses that would make a much-needed difference in today's world.

Conclusion

Behemoth is a film of devastating beauty and splendor. This acknowledgement, however, does not mean that the film "aestheticizes"—and fails to make an ethical response to—the ecological and social ravages of unfettered growth in neo-liberal China. Rather, with its arresting yet unnerving imagery, the film is marked by the quality of the toxic sublime and brings about a tension-ridden experience that, while not involving a direct form of criticism, is capable of triggering ethical reflection and reorientation. In addition, the film uses an allusive narrative structure and poetic symbolism through which the work's critical stance is rendered more concrete (without succumbing to simplistic didacticism). At the same time, by making references to a set of global canonical texts (notably *Divine Comedy* and the Bible) and engaging with certain trends in contemporary film and artistic practices devoted to environmental concerns, the film clearly aims itself not just at viewers in China but at a broader international audience; it can thus be viewed as part of a growing worldwide phenomenon of ecologically engaged cinema and art. Overall, in going beyond traditional documentary approaches and positioning itself within the contexts of global ecological crisis and environmental communication, *Behemoth* opens up new possibilities for a critical ecocinema, one that inspires reflexive thinking and reshapes sensibility and imagination toward a world devastated by our own insatiable desire.

Notes

1.   Along with this proliferation of films devoted to environmental issues has come the growing field of what can be called eco-cinecriticism. Some representative works associated with this trend include Jennifer Fay, *Inhospitable World: Cinema in the Time of the Anthropocene* (New York: Oxford University Press, 2018); Rayson K. Alex and S. Susan Deborah, eds., *Ecodocumentarie: Critical Essays* (London: Palgrave Macmillan, 2016); Tommy Gustafsson and Pietari Kääpä, eds., *Transnational Ecocinema: Film Culture in an Era of Ecological Transformation* (Bristol: Intellect, 2013); Paula Willoquet-Maricondi, ed., *Framing the World: Explorations in Ecocriticism and Film* (Charlottsville: University of Virginia Press, 2010); David Ingram, *Green Screen: Environmentalism and Hollywood Cinema* (Exeter: University of Exeter Press, 2004); and Scott MacDonald, *The Garden in the Machine: A Field Guide to Independent Films about Place* (Berkeley: University of California Press, 2001).

2. Sheldon H. Lu and Jiayan Mi, eds., *Chinese Ecocinema in an Age of Environmental Challenge* (Hong Kong: Hong Kong University Press, 2009).

3. Specifically, this is what Zhao Liang said: "Most of the time, I take some ugly affair and make it 'look beautiful' on film. But isn't our world often packaged to appear beautiful in this way, especially politics?" Quoted in Christian Sorace, "Paradise under Construction," *Made in China* no. 3 (July–September 2016), accessed September 15, 2019, https://madeinchinajournal.com/2016/09/27/paradise-under-construction/.

4. Paolo Magagnoli, "The Civilized Artist Beautifies Pollution: Zhao Liang's *Water* and *Beijing Green*," *Journal of Contemporary Chinese Art* 3, no. 3 (2016): 367–76. The photographs in the two series can be found in Zhao Liang's official website, specifically at http://zhaoliangstudio.com/work/beijing-green-series (*Beijing Green*) and http://zhaoliangstudio.com/work/water-series (*Water*).

5. Michael Hatch, "Zhao Liang: Three Shadows Photography Center," *Artforum International* 47, no. 1 (September 2008): 482–83.

6. Nadin Mai, "*Behemoth*—Zhao Liang (2015)," *The Art(s) of Slow Cinema*, March 14, 2016, accessed October 2, 2019, https://theartsofslowcinema.com/2016/03/14/behemoth-zhao-liang-2015/.

7. Donald Clarke, "*Behemoth* Review: A Chilling Study of China's Current Environmental Malaise," *The Irish Times*, August 17, 2016, accessed October 2, 2019, https://www.irishtimes.com/culture/film/behemoth-review-a-chilling-study-of-china-s-current-environmental-malaise-1.2759408.

8. Susan Sontag, *Regarding the Pain of Others* (New York: Picador, 2003), 76–77.

9. Sontag, *Regarding the Pain of Others*, 81.

10. The "New Documentary Movement" can be traced to the independent (i.e., non-state-sponsored) documentary productions made in the early to mid-1990s, with films such as Wu Wenguang's *Bumming in Beijing: The Last Dreamers* (1990), and Duan Jinchuan and Zhang Yuan's *The Square* (1994). At the outset, these new documentaries tended to downplay overt political content and focused more on personal experiences or on the broad relations of power operating in contemporary Chinese society. But with the coming of the digital era and thus the expanding opportunities in both film production and circulation, the movement started to develop in new directions. For instance, the later documentaries became more socially engaged and provided a forum for grassroots perspectives that often challenged those offered in state-sanctioned representations. Furthermore, the lightweight technology (e.g., digital video) intensified a spontaneous style that can already be seen in their predecessors during the pre-digital era. The documentaries of Zhao Liang fall generally within this later trend toward critical engagement with public issues, even though *Behemoth*, as we are about to see, embraces a more self-consciously experimental approach from a formal and stylistic perspective. For more discussion on the independent Chinese documentary movement, see Dan Edwards, *Independent Chinese Documentary: Alternative Visions, Alternative Publics* (Edinburgh: Edinburgh University Press, 2015).

11. Jie Li, "Filming Power and the Powerless: Zhao Liang's *Crime and Punishment* (2007) and *Petition* (2009)," *China Perspectives*, no. 1 (March 2010): 35.

12. Bill Nichols, *Introduction to Documentary*, 2nd ed. (Bloomington: Indiana University Press, 2010), 150.

13. "Interviewer [sic] with Lu Yangqiao," *Zhao Liang Studio*, October 4, 2015, accessed September 15, 2019, http://zhaoliangstudio.com/p/71.

14. Magagnoli, "The Civilized Artist Beautifies Pollution," 370.

15. Magagnoli, "The Civilized Artist Beautifies Pollution," 371–73.

16. See, for instance, Edmund Burke, *A Philosophical Inquiry into the Origin of Our Ideas of the Sublime and Beautiful* (New York: Simon and Brown, 2013) and Immanuel Kant, *Critique of the Power of Judgement*, ed. Paul Guyer, trans. Paul Guyer and Eric Matthews (Cambridge: Cambridge University Press, 2000). For a general discussion of Burke's and Kant's theories of the sublime, see Robert Doran, *The Theory of the Sublime from Longinus to Kant* (Cambridge: Cambridge University Press, 2015), chaps. 6–12.

17. For Kant's discussions of the concepts, see *Critique of the Power of Judgement*, 131–43, 143–49.

18. Doran, *Theory of the Sublime from Longinus to Kant*, 186–220, 261–66.

19. The epigraph, made up by Herzog himself, was misattributed deliberately to influential French mathematician and philosopher Blaise Pascal in the film. For his defense of this "stunt," see Herzog, "On the Absolute, the Sublime, and Ecstatic Truth," trans. Moira Weigel, *Arion* 17, no. 3 (Winter 2010): 1–12.

20. Janet Maslin, "Werner Herzog's Vision of a World Gone Amok," *The New York Times*, October 25, 1995, https://www.nytimes.com/1995/10/25/movies/film-review-werner-herzog-s-vision-of-a-world-gone-amok.html.

21. This is specifically what Herzog said: "They accused me of 'aestheticizing' horror and hated the film so much that when I walked down the aisle of the cinema I was spat at. They said the film was dangerously authoritarian, so I decided to be authoritarian at my very best. I stood before them and said, 'Mr. Dante did the same in his *Inferno* and Mr. Goya did it in his painting, and Brueghel and Bosch, too.' You should have heard the uproar." Quoted in Eric Ames, *Ferocious Reality: Documentary According to Werner Herzog* (Minneapolis: University of Minnesota Press, 2012), 73.

22. Jennifer Peeples, "Toxic Sublime: Imaging Contaminated Landscapes," *Environmental Communication* 5, no. 4 (December 2011): 375.

23. The photograph can be found at https://www.edwardburtynsky.com/projects/photographs/tailings.

24. The photograph can be found at https://www.edwardburtynsky.com/projects/photographs/mines.

25. Zhao Liang, "Director's Statement," *Grasshopper Film—Behemoth Press Kit*, accessed September 15, 2019, http://grasshopperfilm.com/wp-content/uploads/2016/01/Behemoth---Press-Kit.pdf.

26. Sorace, "Paradise under Construction."

27. Sorace, "Paradise under Construction."

28. Zhao, "Director's Statement."

29. This point echoes the observation made by Jennifer Baichwal, whose documentary *Manufactured Landscapes* (2006) takes as its subject Burtynsky's large-format photographs of factories and industrial blight. According to Baichwal, the overwhelming abstraction of Burtynsky's photographs is provocative but also problematic, and her documentary was designed to balance this abstract detachment with the "innumerable

small parts" and "teeming organic life" that lie beneath the images. See Nadia Bozak, "*Manufactured Landscapes*," *Film Quarterly* 62, no. 2 (Winter 2008): 68.

30. Quoted in Amy Qin, "As China Hungers for Coal, 'Behemoth' Studies the Ravages at the Source," *New York Times*, December 28, 2015, accessed October 2, 2019, https://www.nytimes.com/2015/12/29/world/asia/china-film-zhao-liang-inner-mongolia-coal-behemoth.html.

31. Sorace, "Paradise under Construction."

Part II

Audiences and Reception in Transnational Contexts

4

From *Gone with the Wind* to *The Spring River Flows East*

Melodrama and Historical Imagination in Postwar Chinese Cinema

Kenny Kwok Kwan Ng

The Tears of Yangtze was shown in Shanghai for eighty-four consecutive days, and broke all box-office records of any film ever exhibited in the city. From the four million citizens of Shanghai, eight hundred thousand saw this screen play, which is descriptive of the life of the Chinese people both during wartime and after the Japanese surrender. In another word, every one out of five Shanghai citizens attended the theaters and shed tears . . .

 The Tears of Yangtze is divided into two parts: *Eight War-torn Years* and *The Dawn*, which, when shown together, run for four hours. It breaks the record for film length, as compared with *Gone with the Wind*. But, what is depicted in this picture bears no resemblance to a complicated western romance. It is a true and general account of the life of a family of a petty urban citizen during and after the war.[1]

Commended as "China's best film of 1947" by the veteran leftist critic Xia Yan, *The Spring River Flows East* (*Yi jiang chun shui xiang dong liu*, dir. Cai Chusheng and Zheng Junli, 1947, a.k.a. *The Tears of Yangtze*) was compared with *Gone with the Wind* (dir. Victor Fleming, 1939) for its record film length, grand historical sweep, and enormous popularity. *The Spring River* marked the resurgence of the creativity and popularity of postwar Chinese cinema. But for Xia Yan, there were fundamental differences between this foreign film and the Chinese film: while *Gone with the Wind* appealed to Chinese audiences as a "complicated Western romance," the enormous popularity of *The Spring River* was attributed to its thematic content and artistic style. Xia Yan claimed that the Chinese film's striking power lay in its historical authenticity, with its faithful account of "the life of a family of a petty urban citizen during and after the war." The seriousness of its subject matter made the film stand "unrivaled" when compared with many Hollywood and European productions because of its "broadness and seriousness of communicating the people's true existence, and in its depth of presenting social problems."[2] Xia Yan also compared the Chinese film with another Hollywood production, *The Best Years of Our Lives* (dir. William Wyler, 1946), for the portrayal of the war experience of the common people. All in all, Xia Yan made a patriotic plea to assert the superiority of Chinese films over Hollywood and foreign pictures.

Gone with the Wind and *The Spring River* became big box-office hits in Shanghai's cinema theaters, respectively, before and after the Sino-Japanese War. Both films narrated the war from the perspective of the people's daily lives, blending the developmental plots of history and heartbreaking romance. *The Spring River* offers an encounter with global melodrama that invites comparison and raises questions concerning the affective appeal and ideological effect of storytelling across genres and national landscapes, whereas melodramatic narratives themselves unquestionably thrive on local idiosyncrasies and heterogeneous cultural traditions. This chapter begins by exploring the popularity of *Gone with the Wind* in China and how critics and commentators framed the popularity of the film for the public, engaging in a conversation around melodrama, popular appeal, and politics. It proceeds to inquire how leftist critics and commentators helped to mobilize the audiences to view *The Spring River* as an authentic historical picture, rather than an explicit melodrama with popular appeal.

In her study of contemporary global melodramas, Carla Marcantonio notes, "Melodrama's ties to globalization come first by way of the mode's relationship to nationalism."[3] The case of *The Spring River* poses the challenge of studying Chinese melodramatic film globally within and beyond the demarcation of national cinema. This point brings me to my final analysis of *The Spring River*: how successfully could progressive filmmakers and critics use a melodramatic form to forge a new spectatorship within China's popular cultural sphere amidst the competing interests of commercialism, political activism, and nationalism? Significantly, the popular epic exploits the roles and representation of women to offer a political discussion of national identity. How does the film's particular melodramatic representation work or not work for a leftist film and its discourse of nationalism? I will analyze the representational strategies of *The Spring River* to delineate how the film shapes the discourse of nationhood rooted in a conservative vision of family and womanhood, and reveal the inherent conflicts and tensions of the melodramatic film.

In Dialogue with Melodrama: Left-Wing Interventions

The Spring River was released on October 9, 1947 (on the eve of National Day) to tremendous box-office success. The film was screened for three months, from October 9, 1947 to January 23, 1948, drawing a record-breaking attendance of 712,874.[4] The film was explicitly advertised as "the Chinese version of *Gone with the Wind*" and was a famous "twelve-hankies" movie when it was released in Hong Kong and southeast China.[5] Another advertisement promoted *The Spring River* as a heartrending movie: "The film will move thousands of people! Will enthuse thousands of people! Will make thousands of people feel sad! Will move thousands of people to tears!" To address the audience, it said, "What is described in this movie—is your concern, and my concern as well. It is the concern of everyone. You and I have experienced what is described in this movie; you and I will feel very close to it!"[6]

In the wake of the popular reception of *The Spring River*, *Gone with the Wind* was re-released on December 10, 1947, and ran until January 6, 1948. Before that, the American movie had already enjoyed a prewar popularity when it was given its first Chinese screening on June 18, 1940, only seven months after its US premiere in Atlanta, Georgia. The Hollywood movie became an enormous favorite for Shanghai's filmgoers, screening in cinema theaters for 43 days until July 30. In Shanghai, *Gone with the Wind* topped all other Hollywood full-house big hits amid a pre–Pearl Harbor boom of American films.[7] Both the novel and film began to gain public attention in local newspapers.

Cinematically speaking, *Gone with the Wind* follows the conventions of women's romance. Scarlett O'Hara (Vivien Leigh) suffers from unrequited love in the course of the Civil War that brought about the demise of the Old South (a paradise lost). The film is the "great White American melodrama": Scarlett embodies the modern White self, the resilient survivor, and the capitalist entrepreneur who uses any means to rebuild her home from the ashes of war.[8] The Hollywood blockbuster was popular in 1940 Shanghai, it is argued, because film audiences could easily map their harrowing experiences and war-torn homeland onto the images of Atlanta's destruction. "Its narrative of faded nobility on the wrong side of history, of individual suffering and families brought low," offered compelling storytelling for Chinese spectators to conjure the traumatic experiences and memories of the war.[9]

Nonetheless, Shanghai's newspaper advertisements exhibited a de-historicized promotion of *Gone with the Wind*. Media campaigns for the Hollywood hit apparently disregarded the historical sweep of the movie and American Southern history, and media publicity catered to Chinese audiences that consumed the war epic largely as a historical romance: Chinese readers and viewers tended to identify with the blockbuster as the melodrama of the heroine and her misadventure. In Shanghai's newspapers, the quick-witted and tough Scarlett was associated with the unfortunate Lin Daiyu in *Dream of the Red Chamber* (*Hongloumeng*)—the famous literary prototype of tragic beauty in vernacular Chinese fiction. These advertisements compared *Gone with the Wind* with the fetching love story in *Dream* by virtue of its sentimentalism and profound portrayal of the heroine. The Chinese title of the film, *Luanshi jiaren*, which means "the beautiful maiden in a time of turmoil," recalled the traditional literary prototype of "scholar-beauty" (*caizi jiaren*) in traditional popular fiction.[10] This title was adopted so as to promote the romance of a charming but ill-fated Scarlett who marries three times in *Gone with the Wind*.

In this regard, it is illuminating to see how Xia Yan exploited the different melodramatic and popular appeals of *Gone with the Wind* and *The Spring River* to engage in a diametrically different public discussion of melodrama and politics. The leftist critic instructed the viewer on how to see a Chinese picture and differentiate it from a Hollywood/foreign one, as well as constructing an empirical mass audience for the film (who were patriotic, serious, and progressive). Xia Yan used the Chinese popular reception of *Gone with the Wind*—which had tended to de-emphasize the Hollywood film's historical aspect—to debunk the frivolous nature of all Western films. On the other hand, he evaded the sentimental and romantic strains of the Chinese melodrama that he praised. In the leftist discourse, any indigenous film and serious artistic production had to be associated with the representation and dissemination of images of the nation. Xia Yan argued that *The Spring River* was not just a commercial enterprise, but a national cultural project and an achievement in leftist cinema. He gave different reasons, though, for the phenomenal success of *Gone with the Wind* and *The Spring River* at the box office. Xia Yan maintained that *Gone with the Wind* owed its attractiveness entirely to its entertainment value, whereas the favorable reception of *The Spring River* came from its artistic quality and patriotism; in so doing, he chose to neglect the melodramatic pathos of the Chinese picture.

Xia Yan's remark resembled the tactic adopted by those newspaper advertisements that stressed the potential of the Chinese movie to match Western films and outperform other Chinese films. These ads claimed that the Chinese film swept away all mediocre techniques because of its quality—"the highest artistic achievement of screenplay, direction, performance, and music"—and because of the film's spirit of patriotism, which made it "a grand masterpiece dedicated to the nation by China's outstanding film artists."[11] In short, big Hollywood productions held the Chinese audience's interest by the sheer visual amplitude of the exotic. The major function of such advertising was to distinguish Chinese films from foreign films: "Chinese films were 'real' where foreign films were 'spectacle.' Chinese films were 'innovative' and had claims to 'quality' where foreign films were full of technological novelty (such as color) but were entertainment pieces only. Chinese films were 'patriotic' where foreign films were 'exotic.'"[12]

Xia Yan deliberately slighted melodrama's powerful affective recall of wartime memories in both the Hollywood and Chinese pictures, and framed *The Spring River* for audiences as a genuine Chinese national story without acknowledging the film's star appeal. *The Spring River* had a strong cast that included famous film stars: both Tao Jin and Bai Yang, who played the hero and heroine in the film, were celebrities in Shanghai cinema. The production of many left-wing films counted on the star system, film songs' popularization, film advertisements, and movie magazines for promotion in an urban, commercial setting. Further, contemporary critics believe that what made the postwar Chinese epic films achieve spectacular success—such as *The Spring River* and *Eight Thousand li of Clouds and Moon* (*Ba qian li lu yun he yue*, dir. Shi Dongshan, 1947)—was the inscription of war memories, which could have captured the mood of bitterness and despair of the spectators.[13] Paul Pickowicz explicates the enormous appeals of postwar Chinese epic films by saying that "the primary target for these films was people who stayed behind and endured the harsh Japanese occupation."[14] For the Chinese audience of the late 1940s, a film like *The Spring River* must have unleashed strong identifications with the traumatic experience of the war in people's everyday lives.[15]

Since *The Spring River* has been considered a landmark in "leftist film" (*zuoyi dianying*),[16] a balanced view on this leftist cinema is needed in order to do full justice to the artistic achievement and historical significance of the film.[17] The core narrative of Chinese film history, as represented by Cheng Jihua, Li Shaobai, and Xing Zuwen's *The History of the Development of Chinese Film* (*Zhongguo dianying fazhan shi*), placed an exclusive emphasis on the development of a leftist, progressive national cinema.[18] This established narrative of film history dictated an antagonistic struggle of China's national film industry against the cultural domination of American film. It hinged upon a storytelling of how the left-wing film workers had capitalized on growing patriotic sentiments in the wake of the Japanese invasion that began in September 1931, and succeeded in revolutionizing the film medium into a mass art of conscious social criticism.

Cheng, Li, and Xing's partisan view of Chinese film history has been challenged from divergent critical perspectives. The authors of the 1963 work seemingly have overemphasized the influence of leftist cinema, characterized by a categorical denial of commercial considerations in the film market. While China's left-wing cinema took the view that film ought to promote the audience's awareness of social ills and advocate for radical social reform, it nonetheless relied heavily on sentimentalism and populism as a form of mass entertainment. Scholars have reassessed the tradition of leftist cinema as an amalgam of multigeneric forms of representation. Pickowicz defines the nature of Chinese leftist cinema as a "marriage between classic melodrama and elementary Marxism," as it underscored the new subject of the laboring masses and the sympathy for them.[19] Ma Ning argues that while leftist filmmakers were influenced by Hollywood melodrama, they incorporated more radical Soviet editing with local popular discourses of the time in their films. Progressive and nationalistic as these films were, the leftist mode of filmmaking excelled at exploiting Hollywood conventions to achieve popular film narration with radical leanings.[20] Laikwan Pang proposes that the commercial success of some leftist films actually rendered these films more effective in disseminating the ideas of left-wing intellectuals to a wide audience.[21]

A comparative view of the melodramatic mode in film is called for to discuss a culturally distinct variant like *The Spring River*. The notion of melodrama as conceived in the Western context is used to refer to a historically discredited film genre of inferior works of art that subscribed to an aesthetic of hyperbole, ones that were given to sensationalism and the crude manipulation of audience emotions.[22] Melodrama brought into play a series of bipolar extremes between good and evil, marked by stereotypical characters, heightened emotions, and exaggerated actions, and providing the clear moral meaning missing in the bourgeoisie's daily, lived experience.[23] Historically, as Peter Brooks argues, melodrama emerged as a theatrical form dating back to the French Revolution, and was most vibrant in transitional and uncertain times when the genre functioned to negotiate moral values and truth.[24] Maintaining a global perspective, Marcantonio emphasizes that melodrama has provided a shorthand form for national history to be represented in fiction narratives.[25] In modern China, Pickowicz observes that melodrama became entrenched in China before and after the 1911 Revolution, just as it had once become a popular cultural response to anxieties and moral confusions during the French Revolution.[26]

It is fascinating that the promotion of *The Spring River* was linked directly to its status as China's *Gone with the Wind* in Shanghai's popular sphere, even as the ways in which the Chinese film engages melodramatic forms with national implications demonstrate local and cultural idiosyncrasies in terms of politics and identity. How could a Chinese melodramatic film represent traumatic events and meet the conflicting demands of nationalism (the sovereignty of a nation), commercialism (the rising urban middle class), and left-wing internationalism, which first and foremost needs the vanguard of the enlightened working class and intelligentsia to lead the revolution?

The popularity of *Gone with the Wind* revealed that the dominance of Hollywood movies could serve both as a model and as a foil for native filmmakers. Xia Yan's remarks showed the influences and resonances of the Hollywood popular epic brought to bear on native production. As Chinese filmmakers could not vie with their Hollywood counterparts in terms of financial budget and technical film-production competence, a popular epic like *Gone with the Wind* showed them the public preference for the grandiose and the romantic. This inspiration from the audience's penchant for foreign films—combined with the war experience that drove the Chinese to remember and reconfigure the past—would give them enough incentive and drive to create a modern Chinese epic saga of extensive film length and broad historical scope comparable to the Hollywood film. However, to produce a Chinese popular epic, filmmakers had to abide by the leisure principle of film consumption, inasmuch as they were devoted to making movies as a way to advocate social reform. If Chinese filmmakers could not afford such elaborate mise-en-scène and visual splendor as achieved by the Hollywood big-budget production, they had to turn to film's fictive constructs and its potential power in storytelling, by constructing a family melodrama with epic ambition, and incorporating social and historical references in a film tailored for local tastes.

Family Melodrama, Gender, Nationhood: *The Spring River Flows East*

The Spring River opens with a beautiful scene of the flowing river with the chorus singing the famous Chinese lyric by Li Yu (AD 937–978): "Asked how much sorrow you can take. Alas, it is like a river of spring water running eastwards!" The lyrical as well as the melancholic tone of the opening, however, is followed by a few documentary shots of Shanghai's factories and the lives of the working class, which establishes the realistic time and scene: Shanghai in the wake of the Japanese occupation. Significantly, the opening of the film presents an industrial picture of Shanghai (instead of a metropolitan cityscape), a view that suggests the oppressive conditions of the Shanghai industry and the working class.

Our focus shifts to the female protagonist. We see Sufen (played by Bai Yang), the female worker (proletariat), laboring in a textile factory. Then, romantic music sets in to introduce the sentimental plot of the film. We see Sufen attending an evening school (she probably looks like a "progressive" woman at this point; a worker eager to acquire new knowledge). Our young patriotic hero, called Zhang Zhongliang (a worker intellectual), is the tutor of the class: he is teaching Chinese history, and there is a Chinese map drawn on the chalkboard. We look at the young and handsome man from the female student's perspective, while the woman's gaze shows her desire for the man. In a formulaic romantic plot, Sufen and Zhongliang soon fall in love, marry, and have a son, Kang'er (literally "son of resistance").

In the beginning, the couple has a happy family, but melodramatic twists and turns soon set in and force the couple apart at the outbreak of the Sino-Japanese war in mid-1937. Zhongliang decides to leave for the front and join the Red Cross. Sufen and her mother-in-law and son flee to the family village, but they return to Shanghai during the war period. Meanwhile, Zhongliang is captured by the Japanese during the Red Cross mission. He manages to escape and flees to Chongqing in 1941, but becomes penniless as well as disillusioned with the country. He seeks out his former acquaintance Wang Lizhen (the second woman) for help; there, the young patriotic hero dramatically gives himself up to a life of dancing, drinking, eating, and romancing in Chongqing's high-society circles. Worse, he surrenders to Lizhen's seduction and ends up in her bed, marries her, and leaves his helpless wife and family behind in occupied Shanghai. As we may begin to accept Zhongliang's dramatic change in identity, the male character shows us more than we will expect to see. After the Japanese surrender in 1945, Zhongliang returns to liberated Shanghai to exploit its economic opportunities. In Shanghai, he quickly gets involved in an affair with Lizhen's cousin, He Wenyan (the third woman), who immediately becomes his mistress. A patriotic hero forced to leave his wife on a war mission, Zhongliang goes through a life of hardship and finally becomes a disheartened and "fallen" hero.

E. Ann Kaplan argues that "melodramas" in contemporary Chinese films show grave concerns with the relationship of the individual subject to the state in ways quite different from those found in Western melodramas and film theory. These films portray the "domestic" sphere as the social space, entailing "the level of love/sex, marriage/motherhood, jealousy, loss, murder or other violence; infidelity, preoedipal/oedipal relations" in which the human subjects find themselves in moral and ideological conflicts with larger social forces beyond their control.[27] Nick Browne argues for the specifically Chinese way of ideological negotiation and subversive potential in considering the "political economy" of contemporary Chinese melodramas as "the most complex and compelling popular film form that embodies the negotiation between the traditional ethical system and the new state ideology."[28] In *The Spring River*, the Chinese melodramatic mode serves as a powerful tool for the examination of interpersonal relationships both within the confines of family and the larger parameters of social/national communities. The film storytelling mobilizes powerful melodramatic codes to have the symbol of the nation associated with a domesticated woman. The maternal innocence of Sufen, who is, after all, devoid of any radical leanings of a proletariat, has much to do with the left-wing filmmakers' strategy to appeal to a broader audience by constructing the traditional type of heroine in a way that conformed to the traditional "scholar-beauty" (*caizi jiaren*) trope of fictional discourse. In addition, the film documents a crisis of female subjectivity around the figure of Sufen: her thwarted desires for love and family, her suffering, and finally her tragic sacrifice become representative of victimhood and national humiliation. Through the deployment of cultural codes of female chastity and Confucian ethics, the film projects a figuration of the heroine for the national imaginary with an allegorical Chineseness based on the virtues of loyalty and purity. Prasenjit Duara reveals that in twentieth-century Chinese history, nationalists and social reformers continued to exploit the image of self-sacrificing women in this tradition and redirected the spirit of self-sacrifice to the service of the nation and tradition.[29] Ironically enough, the leftist creation of such a submissive heroine image might seem embarrassing for their progressive colleagues. As Jay Leyda points out, "Most left critics had praised the film and no one seems to have worried or remarked that the loyal, unchanging wife is as feudal a character as her disgraceful husband."[30]

Melodrama is defined in Hollywood cinema as the "women's cinema." Western feminist scholars consider women's pictures as being directed toward a female audience. These films mainly deal with a crisis of the subjectivity of a female figure and problems defined as "female"—problems revolving around domestic life, the family, children, motherhood, and self-sacrifice.[31] In a similar vein, the Chinese film's melodramatic operation has its narrative arc, the falling (whether moral or social) of a female heroine, woven into the epic structure. The weight of sentiment and pathos of *The Spring River* centers on the heroine, as her once loyal and idealistic husband abandons her after remarrying a high-society hostess and establishes a new bourgeois life for himself. In its Sinification of the melodramatic imagination, the Chinese epic portrays a suffering woman as deserted wife, good mother, and virtuous daughter-in-law emblematic of both individual victimhood and national humiliation.

In the film's lyrical treatment, the figure of the longing wife (Sufen) is intimately linked to the images of nature—the moon and river—to evoke the sense of "Chineseness." The lyrical scenes of moonlit nights recall the romantic motif and sorrowing sentiment of the whole film. In its first appearance early in the film,

Zhongliang is asking Sufen to marry her. He gives her a diamond ring, vowing that they will stick with each other—like the moon and the star in the sky—until death. As in classical Chinese poetry, the imageries of the moon and the river become signals to invoke human emotion. However, a sense of irony gradually grows on the natural symbols, marking not the lovers' remembrance of each other but the man's forgetting of his wife. In the middle of the film, when Zhongliang gives in to the temptation of Lizhen and sleeps with her, it smoothly switches to the scene of Sufen, who is staring at the moonlit sky, longing for reunion with her husband without knowing what has become of him. A similar crosscutting happens again when Zhongliang is sleeping with the third woman, Wenyan. This second scene of the man's infidelity takes place simultaneously with Sufen reminiscing in her bed about her long-lost husband, her face bathed in the silvery moonlight.

If these images seem all too conventional for today's contemporary audience, let us be reminded that the legendary actress Bai Yang's impressive performance is what captivates the spectator and delivers all that a melodrama can ask for: the lure of the image of an innocent woman yearning and waiting for her lost lover. It is also due to the director's skillful editing and mise-en-scène treatment that the spectator is drawn to the film's various suspenseful moments. The husband has betrayed his good wife, while the heroine is still indulged in her waiting and dreaming; the artful presentation means that the audience would always know more than the couple knows about each other. The spectator is drawn into the narrative via the techniques of identification with desire and loss in a manner similar to Hollywood strategies.

At this climactic point, then, the spectator who has identified with the heroine is eager to follow her to see what happens to her in the next scene. By an amazing twist of fate, Sufen is employed as a maid at Wenyan's house. It so happens that by now all three women are literally staying under the same roof with the man. The climax of the drama takes place in 1945 on National Day (October 10), at a sumptuous banquet held at Wenyan's big house. In the dining hall, Zhongliang is flirting with his wife Lizhen and his mistress Wenyan, not knowing that Sufen is working in the kitchen as a servant. As fate would have it, Sufen goes out to the dining hall, serves drinks to the guests, and brings fruit dishes to her husband and the women. At this point, the audience would be anxious to see the confrontation between the man and his three lovers, and wonder how he would work his way out of these entangled relationships. What is more remarkable is the suspenseful moment created to hold the viewer's attention. The first time Sufen walks out to the dining hall to serve the guests, she fails to notice her husband at the table. It is at this moment of misrecognition that the spectator is tempted to be involved emotionally in the heroine's psychological state—how will she react when she discovers the naked truth? Will she collapse or accuse her husband? There is a beautiful shot lingering in this sequence, in which the heroine is posed as leaning back against the curtains that separate the hall and the kitchen. Shadows of the dancing figures are reflected on the curtains, or projected on the "screen" behind the heroine.

Surrounded by exuberant noises and music, we follow our heroine's gaze as she looks at the dancing hall as an alienated spectator. All we also observe, however, is the amazing spatial configurations of social classes in the hall's interior space. As a servant of the working class, she is made to stand backstage at a high-society venue. In this long, roughly twenty-minute sequence that takes place toward the end of the film, we are drawn to follow the heroine's visual perspective, from which we look at the decadent life of Chongqing's upper class. With parallel editing, the film cuts to the outside of the house, where Sufen hears a beggar boy singing the folk song "Song of the Moonlight," which laments the separation of family and couples. The visual complexities in the sequence are subtly conveyed by emphasizing the contrast, as observed by the heroine, between the rich and the poor—inside and outside the house.

The camera then leads the spectator back to the dining hall. Amid boisterous music and cheering crowd noises—in a melodramatic time mode of "too late" and "in-the-nick-of-time"—our heroine finally sees her husband, who has left her alone all these years. Unable to believe what she is seeing, Sufen almost passes out. She cannot help collapsing to the floor, and smashes the glasses and the tray she is holding—along with all the hopes she has carried for these many years. The fateful encounter between the hero and the heroine peaks in a "confession scene," in which the suffering heroine is asked to "confess" her long marital relationship with the man. In the famous finale in D. W. Griffith's *Way Down East* (1920), the heroine (Lillian Gish), a country girl seduced (in a mock marriage) by an urbane playboy who becomes an illegitimate mother (the "fallen woman"), confronts the man and accuses him of his marital deception in an impassioned speech.[32] In *The Spring River*, however, Sufen, deeply shocked and humiliated, is speechless and does not even know how to accuse her husband before the guests. Rather, she is "accused" by the people around her for disrupting the party. The framing of the heroine amid the crowd is very subtle in this scene. Crouching down on the floor, Sufen is situated in the center of the crowd of banquet guests from high society. Obviously, the heroine embodies the double personae of both an abandoned wife and an exploited worker, which are effectively expressed by the film's framing and camerawork.

The film's plot is undermined by its own breakdown of the melodramatic narratives, infused as it is with breached understandings, betrayals and infidelity, misrecognition, moral transgressions, and dysfunctional families. The encounter between Sufen and her husband leads to the woman's tragic suicide, which appears most satirical if we recall Zhongliang's endearing words to Sufen in the beginning of the story, when he vows to her, "From now on, in every moonlit night, I will miss you." Sufen then responds, "I will remember what you have just said forever." No matter how determinedly the woman tries to remember the man's promise, the appointment he makes with the woman is doomed to be her disappointment. In short, the woman's private memory of the past is in crisis, being swallowed up by public time of history. In her *The Desire to Desire*, Mary Ann Doane argues that although women's films foreground female characters, they ultimately circumscribe and frustrate their desire, leaving them with nothing to do but "desire to desire."[33] The story of Sufen is more complicated than what Doane has analyzed, however; the cruel irony of Sufen's fate projects larger figurations and allegory in historical terms. The heroine's social situation is getting worse with the passing of "history," and her social downfall is emblematic of the humiliated nation.

According to the memoir of Zheng Junli, the co-director of the film, *The Spring River* was originally titled *The Three Madames of Resistance* (*Kazhan san furen*).[34] The protagonist's first wife, Sufen, is the "Fallen Madame" in occupied Shanghai, representing the working class. His second wife, Lizhen, is the "Resistance Madame" in Chongqing, connected with a web of profiteers and Kuomingtang (KMT) officials. His mistress, Wenyan, is the "Secret Madame" in liberated Shanghai, who entangles him in a human web of traitors and collaborators. These typologies of the female figures in the film's melodramatic plot make an easy binarism (good and evil) for audience reception. The two opposite kinds of femininity (Sufen as the self-sacrificing mother and Lizhen as the adulteress; one representing maternal innocence, the other promiscuous sexuality) enact the historical contradiction of nationhood and modernity. If Sufen is the symbol of the "nation" and "tradition," Lizhen is aligned with the "modern" as its most malicious incarnation. Finally, the tragic death of the saintly Sufen stands for the failure to bind the distraught family and the nation in unity.

Lizhen is best described as a "performer," with all the clichéd stereotypes of a fallen woman—costume and makeup, physical attraction, body, exteriority. The female seducer incarnates the modern Westernized woman associated with sexuality and hedonism. At the very beginning, we see Lizhen appear "on the stage" performing a Spanish dance at a national gala, betraying her sensuousness and charm. As a social flapper, she "plays" her role well to enthrall and threaten powerful men. She seduces and corrupts our "war hero," and "performs" a suicidal drama toward the end of the film to manipulate Zhongliang into divorcing his former wife. In her appearance as the femme fatale, Lizhen jeopardizes the moral and legal codes of marriage and family: the woman's corruption of the hero disintegrates the traditional family order as well as wreaks havoc on the nation. Interestingly, it is this evil woman who embodies the popular imagination of the modern (Shanghai) woman in both left-wing and popular discourses. Under the film's ideological scheme, the modern woman has to "play" the villain in order to conform to the leftist film's social and ideological critique.

The image of the seductress is contrasted with that of the self-sacrificing woman played by Sufen. Lizhen is the villain who threatens to do violence to Zhongliang's family as well as to Chinese tradition, while Sufen as the saintly figure struggles to maintain the unity of the family, which makes her go through many trials and tribulations. The heroine's tragic death at the end no doubt bespeaks the failure of Confucian ethics to bind the distraught family as well as the nation in unity. In *The*

Spring River, the most damaging assault on the family comes not so much from the effect of the war's physical violence on its members as from the fatal violation of familial relationships and values. The traumatic war experience is subtly transfigured from personal suffering to historically irreparable damage to the family and social structure.

As the disintegration of the family mirrors allegorically the chaos of the country, the film's reconfigurations of urban spaces and female images as they are interconnected in the family structure are also revealing. The figurations of women as absolutely good and evil are intertwined with the binary typification of social spaces—namely, the opposition between occupied Shanghai and KMT-controlled Chongqing. One interesting point about the film's allegorical labeling is its representation of the less glamorous space of urban Shanghai in order to serve its ideological bias; one even notices that Shanghai appears very much like a rural locale on screen. The film uses the traditional heroine Sufen to represent occupied Shanghai and its occupied subjects. By contrast, Lizhen becomes the emblem of Chongqing social life with its glamour and decadence. It is precisely because of the film's implicit criticism of the state that Chongqing displaces Shanghai as the "modern" social space. To be sure, the Chongqing episode has a crucial strategic function for leftist filmmakers as the spatial embodiment of the KMT state that they indict. Chongqing symbolizes the bastion of state corruption, where our one-time war hero, Zhongliang, succumbs to the temptations of dancing, womanizing, and Western styles of living, and adopts a life of hedonism and excess. Yet for all the film's critique of the decadent history of the Chongqing period, its depiction is invested with a nostalgic feeling for the glamour of a "prewar" Shanghai. It is curious that in this epic film, we see a magnificent invoking of old-time Shanghai in the Chongqing scenes with art deco settings, elegant mansions, dances, and extravagant banquet scenes held by state officials and the rich. These cinematic treatments are so beautifully done that the film betrays the melodramatic contradictions in its simultaneous fascination with the modern and critique of state politics.

The film's allegorical structure is also closely linked with its aesthetic styles to represent a city-country antithesis, a prevalent trope in left-wing literary and film culture. Earlier in the film, a few episodes of rural resistance are done in a manner similar to the Soviet-style montage. In one remarkable scene, we see Sufen and her parents-in-law plowing the field like cows as they are tortured by Japanese soldiers: a close-up shot of the three characters' faces nonetheless captures their expressions of dignity and determination in the face of danger as they toil across the field. But then it cuts to a scene in which Zhongliang and his colleagues are captured by the Japanese troops. They are treated like slaves, cruelly beaten up along the way, and scramble for water at the side of the road. In this episode, however, Zhongliang's weakness in withstanding the physical assaults foreshadows his mental powerlessness to resist later temptations.

In another episode, we see Zhongliang and Lizhen dancing tango steps in the banquet hall during an occasion that celebrates their new and luxurious mansion. The sight of their tango steps then shifts to the marching steps of the Japanese soldiers, as it is crosscut with the scene of occupied Shanghai, where Sufen and her family still suffer under Japanese custody. Throughout the film, the narrative vacillates between the wanton lives of Chongqing officials and businessmen and the dreary condition of Shanghai citizens in order to highlight the confrontations between the oppressor and the oppressed, the rich and the poor, and the evil and the virtuous. Largely adhering to Western models of continuity editing and melodrama, director Cai Chusheng skillfully manipulated the technique of parallel/contrast editing in the melodrama to open up progressive possibilities for the film. It is through a powerful aesthetic and the excess of melodramatic emotion that the hybrid film text sought to negotiate all these clashes between traditional and modern values and lifestyles.

The dilemmas confronting the corrupt intellectual-hero are emblematic of the confusion and dislocation of the time. Symbolically enough, the man's meteoric rise to high society is closely tied to his entangled relationships with the three female characters, who themselves represent three different temporalities: the man abandons his "prewar" wife (Sufen), has a second marriage with the "wartime wife" (Lizhen), and has an affair with his "postwar" mistress (Wenyan). For all his characteristic frailty and vice, it is the war that has become the crucial historical moment against which the hero-intellectual is driven to go through not only the hard times of the nation, but also a drastic identity change in the individual's struggle for survival. Once a witness of history through his journey with the Red Cross, Zhongliang finally becomes an opportunist of history when he capitalizes on the war experience to achieve social mobility and personal gain.

The Spring River depicts the corruption of a wartime hero who surrenders to greedy capitalists in KMT-controlled Chongqing, a once-loyal husband caught up in his perplexed relationships with three women characters, all of whom take on an allegorical significance in Chinese wartime history. However, because the men in the film lose their power to maintain their family and nation in security—while women appear more assertive and enduring to take their place—leftist critics began to be worried about the film's sensationalism and emotional excess, as they might conceal its traumatic motif and hence undermine the progressive messages that the film intended to convey. They discredited the film for its subservience to popular tastes to the extent that it had lost the intended thrust of social criticism. Tian Han, an eminent left-wing dramatist and screenwriter, disapproved of the film's palpable dramatic elements. He believed that they could only make the film seem less "progressive." The leftist critic also feared that a close affinity between the young intellectual Zhongliang and the Confucian scholar-husband in a traditional Yuan drama would tarnish "the real image of a saintly, anti-resistant figure of intellectual."[35] The film's broad appeal was arguably attributed to its narrative affinity to the famous Yuan drama *The Lute* (*Pipa ji*), one of the most popular Chinese plays of the traditional repertoire. The film's "dramatization" as a hybrid model in traditional Chinese drama and family melodrama, Tian claimed, could only enhance the popular appeal of the movie to the great detriment of its "epic" intent. Another critic, similarly, saw the film as seriously flawed by its narrowing focus on family drama as the spectacular war experience and its epic sweep were vaguely figured on screen. This critic believed that *The Spring River* failed to become a historical account of the great epoch since the interactions of the characters simply did not take root in the story.[36] In short, left-wing commentators were troubled by the film's richly generic elements, intriguing plots, and stereotypical characters, which they saw as weakening the film's historical intent.

These critical comments reflected the leftist film discourse of radical cinema—namely, the film's affinity with classical Hollywood and classical Chinese theater rendered it an inferior work of historical visualization as it shared similar scenarios of ideological closure, stereotypically conservative ending, containment of individual desire, and wishful fulfillment of social ideal. Irrespective of the film's sympathy with the Hollywood paradigm and its generic memory in traditional repertoire, however, I venture to argue that it is precisely the film's uneasy resolution or rather irresolution of the "conservative" and "radical" strains of cinema that bespeaks its ideological shakiness vis-à-vis the imaginary of tradition, modernity, and nationhood. *The Spring River* turned out to be a hybrid cinema of the individualistic (bourgeois) family drama, a conventional tragedy, social allegory and criticism, with documentary traces of the war—a film imbued with the trenchant feelings of loss, frustration, and defeat despite its original intention to rescue the memory of the past and foresee the future. In trying to remember and document history, the hybrid epic, in spite of its own form, betrayed the traumatic fear of history and the obsessive enticement of the modern. The film projected a strong sense of uncertainty and confusion onto the hero's fragility and indecisiveness in committing himself to the "right" woman and the "correct" path of life toward the end of the film. The most gripping moment, no doubt, is when Zhongliang has to resolve Hamlet's dilemma: should he return to the past (Sufen, the family, and traditional ethics and values), or should he continue to embrace the new life of the nouveau riche (Lizhen, contemporary fashionable femininity, modern values and lifestyles)? In the tragic ending, Zhongliang rushes to the waterfront and realizes that Sufen has committed suicide. Lizhen arrives at the scene in her first-class automobile. Without a guilty conscience, Lizhen urges her man to come back with her. Although the audience will never know what the protagonist decides to do in the end, Zhongliang's previous weakness and cowardice only convince the audience that he will continue to surrender to the power and control of Lizhen. Hence, the ending did not give a satisfactory sense of binding the family back into the nation, nor did it present any solution to the plight of the people. The film conveyed the vision of a dystopian future of China rather than the triumph of nationalism in the aftermath of war.

Reflections

The story of *The Spring River* is about how a local picture competed effectively with foreign film genres for Chinese audiences. It used established stars and the form of family drama built on local histories, in dialogue with Hollywood big-budget films and globally popular melodramas like *Gone with the Wind*. The film's interactions with foreign cinematic aesthetics, popular tastes, and local histories reveal the inherently cosmopolitan culture of Chinese cinema in the 1930s and 1940s. In examining Hollywood's dominant presence in Republican China, Zhiwei Xiao points out that Hollywood was often used as a yardstick to measure the quality of domestic productions: "The cinematic style and narrative strategy of the native film productions were developed in a conscious effort to compete with American films for the Chinese audience."[37] The crisscrossing of *The Spring River* and *Gone with the Wind* reveals another global instance of a Sino-Hollywood encounter in Chinese film history. In this vein, I have examined the discursive tactics deployed by Chinese critics to construe a dichotomy between local Chinese films (which are essentially patriotic and nationalistic) and foreign, especially American, movies (which bear the imprint of Western imperialism), and how left-wing intellectuals framed the popularity of the Hollywood and Chinese films differently for audiences in favor of the native production. Yet the criticism of *The Spring River* bespeaks the dilemma of leftist filmmakers, when they sought to balance the film's ideological vigor with its melodramatic input and popular appeal in creating at once a progressive and mass-oriented picture.

Melodrama as a historically discredited film genre has witnessed a passionate revival in film scholarship over the past decades. Indeed, acknowledging the favorable Chinese reception of American films could provide comparative insights into the aesthetics, film form, and narration of native filmmaking. My reading of *The Spring River* shows how a 1940s' Shanghai picture could enrich as well as complicate the Western notion of melodrama by exploiting the capacity of the genre for a wider socio-cultural embrace. The melodramatic mode becomes a potential social imaginary to respond to representations of gender and the nation as they are enacted both in a different social arena and in historical China. While Chinese filmmakers were propelled by the war experience to create epic narratives to reimagine the national past, what made *The Spring River* a cinematic monument is not only its epic scale but also its enormous emotional impact on the audience. It is the film's narrational style and generic appeal that enhanced its capacity for capturing the collective psyche of an audience. A popular historical film cannot be viewed simply as a transparent text of the social and historical experience per se. As a popular epic,

The Spring River is a complex audiovisual artifact that draws on a cultural repertoire of generic forms and narratives to appease the tastes of Chinese spectators.

Situated in different political, ideological, and economical contexts, the "melodramatic imagination" in Chinese cinema is more than simply realistic or "melodramatic." In *The Spring River*, the anti-hero's fall from grace reflected a state of cultural disorder when there seemed to be no utopian future for the nation in the postwar present. The film intended to level a charge at the morally weakened intellectual, who has become a greedy and heartless man in pursuit of the bourgeois ideal of the good life. By a historical paradox, it is the film's uncomfortable portrayal of the protagonists' (the corrupt man's and the evil woman's) Western styles of living and mentality—their pursuit of bourgeois life and prosperity—that conveys a historical aura of Chinese bourgeois modernity. Chinese cinema's dialogues with Hollywood cinema and Western culture not only committed itself to its melodramatic plotline and popular storytelling, but it also opened up a horizon of what Miriam Hansen has called "vernacular modernism," a matrix for the articulation of fantasies, anxieties, and uncertainties of the modern in the Chinese film world, particularly the cosmopolitan cinema in 1930s and 1940s Shanghai.[38] In contemporary parlance, *The Spring River* was produced in an inherently globalized market when Chinese filmmakers had to respond to the pressures of nationalistic sentiments, local tastes, and a worldly cinematic regime of Hollywood in China. It was in its varied context of global capital and production that the Chinese melodramatic film sought to address its own past and present, and negotiate issues of nationhood and modernity. The Chinese melodramatic input helps us to rethink the intricacies of gender, commercialism, historical memory, and social identity as much as it casts light on the new age of globalized media publics.

Notes

1. Xia Yan, "A Modern Chinese Film: *The Tears of Yangtze*," *China Digest* 3, 6 (Hong Kong), February 9, 1948: 18–19.

2. Xia, "A Modern Chinese Film," 18–19.

3. Carla Marcantonio, *Global Melodrama: Nation, Body, and History in Contemporary Film* (New York: Palgrave Macmillan, 2015), 7.

4. Cheng Jihua, Li Shaobai, and Xing Zuwen, *Zhongguo dianying fazhan shi* [History of the development of Chinese film], Vol. 2 (Bejing: Zhongguo dianying chubanshe, 1963), 222.

5. Li Yizhong, *Cai Chusheng* (Shanghai: Shanghai jiaoyu, 1999), 179.

6. *Dianying zazhi* [Picture news] no. 2, October 19, 1947.

7. Jay Leyda, *Dianying: An Account of Films and the Film Audience in China* (Cambridge, MA: MIT Press, 1972), 143.

8. Hernán Vera and Andrew M. Gordon, *Screen Saviors: Hollywood Fictions of Whiteness* (Lanham, MD: Rowman & Littlefield, 2003), 23–25.

9.   Michael Raine, "'You Can't Replace *Gone with the Wind* with Chūshingura': *China Nights* and the Problem of Japanese Film Policy in Occupied Shanghai," *Film History* 30, no. 2 (Summer 2018): 190.

10. *Shen pao*, June 20, 1940, 12.

11. *Shen pao*, October 8, 1947, 3.

12. Bret Sutcliffe, "*A Spring River Flows East*: 'Progressive' Ideology and Gender Representation," *Screening the Past*, no. 5 (1998), accessed December 30, 2019, http://www.screeningthepast.com/2014/12/a-spring-river-flows-eastprogressive-ideology-and-gender-representation/.

13. Yingjin Zhang, "From 'Minority Film' to 'Minority Discourse': Questions of Nationhood and Ethnicity in Chinese Cinema," in *Transnational Chinese Cinemas: Identity, Nationhood, Gender*, ed. Sheldon Hsiao-peng Lu (Honolulu: University of Hawaii Press, 1997), 87.

14. Paul Pickowicz, "Victory as Defeat: Postwar Visualizations of China's War of Resistance," in *Becoming Chinese: Passages to Modernity and Beyond*, ed. Wen-hsin Yeh (Berkeley: University of California Press, 2000), 386. Susan Daruvala argues that Fei Mu's *Spring in a Small Town* (*Xiaocheng zhi chun*, 1948), which centered on a love affair and was thus condemned for its petit-bourgeois decadence and pessimism, shared a general postwar exhaustion and fear of the future with a string of Chinese war epics produced in the period. See "The Aesthetics and Moral Politics of Fei Mu's *Spring in a Small Town*," *Journal of Chinese Cinemas* 1, no. 3 (September 2007): 181.

15. The emotional impact of *The Spring River* on the overseas Chinese audience is also testified to by Leo Lee: "Despite the film's obvious sentimental clichés, an audience consisting mostly of Chinese at a recent showing of the film at Berkeley, California wept intermittently during the film and profusely at the end, whereas a few American members of the audience walked out." See Leo Ou-Fan Lee, "The Tradition of Modern Chinese Cinema: Some Preliminary Explorations and Hypotheses," in *Perspectives on Chinese Cinema*, ed. Chris Berry (London: BFI, 1991), 14.

16. In light of this appraisal from the left-wing camp, one may note the irony that *The Spring River* was awarded the Chiang Kai-Shek Film Prize in 1947. Notwithstanding the film's mockery of official corruption in Chongqing, the production was funded by the Nationalist government that aimed to support the film industry after the war.

17. The beginnings of the leftist cultural movement were generally traced to the 1931 formation of the League of Leftist Performing Arts. As Laikwan Pang notes, the exact title of "left-wing cinema movement" (*zuoyi dianying yundong*) was first used by Cheng, Li, and Xing in their *History of the Development of Chinese Film* (1963) to define a progressive film culture in the 1930s and '40s. See Pang, *Building a New China in Cinema: The Chinese Left-Wing Cinema Movement, 1932–1937* (Lanham, MD: Rowman & Littlefield, 2002), 3–6.

18. Cheng, Li, and Xing, *Zhongguo dianying fazhan shi*, Vol. 2, 137–336.

19. Paul Pickowicz, "Melodramatic Representation and the 'May Fourth' Tradition of Chinese Cinema," in *From May Fourth to June Fourth: Fiction and Film in Twentieth-Century China*, ed. Ellen Widmer and David Wang (Cambridge, MA: Harvard University Press, 1993), 304–5.

20. Ma Ning, "The Textual and Critical Difference of Being Radical: Reconstructing Chinese Leftist Films of the 1930s," *Wide Angle* 11, no. 2 (1989): 22–31.
21. Pang, *Building a New China in Cinema*, 9.
22. Wimal Dissanayake, "Introduction," in *Melodrama and Asian Cinema*, ed. Wimal Dissanayake (Cambridge: Cambridge University Press, 1993), 1.
23. Peter Brooks, *The Melodramatic Imagination: Balzac, Henry James, Melodrama, and the Mode of Excess* (New York: Columbia University Press, 1985).
24. Brooks, *The Melodramatic Imagination*.
25. Marcantonio, *Global Melodrama*, 2.
26. Pickowicz, "Melodramatic Representation and the 'May Fourth' Tradition of Chinese Cinema," 302.
27. E. Ann Kaplan, "Melodrama/Subjectivity/Ideology: Western Melodrama Theories and Their Relevance to Recent Chinese Cinema," in *Melodrama and Asian Cinema*, ed. Wimal Dissanayake (Cambridge: Cambridge University Press, 1993), 10.
28. Nick Browne, "Society and Subjectivity: On the Political Economy of Chinese Melodrama," in *New Chinese Cinemas: Forms, Identities, Politics*, ed. Nick Browne, Paul Pickowicz, Vivian Sobchack, and Esther Yau (Cambridge: Cambridge University Press, 1994), 40.
29. Prasenjit Duara, "Of Authenticity and Woman: Personal Narratives of Middle-Class Women in Modern China," in *Becoming Chinese: Passages to Modernity and Beyond*, ed. Wen-hsin Yeh (Berkeley: University of California Press, 2000), 342–64.
30. Leyda, *Dianying*, 167–68.
31. Mary Ann Doane, *The Desire to Desire: The Woman's Films of the 1940s* (Bloomington: Indiana University Press, 1987), 1–38.
32. Lucy Fischer, "*Way Down East*: Melodrama, Metaphor, and the Maternal Body," in *Cinematernity: Film, Motherhood, Genre* (Princeton: Princeton University Press, 1996), 56–59.
33. Doane, *The Desire to Desire*, 1–38.
34. Zheng Junli, *Hua wai yin* [The sounds beyond the images] (Beijing: Zhongguo dianying, 1979), 4.
35. Tian Han, review of *The Spring River Flows East*, in *Tian Han wenji* [Collected essays of Tian Han], Vol. 15 (1947; repr., Beijing: Zhongguo xiju chubanshe, 1983), 591–96.
36. Wei Zhi, "Lun guochan yingpian wenxue de luxian" [On the literary trend of Chinese films], *Dianying zazhi*, no. 7 and 9 (January and February 1948).
37. Zhiwei Xiao, "American Films in China Prior to 1950," in *Art, Politics, and Commerce in Chinese Cinema*, ed. Ying Zhu and Stanley Rosen (Hong Kong: Hong Kong University Press, 2010), 56.
38. Miriam B. Hansen, "Fallen Women, Rising Stars, New Horizons: Shanghai Silent Film as Vernacular Modernism," *Film Quarterly* 54, no. 1 (Fall 2000): 10–22.

5

Spatial Perception

The Aesthetics of *Yijing* in Transnational Kung Fu Films

Xi W. Liu

This chapter searches for a new mode of analyzing the perception of Chinese aesthetics beyond national boundaries and questions of geography in transnational cinema. Transnational cinema has been primarily theorized as a geographic phenomenon. Will Higbee and Song Hwee Lim, for example, have summarized three central strategies for theorizing the transnational: focusing on the limitations of the national, seeing the transnational as a regional phenomenon, and establishing diasporic and postcolonial cinema.[1] These three approaches contain different angles from which to explore transnational cinema, such as economics, geopolitics, cultural identity, and film representation.[2] All three approaches are typically production-based explorations, and all are essentially geographic approaches to mapping the trends of cultural flows. How then do we analyze the emotional resonance of transnational Chinese cinema and transnational cinema about the Chinese? When the emotional resonance is beyond the geographic register in transnational flows, how do we cross national boundaries and track emotional flows?

To answer these questions, this chapter looks to one of the concepts of sensation in Chinese aesthetics called *yijing*, which literally means the state of ideation and the embodiment of subtle emotional resonance in art. Chinese aesthetics are heavily influenced by Taoism, and the idea of *yijing* highlights the union of *xü* (absence) and *shi* (presence), which closely refers to the Taoist doctrine of *xü* (emptiness) and *jing* (stillness).[3] I apply the idea of *yijing* here to articulate an analytical framework charting sensory and emotional flows in transnational cinema.

Kathleen Newman has applied the idea of a "contact zone" to interrogate "how film registers" within the world economy on both regional and global scales; she argues that transnational cinema provides a sphere in which momentary but meaningful connections can be forged across national borders.[4] To expand on this idea, I argue that charting the perception of *yijing* can extend our understanding of national-registered representational filmic elements in transnational cinema because the sensation of *yijing* can provide a new "contact zone" of film reception on both regional and global scales.

In this chapter, I examine the Chinese film *The Grandmaster* (*Yidai zongshi*, dir. Wong Kar-wai, 2013) and the American animated film *Kung Fu Panda* (dir. Mark Osborne and John Stevenson, 2008) as a way of exploring how the spatial perception of *yijing* is formed in transnational cinema and how this film perception extends our understanding of emotional resonance in transnational processes. Rather than examining orthodox Chinese kung fu and Chinese culture in transnational cinema, this chapter aligns with the idea of *yijing* to examine the sensory emotional resonance of the films, which goes beyond an analysis of national boundaries to explore cultural and aesthetic performances.

The starting point for analysing *The Grandmaster* and *Kung Fu Panda* is emotional resonance. This concept does not only go beyond the emotions triggered by victory or loss in the kung fu genre but also the geographical borders of film production. Next, I theorize the idea of *yijing* and align it with affect theory to clarify how presence and absence configure spatial perception, thereby triggering the emotional resonance of *yijing*. For the following two cases studies, I mainly focus on the snow scene in *The Grandmaster* and the scene of flowers in *Kung Fu Panda*. I argue that the emotional resonance in these scenes is not only triggered by the emotional appeal of filmic figures but is also affected by the perception of the cinematic spaces surrounding them. In so doing, this chapter explores the sensation of *yijing* in a transnational journey.

Emotional Resonance in Transnational Cinema

Both *The Grandmaster* and *Kung Fu Panda* tell stories about Chinese kung fu. However, this chapter focuses on the emotional resonance in the two films instead of kung fu itself. This is not to deny the importance of kung fu in these narratives; rather, it is precisely because kung fu is a transnational object desired by global audiences that prompts questions of transnational reception. Do global audiences perceieve more than the excitement of fighting, more than fantasy Chinese culture, and more than national concerns?

From Bruce Lee (1940–1973) to Jackie Chan, Jet Li, and Donnie Yen—and then to films like *The Matrix* (dir. Lana Wachowski and Lilly Wachowski, 1999), *Charlie's Angels* (dir. McG, 2000), and the *Kung Fu Panda* series (2008–2016)—the popularity of kung fu stars have promoted this film genre in the global market, in turn making kung fu a popular element in global films. According to Simon During's idea of the "global popular," the kung fu film as a globally popular genre can convey certain kinds of cinematic imagery, which generate an affective appeal across national borders.[5] During utilizes Arnold Schwarzenegger as an example to argue that "the appeal of the audiovisual global popular is finally to be read in terms of the limited capacities of particular media to provide for individual's needs and desires, especially male needs and desires, across the various territories that consti-tute the world image-market."[6]

Arguably, the cinematic and affective appeal of kung fu is not simply about an individual's needs. Bruce Lee's anti-colonial kung fu films, for example, are an icon of Chinese pride in Stephen Teo's nationalist reading.[7] In a broader sense, "the blatant and exultant advocation of national identity was congenial not only to Chinese but literally to all people who felt that they had been degraded by Western Imperialism."[8] Contemporary kung fu films, such as Donnie Yen's *Ip Man* series (2008–2019), in many ways follow the traditional form of early kung fu films that re-emphasize the specific image of national pride. Dorothy Lau notes that "the Chinese-fight-against-invaders theme positions the character of Ip Man in an explicitly nationalistic frame."[9] Thus, kung fu film speaks not only to individual desire but to the collective consciousness of anti-colonial sentiment in the post-colonial era.

A different perspective can be seen in the "kung-fu craze" in America in the 1970s, which presented "Asian culture as mysterious and outlandish, exhibit-ing entirely alien social practices."[10] Then, the popularity of Jackie Chan's kung fu comedy presented a re-defined Asian masculinity where "Chan humanises the Asian and Asian American male and unwittingly challenges the stereotypes per-petuated by Orientalism in the process."[11] Also, as Shu Yuan suggests, "Chan's chal-lenge to the hard body of the American action cinema should be considered more in artistic and commercial terms than in political and cultural ones."[12] For Shu, a film is a commercial product, and a popular filmic icon is not just for cultural and political representation but also for sharing profit in the global economy.

I will not delve into this complex debate on globalization here, but I want to suggest that the kung fu genre does not simply convey a single, monolithic essence defining kung fu that makes it globally popular. Rather, kung fu action satisfies various cultural, political, and historical appeals in the global sphere. In this way, the globally popular kung fu genre is still partitioned by national borders. Even though a transnational kung fu film might be a coproduction across multiple nations, it does not mean the popularity of kung fu films are unified by "loving kung fu"—the appeal of the kung fu genre is certainly varied.

However, does this mean that when transnational kung fu cinema crosses national borders we don't consider the shared emotional resonances of film? I suggest that the emotional resonance created in *The Grandmaster* and *Kung Fu Panda* can cross national borders via the the spatial perception of *yijing*. What tran-spired in the production and distribution processes of these two films is not the only way of understanding the transnational meanings of the films; we should also consider the emotional resonance triggered by the films. The emotional resonance here does not lie with the cognition of kung fu, but rather focuses on the agents of kung fu: the kung fu masters.

The Grandmaster is directed by Hong Kong filmmaker Wong Kar-wai, who is famous for his transnational art-house style on the international stage. Ken

Provencher has noted that "Wong's transnational cinema is not a measure of the various ways in which his films import cultural influences, funding, and distribution revenue into China. It is a measure of the distance and the potency of his cinema's influence across national borders."[13] According to Provencher, transnationalism for Wong is maintained in the whole chain of production and reception, as well as being embodied in film content. The filmmaking team of *The Grandmaster*, for example, includes French cinematographer Philippe Le Sourd, Japanese composer Shigeru Umebayashi, French film composer Nathaniel Méchaly, American special effects studio BUF, and transnational stars such as Hong Kong actor Tony Leung Chiu-wai, Taiwanese actor Chang Chen, and mainland China's actress Zhang Ziyi. *The Grandmaster* tells a story about kung fu masters in the period of the Republic of China (1912–1949) and primarily surrounds two masters: Ip Man (Tony Leung Chiu-wai) and Gong Er (Zhang Ziyi). *The Grandmaster* has four versions for global audiences in different regions, which include one general 130-minute 2D version, one 122-minute European version, one 108-minute American version, and one 111-minute 3D version (released in mainland China in 2015). This chapter utilizes the American version, because it depicts a clear storyline that tracks the poetic relationship between Gong Er and Ip Man and was released outside China.

In history, Ip Man is the grandmaster of the Wing Chun style of kung fu, famous for being the teacher of Bruce Lee, who later became a global icon of Chinese kung fu. Ip Man is from Foshan (Guangdong province). The film follows Ip Man's life story, showing the kung fu master's honor, belief, and philosophy in a turbulent age. In contrast to Ip Man, Gong Er is a fictional female figure from northeastern China known as the master of Bagua Zhang. The ambiguous romance in the film is shown by Gong Er's explicit affection for Ip Man without equivalent desire in return. For Ip Man, we can only explicitly recognize his longing for Gong Er's kung fu, but we hardly notice any other clear desire. I suggest that Ip Man and Gong Er's subtle romantic relationship creates a site from which to understand the emotional resonance of the film, one that necessitates a deep reading of the nuanced perception beyond the typical representations of transnational cinema.

Kung Fu Panda tells the story of how Po (the panda), who cannot perform any kung fu, becomes the Dragon Warrior (the kung fu master). *Kung Fu Panda* has been released in sixty-nine film markets across Europe, the Middle East, Africa, the Asia-Pacific, and North and South America. Its worldwide box office sales reached $631.7 million in 2008, with round to 66% from international markets (round to $416.3 million)[14]; in mainland China, it was the highest-grossing imported film in 2008.[15] One could certainly say that this American-produced kung fu story is widely accepted by global audiences. Its global success raises questions about the transnational depiction of Chinese kung fu and the image of Chineseness, because what global audiences saw was not a simple representation of Chinese kung fu. Instead, it is a digitalized animated fantasy of China, the Chinese, and Chinese culture, including landscape, architecture, animals, clothing, food, and philosophy.[16] Here, again, my curiosity is piqued by the sensation and aesthetics of the film. Before analyzing the emotional resonance in both *The Grandmaster* and *Kung Fu Panda*, however, we need to clarify the idea of *yijing*, which provides a special view of emotional resonance across national borders.

Theorizing *Yijing*

Yijing is an ambiguous, abstract, aesthetic term that gets entangled in the expression of ideation and emotions. In this section, I explore the idea of *yijing*, its aesthetic background, and embodied forms, and then detail its usage in charting subtle emotional resonances in these two films.

What is the relationship between *yijing* and Chinese aesthetics? To answer this question, we need to nail down that the term *yijing* and the aesthetic essence of *yijing* are formed and developed in different contexts. *Yijing* as a critical aesthetic term was derived from Chinese philologist Wang Guowei's (1877–1927) literary criticism *Renjian Cihuai* (Notes on *Ci* Poems in the World) in the 1910s. Wang Guowei was influenced by Immanuel Kant (1724–1804) and Arthur Schopenhauer (1788–1860). Scholars have seen *Renjian Cihuai* as a cross-cultural dialogue between Chinese literary criticism and Western philosophy.[17] In his criticism, Wang used the term *jingjie* (realm) to examine the aesthetics of the *ci* poem. In many ways, *yijing* and *jingjie* are interchangeable; that is, the term *yijing* can be seen as the reflection of an earlier aesthetic in Chinese literacy. On the other hand, it is still a debatable topic that the essence of aesthetics or the philosophical foundation of *yijing* is formed by either the interaction between Confucianism, Taoism, and Buddhism, or independently influenced by Taoism or Buddhism.[18] No matter which foundation we follow, the essence of *yijing* has been formed by Chinese philosophy since the time of ancient China. It is hard to say that *yijing* is fully representative of Chinese aesthetics, but I claim that Chinese philosophy can provide plenty of sources to examine the aesthetics of creation and perception of *yijing*.

In this chapter, I want to align with Taoism to examine the usage of *yijing* in film studies. Peng Yuping has pointed out that the link between Wang's idea of *jingjie* and Taoism has been shown in the name of his book. *Renjian* (the World) for *Renjian Cihua* refers to Taoist philosopher Zhuang Zi's (369–286 BCE) essay "Renjian Shi" (Out and About in the World) because they show a similar critique of "the World."[19] In this light, I would like to place Taoist aesthetics as the core that puts the stillness of emotional resonance into play—charting the perception of *yijing*.

"What is *yijing*?" is perhaps the essential question. I suggest that we need to understand *yijing* through its relationship with objects and feelings. The term *yijing* appeared before Wang Guowei's criticism; *yijing* as a Chinese poetic term was originally written in poet Wang Changling's (698–757) *Shige* (which literally means "poem format"). Wang Changling divided the realm of poems into three levels: *wujing* (the realm of objects), *qingjing* (the realm of feelings), and *yijing* (the realm of ideation). Wang Changling's concept of the realm of ideation goes a step further than just objects and feelings. Objects refers to the views we can see, and feelings are the emotional reactions to those views. For Wang Changling, the goal of the realm of ideation is not just the expression of the world that we see or the emotions that we have, but the sincere feeling of the essence of this world from the true heart. In Wong's reading of these three realms, "*yi* is a general concept describing the highest aesthetic experience while *yijing* is a specific term for the theorization of ideation in the aesthetic discourse."[20]

However, this does not mean that objects and feelings are not important; objects and emotions are the two necessities for the sensation of *yijing*. According to pioneering works, the mechanism of having the sensation of *yijing* is based on the convergence of subject and object, and the convergence of presence and absence.[21] The convergence of subject and object means the fusion of objects and the emotional reaction to objects. *Yijing* is neither decided by an object nor a pure subjective imaginary, but rather by a collaboration with subjective feelings and objective views. For the convergence of presence and absence, the presence refers to objects. Yet, the key point for *yijing* is how to understand absence and the interaction between feelings and objects.

Chinese scholar Pu Zhenyuan has summarized three characteristics of absence for *yijing*.[22] First, absence is indirectly signified as objects: that is, absence is embodied by objects with aesthetic imagination. In other words, absence is not any concreteness that has certain images but rather is associated with the aesthetic imagination of the objects. For example, a harmonious atmosphere can be seen as a sort of absence, which might be triggered by various scenes such as mountains and lakes, as well as fallen leaves. Here, the atmosphere does not have a direct relationship with mountains, lakes, or fallen leaves but can be triggered through them, thereby having the realm of absence. Second, since the absence does not directly refer to an object, it is uncertain and unlimited. In the meantime, the third characteristic, the feeling of absence, is a reason that follows the experience—in other words, the uncertainty and limitless of absence does not mean random illusions.

In the light of Pu's conceptualization, the convergence of subject and object and the convergence of presence and absence blur the cognition of a certain image. The sensation of *yijing* as the feeling of the convergence of presence and absence is not to evoke an emotion but rather ceases the process of having an emotion. According to Eric Shouse, "a feeling is a sensation that has been checked against previous experiences and labelled" and "an emotion is the projection/display of a feeling."[23] *Yijing* keeps the feelings of presence and simultaneously blurs the projection of feelings. Instead of saying the sensation of *yijing* is the enemy of cognition, I suggest that *yijing* shows the relaxation of perception rather than the stimulation of having a certain emotion. Keeping a distance from certain emotions shows the aesthetic view of emptiness and vacancy.

The interests of absence embodies the spirit of Taoism, which highlights the *xüjing* (emptiness and stillness) as the essence of life.[24] In *Tao Te Ching*, the fundamental book for the philosophy of Taoism, the ancient Chinese philosopher Lao Zi said "*zhi xü ji, shou jing du*" (keeping emptiness as their limit and stillness as their center). Zhuang Zi developed Lao Zi's thoughts and raised the idea of *xinzhai* (fasting of the heart):

> Your mind must become one, do not try to understand with your ears but with your heart. Indeed, not with your heart but with your soul. Listening blocks the ears, set your heart on what is right, but let your soul be open to receive in true sincerity. The Way is found in emptiness. Emptiness is the fasting of the heart.[25]

For Zhuang Zi, *xinzhai* seeks the spiritual stillness in front of objects. Xu Fuguan notes that the perception within the stillness frees the heart from both the influence of the objects and the judgement toward the objects.[26] In this light, the perception of *yijing* is the spiritual realm triggered by the fasting of the heart. The emotional resonance of *yijing*, therefore, is the perception of stasis that transcends the emotional reaction to the objects and achieves the *ji zi de chaoyue* (self-transcendence).[27] In short, *yijing* stems from the feelings of presence and achieves spiritual stillness.

For the process of charting *yijing* in a film, we can categorize the emotional reaction to the perception of *yijing* via a spatial mode. Xu argues that we can divide perception of absence into a foreground level and a background level.[28] For Xu, the foreground level shows sensual activities in terms of the feelings of views; the background level transcends sensual activities by spiritual activities. "The perception is the spiritual production that is triggered by the visible presence but approaches to a completely different form."[29] The background level is where the sensual activities are transcended and get into the realm of absence. Following this, what we need to chart for *yijing* are the feelings that the foreground appeals to and the absence that the background forms. The foreground and background here are different from the same terms used in a filmic scene, which shows a physical positional relationship between the front and the back. To avoid the polysemy of the terms, we must examine how the cinematic techniques fast or abstain from the emotional appeal of the films. In this chapter, then, I present how the cinematic spaces dissolve emotional appeal away from the people on the screen.

In addition, as the perception of a film is based on the collaboration between the film and viewers, you may ask how to bridge the gap between a screen and a human body, or how the sensory perception happens for the viewers. Affect theory is relevant here. Brian Massumi has noted that "*L'affect* (Spinoza's *affectus*) is an ability to affect and be affected. It is a pre-personal intensity corresponding to the passage from one experiential state of the body to another, and implying an augmentation or diminution in that body's capacity to act."[30] For Massumi, affect is a sort of invisible intensity transmitted as an in-betweenness. Affect for film perception can therefore be seen as a production—one generated by audio-visual images and embodied as perceived feelings. As Teresa Brennan emphasizes several times in *The Transmission of Affect*, "there is no distinction between the individual and the environment" when affect is transmitted.[31] During the experience of watching a film, although there is some physical distance between the viewer and the screen, there is still intensity in-between. The space portrayed by cinematic techniques can be seen as the environment for film viewers; the perception of the film, therefore, is the perception of a digitalized audio-visual space.

Via the lens of affect, the perception of *yijing* shows the transmission from the cinematic absence to the embodied feelings of absence. During an affective film watching experience, I argue that filmic perception goes beyond national borders, as the viewer is affected by the stillness of emotional resonance that is not triggered by certain national images but instead by affective absence.

Yijing and Snow

In *The Grandmaster*, the platonic relationship between Ip Man and Gong Er starts with kung fu and ends with their personal beliefs of kung fu: Ip Man, as the representative of southern martial arts, against Gong Er's father, Gong Yutian (Wang Qingxiang), who represents the northern martial arts. Ip Man ultimately wins the contest. Gong Er cannot accept her father's defeat, so she challenges Ip Man in order to restore family honor. Gong Er defeats Ip Man by means of her unique skill, the "Sixty-Four Hands" (a fictional kung fu technique referring to the canon of Taoism). Gong Er and Ip Man come away from the contest with an appreciation for each other.

When the Second Sino-Japanese War (1937–1945) sweeps China, Ip Man moves to Hong Kong, while Gong Yutian is killed by his student Ma San (Zhang Jin), as Gong Yutian had prevented Ma San from devoting the northern kung fu group's reputation to the Imperial Japanese Army. To take revenge for the murder of her father, Gong Er vows to remain alone, renouncing marriage, children, and teaching; she breaks off her existing engagement, even though it will be a blow to her family's reputation. Gong Er utilizes this revocation to express her determination for revenge. Afterward, Gong Er moves to Hong Kong to become a doctor. In their last meeting, Ip Man still wishes to see the "Sixty-Four Hands," but Gong Er says that she has already forgotten. Gong Er confesses that she cared about Ip Man, but that is all it could ever be. Two years later, Gong Er dies in Hong Kong, keeping her vows to the end.

Before the Second Sino-Japanese War, Gong Er goes back to northeastern China; the romantic relationship between Ip Man and Gong Er is maintained through letter writing. Although the two figures are far from each other, there is a montage sequence that connects Gong Er and Ip Man through scenes of snow. I argue that on the one hand, this letter writing sequence emotionally shortens the distance between Gong Er and Ip Man, showing the presence of their poetic

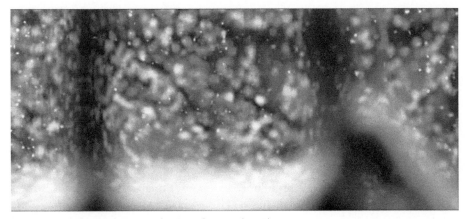

Figure 5.1: A snow scene in *The Grandmaster* (2013).

relationship. On the other hand, the snow scene—as the extended cinematic space in the sequence—removes the emotional stimulus by dissolving the emotional connection.

I call the snow scene a cinematic space as it is a hybrid of real natural snowy scenery and digitalized snow. *The Grandmaster* collaborated with the American visual effects studio BUF as part of its global post-production chain. Ultimately, digital technology is not new to kung fu films; martial arts has already been turned into "cinematic artistry through digital technology."[32] BUF's website, in fact, documents the difference between the original film material and the visual effects rendering.[33] BUF aestheticizes snow in slow motion for *The Grandmaster*, which makes the texture and the motion of snowflakes more obvious. I argue that this usage of snow creates the union of presence and absence for the poetic relationship between Gong Er and Ip Man.

The presence in the snow sequence manifests as the two kung fu masters battle with their individual repressed romantic states. In a non-diegetic sound sequence, which only relays background music, the film suppresses the protagonists' emotions by erasing their voices. The two protagonists never get to speak of their longing for each other, nor do they get to express their feelings directly. To implicitly show the affection between Gong and Ip, the film uses two strategies. First, the protagonists are connected by montage, which conceptually counters the fact that they are not physically together. For example, when Ip practices kung fu, he is motionless and filmed using a zoom-in medium shot. This is followed by a long shot of Gong walking away from the camera under falling snow. This sequence creates a purposeful combined visual effect.

The second strategy shows Gong Er and Ip Man together in a fantasy state. A tracking step-printing shot documents a martial arts practice between the two protagonists in Gong's home, but in reality Ip Man never went to Gong's home. Mechanically, step-printing shoots a scene at a lower frame rate and then projects in a higher frame rate. Visually, through the "magic" of time and speed, the characters' movements are no longer smooth. Even though Gong and Ip appear together, the visual cognition seems foreign in comparison to other shots, thereby functioning as a dream image that would fail to materialize in actuality.

In their letters, Ip Man writes, *"yedi canghua yidu, mengli taxue jihui"* (I dream of seeing the "Sixty-four Hands" again in the snow).[34] In Chinese, *yedi canghua* (literally meaning to hide the flower under the leaves) is a paronomasia. On the one hand, it is the name of Gong's martial arts movement. On the other hand, if *"ye"* refers to Ip (in Cantonese it is pronounced as *Ip*, meaning "leaves"), then the question that remains is who the *"hua"* (flower) he refers to? As a result of this linguistic subtlety, viewers are required to cognitively interpret the presence of the inferred affection between Ip and Gong.

However, the film does not stop at establishing the connective presence between Gong Er and Ip Man; it simultaneously dissolves the emotional appeal to maintain the stillness of emotional resonance. Representationally, one could say that the romantic relationship between Gong Er and Ip Man presents the traditional Chinese poetic preference of the feeling of love—the ideation of stasis. The *Daxu* (the commentary of the *Shijing*) commented that *"fa hu qing . . . zhi hu li yi"* (the feelings that are from the true heart do not go beyond the disciplines of ritual and justice).[35] In the film, Gong Er restrains her desire initially because she is engaged to another man; ritual and custom would not allow her to break off an engagement because of Ip Man. Then, in order to protect her justice to avenge her father, Gong Er keeps the vows in that she neither gets married nor maintains the ambiguous relationship with Ip Man. For Ip Man, his obsession with kung fu is more than his desire for Gong Er. Thus, the poetic relationship between Gong Er and Ip Man is maintained within the ideation of stasis. Moreover, I argue that the emotional resonance of the film is not limited to the literal understanding of Chinese poetry but can be directly affected through audiovisual images.

The snow sequence in *The Grandmaster* forms an atypical emotional affection. It does not mean that the snow sequence is anti-feelings or going against the emotional desire of global audiences; rather, it creates a feeling that goes beyond cultural-based understanding. Considering this, even without the snow scenes, the storyline remains narratively comprehensible; that is to say, the digital snow goes beyond the function of the narration. I suppose it could be said that the snow enables a shift to the state of absence, overriding the affection between the two protagonists and triggering the sensation of *yijing*. In the film, the scenes with the digital snow can be seen as space beyond the place that carries the romantic relationship between Gong and Ip.

For the perception of the snowing space that is empty and still, Wang and Wang note that "emptiness makes the scene on the screen transcend the bounds of space and time and combine with the perception of the spectator; at the same time, spectators transfer their role from perceivers to participants."[36] Following Wang and Wang, what the participants experience in the cinematic space of emptiness is nothing more than the state of stasis, where the emotional appeal is dissolved within the emotional resonance of absence. Thus, the perception of the digital snow is neither the snow nor the affection generated from the protagonists, but rather the state of absence.

Yijing and Flowers

In *Kung Fu Panda*, Master Oogway, the kung fu legend, has had a vision that Tai Lung (the snow leopard) will return. Tai Lung wanted to win the Dragon Scroll and become the Dragon Warrior, but Oogway rejected him because he was aggressive, arrogant, and had darkness in his heart. However, Oogway knows he does not have time to stop Tai Lung again and chooses Po as the Dragon Warrior, tasking Master Shifu with training him. In the film, Oogway is the founder of kung fu and is gentle, wise, patient, and reliable, but his time has come; he leaves all others' trust, doubt, and hope behind, and ascends amid drifting peach blossoms (in Taoism, ascension does not mean death but rather shows the moment of reaching Heaven). The emotional resonance in this ascending scene is more than the emotional appeal of farewell, showing the ideation of loss.

Oogway's ascension may appeal to feelings such as sadness, grief, and sorrow. In the film, Oogway is the icon of kung fu and he is the only one who believes that Po can be the Dragon Warrior. Heroic films always show a normal character being trained by a master and becoming a hero, such as Neo (Keanu Reeves) in *The Matrix* and Jian Fu (Jackie Chan) in *Snake in the Eagle's Shadow* (*Shexing Diaoshou*, dir. Yuen Woo-ping, 1978). In *Kung Fu Panda*, Oogway is in the role of the master who would normally teach Po, but he leaves. Although Shifu accepts Oogway's instruction to train Po, in the beginning he does not believe that Po can be the Dragon Warrior. Thus, Oogway's ascension to a great extent takes away hope, belief, and the grace of trust of making someone into a hero.

Representationally, Oogway's ascension does not mean that the age of kung fu has come to an end. Rather, he has finished his work in the earthy realm, and it is time for him to achieve the higher spiritual level. Following this idea, the feeling of this ascending moment is not the same as the feeling of farewell. The spiritual level of ascension could present the Taoist idea "Heaven and Earth and I were born at the same time, and all life and I are one."[37] At the ascending moment, Oogway's body is dissolved within the drifting peach blossoms, which can be seen as the union of "Heaven and Earth and I." In the meantime, the dissolving of the body presents a crucial idea of *sangwo* (lose myself); *sangwo* is one of the fundamental representations of *xinzhai* (fasting the heart). Through the loss of body, the spirit can be freed to achieve the state of "all life and I are one." Ideally, *xinzhai* and *sangwo* require a negative attitude toward emotions and desires.[38] As Zhuang Zi said of the sage:

> He has the form of a man, but not the emotions of a man. Because he has the form
> of a man, he can be amongst men, but not having the emotions of a man, he does
> not have to follow the ways of right and wrong. Inconsequential and small, he stays
> amongst me! Substantial and large, he is at one with Heaven![39]

In the light of Taoism, the ideation of *she* (loss) is sometimes presented as the ignorance of fame and fortune. For example, in his "Taohua an ge" (Peach Blossom Song) Tang Yin (1470–1524) said:

> Hope to die under the flowers with wine, but do not want to run around. A steed
> is the business of a dignitary, wine and flowers are for the life of a hermit. If you
> compare a dignitary and a hermit, one is on the earth; the other is in the sky. If you
> compare a steed and wine, how busy you are, and how relaxed am I? People laugh
> at my madness, but I laugh at those who are muddled. There is no Wuling Heroes'
> tomb anymore, no flowers, no wine, all that is left is the farm.[40]

The main premise behind Tang's song is to present his indifference toward both riches and honor. As he loves peach blossoms, he chooses to stay alongside the blossoms and revel in his happiness. When Oogway is ascending in *Kung Fu Panda*, he does not seem unwilling to leave; nor does Oogway show strong emotional reactions to what happens in the world, even though he knows that Tai Lung is coming back and people will be in danger. He no longer frames himself as a kung fu master who must protect others—or we could say that he is not framed by heroism. Oogway's ascension can be understood as being indifferent to his status, in that he is in the state of *xinzhai*.

Instead of saying that peach blossoms in the film must refer to Chinese poetry and Taoism, I suggest that the affect of the peach blossoms configures the similar state of absence as the aesthetics of Taoism. Spatially, peach blossoms are an icon of the spiritual world. In addition to the ascending scene, peach blossoms also fly to bring down the Dragon Scroll from the roof of the Jade Palace with a sense of ceremony. When Tai Lung breaks the staff that Oogway left to Shifu, peach blossoms appear and fly again. On the one hand, peach blossoms represent the connection between the real world and the spiritual realm. If the film failed to use peach blossoms as a visualization tool, the realization of the spiritual realm would also fail; for example, if Oogway were shown to merely fade away as opposed to dissolving with flower petals, the connection between the spiritual and the physical world would disappear, and it would lack the spatial perception of a spiritual world.

On the other hand, the ascending scene dissolves the emotional appeal of farewell by switching the spaces that are perceived. The scene of Oogway dissolving within the flying peach blossoms is followed by an extreme long shot of flowers flying upward into the air and then changing into the starry sky. In this sequence,

Figure 5.2: Peach blossoms becoming the stars in the night sky in *Kung Fu Panda* (2008).

the visual space is continuously extended. Following the peach blossoms, the sense of the body is switched to the sense of sky, because the affected feeling switches from empathy with the character to the perception of natural scenery. This process triggers the ideation of loss. This loss does not mean missing something, but rather liberating the feelings that are blocked by a farewell. The perception of *yijing* here can therefore be affected by the emotional resonance of the ideation of loss. The affection is not only triggered by the characters and peach blossoms, but also the spatial transformation of the scenes.

Conclusion

Instead of saying that the perception of *yijing* is universal, I stress that the perception of *yijing* is caused by bodily reactions to moving images. As a byproduct of coproduction, the ability to perceive *yijing* stresses that the individual spectator's capacity can be affected. However, I suggest that via the lens of *yijing*, we can chart the global audience's perception beyond cultural recognition in transnational contexts. Within a transnational trend, the perception of *yijing* is more than the cognition of a genre and the image of a specific cultural icon.

In *The Grandmaster* and *Kung Fu Panda*, the digitalized snow and the aminated peach blossoms are crucial images for charting *yijing*, but they are not representations of *yijing*. Rather, they are a cinematic presence, and they trigger *yijing* by creating the emotional reactions to them in their absent state. The aesthetic states of snow and peach blossoms go beyond their visualized images. Whatever the presence is on the screen, the mechanism of triggering *yijing* relies on the emptiness and stillness of presence.

Indeed, the term *yijing* is Chinese and this chapter has utilized Taoism to explore the ideas of emptiness and stillness; *yijing* is the bodily perception that can be broadly discussed in different aesthetic trends. It is worth noting that the focus of this chapter is on cross-border perceptions within transnational processes, but this chapter only utilizes the perception of space as an example to chart *yijing*. However, space and time cannot be separated in cinematic products, as whatever we see on the screen—movement, or stillness in a space—all indicate time. The perception of time is much more implicit than the perception of space, because time is identified through spatial change. Aligning with Buddhist ideas, Victor Fan has argued that the pathway to *wudao* (enlightenment) indicates "a passage of time-passed."[41] The perception of *yijing* in this chapter is seen in a similar fashion of *wudao* but in a Taoist text, although it is worth looking into how time-passing triggers the perception of *yijing* and how time-passing can create a state of absence. These aesthetic debates would interrogate the film perception at the cross-border stage and therefore re-configure cultural representations in transnational cinema.

Notes

1. Will Higbee and Song Hwee Lim, "Concepts of Transnational Cinema: Towards a Critical Transnationalism in Film Studies," *Transnational Cinemas* 1, no. 1 (2010): 7–21.
2. Andrew Higson, "The Limiting Imagination of National Cinema," in *Cinema and Nation*, ed. Mette Hjort and Scott MacKenzie (London: Routledge, 2000), 63–74; Sheldon Hsiao-Peng Lu, ed., *Transnational Chinese Cinemas: Identity, Nationhood, Gender* (Honolulu: University of Hawai'i Press, 1997); see also Zakir Hossain Raju, "Indigenization of Cinema in (Post)Colonial South Asia: From Transnational to Vernacular Public Spheres," *Comparative Studies of South Asia, Africa and the Middle East* 32, no. 3 (2012): 611–21.
3. In the *Tao Te Ching*, Lao Zi said "*zhi xuji, shou jingdu*" (keeping emptiness as their limit and stillness as their center). Red Pine [Bill Porter], trans., *Lao-Tzu's Taoteching* (Port Townsend, WA: Copper Canyon Press, 2009), 32.
4. Kathleen Newman, "Notes on Transnational Film Theory: Decentered Subjectivity, Decentered Capitalism," in *World Cinemas, Transnational Perspectives*, ed. Nataša Ďurovižová and Kathleen E. Newman (London: Routledge, 2009), 3–11.
5. Simon During, "Popular Culture on a Global Scale: A Challenge for Cultural Studies?," *Critical Inquiry* 23, no. 4 (1997): 808–33.
6. During, "Popular Culture," 815.
7. Stephen Teo, *Hong Kong Cinema: The Extra Dimensions* (London: BFI, 1997), 110.
8. Chiao Hsiung-ping, "Bruce Lee: His Influence on the Evolution of the Kung Fu Genre," *Journal of Popular Film and Television* 9, no. 1 (1981): 37, quoted in Yuan Shu, "Reading the Kung Fu Film in an American Context: From Bruce Lee to Jackie Chan," *Journal of Popular Film and Television* 31, no. 2 (2003): 50–59.
9. Dorothy Lau, "Donnie Yen's Wing Chun Body as a Cyber-Intertext," *Journal of Chinese Cinemas* 7, no. 2 (2013): 168.
10. Martin Daniel, "The Americanization of the Hong Kong Kung Fu Hero: Orientalism and Social Class in Marvel Comics' *Iron Fist*," *Journal of Popular Culture* 51, no. 6 (2018): 1521.

11. Shu, "Reading," 56.
12. Shu, "Reading," 58.
13. Ken Provencher, "Transnational Wong," in *A Companion to Wong Kar-Wai*, ed. Martha P. Nochimson (Chichester: Wiley Blackwell, 2016), 41–63.
14. "Kung Fu Panda," Box Office Mojo by IMDbPro, accessed January 7, 2021, https://www. boxofficemojo.com/title/tt0441773/?ref_=bo_se_r_1.
15. Xiaoyan Bu, "An Intercultural Interpretation of *Kung Fu Panda*: From the Perspective of Transculturation," *Sino-US English Teaching* 9, no. 1 (2012): 878.
16. Naomi Greene, *From Fu Manchu to Kung Fu Panda: Images of China in American Film* (Hong Kong: Hong Kong University Press, 2014); Hye Jean Chung, "*Kung Fu Panda*: Animated Animal Bodies as Layered Sites of (Trans)National Identities," *The Velvet Light Trap* 69, no. 1 (2012): 27–37.
17. Christopher K. Tong, "Nonhuman Poetics (By Way of Wang Guowei)," *Chinese Literature, Essays, Articles, Reviews* 37 (2015): 5–28.
18. Wu Bili, "Rang chuantong zouxiang weilai 2000 nian yilai de yijing lilun yanjiu zongzhu" [A summary of the research on the theory of yijing since 2000], *Wenjiao ziliao lunwenji* 15 (2004): 34–39.
19. Yuping Peng, ed., *Renjian Cihua* (Beijing: Zhonghua Book Company, 2010), 4–5.
20. Wayne Wong, "Action in Tranquillity: Sketching Martial Ideation in *The Grandmaster*," *Asian Cinema* 29, no. 2 (2018): 203.
21. Zhenyuan Pu, *Zhongguo yishu yijing lun* [Chinese art yijing theory] (Beijing: Peking University Press, 1994).
22. Pu, *Zhongguo*, 29–30.
23. Eric Shouse, "Feeling, Emotion, Affect," *M/C Journal* 8, no. 6 (2005), https://doi. org/10.5204/mcj.2443.
24. Xu Fuguan, *Zhongguo yishu jingshen* [Chinese art spirit] (Beijing: The Commercial Press, 2010).
25. Zhuang Zi, *Book of Chuang Tzu*, trans. Martin Palmer, Elizabeth Breuilly, Wai Ming Chang, and Jay Ramsay (London: Penguin Classics, 1996), 29.
26. Xu, *Zhongguo*, 86.
27. Xu, *Zhongguo*, 106.
28. Xu, *Zhongguo*, 88.
29. Xu, *Zhongguo*, 88, my translation.
30. Brian Massumi, "Translation Notes," in *A Thousand Plateaus: Capitalism and Schizophrenia*, by Gilles Deleuze and Félix Guattari (London: Bloomsbury Academic, 2013), xv.
31. Teresa Brennan, *The Transmission of Affect* (Ithaca, NY: Cornell University Press, 2004), 6–7.
32. Jessica Ka Yee Chan, "Anticipating Action: The Evolving Grammar of Action and Montage in Hong Kong Cinema," *East Asian Journal of Popular Culture* 1, no. 3 (2015): 412.
33. "The Grandmaster," BUF, accessed March 5, 2019, http://buf.com/films/the-grandmaster/.
34. This is the official translation in the film. "64 Hands" is the name of Gong Er's kung fu.

35. The *Shijing* is a collection of ancient Chinese poems (eleventh to sixth centuries BCE). The *Daxu* literally means the main preface of the *Shijing* and stresses the collection's core information. "Daxu," in Zhu Xi, ed., *Shijing* [Book of Songs] (Shanghai: Shanghai Classics Publishing House, 2013), 9.

36. Wang Di and Wang Zhimin, *Zhongguo dianying yu yijing* [Chinese cinema and yijing] (Beijing: CFP, 2000), 225.

37. The original Chinese is "tiandi yuwo bingsheng, er wanwu yuwo weiyi." Zhuangzi, *The Book of Chuang Tzu*, 15.

38. Xu, *Zhongguo*, 93.

39. Zhuang Zi, *Book of Chuang Tzu*, 44.

40. Translated by author.

41. Victor Fan, *Cinema Approaching Reality: Locating Chinese Film Theory* (London: University of Minnesota Press, 2015), 104.

6

Global Network, Ecocinema, and Chinese Contexts

Wolf Totem as a Successful Model of Transnational Coproduction

Wendy Su

Transnational coproduction has become a very trendy and remarkable phenomenon in China's film industry. *Coproduction* refers to a partnership between two or more different national production entities aimed at pooling resources while taking advantage of tax incentives, funding opportunities, locations, and popular talent in order to better compete in international markets. Coproduced movies have not only become major contributors to domestic box office revenue and the backbone of China's film industry, but they have also enabled foreign studios, especially Hollywood, to bypass the tight quota limit on film imports in China. In 2015, international coproductions approved by China outnumbered the sum of all coproductions launched in China in the prior three years, and Hollywood was China's biggest partner in these coproductions.[1] A record high eighty-nine shooting permits were issued by China's film administration in 2016 for coproductions, an increase of 11 percent over the 2015 figure.[2] By the end of 2017, coproduction treaties had been signed between China and twenty other countries.[3]

Coproduction is not something new. From its inception, the film industry has been inherently transnational, involving collaboration among various countries. Postwar cinema especially relied on transnational and transregional collaboration, and the trend has become increasingly prominent since the 1990s, driven by booming cultural industries in Asia. Coproductions have also been supported by China's unstoppable ascendance as the world's largest film market and one of the top film producers, backed by its rapidly increasing economic power and constantly growing middle class. Under China's quota system, only thirty-four foreign movies are allowed to be imported into China on the revenue-sharing basis every year, and the revenue-sharing system enables producers of these foreign imports to earn 25 percent of the total revenue. However, a coproduction is exempt from the quota limit and can be released in China as a domestically made movie, which can earn the studio as much as 43 percent of the total revenue. This significant profit difference encourages foreign studios to obtain coproduction status for their movies.

Coproduction is also greatly supported by the Chinese state and is part of its long-practiced strategy of "going to sea by borrowing a boat" initiated at the turn of the twenty-first century. China hopes to draw on foreign resources to transform its domestic film industry, export Chinese culture, and enhance its soft power in the world. Miao Xiaotian, president of the China Film Co-Production Corporation, speaking at the 2015 US-China Film Summit, said that what China desires from the coproduction process is for Chinese movies to be seen by the world to gain influence and reputation.[4]

While "international collaboration is normal practice for filmmakers and financiers through formal coproduction agreement or business partnerships,"[5] and coproduction is an effective operating mode for film producers to pool resources and talents, avoid quota limit and taxes, and share markets, these "border-erasing free-trade economics" nevertheless butt up against "border-defining cultural initiatives under the unstable sign of the nation."[6] Coproduction thus has an inherent tension between its pursuit of economic benefits and of seeking international appeal across national borders. This is especially true if coproducers are from entirely different cultures and hold quite disparate value systems, ethics, or customs. Miao Xiaotian once concluded that "the biggest obstacle facing coproductions is a cultural barrier."[7] James Pang, CEO of China's Kylin Network Movie and Culture Media Co. Ltd., contends that coproduction is a form of cultural "kidnapping" or the imposition of one's own culture and value system on another partner.[8]

Although Sino-foreign coproductions have become an integral part of global film production and consumption networks, the cultural barriers facing coproduction as a practice have meant that very few Sino-foreign coproductions have acquired both critical acclaim and box office success in China and the partner country, as demonstrated by the unsatisfactory market performance of *The Great Wall* (*Changcheng*, 2016), a Sino-US coproduction directed by China's famous director Zhang Yimou. One film that did acquire critical acclaim, however, is *Wolf Totem* (*Lang tuteng*, dir. Jean-Jacques Annaud, 2015), a Sino-French coproduction.

This chapter takes *Wolf Totem* as a case study, analyzing its cross-cultural aesthetics as well as its global network of production, circulation, and consumption. *Wolf Totem* achieved impressive box office successes in both Chinese and European film markets, generating 700 million yuan (approximately US$1.07 million) within a month of its release and $125.6 million globally. The $125.6 million revenue included $110 million from China and $8 million from France, given that the director is a renowned French director. The film, however, earned only $210,591 in the US. As such, the film's international revenue outside North America accounted for 99.8 percent of total box office receipts, whereas China accounted for 88% of the total box office.[9] The movie is about the experience of China's "sent-down" generation in Inner Mongolia during the Cultural Revolution era, highlighting the relationships among human beings, animals, and nature. The film experiments with a plausible way to do coroductions—a universally acceptable theme in a China context, and thus opens up the space for aesthetic and artistic success if not box office success in North America.

Drawing on the emergent field of "ecocinema" studies that examines cinema from a broad ecological perspective,[10] this chapter argues that the artistic success of *Wolf Totem* lies in its incorporation of the transnational theme of environmentalism in a specific Chinese historical context. I will decipher the factors contributing to the success of this transnational coproduction, including its universally appealing theme of ecological consciousness and environmental protection, a touching story deeply rooted in China's Cultural Revolution, and a director-centered model with a high degree of professionalism and division of labor in global networks of production and distribution. I argue that the film grounds its ecological consciousness in a historically specific Chinese setting, thus embedding its transnational theme in a local Chinese context. Standing at the meeting point of transnationalism and national politics, this movie is both Chinese and global. I, therefore, suggest in this chapter that *Wolf Totem* may have paved a path for future Sino-foreign coproductions.

Coproduction and Confining Cultural Factors

Because of the inherent tension in film coproductions between the cultural specificity of filmmakers and the cultural universality needed to appeal to international audiences,[11] previous researchers have proposed the notions of "cultural proximity"[12] and "cultural discount"[13] to try to explain the reasons behind the success or failure of a coproduction.

Cultural proximity refers to "the tendency to prefer media products from one's own culture or the most similar possible culture,"[14] for the obvious reason of easy apprehension, mutual understanding, and cross-border appeal. This notion can be used to explain why there are more coproductions among European countries such as Britain, France, Italy, and Spain, who enjoy geographic proximity and cultural similarity. More Asian coproductions among Japan, China, and Korea may also testify to this notion.

However, cultural proximity cannot guarantee the success of a coproduction in different national and cultural contexts and cannot explain why, in the same country, some coproduced movies or imported programs are successful while others aren't. As Koichi Iwabuchi argues, cultural proximity is "an ahistorical and totalizing way of conceiving culture" and risks seeing culture as a set of static and essentialized attributes that would automatically attract audiences."[15] Iwabuchi maintained that "cultural proximity" should be understood as a dynamic process of "becoming culturally proximate" when "audiences identify cultural similarities in a specific programme and context."[16]

I would further argue that cultural and geographic proximity cannot erase cultural differences, historical conflicts, and nationalistic sentiment; this concept may only apply to certain cross-border productions and has its limitations. For example, among a number of China-Korea coproductions, only two movies, *A Wedding Invitation* (*Fenshou heyue*, dir. Oh Ki-hwan, 2013) and *20 Once Again* (*Chongfan ershisui*, dir. Chen Zhengdao, 2015), achieved relative commercial success, mainly in the Chinese market, despite the seeming "cultural proximity" between China and Korea. Similarly, Chinese remakes of Japanese original titles face the difficulty of transplanting authentic Japanese cultural elements into the Chinese context. For example, *What a Wonderful Family* (*Mafan jiazu*, dir. Huang Lei, 2017), a movie of family conflicts and relationships based on Yoji Yamada's novel, suffered both box office failure and criticism. Critics complained that the film merely copied the Japanese version without a sufficient localizing process. The major conflict between the old couple—in which the wife demands a divorce for being neglected by her husband and spends her time learning how to write—does not fit well into the Chinese context in which women are more often independent working mothers. Historical memories and political conflicts also often come into play, as in the case of Lu Chuan's 2009 movie *Nanjing! Nanjing!*, which most Japanese theatres refused to screen. The Japanese actors who participated in this Sino-Japanese coproduction were severely lambasted in Japan.[17]

The counterpart to theories of cultural proximity is the concept of cultural discount, which refers to a reduction in the value or appeal of cultural imports crossing national borders. Imported films' appeal to the audiences of other countries tends to decrease due to audiences' insufficient background information as well as cultural and linguistic barriers.

Language is considered a critical factor in measuring cultural discount, as audiences do not enjoy dubbed foreign films and do not prefer reading translated subtitles. As a pioneer in Sino-US coproductions, Janet Yang observed that American audiences "have been spoiled and are provincial and rarely embrace foreign-language films." Overall, "there is simply a lack of familiarity and exposure to Chinese cultural icons. The Western education system has not given filmmakers or audiences a strong basis for understanding the core Chinese visual and dramatic language."[18]

However, some genres—action, crime/detective/thriller, and science fiction—have lower degrees of cultural resistance.[19] For example, the Chinese remake of the Japanese movie *The Devotion of Suspect X* (*Xianyiren X de xianshen*, dir. Su Youpeng, 2017), a thriller based on Keigo Higashino's novel, garnered more than 400 million yuan at the box office and was critically acclaimed, among all other unsuccessful adaptations and remakes. Its success can be attributed to the genre. The plot, full of suspenseful twists and turns, completely caught the attention of viewers. The thriller genre itself is a selling point because the context and cultural differences can either be largely neglected or localized without major revisions. The narrative unfolds around two or three main characters and centers on their homes or workplaces, requiring little interaction with specific cultural and national contexts. The storyline is thus largely devoid of cultural uniqueness and can easily be transplanted into a different cultural context. Science fiction films may be another possible genre for coproduction. Netflix announced its high-profile plan to have *Game of Thrones* (originally broadcast on HBO, 2011–2019) creators David Benioff and D. B. Weiss adapt Chinese writer Liu Cixin's bestselling sci-fi trilogy *The Three-Body Problem* in 2020;[20] whether the movie adaption will be successful remains to be seen. On the other hand, dramas and comedies are not as easily apprehensible as action and thriller movies because the content is rooted in specific cultural and national contexts.

The most crucial component of coproduction is to make movies that appeal to as broad of an audience as possible. As acknowledged by another pioneering coproducer, Peter Shiao, "a good story always transcends cultures."[21] As such, some scholars argue that coproductions should be about "global stories" that "are defined neither by spatial nor temporal dimensions but occur 'anywhere'—out in space, in prehistoric times, or in changing locations and temporal dimensions."[22] However, it is dubious that such decontextualized stories would have any relevance to the audiences bounded by specific cultural traditions and historical conditions.

The China-US coproduction *The Great Wall* speaks to the difficulty of a cross-border appeal. The film received predominantly negative comments in both the US and China. On Douban, China's audience-generated movie review platform similar to Rotten Tomatoes, it received a rating of 4.9 out of 10. Over 40 percent of the over 70,000 reviews rated the film either one or two stars out of five. They described the movie as "messy, mindless and illogical."[23] On Rotten Tomatoes, it received an Audience Score of 3.4 out of 5. The main problem with the movie seems to be the misperceptions it gives to both American and Chinese audiences: Chinese and Asian-American audiences misinterpreted this movie to be an outdated myth of a "white man saving China," while mainstream American/white audiences believed this movie to be an advocate of the Chinese philosophy of "faith and trust" that transforms the white protagonist, but in a very awkward and badly developed storyline. With these conflicting movie receptions, the movie has pleased neither Chinese nor American audiences.

I believe that the existing theories of cultural proximity and cultural discount are too simplified and static to serve as a strong theoretical framework for analysing the contributing factors to coproductions. On the other hand, the so-called "global stories" that have been advocated by some scholars to be used for coproductions that can occur "anywhere" decontextualize films and can hardly relate to the audiences' specific cultural traditions and historical conditions, therefore, audiences would find it almost impossible to resonate with them. I would argue that coproductions should produce "global stories" that do not deprive of any cultural and historical references. "Global stories" should be defined by "universally appealing" themes and a kind of transnational touchstone that transcend national boundaries and cultural barriers, and are able to find wide resonance in global audiences. *Wolf Totem* is such a movie that boasts a universally appealing theme: environmentalism and an ecological consciousness.

Wolf Totem: Ecocinema and Environmentalism Embedded in Chinese Politics

The movie *Wolf Totem* is based on a 2004 Chinese semi-autobiographical novel about the experiences of a young Beijing student who was sent to the countryside of Inner Mongolia in 1967 to be "re-educated" at the height of China's Cultural Revolution. The author, Lü Jiamin, wrote the book under the pseudonym Jiang Rong. The novel describes folk traditions, rituals, and the life of the ethnic Mongolian nomads on the steppe, praising their freedom, independence, respect for Mother Nature, and unyieldingness before hardship. The novel condemns the agricultural collectiviza-tion imposed on the nomads by the local authorities and the ecological disasters it caused, ending with a sixty-page "call to action" disconnected from the main thread of the novel. Named one of the "Ten Best Chinese-language Books of 2004" by international newsweekly *Yazhou Zhoukan* (*Asian Weekly*)[24] and the recipient of the first Man Asian Literary Prize in November 2007,[25] the novel was a best-seller and was read by more than 10 million people before its film adaption. It has been translated into thirty languages and published in 110 regions and countries.

The movie adaption *Wolf Totem* was formally approved by the Film Bureau in 2007 and was released in 2015 after eight years of arduous production. It was directed by French director Jean-Jacques Annaud, who was also one of the French producers and who co-wrote the screenplay with Alain Godard, John Collee, and Chinese writer Lu Wei. Two other Chinese producers, Wang Weimin and Xu Jianhai, a French producer, Xavier Castano, as well as an assembly of international production and post-production teams constituted the major production crew. As such, the movie is truly a global, collaborative project.

Producers from both France and China are centrally concerned with how to make an internationally appealing movie. Based on an interview with French producer Xavier Castano, the primary market for this movie is China; the second-ary focus is France and international markets. He said that *Wolf Totem* tells a very Chinese story but with a worldwide perspective. For the Chinese audience, the most appealing part may be the story of wolves and their relationship with human beings. For the foreign audiences, the most interesting part may be the history and the destiny of young generations during the Cultural Revolution, as well as the film's depiction of Chinese culture.[26] By combining a typically Chinese story with a worldwide perspective, the movie may be marketable to various audiences. The appeal of the movie thus lies in the incorporation of this worldwide perspective—a universally appealing theme of strong eco-consciousness—into a Chinese historical backdrop.

In this way, *Wolf Totem* exemplifies the concept of "ecocinema," a fledgling, emergent field in film studies. As Sheldon Lu defined in the first book bearing the title of "ecocinema," *Chinese Ecocinema in the Age of Environmental Challenge*:

> In the simplest terms, ecocinema is cinema with an ecological consciousness. It articulates the relationship of human beings to the physical environment, earth, nature and animals from a biocentric, non-anthropocentric point of view. In the final analysis, ecocinema pertains nothing less than life itself. Last but not least, the study of Chinese ecocinema specifically should be placed squarely within specific Chinese intellectual and socio-historical contexts that may be different from Euro-American settings in significant ways.[27]

With transnational collaboration in full swing, ecologically oriented visual culture is not just seen "as a national phenomenon limited to mainland China, but in the broad context of transregional Chinese-language cinema and the global network of commodity production, circulation and consumption."[28] Against the backdrop of increasingly severe environmental pollution and deteriorating ecosystems in China, film producers aim to use cinema as a venue to capture the gravity of pollution and natural disasters so as to help raise environmental consciousness. Chinese ecocinema thus includes both feature films and documentaries. From *Yellow Earth* (*Huang tudi*, dir. Chen Kaige, 1984) and *Old Well* (*Laojing*, dir. Wu Tianming, 1987) of the fifth generation, to Jia Zhangke's *Still Life* (*Sanxia haoren*, 2006), and, most recently, Chai Jing's documentary *Under the Dome* (*Qiongding zhi xia*, dir. Fan Ming, 2015), Chinese filmmakers have evoked profound reflections on the impact of water shortages, the environmental consequences of building the Three Gorge Dam, and air pollution on human life and environmental disasters (for a further discussion of global Chinese ecocinema, see chapter 12). Filmmakers have also rethought the relationship between human agency and the treatment of nature as an object of human appropriation, as well as modernity's discontentment.[29]

Chinese filmmakers' environmental consciousness aligns with a rising consciousness worldwide, as indicated by the similar book *Ecocinema Theory and Practice*, which claims cinema itself is a form of negotiation and meditation between the world as it "consumes and itself is consumed."[30] The book also states that "ecocinema studies is not simply limited to films with explicit messages of environmental consciousness, but investigates the breadth of cinema from Hollywood corporate productions and independent avant-garde films to the expanding media sites in which producers, consumers, and texts interact."[31] And the book believes "*all* films present productive ecocritical exploration and careful analysis can unearth engaging and intriguing perspectives on cinema's various relationships with the world around us."[32] In fact, the term "ecocinema" was coined by Scott MacDonald in his 2004 *ISLE* article, "Toward an Eco-Cinema," in which he used the term to describe films that provide "something like a garden—an 'Edenic' respite from conventional consumerism—within the machine of modern life, as modern life is embodied by the apparatus of media."[33] According to *Ecocinema Theory and Practice*, five book-length studies published at the turn of the twenty-first century mark the beginnings of an "unprecedented swell in eco-film criticism": Jhan Hochman's *Green Cultural Studies: Nature in Film, Novel and Theory* (1998), Gregg Mitman's *Reel Nature: America's Romance with Wildlife on Film* (1999), Derek Bousé's *Wildlife Films* (2000), David Ingram's *Green Screen: Environmentalism and Hollywood Cinema* (2000), and Scott MacDonald's *The Garden in the Machine: A Field Guide to Independent Films about Place* (2001). This scholarly interest in ecocinema reflects the increasing size and scope of the environmental movement in the US, Europe, and Asia, starting from the twentieth century, when environmental ideas continued to grow in popularity and recognition.

To be honest, the movie *Wolf Totem* may not be a well-conceived project for advocating environmentalism or a voluntary cinematic participation in the grassroots environmental protection movements nationwide and worldwide. The movie is a commercial cross-border production for making profits. But the movie contains a strong eco-consciousness and uses cinematic language to create an ecological lens to look at nature and human beings. As producer Wang Weimin said: "*Wolf Totem* concerns the human-animal relationship and the human-nature relationship. We human beings are not smarter than animals when facing Mother Nature. We should humbly learn from animals. In contemporary times, greedy human beings only take without giving, which caused irreversible damage to the environment. We can see all these from this movie."[34] Because of the producers' strong environmental self-consciousness—as well as the movie's tremendous artistic achievement and stunning visual effects displaying environmental disasters arousing an environmental consciousness—the movie perfectly exemplifies what ecocinema means.

Situating itself within the historical era of China's Cultural Revolution under Mao's reign in the 1960s, the storyline of *Wolf Totem* unfolds following the footsteps of two Beijing students, Chen Chen and Yang Ke, who were "sent down" to Inner Mongolia to be re-educated. From their eyes, the grandeur of the grasslands and the rituals and folk traditions of nomads deeply intrigued them. They lived with a nomad family whose old father, Bilig, served as their guide to the myth of the nomads' spiritual world and their relationship with their totem wolf and the steppe. After witnessing packs of wolves chasing large flocks of Mongolian gazelles and cornering them to be trapped by deep snow holes, Bilig explained to Chen Chen—who was angry at the cruelty of wolves—that Mongolian gazelles were the ones who were actually destroying the steppe and that wolves, in fact, helped sustain the grasslands. When the nomads pulled the Mongolian gazelles out of the snow holes and carried them away for their food storage, Bilig told them to leave some for the wolves so that they would not attack humans and their herds of sheep. However, a group of settlers from the disaster-ridden eastern parts of Inner Mongolia dug all the gazelles out and sold them to the hungry people without leaving any for the wolves. As a result, the hungry and irritated wolves launched their war against human society and attacked the military horses that Bilig's family took care of. In what appeared to be an unprecedented war between the wolves, the herdsmen, and the military horses, Bilig's son dies from a wolf attack, and hundreds of horses are trapped to their death in a large ice lake. The retaliation from the wolves gave the greedy human beings their first bloody lesson about disrespecting the ecosystem of the steppe.

Yet people of that era did not learn their lesson and continued to erase the grasslands. New settlers occupied the last uncultivated Swan Lake area, exterminating the grasslands to cultivate arable land, annihilating various species and baby wolves in order to sell their soft hide. Local officials and civilian guards even drove jeeps and carried rifles to chase down exhausted wolves and shoot them one by one. The entire ecological chain of the steppe was cut off, and the local environment was completely and irreversibly jeopardized. Torn by what he was instructed to do as part of "re-education" by local officials and by his love for the wolves and the steppe, Chen Chen set free a baby wolf that he had been raising. He realized later that a free-spirited creature like the wolf cannot be kept in human society. The baby wolf escaped into the deep mountains, bearing the hope for the rejuvenation of wolf packs and for the recovery of the ecosystem.

The movie contains a fundamental feature of ecocinema: a strong ecological consciousness and a profound reflection on the relationship of human beings with the physical environment—earth, nature, and animals—"from a biocentric, non-anthropocentric point of view."[35] In response to the rising trend of global ecocinema studies, the movie thus boasts a universally appealing theme. However, this theme is not affected by a so-called abstract "global story" that is deprived of spatial-temporal dimensions and can occur "anywhere" and thus is not relatable to any audience. On the contrary, the storyline is deeply rooted in a specific Chinese socio-historical context: the disastrous Cultural Revolution era that is notorious for its political terror, cultural and intellectual annihilation, and environmental crisis. The scenes of defacing the grasslands to cultivate arable land and the stress on human agency over natural restraints are familiar to the Chinese audience and resonate deeply within their minds and hearts. The movie is therefore both universal and local enough to find very receptive audiences, both domestic and international.

State Support, Director Autonomy, and Professional Division of Labor

A coproduction will not proceed well without collaborative efforts from various partners and participants. A global network from production to distribution is imperative for the success of a coproduction.

The production of *Wolf Totem* obtained strong and almost-unreserved support, and the blessing of the Chinese state Film Administrative Bureau and state-backed China Film Group Corporation (CFGC). It took almost ten years from the approval of the production to its final completion, which involved much enthusiasm, commitment, and effort. In the words of La Peikang, president of CFGC, *Wolf Totem* represents a dream of all Chinese film professionals and the trust bestowed on CFGC that they couldn't fail to live up to: "No matter how much money and resources to be invested in this movie, it is all worthwhile. This is our commitment to the movie, and our task to fulfil a dream for Chinese cinema."[36]

China's desire for collaboration and to excel in global film industries is so strong that at times it has shown political flexibility and even a willingness to compromise. As Peter Shiao said: "Both Chinese and American (foreign) partners are willing to tolerate any unpleasant experiences to get there for their own benefit."[37] The invitation China extended to well-known French director Jean-Jacques Annaud to make the film *Wolf Totem* testifies to this political tolerance and flexibility.

One of the producers, The Beijing Forbidden City Film Corporation, initially sought to hire a Chinese director, but the act of filming humans with live wolves was considered too difficult to accomplish. Several big-name directors in China, including Zhang Yimou and Ang Lee, refused to direct this film due to the extreme difficulty of training Mongolian wolves. New Zealand director Peter Jackson was approached as well, "but the production did not take place."[38] Just after the novel was released in France, a friend called Jean-Jacques Annaud, recommending the novel and telling him "it was as if the book was prepared for him." Not long after, the French director received a call from a Chinese representative. Annaud's 1997 movie *Seven Years in Tibet* had been banned in China, so he was shocked when he was contacted by film producers from the Beijing Forbidden City Film Corporation. They assured him that "China has changed. We are pragmatists. We don't know how to do the job you are good at. We need you." Annaud even had the right to determine the "final cut," which is quite unusual in China under the country's strict censorship. He expressed surprise at how flexible China's censorship system can be and he found it difficult to understand why he enjoyed such a high level of autonomy without much governmental intervention.[39]

Annaud boasts a record of making movies in Asia such as *The Lover* (1992), which made him fall in love with Asia and appreciate the way that Asian people interact. He also became an experienced animal movie director through directing *The Bear* (1988) and *Two Brothers* (2004). As early as 1981, he directed a movie about primitive human tribes, *The Quest for Fire*, in which he found a lot of similarities between human beings and animals. "*Wolf Totem* is like a center of all my movies and contains all key components that I am interested in," he said.[40] He had full control of the production process, from self-writing the screenplay and soliciting animal trainers, to selecting actors and actresses. He had many chances to talk to the writer of the novel, Jiang Rong, and travelled to Inner Mongolia to personally experience the rituals and cultural traditions there. Based on his experience of writing screenplays and his sense of fundamental generic differences between novel and movie, he made three major revisions to the original novel and wrote as many as eleven draft screenplays before it was finalized.

The first major revision in Annuad's screenplay was to shift the entire focus to the ecosystem and environmental protection. Jiang Rong's original novel features lengthy discussions of the different characters of nomadic civilizations and agrarian civilizations, sometimes including judgmental comparisons of the superiority and inferiority of nomadic culture and agriculture. Through a profound reflection on the historical myth of nomads' expeditions and the establishment of the unprecedented Mongol empire by Genghis Khan crossing Asia and Europe, the novel seeks to discover the ethos and characters of the nomadic people and praise their superior, conquering, and triumphant spirit, in accordance with the character of the wolf, their totem. Jiang Rong said that he aimed to disclose and condemn the damage to the grasslands inflicted by agriculture, to arouse people's awareness to the weakness of the Han nation, and to learn from the wolf's unyielding toughness, determination, teamwork, and freedom-loving spirit.[41] His major argument is uttered through Chen Chen's conversation with Yang Ke:

> The peasant economy of Han China fears competition and features peaceful farming. Confucianism stresses the unconditional submission to the authority and hierarchy to eradicate competition in order to uphold the imperial power and peaceful agriculture. The peasant economy and Confucianism both weaken the character of the Han Chinese from the existence and ideology. The brilliant civilisation of ancient China is at the cost of national character and the potential for advancing. When the world history surpassed the lower stage of agrarian civilizations, China is doomed to be attacked.[42]

Chen Chen accordingly concluded, "If Han Chinese hope to stand out of all 'world wolves,' it is imperative for them to completely eradicate the character of sheep and domestication existing in farming communities, and to turn themselves into doughty wolves."[43]

As such, the main purpose and concern of the original novel was the rebuilding of the national character to stand strong among world competitors, and the wolf is a symbol of not only nomad tribes but should also be the symbol of all admired national characters in a modern world. However, this conclusion and its historical worldview, at their best, are subjective, simplistic, judgemental, and controversial; at their worst, they are fascist and socially Darwinist.

Annaud's screenplay makes major cuts to the above-mentioned sensitive and controversial topics and themes, and entirely refocuses on the theme of a strong eco-consciousness and environmental protection. This refocus not only avoids causing discomfort and controversies among Han Chinese, who constitute the majority of Chinese audiences, but also rebuilds the film on a consensus of environmental protection that is globally appealing without controversies and political sensitivity. The screenplay therefore lays a solid foundation for a marketable movie. Jiang Rong said the environmental issue is also an important component of the novel, and Annaud's cuts were acceptable to him.[44]

The second major revision Annuad made was to add a love story. The screenplay foregrounds the female lead Gasma and adds a love story with the Beijing student that did not exist in the original novel. The aim was to put human emotions on par with the emotions of the wolves, and to add a romantic flavor that would better appeal to international audiences.

The third major revision was the deletion of the very primitive, cruel and ugly scenes of the novel—such as the bloody slaughter of horses by the wolves—in order to focus more on the vitality, beauty, grandeur, and future hope of the grasslands in cinematic language, which enables the movie to be very picturesque and painting-like. At the end of the original novel, Chen Chen strikes the baby wolf to death because the free-spirited wolf tried to break its chains too many times and had fatally hurt itself: to honor the spirit of wolf, Chen Chen personally killed it to preserve its dignity. In the screenplay, however, Chen Chen releases the wolf to allow it to live in deep mountains.

Annaud explained that this is the difference between a movie and a book. Movies use stories and pictures to bring the audience into its context; therefore, it is important to touch the audience's soul and make them understand and respect nature, and understand more about love. He said he did not like the ending of the novel because nobody wished to see such a lovely little creature killed on screen. He said, "All my movies usually have an ending full of hope, because I am that kind of person. . . . I hope the audience can fully understand the message conveyed by the original novel, understand the significance of maintaining a balance between nature and human beings, and respect all species."[45]

From the beginning, Annaud decided to use real Mongolian wolves in the movie and train those wolves to become real actors. Thus, finding a good animal trainer was the most challenging task and crucial for the movie's success. Luckily, Canadian animal trainer Andrew Simpson recommended himself to Annaud. Simpson has participated in more than 150 movies and 200 TV dramas; he is considered the world's greatest and most experienced animal trainer. The film crew spent three years, from 2011 to 2013, raising three generations of thirty-five Mongolian wolves and setting up four animal-raising bases. Seventeen wolves were trained and starred in the film.[46] Headed by Simpson, a ten-person team took good care of the wolves and trained them on performing complicated gestures, procedures, and mechanisms. The movie could not have been successful without the hard work and coordination of Simpson's team. As an interesting anecdote, sixteen wolves and a dog stunt double immigrated to Canada after retiring from filmmaking; they currently live on the ranch owned by Simpson.

The movie *Wolf Totem* features breathtaking visuals and special effects in the human-wolf war and the horse-wolf war: chasing shots, close-ups, facial expressions of wolves, and numerous scenes of wolves howling at the midnight moon. More than

1,000 shots needed CGI technology and 3D technology, so digital artists from more than forty foreign countries, 160 Chinese domestic digital artists, and more than thirty visual effect teams joined the production and post-production process. This global coproduction network includes Hollywood's Base FX (*American Capital 2: The Winter Soldier* [*Meiguo duizhang 2: dongri zhanri*], dir. Anthony Russo and Joe Russo, 2014; *Transformers 4: Age of Extinction* [*Bianxing jingang 4: jueji chongsheng*], dir. Michael Bay, 2014), Plxomondo (*Hugo*, dir. Martin Scorsese, 2011), Singapore's VHQ (*Harry Potter* series), France's LUX, as well as China Film Group's special effects team and ILLUMINIA.[47] This professional division of labor and close collaboration on a global scale ensured the film's high-quality and breathtaking visual effects; additionally, the international team helped bring a global perspective on ecology that impacts the visual construction of the film.

Conclusion

As the above analysis indicates, the film *Wolf Totem* may have paved a path for Sino-foreign coproductions. It is Chinese in that its touching story is deeply rooted in China's Cultural Revolution; it is global in its universally appealing theme of ecological consciousness and environmental protection. Its global appeal is manifested and perfectly integrated into its local context. The film therefore overcomes the inherent tensions and confining cultural factors that usually plague a coproduction: the cultural specificity of a film storyline and the cultural universality needed to appeal to international audiences.

Furthermore, the film's production process features a director-centered model and a high degree of professionalism and division of labor. Its production is integrated into the global network of production and distribution, involving joint efforts of film professionals coming from a number of countries. This transnationalism and internationalism highlight a true cross-border collaboration and coproduction.

Wolf Totem's production acquired strong support from the Chinese state. The issue of state intervention brings up the question of film censorship that potentially concerns many international film coproducers. The film's universally appealing theme of environmental protection fits into the Chinese state's strategic development plan and environmental protection plan, however, and was therefore approved by the state film administration. Furthermore, the film is situated in the historical era of Mao's disastrous Cultural Revolution instead of a contemporary time, which avoids a direct criticism and clash with current Chinese economic growth policies that are often at the expense of environmental protection and nature preservation. Mao's Cultural Revolution had been officially concluded a national disaster; thus, the film does not run counter to the state's stance and is acceptable to the Party. In addition, *Wolf Totem* is not radical in terms of its conveyed message: it offers just enough eco-consciousness to attract audiences without venturing into too much political critique. Compared with other cinematic works such as Chai Jing's documentary

Under the Dome (*Qiongding zhi xia*, 2015)—which provides a far gloomier picture of contemporary China's environmental disaster and a more pungent criticism of China's policy and social circumstances—*Wolf Totem* is historically reflective, visually stunning and spectacular, highly entertaining and enjoyable, but politically non-provocative. In this sense, its global-local interaction is positive.

So what would happen if a coproduction's global theme is not approved by the state and the global-local interaction is not positive? Under such circumstances, the global-local interaction would be conditional and contextual. One can only hope for fast-changing social and political conditions and an increasing level of governmental tolerance and flexibility, as implied by the production experience of *Wolf Totem*. With this hope and optimism, the space for coproduction remains wide open, and the path may be repeated by other coproductions.

Notes

1. Miao Xiaotian, speech at the 2015 US-China Film Summit, Los Angeles, November 1, 2015.
2. Steven Schwankert, "2016 Sets Record for Shooting Permits in China," *China Film Insider*, January 31, 2017, https://chinafilminsider.com/2016-sets-record-co-production-permits-china.
3. L. Zhao, "Zhongguo yu ershiyi ge guojiadiqu de hepaipian zheng jianjianhepai" [China on track to coproduce films with 21 countries], *China Film News*, January 11, 2018, https://www.sohu.com/a/216069631_388075
4. Miao, speech at the 2015 US-China Film Summit.
5. Ben Glodsmith and Tom O'Regan, "International Film Production: Interests and Motivations," in *Cross-Border Cultural Production: Economic Runaway or Globalization?*, ed. Janet Wasko and Mary Erickson (Amherst, MA: Cambria Press, 2008), 13.
6. Toby Miller et al., *Global Hollywood 2*, 2nd ed. (London: British Film Institute, 2005), 209.
7. Miao, speech at the 2015 US-China Film Summit.
8. James Pang, personal communication, November 1, 2015.
9. "Wolf Totem," Box Office Mojo by IMDb Pro, https://www.boxofficemojo.com/release/rl561874433/weekend/.
10. Sheldon Lu, "Introduction: Chinese-Language Ecocinema," *Journal of Chinese Cinemas* 11, no. 1 (2017): 1–12.
11. Paul W. Taylor, "Co-productions—Content and Change: International Television in the Americas," *Canadian Journal of Communication*, 20, no. 3 (1995): 411–16.
12. Joseph D. Straubhaar, "Beyond Media Imperialism: Asymmetrical Interdependence and Cultural Proximity," *Critical Studies in Mass Communication* 8, no. 1 (1991): 39–59.
13. Colin Hoskins and Rolf Mirus, "Reasons for the US Dominance of the International Trade in Television Programmes," *Media, Culture & Society* 10, no. 4 (October 1988): 499–515.
14. Joseph D. Straubhaar, "Choosing National TV: Cultural Capital, Language, and Cultural Proximity in Brazil," in *The Impact of International Television: A Paradigm Shift*, ed. Michael G. Elasmar (Mahwah, NJ: Lawrence Erlbaum Associates, 2003), 85.

15. Koichi Iwabuchi, "Becoming 'Culturally Proximate': The A/scent of Japanese Idol Dramas in Taiwan" in *Asian Media Productions*, ed. Brian Moeran (Honolulu: University of Hawai'i Press, 2001), 57.

16. Iwabuchi, "Becoming 'Culturally Proximate'," 58.

17. Stephanie M. Brown, "Victims, Heroes, Men, and Monsters: Revisiting a Violent History in *City of Life and Death*," *Quarterly Review of Film and Video* 32, no. 6 (July 2015): 527–37, https://doi.org/10.1080/10509208.2015.1046350.

18. Janet Yang, personal communication, August 1, 2016.

19. Hoskins and Mirus, "Reasons for the US Dominance."

20. Patrick Brzeski, "GOP Senators Send Letter to Netflix Challenging Plans to Adapt Chinese Sci-Fi Novel 'The Three Body Problem'," *The Hollywood Reporter*, September 24, 2020, https://www.hollywoodreporter.com/news/gop-senators-send-letter-to-netflix-challenging-plans-to-adapt-chinese-sci-fi-novel-the-three-body-problem.

21. Peter Shiao, personal communication, August 17, 2016.

22. Doris Baltruschat, "International TV and Film Co-production: A Canadian Case Study," in *Media Organization and Production*, ed. Simon Cottle (London: SAGE, 2003), 156.

23. Josh Horwitz and Echo Huang, "'Messy, Mindless, Illogical': Chinese Moviegoers Review Matt Damon's Film 'Great Wall'," *QUARTZ*, December 20, 2016, https://qz.com/866485/matt-damons-the-great-wall-is-a-hit-at-the-chinese-box-office-but-critics-hate-it/.

24. Zhang Hailing, "2004 *Yazhou Zhoukan* shi dahao shu jiexiao" [Announcement of *Yazhou Zhoukan*'s 10 Best Chinese Books of 2004], *Yazhou Zhoukan*, January 16, 2005.

25. "Chinese Author Scoops Book Prize," BBC News, November 11, 2007, http://news.bbc.co.uk/2/hi/entertainment/7089513.stm.

26. Xavier Castano, "Shijiedianying de weilai shi Zhongguo" [The future of world cinema is in China], in *Langtuteng dianying quanjilu* [The entire record of the production of *Wolf Totem*], ed. Yang Sixuan (Beijing: China Broadcasting, Film and Television Press, 2015), 54–62.

27. Sheldon Lu, "Introduction. Cinema, Ecology, Modernity," in *Chinese Ecocinema: In the Age of Environmental Challenge*, ed. Sheldon Lu and Jiayan Mi (Hong Kong: Hong Kong University Press, 2009), 2.

28. Sheldon Lu, "Introduction: Chinese-Language Ecocinema," *Journal of Chinese Cinemas* 11, no. 1 (2017): 2.

29. Sheldon Lu and Jiayan Mi, eds., *Chinese Ecocinema In the Age of Environmental Challenge* (Hong Kong: Hong Kong University Press, 2009).

30. Stephen Rust, Salma Monani, and Sean Cubitt, eds., *Ecocinema Theory and Practice* (New York: Routledge, 2013).

31. Rust, Monani, and Cubitt, *Ecocinema Theory and Practice*, 3.

32. Rust, Monani, and Cubitt, *Ecocinema Theory and Practice*, 3.

33. Scott MacDonald, "Toward an Eco-Cinema," *ISLE: Interdisciplinary Studies in Literature and Environment* 11, no. 2 (2004): 107–32.

34. Yang Sixuan, ed., *Langtuteng dianying quanjilu* [The entire record of the production of *Wolf Totem*] (Beijing: China Broadcasting, Film and Television Press, 2015).

35. Lu, "Introduction," 2.

36. La Peikang, "Xu: wei zhongguo dianying yuan yigemeng" [Preface: Fulfill a dream for Chinese cinema], in *Langtuteng dianying quanjilu*, ed. Yang Sixuan, 1.

37. Peter Shiao, personal communication, August 17, 2016.

38. IMDB, "*Wolf Totem* Trivia," https://www.imdb.com/title/tt2909116/trivia?ref_=tt_trv_trv.

39. Amy Qin, "Jinpan daoyan zhidao langtuteng lingrenyiwai" [Director of banned movie to direct *Wolf Totem*], *New York Times Chinese*, February 28, 2015, https://cn.nytimes.com/film-tv/20150228/t28wolftotem/zh-hant/.

40. Yang, *Langtuteng dianying quanjilu*, 5.

41. "Zhongren zhiyi langtuteng Jiang Rong: wo juebu tuoxie" [Jiang Rong refutes public suspicion of *Wolf Totem*], *Xin Jing Bao*, February 26, 2015, http://culture.ifeng.com/a/20150226/43223694_0.shtml.

42. Lü Jiamin, *Wolf Totem* (Wuhan: Changjiang Literature and Arts Publishing House, 2004), chapter 20.

43. Lü Jiamin, *Wolf Totem*, chapter 28.

44. Amy Qin, "Jiangrong: caoyuan, yijing huibuqule" [Jiangrong said to nowhere in the steppe that he can go back], *New York Times Chinese*, March 3, 2015, https://cn.nytimes.com/film-tv/20150303/tc03jiangrong/zh-hant/.

45. Yang, *Langtuteng dianying quanjilu*, 14.

46. Yang, *Langtuteng dianying quanjilu*, 21.

47. Yang, *Langtuteng dianying quanjilu*.

Part III

Globalization and Chinese Identities

7

The Sound of Chinese Urban Cinema

Multilingualism and the Re-globalization of Shanghai in the 1990s

Lin Feng

Although China's economic reform started in the late 1970s, it did not come into full blossom until the 1990s when China's then-paramount leader Deng Xiaoping (1904–1997) made his famous Southern Tour in 1992. Since then, China's economic development has featured rapid urbanization, marketization, and globalization. The nationwide reform and social changes inevitably impacted Chinese cinema's narrative interests. In her analysis of the rising urban generation during the 1990s, Zhang Zhen regarded Chinese urban cinema as a marginalized "minority" whose significance existed in its resistance to officially sanctioned mainstream cinema of both state-sponsored leitmotif (*zhuxuanlü*) and commercial films. Primarily focusing on indenpent cinema, Zhang claimed that many of those films attempted to capture "the socioeconomic unevenness, psychological anxiety, and moral confusion caused by the upheaval" as well as the struggle and hardship that urban subjects (such as migrant workers) were facing.[1]

Moving away from independent cinema, Guo Shaohua argued that since the late 1990s, Chinese urban cinema did not just function "as a 'vehicle of criticism' of China's urbanization process"; it also provided a "shared platform" for a number of filmmakers to engage with "less confrontational" themes, such as the economic appeal and cultural aspirations of the new middle class.[2] Unlike Zhang, who saw Chinese urban film as a counter-cultural product for a niche elitist market, Guo regarded it as a middlebrow genre that catered to the growing middle-class audience. Despite their different perspectives, both scholars' analyses illustrate contemporary Chinese cinema's effort to capture Chinese citizens' newly acquired urban experience in addition to globalization's impact on the country's changing landscape.

Among the many academic studies concerning contemporary Chinese urban cinema is a clear focus on the relationship between urbanization and social mobility. Hence, small towns, such as Fenyang in Jia Zhangke's *Home* trilogy, were frequently interpreted as a representation of China's torn-down areas, featuring the destruction and demolition of the past and old communities. In comparison, the urban trans-formation in big cities like Shanghai and Beijing in films such as *Beautiful New World* (*Meili xin shijie*, dir. Shi Runjiu, 1999) and *Shower* (*Xizao*, dir. Zhang Yang, 1999) catered to what Sheldon H. Lu called "the tastes, dreams, pursuits, and disil-lusions of a rising Chinese middle class, which is concerned less about politics and more about money."[3] What is missing from this scholarship is the specificity of a city's urban (re)generation. Such local specificity was often overshadowed by the class-bound critiques on social mobility, commodification of urban landscape, and rural-urban division.

However, cities are different, and so are their citizens' urban experiences. Whilst many Chinese big cities have their own unique urban history and characteristics, they are also endowed with specific social, economic, and political roles by the state government. As such, a city's relationship with the local, national, and global con-structs are constantly under negotiation. With this negotiation in mind, I argue that cinematic discourse of a city's local specificity—whether it is foregrounded as a key feature of the story or deliberately removed to serve the officially sanctioned national discourse—is equally important in order for us to understand the eco-nomic and political paradigm of Chinese urban cinema.

To illustrate this point, I have chosen Shanghai as a key case study. To be spe-cific, this chapter examines how Chinese *shijing* comedies in the 1990s used spoken language to shape Shanghai's cultural-political space, both on- and off-screen, when the city was experiencing rapid re-globalization and urban regeneration. Meaning "urban streets" or "urban marketplaces," *shijing* often concerns the urban resident's everyday life.[4] Relatively free from upper- and middle-class social etiquette or political elitists' public manners, *shijing* narrative in Chinese comedies frequently either celebrates common urban citizens' consumer wisdom and their adaptabil-ity to economic and social changes, or humorously highlights their pettiness and cunning in exploring financial advantage. As one of the most-developed cities in the country, Shanghai was not only China's film center for decades; it continues to be highly significant to China's economic development. In this regard, it would be difficult to ignore the city when analyzing Chinese *shijing* comedies or urban cinema as a whole.

Jurg Hausermann pointed out, "Wherever we are, whatever we do, we invaria-bly find ourselves in an acoustic environment" that is "specific to place, culture, and historical period."[5] In comparison to the written form of any language, spoken lan-guage has far more diversified variants, even within the same linguistic family, thus binding it more closely with regional specification of a cultural space. As such, this chapter is not so much about Chinese cinema's contest of rural-urban mobility or a migrant worker's struggle when they adapt to city life. It is more about how Chinese urban cinema (*shijing* comedies in this case) underlines a city's struggle to negotiate its local voice and its national role when both globalization and national unity are increasingly embedded into China's political and economic ambition. Through a detailed analysis of the linguistic soundscape of *Shanghai Fever* (*Gu feng*, dir. Lee Kwok-lap, 1994) and *Four Chefs and a Feast* (*Chunfeng deyi meilongzhen*, dir. Lee Kwok-lap, 1998), this chapter argues that during the 1990s there was an attempt in Chinese popular cinema to capitalize on Shanghai's unique experience of urban regeneration and re-globalization, yet at the same time, such films also revealed that the city's distinctive localness is often offset by its national role showcasing China's image as a unified nation.

Both of the films selected in this chapter were directed by a Hong Kong film-maker, Lee Kwok-lap; there are three reasons for this selection. First, Hong Kong filmmakers made a huge contribution to the development of Chinese commercial cinema during Deng's reform era. Among Hong Kong filmmakers who embraced China's newly opened-up film industry, Lee was at the forefront of exploring China's recent cycle of urbanization. After mainland China adopted the Open Door Policy in 1978, mainland China–Hong Kong film coproduction quickly resumed, with notable examples like *Shaolin Temple* (*Shaolin si*, dir. Zhang Xinyan, 1982), *The Burning of the Imperial Palace* (*Huo shao yuanming yuan*, dir. Li Han-hsiang, 1983), and *Great Shanghai 1937* (*Da Shanghai 1937*, dir. Chang Cheh, 1986). It is through these coproductions that post-Mao China started to gradually re-celebrate com-mercial cinema through popular genre filmmaking. However, many of these films were directed by older-generation filmmakers who migrated from mainland China to Hong Kong at the turn of the 1950s and developed their career in Hong Kong's Mandarin cinema in the 1960s. Understandably, many of these early collaborations not only closely followed Mandarin cinema's monolingualism, but also frequently placed their thematic concern within a historical context when pre-modern China was facing a territorial crisis under external threat or invasion.

It was not until the 1990s that mainland–Hong Kong coproductions started to capture China's latest wave of urban development featuring global mobility. In comparison to the coproductions in the 1980s, many films coproduced in the 1990s were directed by a younger generation of filmmakers who were born in Hong Kong, earned their professional reputation in Hong Kong's Cantonese cinema and televi-sion, and attracted critical attention through their interests in Hong Kong's local urban stories. Accordingly, their films were more often set in big cities, such as Beijing and Shanghai. Unlike his peer Hong Kong filmmakers who often adopted a nostalgic approach of probing Shanghai's cosmopolitan history,[6] Lee was more willing to explore local citizens' quick adjustment to China's newly marketized economy.

Second, although mainland Chinese cinema started to re-embrace *shijing* com-edies' commercial appeal as early as the 1980s, few of those films explored a city's locality through a linguistic soundscape other than Mandarin, as evidenced in all films from the *Er Zi* series (1983–1992).[7] To some degree, Lee's collaboration rein-troduced (non-Mandarin) dialect filmmaking into *shijing* comedies in mainland China. Whereas the Shanghai dialect was generally more tolerated in films with historical settings prior to the People's Republic of China's (PRC) founding in 1949, Lee's films set out to test the linguistic boundary of urban locality in contemporary China.

Third, Lee also represents a group of Hong Kong filmmakers who sought to establish their place in the greater Chinese mainstream cinema through their collaboration with state-owned studios as well as through contributing, negotiating, and even compromising the popular cinema's portrayal of urban specificity with China's leitmotif value of nationalism. As such, Lee's films are also selected in this chapter for their exemplification of contemporary Chinese urban cinema's mediation of a city's complex relationship with the state's local, national, and global agenda.

As I discuss in more detail later, in spite of both *Shanghai Fever* and *Four Chefs and a Feast* intending to capture Shanghai's localness through multilingual filmmaking, the way local dialect (Shangahinese in this case) is used or eliminated reveals the city's struggle in negotiating its local pride with its newly assigned role promoting China's national and global ambitions. In other words, Shanghai's localness remains ambivalently between the visible and invisible—or more accurately the audible and inaudible—in Chinese cinema. Before I venture into a detailed analysis, I briefly review Chinese cinema's language practice in next section in order to provide a historical context of how Chinese cinema has politicized Shanghai's urban image through controlling the usage of local dialect(s).

(The Shanghai) Dialect in Chinese Urban (Comedic) Cinema

Chinese cinema has a long history of producing *shijing* comedies. One of the earliest surviving examples is *Laborer's Love* (*Laogong zhi aiqing*, dir. Zhang Shichuan, 1922). It tells a story of fruit vendor Zheng, who falls in love with the daughter of his neighbor, Doctor Zhu. In order to win over Zhu's approval for his daughter's marriage, Zheng devises a plan to modify the staircase of a nightclub near the doctor's clinic. Zheng's handiwork results in many of the nightclub's customers falling down the stairs and injuring themselves, and thus Zhu's clinic becomes in high demand. Helping Zhu to revive the business, Zheng obtains Zhu's blessing. This film vividly demonstrates Shanghai's status as the birthplace of Chinese *shijing* comedies: not only because the film was set and produced in Shanghai, but also because its comedic narrative is tightly built into the fabric of the city's consumer economy. Unlike a rom-com that primarily focuses on a couple's love encounter or intertwines comedic moments with the couple's misunderstandings of each other, the romantic narrative in *Laborer's Love* is rather minimal. The realization of the couple's marriage is only achieved when Zheng proves his ability to help Zhu to achieve business success. While Zheng's intent to injure innocent people could be seen as ethically flawed, the film rewards the character with a happy ending. This early example illustrates that *shijing* comedies place more emphasis on the narrative of an individual's inspiration of personal gain within a city's economic infrastructure and consumer culture.

Despite *shijing* comedies successfully transferring into the sound era, their articulation with Shanghai's urban locality is severely restricted by the government's language unification policies from the 1920s onward. Film historian Zhong Jin noted that the Nationalist government established a film censorship committee in 1931, and soon after, the committee banned all dialects in Chinese sound films. In 1932 and 1933, the committee issued a number of official notices informing film studios that all new productions must adopt Mandarin as their spoken language.[8] Although the Nationalist government was not able to restrict the production of Cantonese films in Hong Kong and Guangdong province because of its lack of control over those regions, it had a firm grip on the Shanghai film industry, which was then the center of Chinese cinema.

As a result, despite the fact that the majority of *shijing* comedies, and urban films by and large, were produced by Shanghai-based studios and were set in the city, Mandarin was used as a default language from the very beginning of the sound era, whereas a local dialect—Shanghainese—was only used sporadically. Instead of adopting dialects, the portrayal of linguistic differences between various Chinese communities was primarily delivered through accented Mandarin. For instance, in the left-wing classic *Crows and Sparrows* (*Wuya yu maque*, dir. Zheng Junli, 1949) all the tenants of a rented house speak Mandarin, although they have various northern and southern accents to signify Shanghai's image as a migrant city. Shanghainese was used sparingly in only a handful scenes. One such occasion is when Mr. Xiao (Zhao Dan), one of the tenants, murmurs to himself about his daydream of getting rich quick through subletting. Another example takes place when Xiao and his wife (Wu Yin) are thrown out of a black market by local gangsters. In both scenes, the linguistic twist associated Shanghai's localness with urban consumerism and opportunism.

Such linguistic control over mainland Chinese cinema continued after 1949. Despite their political and ideological differences, the Communist government followed the Nationalist government's language policy and regarded Mandarin as a useful tool to enhance national unification and to promote collectivism. In 1956, China's State Council issued official instructions to promote *Putonghua*—that is, standard Mandarin—and mandated that all actors and broadcasters must receive *Putonghua* training.[9] The only exception was for actors from regional Chinese operas and *quyi*—a collective term referring to a variety of traditional Chinese entertainment forms, such as ballad singing, storytelling, cross-talking, and stand-up comedy, of which dialect is an organic element of the performance. In a sense, it would be impossible to remove dialect from those regional art and entertainment forms without destroying them entirely.

As regional Chinese operas and *quyi* collectively had a large fan base, they were tolerated and used as tools to promote the Communist Party's governance, ideologies, and policies. Hence, forcing Chinese operas and *quyi* to adopt standard Mandarin would likely pose a threat to the new regime that still needed to gain support from the public across the country during the early period of the PRC. In addition, the majority of the regional operas and *quyi* have a restricted scope of dissemination on their own, and they are predominantly popular within the region where the language is native. Since many of them do not have nationwide appeal, they are not perceived by the state as threats to national unity. Unlike films that are often distributed nationwide and thus have wider mass impact, regional Chinese operas and *quyi* were protected as a way to symbolize the new government's embrace of cultural and folk diversity within the big Chinese family. In fact, Chinese opera films were the only form of dialect films that were allowed to be produced through-out the Mao era from the 1950s to the 1970s. Dividing the new mass media (including film) and traditional theatre into two tiers of national and regional canons, such linguistic requirements demonstrated that the Communist government prioritized its control over different art forms based on their dissemination reach.

In order to promote standard Mandarin, a number of educational documentaries were produced in the years after the instructions were issued. In these documentaries, such as *Let's Speak Mandarin* (*Dajia lai shuo putonghua*, prod. Shanghai Science Education Film Studio, 1957), Shanghainese was frequently used as a negative example to suggest that regional dialects were responsible for misunderstanding and miscommunication. Accordingly, except for a handful of comedies—such as *Sanmao Learning Business* (*Sanmao xue shengyi*, dir. Huang Zuolin, 1958) and *Such Parents* (*Ruci dieniang*, dir. Zhang Tianci, 1963), both of which were adapted from the local *quyi* form *huaji xi* (Shanghaiese comedy) and cast *huaji xi* actors to perform their stage roles on the big screen for local audiences[10]—Shanghainese was either removed entirely from the soundtrack or depicted as inferior in Chinese cinema. For instance, Xie Jin's documentary *Huang Baomei* (1958) and feature comedy *Big Li, Little Li, and Old Li* (*Da Li Xiao Li he Lao Li*, 1962) were both shot in Shanghainese and then dubbed into Mandarin before their public release. In a similar vein, Yomi Braester pointed out in his study of the film *Sentinels Under the Neon Lights* (*Nihongdeng xia de shaobing*, dir. Wang Ping and Ge Xin, 1964) that "Mandarin and the Shanghai dialect are portrayed as vehicles of two competing ideologies. . . . The Shanghai dialect is construed as an ideological affront and a form of sabotage. The linguistic twist associates Shanghai localism with hypocrisy, political subversion, and resistance to the PLA [People's Liberation Army]."[11] As these examples illustrate, the co-existence of languages in Chinese (urban) films produced during the Mao era was not intended to celebrate Shanghai's local ambience or the diversity of the city's urban cultures. Instead, it sent a clear message to the mass public that Shanghainese as well as the city's marketized economy and cosmopolitan lifestyle were undesirable because of their associations with capitalism, consumerism, and Westernized urban bourgeoisie.

It is within this wider political context that Shanghai-based *shijing* comedies were replaced by what Bao Ying called "eulogistic comedies,"[12] such as *Today, I Rest* (*Jintian wo xiuxi*, dir. Lu Ren, 1959) and *Female Barber* (*Nü lifashi*, dir. Ding Ran, 1962). Unlike *shijing* comedies that draw inspiration from market economy and urban consumerism, eulogistic comedies foregrounded the state's ideological obligation of promoting a worker's devotion to their work, even though they might also appear to focus on common people's everyday life. These attitudes and restrictions probably explain why both Shanghai dialect filmmaking and urban films (including *shijing* comedies) set in Shanghai disappeared entirely from China's big screen during the following two decades.

In contrast to the situation in mainland China, both *shijing* comedies and dialect filmmaking survived in Hong Kong. As a result of many mainland filmmakers having migrated to Hong Kong during and after the Civil War, *shijing* comedies quickly expanded their audiences in those filmmakers' new host city. Examples include, but are not limited to, Zhu Shilin's *The Dividing Wall* (*Yi ban zhi ge*, 1952) and Li Pingqian's *Day Dream* (*Bairi meng*, 1953). Moreover, Hong Kong filmmakers successfully localized *shijing* comedies through adopting Cantonese into their production, as evidenced in *My Intimate Partner* (*Nan xiong nan di*, dir. Qin Jian, 1960), *Master of All* (*Tongtian shifu*, dir. Chen Zhuosheng, 1964), *The House of 72 Tenants* (*Qishi'er jia fangke*, dir. Chor Yuen, 1973), and many of the Hui Brothers' comedies.[13] Successfully articulating Hong Kong's local experiences with the city's transformation into a major financial center, these Cantonese *shijing* comedies enjoyed huge popularity among local audiences in Hong Kong and overseas Chinese communities.

Notwithstanding the lack of commercial films in mainland Chinese cinema from the mid-1960s to the turn of the 1980s, the mainland film industry and market quickly responded to the new social changes after the government reopened the country for marketization in the early 1980s and eventually extended the scale of economic reform across the country to encourage further globalization in the 1990s. In the beginning, an increasing number of Hong Kong and foreign films were imported (legally and illegally). Whereas only a small number of legally imported films were released in theaters with a dubbed Mandarin soundtrack, a large quantity of Hong Kong films (with their original Cantonese soundtracks) were shown in *luxiangting* (video halls) in both big cities and small towns during the 1980s and 1990s.[14] With the help of subtitles, Cantonese films were able to bypass the state control over the language that is permitted in mainland films. Despite the copyright infringement, *luxiangting* culture provided mainland audiences with a valuable platform of appreciating dialect films in popular cinema other than opera films.

Mainland China's film production was gradually decentralized and commercialized after 1984, when the central government formally announced its decision to shift China's centralized planned economy to a market economy.[15] This move encouraged state-owned studios to explore commercial filmmaking and seek international collaboration. As a result of embracing the growth of media markets and swift urbanization taking place across the country—while also competing with popular films from Hong Kong—many state-owned studios started to produce urban-based genre films in order to attract wider urban audiences. Subsequently, Shanghai-based urban films, after nearly two decades of absence from the Chinese big screen, re-emerged.

In simplistic terms, Shanghai-based urban films produced by the state-owned studios during the early years of Deng's reform era can be divided into two main categories. The first group constitutes popular genre films, including comedies, such as *The New Story of Du Xiaoxi* (*A hun xin zhuan*, dir. Wang Weiyi, 1984) and *Romance in Philately* (*You yuan*, dir. Sang Hu, 1984). As with their 1950s and 1960s predecessors, these comedies often used satire to educate the unmotivated youth who struggled to adjust themselves to the reform era—a narrative that continued to follow the eulogistic comedies' thematic concern. The second group contains a large number of social dramas, such as *The Nanpu Bridge* (*Qing sa pujiang*, dir. Shi Xiaohua, 1991) and *City Saxophone* (*Dushi sakesifeng*, dir. Shi Xiaohua and Shi Qicheng, 1994). Often telling stories about how Chinese workers and intellectuals can resist the seduction of consumerism brought on by the globalization and marketization reforms, these films fit well into the officially sanctioned leitmotif narrative model of nation-building.

Although many of these Shanghai-based films involved local residents as main characters, their multilingual features were still primarily delivered through standard Mandarin and a limited use of foreign languages, such as English and Japanese. Local dialect—Shanghainese—continued to be absent. Given that the nationwide promotion of *Putonghua* was written into the country's constitution in 1982, these urban films' emphasis on nationhood and national pride meant that they could easily be set in any city without making too much difference in terms of the portrayal of specific urban experience or locality. This situation did see some changes, however, in 1990s coproductions, which I discuss in more detail in next section.

Revaluing Dialects in Shanghai-Based *Shijing* Comedies in the 1990s

After nearly ten years of China setting up special economic zones in South China near Hong Kong and Taiwan, Shanghai was finally allowed to develop its local economy and to improve its urban infrastructure in the 1990s. Along with the development of the Pudong New Area and re-globalization of the city, local citizens experienced a rapid urban regeneration. As part of this development, both the city and its citizens had to renegotiate their relationships to the global economy. To do so, Shanghai frequently looked to other major world cities, such as New York, Tokyo, London, and especially Hong Kong, for reference and inspiration.[16] Meanwhile, the city's fast urban development and the resurgence of its cosmopolitan culture was accompanied by a rising sense of local pride.

It is in this context that Shanghainese reappeared on Chinese screens, especially through original creations (in contrast to adaptations of Chinese operas or *huaji xi* stage plays), to deliver local stories while at the same time testing the boundaries of linguistic control in Chinese commercial cinema. One example is *Shanghai Fever*, the first mainland project of Hong Kong filmmaker Lee Kwok-lap. Primarily in Shanghainese, the film's original version also contains Cantonese, Mandarin, English, and various dialects from the Wu-language-speaking region, such as Suzhou, Shaoxing, and Yangzhou dialects.[17] Coproduced by a relatively small state-owned studio, Xiaoxiang Film Studio, and Hong Kong's Impact Films Investment Ltd., *Shanghai Fever* depicts Hong Kong businessman Alan's (Lau Ching-wan) encounter with a Shanghai bus conductor Fan Li (Pan Hong). In the film, Fan's Shanghai local citizenship enables her to help Alan get access to and make profit through investing in a newly reinstalled Shanghai stock exchange.[18]

Unlike the new urban-based leitmotif or eulogical comedic characters mentioned in previous section, the protagonist in *Shanghai Fever*, Fan, and her neighbors are no longer ashamed of talking about money and expressing their desire to improve their living conditions through financial means; more importantly, the film doesn't fault its characters for seeking out financial success to improve their lives. In the 1980s and 1990s, Shanghai experienced a housing crisis that stemmed from the city's role, since 1949, as China's major revenue contributor. Between 1951 and 1995, Shanghai contributed an average of 72.5% of its local revenue to the central government.[19] Because of this heavy fiscal burden, the city was not able to develop or renew its urban infrastructure for decades. As a result, many local citizens lived in poor housing conditions, such as accommodating an entire three-generation family in one tiny room or using shared kitchens and toilets with neighbors. These living conditions are vividly captured in the scenes where Fan and her neighbors have daily conversations and even arguments in Shanghainese in the communal areas, including in a shared kitchen and *longtang*—a type of alleyway that connects a number of resident houses in Shanghai. As many local audiences would have recognized the film's portrayal of their own living space, they would also share Fan's desire to have a larger apartment with its own kitchen and bathroom.

This film was set in the time when Shanghai reopened its stock market in 1990. New to many Chinese people who were born after 1949, the transaction of stocks was restricted to citizens of selected cities during its early years. In spite of the financial risk that the index could fall rapidly, the potential of earning high profits appealed to many ordinary Shanghai citizens, who were desperately wishing to earn quick money in order to improve their living conditions. In the film, Fan is a smart and somewhat shrewd opportunist who quickly realizes that she can use Alan's financial knowledge and capital to invest in this booming stock market. As in the two scenes that I mentioned earlier about Mr. Xiao in *Crows and Sparrows*, *Shanghai Fever* also contains scenes in which Fan calculates her financial gain and queues overnight at a stock exchange dealer in order to purchase the warrant certificate that allows the holder to purchase a certain amount of newly listed stocks on the market. Here, the comparison is not to suggest that *Shanghai Fever* borrowed the idea from or made deliberate references to *Crows and Sparrows*, but to note that the film promptly captured Shanghai residents' local mentality when the city's financial sector became vibrant again in the 1990s. Unlike Mr. Xiao, who almost becomes a laughable character and nearly bankrupts himself because of his speculation, Fan is rewarded with a happy ending of moving into a new property in Pudong. Such a happy ending positioned Shanghai as a new financial center full of opportunities for everyone, regardless of their background.

The film's adoption of dialects interestingly establishes a comparable relationship between Shanghai and Hong Kong, then one of Asia's financial centers. In the film, Alan's Cantonese and accented Mandarin clearly mark him as a newcomer to Shanghai, whereas Fan's Shanghainese symbolizes an access to the fast-developing (mainland) Chinese financial market. In a scene where Fan and Alan visit a stock exchange VIP room, the security guard lets Fan enter the room when she flashes her local citizen ID card; however, Alan is stopped for failing to answer a question asked in Shanghainese. Unable to comprehend the question, Alan is denied access until Fan tells the guard in Shanghainese that Alan is with her. Interestingly, during the quick conversation, Alan—a rich businessman with money to invest—is described lightheartedly by Fan as a fisherman from the countryside of Guangdong. In contrast, Fan, a local working-class woman who tries to help with her family's living expenses via stealing her neighbor's tap water and even setting a daily limit on toilet paper usage, is endowed with privileged access to the market.

This scene has three implications. First, it establishes a hierarchical relationship between urban-superiority and rural-inferiority, which reverses the construct in films from previous decades, such as *Sentinels Under the Neon Lights*. Second, it implies Fan's pride in Shanghai's past as one of the most developed and cosmopolitan cities in China. After decades of China's closed-door policy and political chaos, the city's infrastructure and economy had fallen far behind many other major global cities by the 1990s; however, economic reform gave the city an opportunity to reclaim its past glory. Describing Alan as a countryman, Fan thus nostalgically re-connects Shanghai with a time when the city's urban development was more advanced than that of Hong Kong. Third, engaging the conversation with the security guard in Shanghainese that Alan is unable to comprehend, Fan establishes herself as an insider of China's new financial market. In comparison, Alan, despite his financial experience gained in Hong Kong, is portrayed as an outsider who needs an insider's connection to enter China's booming market.

Indeed, Shanghai and Hong Kong have a close link throughout their urban histories. *Shanghai Fever*, though not explicitly portraying the competitive nature of the two cities, subtly captured the affable rivalry from the perspective of Shanghai through Fan's remarks. As Fan becomes adept at navigating the financial market, she quickly transforms herself from a state-employed bus conductor to a private stock investor. As such, Fan's seemingly patronizing comments also reveal her desire, perhaps subconsciously, to see Shanghai outperform its Hong Kong counterpart once again when the city re-engages with the market-oriented economic system. Because Alan is seeking new investment opportunities in Shanghai instead of Hong Kong, Shanghai is portrayed as a land of promise and future opportunities.

Embracing local (urban) pride does not mean the removal of Mandarin entirely from the film; yet, unlike some of the 1950s and 1960s films that associated Shanghainese with linguistic and ideological inferiority, this film uses Mandarin as one of many spoken languages to celebrate the city's cultural flexibility. Whereas Alan and Fan speak their own languages to their own communities—Alan speaking Cantonese and English to his girlfriend and Fan speaking Shanghainese to her family and neighbors—they communicate with each other in accented Mandarin. In other words, mutual intelligibility is established through the agency of Mandarin. Here, Mandarin functions as a bridge between different communities rather than as a tool to suppress local dialects.

Such a shifting attitude about Shanghainese is particularly evident in a scene toward the end of the film where Alan has a conversation with Fan's husband, Xu Ang (Wang Huaying), who attempts to kill himself after losing 200,000 RMB in borrowed money on the stock market. Although Alan is still unable to speak Shanghainese, he can understand Xu's Shanghainese perfectly thanks to his experiences in the city thus far. Being able to comprehend the local dialect, Alan is not only able to communicate beyond his original community, but also gain access to a new cultural space. As the film's ending shows, Alan has been accepted as a true friend to Fan's family and neighbors. In a sense, Alan's newly grasped linguistic skills (at least his listening skills) transform him from an outsider to an insider of a Shanghai community. In this way, the Shanghainese and Cantonese dialects are no longer portrayed in the film as undesirable or an ideologically inferior languages that warrant elimination or enmity. Instead, the co-existence of different dialects and the characters' ability to switch between languages establishes Shanghai as a contact zone where different language speakers encounter one another, celebrating urban citizens' flexible access to diversified cultural spaces. In this regard, Shanghainese, Mandarin, Cantonese, and many other Wu dialects are all placed on a spectrum of Chinese language.

The linguistic flexibility was not restricted to the big screen. As a coproduced film, *Shanghai Fever* was cowritten by Shanghai-based Jia Hongyuan and Kong Kong–based Kwan Jing-Man, who is unable to speak Shanghainese. Although director Lee, scriptwriter Kwan, and their peer Hong Kong filmmakers came into the project with their experiences of making dialect films and commercial popular films (just as Alan brings his financial experience and capital into the film), they had to rely on their mainland partners to grasp the local specificity of China's latest urban development and to access the newly opened-up Chinese film market (and its much larger potential audience).

Like many other languages, colloquial Shanghainese and other Wu dialects are difficult to express precisely in writing. In order to create a soundscape specific to local conditions, Lee decided to cast many Shanghai-based actors, including *huaji xi* performers, who were allowed to improvise their own dialogue based on their experiences and observation of local life. The collaboration was a success. The film was praised for its authentic localness as well as for vividly capturing Shanghai's unique urban experience and the dynamics of Shanghai–Hong Kong mobility in the 1990s.[20] As such, the original version of *Shanghai Fever* not only demonstrates what Zhang Yinjin terms a "polylocality" that "recognizes the existence of multiple, diverse localities," but also illustrates Zhang's concept of a "translocality" that "connect[s] these localities."[21]

Negotiating Localness and Nationhood in a Globalized China

The success of *Shanghai Fever* saw a number of multilingual films being produced in the following years to explore local *shijing* stories, such as *Go for Broke* (*Heng shu heng*, dir. Wang Guangli, 1999), *Family Tie* (*Kaoshi yi jia qin*, dir. Ah Gan, 2000), and *Shanghai Fever*'s sequel, *Love Over Blue Chips* (*Gu a gu*, dir. Zhang Min, 2002). Covering a range of genres and film forms, these films either adopted Shanghainese as their main spoken language or partially used it as one of many languages to map out a rich soundscape that specifically associated their stories with Shanghai's acoustic environment. However, it would be overly optimistic to suggest that local dialects, Shanghainese in this case, did not face any struggles to claim their prominence. The attention paid to Shanghai in these films, after all, stemmed from the city's role in demonstrating the successes of national economic reform, not simply a desire to celebrate local accomplishment or to capture local struggle.

As Braester points out, "Shanghai at the turn of the twenty-first century is forward-looking, in accordance with the policy, launched in 1993, of developing a global center in Pudong New Area under the slogan 'Developing a new Shanghai.' Films now paint Shanghai with new ideological colors."[22] In this context, Shanghai was not merely portrayed as a city in its own right but a city carrying a duty to inspire the entire nation as well as overseas investors, including those from Hong Kong, which by then had not yet returned to China. In *Shanghai Fever*, when Shanghai switches its role to that of a window showcasing the newly opened-up China, Mandarin often takes over the narrative. For instance, in the suicide scene mentioned in previous section, Alan makes a speech to dissuade Xu from killing himself. In this speech, Alan notes that Xu has everything—wife, daughter, a happy family—and more importantly, an identity as a Chinese citizen. According to Alan, his Hong Konger's identity made him a second-class citizen. Delivered in Mandarin, this speech clearly expresses a Hong Kong character's frustration of being an overseas Chinese whose nationality was lacking. Given that Hong Kong was about to return to China in 1997, Alan's speech could be easily interpreted as patriotic remarks about China's growing economic and political power in the new era of globalization. In this regard, the central government's economic strategy of allowing Shanghai's local development and China's nationalism became two sides of the same coin.

Despite *Shanghai Fever*'s commercial popularity and critical acclaims, its producer decided to create a Mandarin version for the film's national release. Strictly speaking, the Mandarin version is multilingual too, as it contains Mandarin, Cantonese, and English. However, all Shanghainese and other Wu dialects are dubbed into Mandarin under the ongoing presumption that dialects created a linguistic barrier in film consumption.[23] To some degree, such an argument is rather flimsy. First, the original dialect version was not just popular in southern and eastern China, which had a large number of native-speaking audiences; it was also popular in northern cities, such as Tianjin, where standard Mandarin and its variants are the dominant language.[24] Second, as mentioned previously, during the 1980s and 1990s video halls became popular across mainland China through showing Cantonese films, which demonstrated that Chinese audiences were not deterred from consuming dialect (and foreign language) films, not to mention the use of subtitling. Third, it is worth noting that *Shanghai Fever*'s Mandarin version only removed Wu dialects (including Shanghainese), whereas Cantonese was kept in the soundtrack. As such, removing the language barrier is not sufficient to explain why only selected dialects were replaced.

In this regard, the studio's justification for releasing a Mandarin version suggests Chinese cinema's discrepancy in delivering the locality of Shanghai's urban experience. In comparison to the linguistic richness in the original version, the Mandarin version sacrifices the diversity of Shanghai's cultural spaces, as represented by various dialects spoken in the city. In this Mandarin version, Shanghai's urban regeneration and re-globalization are no longer a local event but a national affair. The communication between Mandarin-speaking Fan and Cantonese-speaking Alan suggests that the original Shanghai–Hong Kong dimension is now replaced by a domestic-overseas encounter.[25] As such, the Mandarin version not only maps out the screenspace in a different way but also reveals the ambivalent ground upon which Shanghai stands. Whereas the original version underlines the city's ambition of reclaiming its urban distinction and rebuilding its past glory as a popular global city, the Mandarin version stresses the city's national duty to serve as the whole nation's Shanghai (*Shanghai shi quanguo de Shanghai*),[26] serving as a window to showcase the country's achievement.

The cinematic portrayal of Shanghai's national role is not only accomplished by dubbing local dialects into Mandarin in this instance, but is also shown in many other multilingual urban films that choose to use Mandarin as their major spoken language. Four years after *Shanghai Fever* in 1998, Lee directed another film set in Shanghai, *Four Chefs and a Feast*. Coproduced with Shanghai Film Studio, this film was also shot on location in Shanghai. However, despite the film containing Mandarin, Cantonese, Shanghainese, English, and Japanese, local dialects and foreign languages are only used sporadically. Unlike the original version of *Shanghai Fever*, the main characters in this film mainly speak Mandarin, privately and publicly.

The film's main protagonist is a Shanghai chef, Fang Zhenjin (King Shih-Chieh), who is struggling to restore the famous restaurant Meilong Town's past glory when facing competition from fast growing Western fast food chains in China, such as KFC and McDonald's. Similar to Fan's subconscious desire to see Shanghai as a globally competitive metropolis in *Shanghai Fever*, Fang's ambition also traces Shanghai's future prosperity back to the city's urban heritage, as exemplified by the restaurant's past popularity, awards, and its legendary banquet. Coached by the restaurant's former intern, Li Lang (Lung Sihung), who recently returns to Shanghai from abroad, Fang decides to recreate the legendary Victory Banquet in order to improve the restaurant's market competitiveness.

The Victory Banquet was created by the restaurant's three partners in 1945 to celebrate the end of the Second Sino-Japanese War. As the grandson of one of the original partners, Fang successfully locates the whereabouts of the other two partners' descendants, Mei Hua (Wu Chien-lien) and Wu Shaolong (Jordan Chan), and invites them to Shanghai. Interestingly, except for Shanghai-based Fang, the other three key characters' families have respectively migrated to and settled down in Hong Kong (Wu), Taiwan (Mei), and Singapore (Li). These four characters' home locations and the film's celebration of reunification neatly created a metaphor of mainland China's post-1997 ambition to build a greater China that unifies all overseas regions (including the former colonial city Hong Kong, the forthcoming return of Macau, and separately governed Taiwan) as well as invited a sense of cultural belonging from diasporic Chinese communities (such as Singaporean Chinese).

As the film reveals, the protagonists' grandparents used to work together like a family in Shanghai. However, due to a misunderstanding, the partnership broke up and the three families were separated for decades. Since each family kept their own unique recipe, the entire Victory Banquet could not be recreated until Shanghai-based Fang reaches out and reunites all the descendants. Although initially Mei and Wu only accept Fang's invitation for a promise of financial rewards, they are soon moved by Fang's passion and regain their pride in their family heritage. In a sense, it is under Fang's leadership that a harmonious relationship between the descendants and a restoration of the partnership is accomplished.

Their family heritage, however, does not extend to their linguistic skills, as none of the characters in the film speak any Shanghainese: Fang—the Shanghai-based chef—speaks standard Mandarin, Mei speaks Taiwan-accented Mandarin, Wu speaks Cantonese and Cantonese-accented Mandarin, and Li speaks Beijing-accented Mandarin. In this regard, this film withdrew itself from (Shanghainese) dialect filmmaking practices of *shijing* comedies and resumed Chinese cinema's promotion of Mandarin dominance.

However, it is worth noting two sequences where dialects are used, both of which—instead of embracing the richness and diversity of Shanghai's cultural spaces and their associated locales—function as celebrations of a united China. A local dialect is first heard when the film introduces the character Wu in Hong Kong. In this sequence, Wu's girlfriend decides to leave him for an upper-middle class man, whom her rich family considers to be a proper match. In this scene, Wu speaks Cantonese to his friends and girlfriend, highlighting his identity as an overseas Chinese from a former colonial city. Being rejected by his snobbish girlfriend and her family, Wu accepts Fang's invitation to visit Shanghai, where he not only immediately switches his spoken language to Mandarin, but also quickly establishes a sense of belonging. Although Wu's Mandarin has a strong accent, he encounters no trouble in communication or comprehension with his Shanghai colleagues and local citizens, who all speak Mandarin instead of Shanghainese. In a sense, Wu's language switch not only suggests that the character already grasps the official language promoted by the government but also marks his smooth transition from a Hong Konger to Chinese. Given that the film was produced just one year after Hong Kong's return to China, the linguistic transition could be easily seen as a symbol of political assimilation.

Another important scene taking a multilingual approach occurs toward the end of the film. Successfully recreating the legendary Victory Banquet, Fang, Li, Mei, and Wu invite many Shanghai local citizens to taste the menu. The guests are played by Shanghai-based celebrities, such as *huju* (Shanghai opera) actress Ma Lili;[27] *huaji xi* performers Zhou Bochun, Li Jiusong, Nen Niang, and Wen Shuangjie, Jr.; and older-generation film stars Sha Li, Ling Zhihao, Shu Shi, and Feng Huang. Unlike *Shanghai Fever*, in which the use of dialect was a result of cross-regional collaboration between Hong Kong and Shanghai talents, the multilingual soundscape in this scene appears to be contrived. As mentioned above, Chinese operas and *quyi* were exempt from compulsory Mandarin performance due to their regional roots in dialect-infused localness and restricted dissemination scope. Unlike those *huaji xi* actors cast in *Shanghai Fever*, who were able to improvise their dialogue, all *huaji xi* actors in *Four Chefs and a Feast*, together with film stars, spoke Mandarin to praise the quality of the food. Only *huju* actress Ma spoke Shanghainese, suddenly bursting into song right in the middle of the feast.

While the older generation of film stars' standard Mandarin performance continued Chinese mainstream cinema's preference of Mandarin over dialects, *huaji xi* actors' Mandarin performance completes the process of language assimilation from the local to the national in the film. If some films' (such as *Huang Baomei; Big Li, Old Li, and Little Li;* and *Shanghai Fever*) dubbing practice to replace Shanghainese with Mandarin still left traces of localness on their original soundtrack or archived record, this film almost entirely removes the local sound for the sake of national wholeness. However, unlike Chinese cinema in the 1950s and 1960s, where the ridicule and suppression of Shanghainese suggests that the process of reforming and unification was still taking place, *huaji xi* actors' Mandarin performance in *Four Chefs and a Feast* indicates a completion of this transformation.

It is important to note that by the time the film was produced, director Lee had just stepped down from a prominent position as the Production Director at China Film Group—the biggest state-owned film enterprise—and established his own company, Tangren Media, which had its headquarters in Shanghai and operational offices in cities like Tianjin, Beijing, and Hong Kong. As a Hong Kong filmmaker who had resettled his career predominantly in mainland China only four years after he made his first coproduction with a state-owned studio, Lee now is not only familiar with mainland China's film business and politics, but has also become a "model" of a Hong Kong expat who has successfully transformed into a Chinese filmmaker embracing the unified greater China.

As Yin Hong and He Mei point out, despite mainland–Hong Kong coproduction featuring Hong Kongized entertainment of genre filmmaking and localized storytelling strategies in the first half of the 1990s, the dynamics gradually shifted after 1996 when the Chinese government introduced film censorship and production regulations specifically regarding coproductions and adopted the principle of "*yi wo wei zhu*" (I am the main player).[28] Unlike Lee's *Shanghai Fever*, which tested the local/national boundary, *Four Chefs and a Feast*, as Tangren's first project and Shanghai Film Studio's New Year celebration film, consciously embeds China's leitmotif narrative of promoting a harmonized greater China into the popular commercial genre of *shijing* comedies.

In this context, Ma's *huju* performance creates a rather interesting, if not bizarre, effect in the aforementioned banquet scene. Unlike in some Chinese social occasions where a celebrity is invited to perform, Ma appears in the scene merely in the role of a local citizen. Witnessing her neighboring guests—an old couple (played by Ling Zhihao and Sha Li, who are also a real couple off-screen)—who recall their fond memory that a dish from the banquet facilitated their romantic journey in the past, Ma suddenly starts singing as a celebration of the banquet's success as well as the couple's long-lasting love. Not fitting with any main storyline, the couple's love story, delivered in standard Mandarin, not only associates the re-creation of the Victory Banquet with a harmonized relationship, but also romanticizes the notions of togetherness. Ma's Shanghainese singing thus underpins local appreciation of togetherness as represented by the couple's love story and the four chefs' collective effort. However, local expression has only very limited screen time: as soon as Ma finishes her singing, she remains largely silent except for her only spoken line, delivered in Mandarin, appreciating the quality of the food. In this regard, this scene demonstrates that the local sound is strictly controlled and is only permitted to celebrate nationally endorsed harmony.

Indeed, the central government's policy of using Mandarin as a tool to unite the nation and the diasporic Chinese community has not changed from the beginning of Chinese sound cinema. Despite the short period in the early 1990s in which

Shanghai dialect filmmaking saw some success both commercially and critically, Mandarin quickly resumed its dominant role as representing the wholeness of China. In comparison, dialects, especially Shanghainese, were once again reduced to a mere token to signify the multiple cultural spaces that would eventually become part of the whole—if they were not already. As such, Mandarin-speaking Shanghai in this film is to some extent no longer a city; it has become a symbol of a greater China that attracts and unifies everyone.

Conclusion

Mainland Chinese studios' collaboration with Hong Kong filmmakers during the Deng era, to some degree, enriched Chinese cinema's experiments that explored local expression through multilingual and dialect filmmaking. As discussed in this chapter, in the 1990s a number of Chinese *shijing* comedies and urban films adopted Shanghainese to capture the specificity of the city's urban experience and local pride. Unlike those small towns that underwent urbanization for the first time in the 1990s, Shanghai was already a megacity at the time, even though its urban infrastructure suffered severely from poor maintenance during the preceding decades. Rather than functioning as a resistance to or critique of social upheaval, both the city of Shanghai and Chinese cinema embraced the new opportunities brought by the fast re-urbanization and re-globalization. The use of various dialects in the original version of *Shanghai Fever*, as illustrated in this chapter, thus underlines a strong local pride of appreciating the city's past achievement as a cosmopolitan metropolis as well as revealing the city's ambition of rebuilding itself as a competitive global city. Despite their small number and the short period of their existence, the original version of *Shanghai Fever* and other follow-up multilingual urban films and television productions[29] provided an alternative soundscape where local urban experience could be heard.

However, such linguistic experiment was allowed limited scope to extend into the national level. Whereas the inclusion of Shanghainese was not rare in those films that were set in the past, especially in the period before 1949, only a handful of productions set in the present were able to adopt the dialect as their main spoken language. Along with China's growing global influence since the late 1990s, Chinese urban cinema's celebration of localness quickly gave way to the government's growing ambition to promote the PRC as a country unifying different regions, and big cities like Shanghai are often assigned the role of representing and promoting the entire nation. Under such political prioritization, the usage of local dialects—especially the ones from major non-Mandarin speaking cities—are often restricted, if not completely suppressed, so that the local accomplishments and strengths do not overshadow the state agenda of national unification. As such, while multilingual filmmaking is common in today's Chinese urban films, in which foreign languages such as English and Japanese are often used to suggest access to global networks and international mobility, local linguistic variation is still strictly controlled, manipulated, and even sacrificed to serve such political purpose.

This is not to suggest that dialect (especially Shanghainese) filmmaking is entirely ridiculed as it has been in the past. As China embraced speedy urbanization and globalization, urban cinema (including *shijing* comedies) has regained its popularity among Chinese audiences and is no longer condemned as petty bourgeoisie cinema. Instead, it is a city's local specification that is marginalized and even relegated for the sake of a centralized and unified nationhood. It is within this context that the ideological negotiation of the Shanghai dialect between the local and the national was never fully suspended during the 1990s, even as a number of multilingual urban films were produced and released for a nationwide consumption of the local's connection with the global.

Notes

1.   Zhang Zhen, "Bearing Witness: Chinese Urban Cinema in the Era of 'Transformation' (*Zhuanxin*)," in *The Urban Generation: Chinese Cinema and Society at the Turn of the Twenty-First Century*, ed. Zhang Zhen (Durham: Duke University Press, 2007), 1–2.
2.   Guo Shaohua, "Acting through the Camera Lens: The Global Imaginary and Middle Class Aspirations in Chinese Cinema," *Journal of Contemporary China* 26, no. 104 (2017): 314.
3.   Sheldon H. Lu,"Tear Down the City: Reconstructing Urban Space in Contemporary Chinese Popular Cinema and Avant-Garde Art," in *The Urban Generation: Chinese Cinema and Society at the Turn of the Twenty-First Century*, ed. Zhang Zhen (Durham: Duke University Press, 2007), 147.
4.   *Shijing* contains two characters, *shi* and *jing*. The first character means "urban" or "city"; the latter part derives its meaning from the well-field system, which organized a number of dwellings and a shared communal area into a unit during the Warring States period. The shared communal area was often used as a marketplace where dwellers exchanged goods. Thus, the usage of the word *shijing* is often related to an urban marketplace or urban common people's everyday life. See Xu Shen, *Shuowen Jiezi* [Explaining graphs and analyzing characters] (Shanghai: Shanghai Chinese Classics Publishing House, 1981), 214.
5.   Jurg Hausermann, "Auditory Media: Sound Studies and the Political Components of the Auditory," in *The Routledge Handbook of Language and Media*, ed. Colleen Cotter and Daniel Perrin (Oxon: Routledge, 2018), 217.
6.   Hong Kong filmmakers showed a strong interest in Shanghai stories throughout the 1980s and 1990s. Examples include, but are not limited to, Stanley Kwan's *Centre Stage* (*Ruan Lingyu*, 1991), Wong Kar-wai's *Days of Being Wild* (*A fei zhengzhuan*, 1990), Tsui Hark's *Shanghai Blues* (*Shanghai zhi ye*, 1984), and Ann Hui's *City of Fallen Love* (*Qin cheng zhi lian*, 1984) and *Eighteen Springs* (*Ban sheng yuan*, 1997). Although some of those films cast mainland Chinese actors and were even partially filmed in Shanghai (e.g., *Centre Stage*), they were either solely produced by a Hong Kong studio or coproduced between Hong Kong and Taiwan. The majority of these films either traced Shanghai

back to the Republican era before 1949, or focused on the diasporic Shanghai community in Hong Kong. One exception is Ann Hui's *My American Grandson* (*Shanghai jiaqi*, 1991), which was filmed on location in Shanghai, but this film was a coproduction between Taiwan and mainland China. Although this intraregional interaction between Taiwan and mainland China and its impact on Chinese filmmaking practice is also fascinating and warrants further exploration, that discussion is beyond the scope of this chapter.

7. The *Er Zi* series consists a number of films featuring a character called Er Zi, played by Chen Peisi. The series mainly concerns the stories of common Beijing residents' transition to the new economic period featuring marketization and privitization. The first Er Zi image appeared in *Sunset Street* (*Xizhao jie*, dir. Wang Haowei, 1983) as a supporting character. Later on, Er Zi was developed into a main character in five films of the *I Was Born to Be Useful* (*Tiansheng wo cai bi youyong*) series: *Father and Son* (*Fu yu zi*, dir. Liu Guoquan, 1986), *Er Zi Has a Little Hotel* (*Er zi kai dian*, dir. Wang Binglin, 1987), *Silly Manager* (*Shamao jingli*, dir. Duan Jishun, 1988), *Father and Son's Car* (*Fuzi laoyeche*, dir. Liu Guoquan, 1990), and *Father and Son Open a Bar* (*Ye'erlia kai geting*, dir. Chen Peisi and Ding Xuan, 1992). Four of the five films were either produced by the newly established Shenzhen Film Studio or had an investment from private companies based in the Special Economic Zone. The only exception is *Er Zi Has a Little Hotel*, which was produced by Beijing Film Academy's Youth Film Studio, which was initially established as an educational facility to train the Academy's film students.

8. Zhong Jin, *Minguo dianying jiancha yanjiu* [A study of Republican China's film censorship] (Beijing: China Film Press, 2012), 77.

9. State Council, "Guowuyuan guanyu tuiguang Putonghua de zhishi" [State Council's instruction on promoting *Putonghua*], February 6, 1956, accessed April 5, 2019, http://big5.www.gov.cn/gate/big5/www.gov.cn/test/2005-08/02/content_19132.htm.

10. *Huaji xi* is a *quyi* form that is mainly popular around the Wu-language-speaking region. While it includes comedies performed in any Wu dialects, Shanghainese is one of the most frequently used languages in *huaji xi*, and the majority of major *huaji xi* troupes are based in Shanghai. For these reasons, this particular *quyi* form is commonly known as Shanghainese comedy.

11. Yomi Braester, *Painting the City Red: Chinese Cinema and the Urban Contract* (Durham: Duke University Press, 2010), 89.

12. Bao Ying, "Chinese Lighthearted Comedies of the Early 1960s," *International Communication of Chinese Culture* 6 (2019): 265–77, https://doi.org/10.1007/s40636-019-00162-0.

13. *The House of 72 Tenants* is an adaptation of a Shanghai *huaji xi* play of the same title first performed in 1953. Another screen adaptation of the play is a 1963 film (dir. Wang Weiyi) coproduced by mainland China's state-owned Zhujiang Film Studio and Hong Kong's Hongtu Film Studio. The earlier film adaptation was shot in Cantonese, but its release was restricted to Hong Kong, Guangdong province, and overseas. After the Cultural Revolution, the 1963 version was selected for re-release nationwide, but only after it was dubbed into Mandarin. For more detail, see Wang Weiyi, *Nanwang de suiyue: Wang Weiyi zizhuan* [Unforgettable time: Wang Weiyi's autobiography] (Beijing: China Film Press, 2006).

14. *Luxiangting* refers to a small screening space. Without licenses for distributing and exhibiting films, these places usually only showed smuggled and pirated films through video cassettes and, later on, DVDs. Despite their illegal status, *luxiangting* were popular in mainland China, as they provided an alternative entertainment and cultural space where consumers could access a variety of Hong Kong and foreign films that were not available through official channels. For further discussion, see Luzhou Li, *Zoning China: Online Video, Popular Culture, and the State* (Cambridge, MA: MIT Press, 2019) and Jinying Li, "From D-Buffs to the D-Generation: Piracy, Cinema, and an Alternative Public Sphere in Urban China," in *Piracy Cultures: How a Growing Portion of the Global Population Is Building Media Relationships through Alternate Channels of Obtaining Content*, ed. Manuel Castells and Gustavo Cardoso (Los Angeles: USC Annenberg Press, 2013), 239–57.

15. Ding Yaping, *Zhongguo dianying tongshi* [General history of Chinese film] (Beijing: China Film Press and Culture and Art Publishing House, 2016), 151.

16. In 2001, Shanghai's Fudan University teamed up with Hong Kong's Chinese University of Hong Kong and co-established the Shanghai-Hong Kong Development Institute to develop research into both cooperation and competition between the two cities. This cross-regional institute also provides strategic policy advice to both public and private sectors. For further detail, see Shanghai-Hong Kong Development Institute's official website, http://www.cuhk.edu.hk/shkdi/index.html.

17. Wu language is a variant of Chinese. It includes a group of dialects that are native to the eastern regions of China near the Yangtze Delta.

18. Shanghai's stock exchange was shut down shortly after the Communist Party took over the city in 1949 and did not re-open until 1990.

19. For further detail, see Office of Shanghai Chronicles, "Caizheng, Shuiwu" [Finance, tax], *Shanghai Chronicles* 24, July 14, 2008, accessed April 2, 2019, http://www.shtong.gov.cn/Newsite/node2/node2247/node4577/index.html.

20. Que Zheng, "Fangyan fang dianying 'Jie Diqi'" [Dialects make films accessible], *Xinmin Weekly*, November 30, 2018, accessed August 20, 2019, https://m.xinminweekly.com.cn/content/1581.html.

21. Yingjin Zhang, *Cinema, Space, and Polylocality in Globalizing China* (Honolulu: University of Hawai'i Press, 2010), 9.

22. Braester, *Painting the City Red*, 93–94.

23. Zheng, "Fangyan fang dianying 'Jie Diqi.'"

24. Data collection in Chinese cinema was not fully established in the 1990s, so the box office figures before 2000 are rather incomplete and inconsistent. The popularity of many films could only be evidenced through newspapers' or magazines' discursive reports or personal recollection. In Wang Yueyang's article, Wang Rugang—the actor who played a major character in *Shanghai Fever* and participated in the casting process—recalled that the popularity of the film's original version was rather wider spread around the country. See Wang Yueyang, "Huyu ru dianying, jiaohao you jiaozuo" [Making films with Shanghai dialect, winning both critical acclaim and commerical success], *Xinmin Weekly*, June 20, 2018, accessed January 7, 2020, http://www.xinminweekly.com.cn/fengmian/2018/06/20/10464.html.

25. As residents in a former colonial city outside of mainland China's territory, Hong Kongers had been classified as overseas Chinese before 1997.

26. The slogan "Shanghai is the whole nation's Shanghai" appeared in a number of official media outlets. For further details, see *Eastday*, "Suzao chengshi jingshen, Shanghairen yao zuo 'ke'ai' de ren" [Building city spirit: Shanghailanders are to be amiable citizens], February 18, 2003, accessed April 6, 2018, http://sh.sina.com.cn/news/20030218/08275645.shtml; Tu, Zhili, "Xiying shiqida—kexue fazhan, gongjian hexie: Xiting Shanghai xin taosheng" [Get ready for the 17th National Congress—Scientific development, building harmony: Listen to Shanghai's New Wave], *People's Daily*, September 21, 2007, accessed April 6, 2019, https://china.gov.cn.admin.kyber.vip/jrzg/2007-09/21/content_756848.htm; and Lu Qiguo, "Chengshi guannian yu chengshi shenghuo—Shanghai kaibu 170 zhounian zhali" [Urban concept and urban life: Recording 170 years of Shanghai's opening-up as a seaport], *Shanghai Municipal Archive*, November 10, 2013, accessed April 6, 2019, http://www.archives.sh.cn/shjy/scbq/201311/t20131120_39844.html.

27. *Huju* is one of many Chinese operas. It is performed in Shanghainese, and mainly popular in Shanghai and its surrounding areas near the Yangtze Delta.

28. Yin Hong and He Mei, "Zou xiang hou hepai shidai de Huayu dianying: Zhongguo neidi yu Xianggang dianying de hezuo/hepai lichen" [Chinese films after the period of coproduction: The historical development of Mainland-HK coproduction in the Chinese movie industry], *The Chinese Journal of Communication and Society* 7 (2009): 37 and 42.

29. During the 1990s, a number of Shanghai-dialect television dramas were also produced and broadcasted, such as *Sinful Debt* (*Nie zhai*, Shanghai TV Studio, 1995, 20 episodes). Similar to *Shanghai Fever*, *Sinful Debt* was dubbed into Mandarin for the second round of national release.

8

Sound, Allusion, and the "Wandering Songstress" in Royston Tan's Films

Alison M. Groppe

The film credited as Singapore's first to achieve international commercial success since the rebirth or revival of the Singapore film industry in the early 1990s is Glen Goei's *Forever Fever* (a.k.a. *That's the Way I Like It*, 1998), inspired by John Badham's *Saturday Night Fever* (1977). Set in late 1970s Singapore, the film deploys two icons of masculinity, Bruce Lee and John Travolta, to explore challenges faced by its working-class, "national everyman"[1] protagonist Ah Hock: channeling these stars' spirits empowers Ah Hock to surmount his life's obstacles and finally achieve success. The globally circulated images of Travolta and Lee can also be credited with helping *Forever Fever* to overcome challenges of visibility and obtain international success for itself and its filmmaker: its US, British, and Canadian distribution rights were purchased by Miramax for $4.5 million while Goei himself was signed to direct three films over five years for Miramax.[2] As Goei subsequently observed, "I am a first-time director from a small country like Singapore. It was mind-blowing."[3] Indeed, Singapore *is* a small country, and before the revival period its film industry had been dormant for approximately twenty years. Like the other "small nation cinemas" addressed in a recent study by Mette Hjort and Duncan Petrie,[4] Singapore cinema has long struggled for audience and recognition in a cinematic landscape dominated by Hollywood.

Fellow Singaporean filmmaker Royston Tan (Chen Ziqian, b. 1976) has also availed himself of a transnational screen icon—the songstress or singing actress who dominated the cinemas of Republican Shanghai and Hong Kong in the 1950s and 1960s—to grapple with local issues while achieving distinctive visibility on the world stage for his own filmmaking as well as for the filmic network that inspired him, linking Singapore to Hong Kong and Taiwan, two other "small nation cinemas." In this chapter, I argue that Tan's adaptation of this narrative and cinematic trope allows him to "act local" while "thinking globally." In his short films *Hock Hiap Leong* (2001) and *Grandfather* (*Ah Kong*, 2010), Tan uses sound, allusion, and a rhetoric of fandom to lament the passage of time and consequences of economic development while affiliating his films with those of Tsai Ming-liang (Malaysia, Taiwan). In his feature-length movie musicals *881* (2007), *12 Lotus* (*Shi'er lianhua*, 2008), and *3688* (*Xiangru feifei*, 2015), Tan's reconfiguration of the songstress figure allows him to simultaneously explore local cultural and linguistic politics in Singapore while illuminating a broader Sinophone filmmaking tradition born of cultural and cinematic flows between the small nation cinema sites of Hong Kong, Taiwan, and Singapore; such expansion is critical for ensuring Sinophone filmmaking's diversity, distinctiveness, and visibility in global cinema.

The Songstress in Chinese Cinema

The "wandering songstress" in this chapter's title refers to a famous song by one of Chinese cinema's best-loved singing actresses, Zhou Xuan (1920–1957). Variously translated as "Sing-Song Girl at the Ends of the Earth," "The Wandering Songstress," and "Songstress of the World," "Tianya genü" first appeared in *Street Angel* (*Malu tianshi*, dir. Yuan Muzhi, 1937), the film that simultaneously catapulted Zhou Xuan to stardom and made the songstress a prevalent screen icon for Chinese cinema; the song's popularity led it to become the title of Zhou's next important film, *Songstress of the World* (*Tianya genü*, dir. Wu Cun, 1940). In *Street Angel*, Zhou Xuan plays a young woman forced to abandon her hometown because of the Japanese invasion and flee to Shanghai, where a greedy couple compel her to sing in their teahouse and then conspire to sell her to a lecherous gangster. *Street Angel*'s portrayal of the teahouse singer ensured that in subsequent films Zhou Xuan would most frequently be cast as a sympathetic "singer with a sweet voice, a poor upbringing and a tragic disposition."[5] Yet if *Street Angel* can be considered the film that "forged the archetype . . . of the songstress as a tragic figure and victim of society,"[6] the "tragedy-prone life" of the songstress emerges more poignantly in two of Zhou's later, Hong Kong–produced films, *All-Consuming Love* (*Chang xiang si*, dir. He Zhaozhang, 1947) and *Song of the Songstress* (*Genü zhi ge*, dir. Fang Peilin, 1948).[7] While in *Street Angel* Zhou Xuan's character struggles initially but is then granted a happy ending, the songstress-protagonists in *All-Consuming Love* and *Song of a Songstress* begin the films as content and successful but by the end face hardship and unhappiness, as though predestined for sorrow. That Zhou Xuan herself experienced a life of tribulation despite her fame and success—and died prematurely at the age of thirty-seven—has only reinforced her association with the songstress-as-tragic-figure type.

Zhou Xuan's career developed amid turmoil: the Japanese invasion of China, increasing hostilities between the Nationalists and Communists, the Japanese occupation of Shanghai, World War II, civil war in China, and the establishment of the PRC. Consequently, the majority of people associated with Republican Shanghai's popular music and film industries emigrated to Hong Kong. Po-Shek

Fu has identified the period of 1935–1950, when the PRC closed its border, as the "Shanghai–Hong Kong nexus" in order to convey the "extensive movement of people, capital and ideas across the border" during this time.[8] This migration caused Hong Kong's population to nearly quadruple and transformed Hong Kong into a new center of cultural and cinematic production serving Asian markets of Chinese-speaking societies outside of China, including in Taiwan and throughout Southeast Asia. It also allowed the songstress figure to travel to and further develop in Hong Kong.

While Zhou Xuan is credited with making the songstress figure a dominant Chinese cinema icon, in subsequent decades singing actresses in other films introduced variations on the theme. Scholarship on the songstress breaks this figure down into several types. The most important for this chapter are the tragic "sing-song girl," represented principally by Zhou Xuan, and the "Mambo Girl" type, exemplified by Grace Chang (Ge Lan, b. 1933) and named after Chang's breakout vehicle, *Mambo Girl* (*Manbo nülang*, dir. Yi Wen, 1957), in which she plays a popular high school student admired for her singing and dancing.[9] Through vivacious performances in films like *Mambo Girl*—considered "the single most representative work of postwar Mandarin cinema"[10] and that which made Chang "the most popular star in Singapore and Malaya"[11]—and *Air Hostess* (*Kongzhong xiaojie*, dir. Yi Wen, 1959), Chang enabled Motion Pictures and General Investment (MP&GI), the studio that produced her films and made her a star, to "refashion the Mandarin musicals as a hip, youth-oriented cinema."[12] In addition to her movie stardom, Chang recorded over a hundred songs with Hong Kong's Pathé Records and, in 1959, appeared on *The Dinah Shore Show* and released an American LP with Capitol Records. Despite having quickly become, as Yeh puts it, "the first multi-faceted star in transnational Chinese entertainment,"[13] Chang retired in 1964 after marrying the son of a successful businessman in 1961.

By the 1970s, the rise of martial arts cinema caused the male action hero to replace the songstress as the essential screen icon in Hong Kong cinema.[14] Recently, however, important films by major Sinophone auteurs have attested to the songstress figure's persistent appeal. Ang Lee's *Lust, Caution* (*Se jie*, 2007) pays tribute to Zhou Xuan by having the female protagonist sing "The Wandering Songstress" ("Tianya genü") for her lover in a significant scene. Wong Kar-wai named his acclaimed film *In the Mood for Love* (*Huayang nianhua*, 2001) after another of Zhou Xuan's famous songs, "Huayang nianhua" ("The Blooming Years"), originally from *All-Consuming Love*, and similarly featured the song in a significant scene expressing the protagonists' longing. He pays additional tribute to the song, and its songstress, by using it to accompany a montage of clips retrieved from a cache of films discovered in California in a short film titled *Huayang de Nianhua* (*The Blooming Years*), which appears as a special feature on the Criterion Collection's *In the Mood for Love* DVD.[15] Most important for this study, Tsai Ming-liang's *The Hole* (*Dong*, 1998) includes several fantasy musical sequences featuring the female protagonist (played by Yang

Kuei-mei) lip-synching and dancing to the music of Grace Chang that brighten the film's otherwise bleak, dark atmosphere. Similarly, Tsai's *The Wayward Cloud* (*Tian bian yi duo yun*, 2005) features an array of musical sequences that borrow music from Yao Lee, Bai Guang, Chang Loo, and Grace Chang from the many Mandarin musicals that dominated Hong Kong cinema in the 1950s and 1960s. Particularly interesting in light of this discussion is the scene in which an aging porn star lip-synchs to Grace Chang singing "Tong Qing Xin" ("To Keep my Heart True"), a song that poignantly voices the songstress's struggles, from another of her acclaimed films, *Wild, Wild Rose* (*Ye meigui zhi lian*, dir. Wang Tianlin, 1960).[16] Chang's hit "Wo Yao Nide Ai" ("I Want Your Love"), adapted from Louis Jordan's "I Want You to Be My Baby," is also heard in *Crazy Rich Asians* (dir. Jon M. Chu, 2018).

Even as criticism of *The Hole, In the Mood for Love*, and *Lust, Caution* cover these films' allusions to popular music and movie musicals of earlier eras, scholarship on the songstress figure herself has remained sparse and scattered until recently. Jean Ma's 2015 *Sounding the Modern Woman: The Songstress in Chinese Cinema* (2015) amply remedies this neglect. Originally intended to focus just on Grace Chang's films and music, the book evolved to employ the songstress figure to present a more gendered and international perspective on Chinese film history.[17] For Ma, the songstress in recent Sinophone filmmaking is not just a figure of nostalgia but also symbolizes migration, circulation, and cultural and linguistic heterogeneity. For example, Ma points out that the songstress phenomenon "demands to be understood as part of the 'Shanghai–Hong Kong nexus,'" discussed above, and attests to its "continuing impact . . . throughout the 1950s and 1960s."[18] Relatedly, the period of film history that the songstress dominated witnessed the creation of "an émigré generation" comprised of people "steeped in memories of the past and deeply marked by their experiences of dislocation."[19] Finally, though Ma's book concentrates on music and performers in Mandarin cinema, she also notes that "singing actresses and crossover stars appeared across the polylinguistic terrain of diasporic film culture" and were able to flourish "in a milieu constituted by movements across borders, hybridity, and multiple locations (and dislocations) of culture."[20] These are the aspects of the songstress figure that predominantly inform the present analysis of Royston Tan's refashioning of the songstress figure to simultaneously engage with Singapore's language and cultural politics and forge connections with other Sinophone centers of cultural production, namely Hong Kong and Taiwan.

Sound, Allusion, and the Songstress in Royston Tan's Short Films

A graduate of Singapore's Temasek Polytechnic, Royston Tan first gained attention for his short films *Sons* (2000), *Hock Hiap Leong* (2001, discussed below), and *15* (2002).[21] The latter became the basis for Tan's debut feature film, *15* (2003), which was commercially successful upon its local release by Shaw and also launched Tan onto the international film festival circuit.[22] Featuring Singaporean fifteen-year-old boys skipping school, composing and practicing "gangsta"-like raps for a talent show, getting tattoos and body piercings, fighting, watching pornography, smuggling drugs from Malaysia, and searching for ideal suicide spots, *15* resembles other revival films in demonstrating an interest "not so much in the Singapore Success Story as in the Singapore Failure Story, with success and failure measured chiefly in academic and economic terms."[23] Having been screened in its original form for a sold-out crowd at its 2003 Singapore International Film Festival premiere, for its general release Singapore's Board of Film Censors reportedly demanded that Tan make twenty-seven cuts.[24] In response Tan became, as he put it, "'the poster-boy of the anti-censorship movement,'"[25] particularly as evinced by his short film *Cut* (2004). In *Cut*'s first half, an obsessive film buff hounds a film censor while she shops for groceries. Sarcastically praising the Board's willingness to censor films screened in Singapore, the cinephile brings up *15* as an example of the Board's greatest accomplishment: "27 cuts! I'm so proud of you, your highest record so far!"[26] The short film's second half features flamboyant musical numbers set to familiar popular songs whose lyrics have been rewritten to satirize censorship: a verse from ABBA's "Thank You for the Music," for example, becomes "Thank you, Board of Censors, I really owe you / . . . / To keep my conscience so free, choosing for me / Without your slice of advice, what are we? / So I say thank you, Board of Censors / For giving your PG [Parental Guidance rating]."[27] Kenneth Paul Tan has praised *Cut* for being "highly cathartic for the arts community [in Singapore]," citing the "thunderous applause [he] observed after its screening at the opening of the 2004 Singapore International Film Festival [that] attested to the emotional connection [the film] enjoys with frustrated artists in Singapore."[28] That same year Royston Tan was among the twenty "Asian Heroes" under the age of forty identified by *Time Asia*.[29]

Several successful feature films later, short film production still comprises a significant portion of Tan's output; two of Royston Tan's short films, *Hock Hiap Leong* and *Grandfather*, strongly suggest it was Tsai Ming-liang's use of Grace Chang's music in *The Hole* that inspired Tan's interest in the songstress. As Ma aptly puts it, Grace Chang's music provides *The Hole* with a "colorful past" which, "amidst the bleakness and anonymity of contemporary life . . . promises a last refuge for feeling and intensity, triumph of fantasy over banality, and the survival of humanity in a literally dehumanizing universe";[30] it also serves to chart "movements across a territorial expanse," registers the "temporal rifts"[31] consequently created, and highlights the production/consumption network created by Sinophone popular culture.[32] Commonly considered a tribute to *The Hole*, Tan's *Hock Hiap Leong*[33] uses Chang's music similarly. In a coffee shop (called Hock Hiap Leong) about to be demolished because of urban development, a young man reflects on the coffee shop's importance for its customers. Grace Chang singing "Wo Bu Guan Ni Shi Shui" ("I Don't Care Who You Are"), also in *The Hole*, enters the ambient sound as the man comments on the café's sensory delights and the emotional relief it provides while the camera pans over the customers, vendors, food, and drinks. As Chang's song becomes louder, the man laments the passage of time and the coffee shop's soon-to-transpire demise. The film then uses the first lyric from Grace Chang's "Jajambo" ("Too Happy for Words")—a hit from *The Wild, Wild Rose* noted for being "the first and only Chinese song . . . [on] the top ten list of Radio Hong Kong's Hit Parade in 1961, then devoted exclusively to English language songs"[34]—to accentuate a shift in the film's tone. Next, performers dressed in costumes ranging from 1960s go-go and 1970s disco dancing outfits to those worn by older, working-class men in Singapore, T-shirts and pajama bottoms, dance and lip-synch to Grace Chang singing "I Love Cha-Cha" from *Mambo Girl*. Khoo insightfully suggests this song-and-dance sequence is Tan's way of "render[ing] everyday life in the *kopitiam* [coffeeshop] as a campy 1960s musical";[35] of course this stylistic shift forms yet another connection to the filmmaking of Tsai Ming-liang, also known for his interest in camp.[36]

A similar rhetoric of fandom and nostalgia characterizes Tan's short film *Grandfather*,[37] which opens and closes with Grace Chang singing "I Don't Care Who You Are." Commissioned by Singapore's Health Promotion Board, the film explores the challenges of dementia by featuring a grandson interacting with and learning more about his dementia-afflicted grandfather. In the first half, the grandson inter-views those that knew his grandfather as a younger man. One of the interviewees, a fishmonger in a wetmarket, tells the grandson/camera, "Your Grandpa used to love Ge Lan's [Grace Chang's] songs. When he heard her songs like 'Shangri-La' or 'I Don't Care Who You Are,' he would start to dance, even better than the *kampung* [village] geese," thus highlighting the reception of Chang's music in Singapore. Chang's "I Don't Care Who You Are" recurs non-diegetically in the film's closing sequence, much as it does in the final sequence of Tsai's *The Hole*. However, instead of a couple dancing, as in *The Hole*, in *Grandfather* it accompanies a touching record of the grandson's love and caring for his grandfather. Chang continues to croon "I don't care who you are" as the image switches to an image of clouds, over which floats a message written in Chinese calligraphy: "All that you love most is still there / Dementia doesn't change who they are." This message evokes *The Hole*'s conclusion, in which a black screen presenting Tsai Ming-liang's calligraphy asserts, "We are fortunate that, in the year 2000, we still have Grace Chang's music to comfort us." In Tsai's film, the final shot explains why Chang's songs "graced" the film while also acknowledging his consumption of and fandom for Grace Chang's music in Taiwan, where he has been based since college, and in Kuching, where he grew up.[38] Both of Tan's short films, particularly in their final sequences, simultaneously amplify the circulation of Chang's music into Singapore as well as Tsai's cinematic influence on Tan,[39] reinforcing the sense of a network of cultural production linking Hong Kong, Singapore/Southeast Asia, and Taiwan.

Sound, Allusion, and the Songstress in Tan's Feature Films

In her heyday, the songstress took on numerous cinematic roles ranging from teahouse and nightclub singers and showgirls to modern teenagers, country girls, and revolutionaries—diverse types that, as Ma reminds us, must be analyzed with reference to the particular historical and cultural contexts in which they were imagined.[40] In *881* and *12 Lotus*, Tan engages language politics in Singapore by featuring songstress-protagonists that are *getai* (song-stage) singers, performers in public outdoor concerts held annually in Singapore (and Malaysia) during the Hungry Ghost festival (in the seventh lunar month, or August) to entertain roaming ghosts temporarily released from the underworld. Originally consisting primarily of traditional Hokkien and Teochew operas, since the 1960s Singaporean *getai* have evolved into popular entertainment shows staged on public housing estate land and featuring "dazzling lights, flamboyant costumes, and raunchy acts and comedy mainly in Hokkien."[41]

In *881*, two young women, Big Papaya (played by Yeoh Yann Yann) and Little Papaya (Mindee Ong), are brought together by their love of *getai* and fandom for Chen Jin Lang (1961–2006), a famous *getai* performer and singer of Hokkien (and Mandarin) pop whose actual 2006 death from cancer is depicted in *881*. Helped by a seamstress named Aunt Ling (played by Liu Ling Ling, another famous *getai* performer in real life) and her mute son (Guan Yin, played by Qi Yuwu), the Papaya Sisters form a singing duo but are judged unready for the stage until Aunt Ling takes them to see her estranged sister, the Goddess of *Getai* (also played by Liu Ling Ling). Before the Papaya Sisters can receive divine abilities from the Goddess, they must agree to five rules, the most important being that they must "stay pure, and no man love." They agree and become *getai* stars. Similarly, *12 Lotus* presents the tragic life of an aspiring *getai* singer (played by Mindee Ong as she is rising to fame). Though she achieves this dream, it turns out that her aspiration to learn the well-known Hokkien song "Shi'er lianhua" ("Twelve Lotus"), which recounts twelve chapters in the title character's life of suffering, has doomed her to a tragic fate. She ends the film in a state of mental illness and abandonment (Liu Ling Ling plays the character in her mentally ill state).

Spotlighting *getai* and Hokkien through music and dialogue is the most obvious way that *881* and *12 Lotus* engage with language politics in Singapore. As Tan remarked of *881*, "[T]he thing was to bring out our very repressed dialect, one of the languages that we have not spoken for a very long time."[42] Singapore's colonial legacy and recent language policies have created a linguistic hierachy in which English, the language of business and government, outranks Mandarin—the "official 'ethnic language' for Chinese Singaporeans but [which] is considered of little importance to educational and career achievement"—which in turn outranks the "systematically marginalized" non-Mandarin Sinitic languages, like Hokkien and Cantonese.[43] Brought to Singapore by emigrants from the southern mainland Chinese provinces of Fujian and Guangdong, languages like Hokkien, Cantonese, and Teochew were the first languages of earlier generations of Sinophone Singaporeans; Hokkien was this community's *lingua franca*. But with the start of the Speak Mandarin campaign in 1979, non-Mandarin Chinese languages were banned from radio, print media, and television; Mandarin was designated as the second language after English in school for Sinophone Singaporeans.[44] Though restrictions relaxed in the 1990s, allowing increased use of Hokkien, Cantonese, and Singaporean English (or "Singlish," another restricted language in Singapore media) in films by Eric Khoo and Jack Neo,[45] by 2011, language-use statistics showed English and Mandarin supplanting the speaking of non-Mandarin languages for most Singaporeans identifying as ethnic Chinese.[46] Hence Tan's lament that "in the new current generation they are not exposed to the beauty of such a wonderful language [Hokkien]."[47]

Featuring substantial amounts of dialogue in Hokkien (along with Mandarin and Singaporean English), soundtracks dominated by Hokkien *getai* songs, and, in the case of *12 Lotus*, using the story and structure of a popular Hokkien song, *881* and *12 Lotus* challenge these linguistic trends. After *881* became 2007's highest-grossing locally produced movie[48] and the tenth most-viewed film in Singapore, its soundtrack sold out; audiences for *getai* expanded; STOMP—an online content portal for *The Straits Times*—launched a *getai* website called Getai A-Go-Go;[49] and the popular press credited the movie with "revitalizing the dying Hokkien language" in Singapore.[50] This latter claim may be hyperbolic: in their trenchant study of Hokkien popular music published several years after *881* and *12 Lotus*, Khiun and Chan conclude that in Singapore Hokkien has largely become "vestigial": "'functionless' and 'irrelevant' against the pervasiveness of English and Mandarin and in [Singapore's] public sphere."[51] Even if Tan's films cannot be credited with achieving empirical gains for Hokkien, however, his reinvention of his songstresses as *getai* singers in order to "expose new generations to the beauty of Hokkien" and to "immortalize a little bit of myself, because I am Hokkien"[52] confirms the capacity of the songstress trope to represent linguistic heterogeneity and engage with local language politics.

The linguistic hierarchy described above maps onto a broader cultural hierarchy in Singapore that is typically explained with reference to a 1999 National Day Rally speech made by former Prime Minister Goh Chok Tong (1999–2004) in which he identified two types of Singaporeans. One is the "elites" or "cosmopolitans": the English-speaking, bilingual class that "have skills that command good incomes—banking, IT, engineering, science and technology," "produce goods and services for the global market," and "can work and be comfortable anywhere in the world."[53] The second is the "heartlanders," referring to the majority of Singaporeans who live in public housing estates built by Singapore's Housing Development Board (HDB). According to Goh, "heartlanders" generally include "taxi-drivers, stallholders, provision shop owners, production workers and contractors" who have "orientations and interests [that] are local rather than international," and whose "skills are not marketable beyond Singapore."[54] Goh proposes that both heartlanders and cosmopolitans "are important to Singapore's well-being": "Heartlanders play a major role in maintaining our core values and social stability. They are the core of our society. . . . Cosmopolitans . . . are indispensable for generating wealth for Singapore. They extend our economic reach. . . . Without them, Singapore cannot run as an efficient, high performance society."[55] Still, scholars agree that these classifications have created a hierarchy in which elites/cosmopolitans outrank heartlanders. Tan and Fernando discern an "elitist bias towards the cosmopolitan" and note that Goh's binary logic and "privileging of the cosmopolitan over the heartlander reflects institutionalised social divisions along the lines of class, language, education and occupation in contemporary Singaporean society."[56] Relatedly, Edna Lim interprets Goh's statements as, in effect, excluding heartlanders from exemplifying success in Singapore: "[H]eartlanders are important for local identity, and cosmopolitans are crucial to and participants of Singapore's performance of success."[57]

881 challenges these hierarchies not just by promoting Hokkien but also by defining success in terms of a sisterhood forged and sustained by the heartlanders' vernacular culture, represented here by *getai* and the Hungry Ghost Festival (when *getai* occurs). Much of the film's plot involves a *getai* contest between the Papaya Sisters and their rivals, the Durian Sisters. Being speakers of Mandarin and Hokkien links the Papaya Sisters linguistically with Singapore's Chinese-speaking "heartlander" class; the film's opening sequence pairs sound and image to make their origins in the heartland even more apparent and meaningful. As a male voice-over (the interior voice of Aunt Ling's mute son Guan Yin)[58] announces their births, medium shots of a male stallholder holding loaves of bread and a female fishmonger holding a large fish liken the girls to products of the traditional market in which the shots were taken. Fast-forward in the plot: the Papaya Sisters' success on the *getai* circuit sparks the jealousy of the Durian Sisters, another popular act. They become antagonists to the Papaya Sisters when they launch a campaign of harassment against them. As English speakers who speak Mandarin awkwardly and struggle with the Hokkien in the most popular *getai* songs, the Durian Sisters (played by Eurasian twins Teh May Wan and Tey Choy Wan)[59] represent Singapore's elite, "cosmopolitan" class; notably, their villainy is marked by, among other things, a lack of respect for the Goddess of *Getai*, whom they mock as a "retired old fart," and their lack of fluency in Hokkien, as seen in their inability to lip-synch Hokkien songs properly.

To settle the dispute, a contest is set up, which Chan aptly reads as an allegory for tensions between the Sinophone and Anglophone communities in Singapore as well as for "the class-based contradiction between the working-class heartlanders and the middle-class English-speaking cosmopolitans."[60] After an intense competition, the Papaya Sisters are eventually bested by the Durian Sisters' technical powers; it turns out that Big Papaya has lost the abilities granted to her by the Goddess of *Getai* because she fell in love with Guan Yin. Little Papaya, who has battled leukemia her whole life, has to exhaust her energy to save them both; the effort proves too much and she ends up hospitalized, dying shortly thereafter. Though the contest ends badly for the Papaya Sisters, by the film's conclusion we see that not only has Big Papaya achieved her dream of becoming a successful *getai* singer, but that during the Hungry Ghost festival, when ghosts are permitted to revisit the mortal world, she is able to sing once again with Little Papaya. Thus does *881* propose that their allegiance to *getai* has ultimately fulfilled the Papaya Sisters' fantasies and granted them a transcendent sisterly bond. Meanwhile, Big Papaya was introduced in the film's opening sequence as having achieved the kind of academic success that theoretically could have moved her into the "elite, cosmopolitan" category. That she locates her own success and personal fulfillment in the world of *getai*, even after Little Papaya's death, further underscores the film's endorsement of heartlander culture.

Clearly, Tan's *getai* songstresses and their narratives need to be analyzed with respect to Singaporean linguistic and cultural politics. Equally important, however, are the traces of earlier songstress films in Tan's films that bring into view the continued circulation and adaptation of the songstress as a cinematic trope in Sinophone filmmaking. All of Tan's songstresses evoke "a key motif of the songstress genre," namely, as Linda Chiu-han Lai puts it, "the self-sacrificing woman condemned to a life of poverty, suffering, and humiliation in the entertainment industry because of economic pressures, or in order to protect her family or her lover."[61] The songstress's narrative in *12 Lotus* most clearly fits this description in that her suffering stems largely from her willingness to support her abusive father, whose gambling racks up large debts. After his death, the gang to which her father owed money demands repayment from her and her new husband, Ah Long (played by Qi Yuwu), who, we soon learn, has been conspiring with the gang all along. Unaware of Ah Long's betrayal and to prevent the gang from killing her beloved, Sister Lotus sacrifices herself and is subjected to a night of humiliation, violence, and rape; when she returns, Ah Long has vanished. As mentioned, the film structures its plot according to the lyrics of a Hokkien popular song called "Twelve Lotus"; following the plot developments just described, the film features the protagonist singing: "Chapter Six of Pitiful Lotus / Money has caused her downfall and ruined her name / There is no way out for her." Soon other voices join in to sing verses seven and eight of the song, which recount a descent into despair and isolation; thus does the film use the song lyrics to indicate the passage of time and Sister Lotus's succumbing to mental illness and agoraphobia.

As mentioned, the motif of a songstress as a self-sacrificing, tragic figure is seen as originating with Zhou Xuan, but it persisted in later Hong Kong films even as other songstress types joined the stage. Having risen to fame playing a generally fortunate "mambo girl" and "air hostess," for example, in *Wild, Wild Rose* Grace Chang plays a nightclub singer whose exploitation and abuse at the hands of men, combined with her loyal heart and self-sacrificing nature, memorably reprises the role of the songstress as a tragic victim of fate and patriarchal society. On its heels appeared *Love Without End* (*Bu liao qing*, dir. Tao Qin, 1961), starring Linda Lin Dai as Li Qingqing, another nightclub singer willing to sacrifice herself to save her lover from bankruptcy. Compounding her tragedy, just as marriage to her beloved is within Qingqing's grasp, she is diagnosed with and then soons dies from leukemia. As Law and Bren remark, "Once again, [in *Love Without End*] the songstress is a friend of misfortune, sacrificed for an ideal or for her integrity in love."[62] *Love Without End* was a huge hit and earned Lin her fourth and final Best Actress Award in the Asian Film Festival (Seoul, 1962).[63] It also inspired Derek Yee's (1993) *Xin bu liao qing*, literally translated as "new love without end" but also referred to as *C'est la vie, mon chéri*, featuring multiple female characters who sing, but whose protagonist is afflicted with (and dies from) leukemia, as in *Love Without End*.

The influence of these two Hong Kong–produced songstress films on *881* and *12 Lotus* can be discerned through narrative, characterization, and shot selection. Little Papaya's suffering and death from leukemia forms an obvious connection to both *Love Without End* and *C'est la vie, mon chéri*. More interesting, Lai suggests that, in featuring a story involving multiple female singers, "*C'est la vie, mon chéri* self-consciously splits the figure of the songstress into four different female characters that embody a complex historical temporality" and allows it to express a "gap between the 1960s and contemporary Hong Kong while nonetheless holding on to a nostalgic, modified version of old genres."[64] *881* similarly splits its songstress figure into multiple female characters that evoke rifts and distinct associations, but which, taken together, exalt a heartlander-based sisterhood and a dedication to *getai*: Little Papaya, who dies tragically and prematurely; Big Papaya, who manages to survive as a *getai* singer but perpetually mourns her sworn sister; Aunt Ling and her sister, the Goddess of *Getai*, whose reunion at the film's conclusion reinforces the film's celebration of sisterhood; and finally, Big Papaya's mother, a former *getai* singer herself who initially rejects Big Papaya for her *getai* dreams but is eventually supportive. *12 Lotus* acknowledges its debt to *Love Without End*, filmed in black and white, with a sepia-toned shot following the father's death. In the shot, whose warm sepia tones conspicuously contrast with the cool blue-green shades of the hospital scene that precedes it, Sister Lotus holds her father's picture while standing on a rock in the ocean. Her pose, along with the shot's composition, location, and tone, powerfully recall the final shot in *Love Without End* in which Qingqing's lover mourns her while also gazing out at the sea.

Though Tan's latest feature, *3688*, leaves the *getai* world behind, it bears thematic and aesthetic connections to *881* and *12 Lotus* that demonstrate Tan's ongoing interest in reinterpreting the songstress figure to engage with local issues while highlighting transnational connections with other "small nation cinema" sites. *3688*'s songstress-protagonist is a parking enforcement officer named Xia Fei Fei, avid fan of Taiwanese singer Fong Fei-Fei (1953–2012),[65] who eventually works up the courage to sing Fong's songs in a televised singing contest. The film's Chinese title, *Xiangru feifei* exploits the homophone *feifei* in a Chinese idiom meaning "to indulge in fantasy" (*xiangru feifei*) to imply "Dreaming of [Fong] Fei-Fei." Though *3688*'s sound contains considerably less Hokkien dialogue than *881* or *12 Lotus*, it still comments on Singapore's language politics and linguistic hierarchies through the storyline of Xia Fei Fei's father, a retired Rediffusion (*lidehusheng*) subscription salesman nicknamed "Uncle Radio" by neighbors. Established in 1949, Rediffusion gained popularity among Sinophone Singaporeans because of its dialect programming, but went into decline after having to cease this programming because of the Speak Mandarin Campaign.[66] It finally closed in 2012, leading many to express concerns over the loss of this "integral aspect of dialect culture."[67] If *3688*'s primary plot pays homage to Fong Fei-Fei, then its secondary one—featuring Uncle Radio clinging to his past life, extolling the talents of the Hokkien storytellers he used to listen to on Rediffusion, and perpetually repairing old radios—notably pays homage to Rediffusion and its contributions to Hokkien cultural production in Singapore.

Like *881*, *3688* stages a contest to symbolize class tensions while exalting heartlander culture: being a parking attendant and unable to afford lavish costumes earns Xia Fei Fei mockery from others involved with the contest, while her sincere renditions of Fong Fei-Fei's hits win over the audience and judges nevertheless. Also like *881*, *3688* splits the songstress figure into multiple female characters, functioning here to stress Singapore's multilingualism and multiculturalism. Besides Joi Chua as Xia Fei Fei singing Fong's Mandarin hits (like "Wo shi yi pian yun" ["I am a cloud"] and "Zhangsheng xiangqi" ["When I hear applause"]), the film also casts Liu Ling Ling as a cafe owner named Ah Luan.[68] Though not a singer in the film, her outlandish costumes hint at the *getai* world from which Liu hails. Playing the role of Jenny, Fei Fei's colleague and rival, is Malay Singaporean Rahima Rahim (b. 1955), one of Singapore's most popular singers during the 1970s and 1980s who sings in Malay, English, and Mandarin. Like the songstresses in *881*, *12 Lotus*, and earlier films, Xia Fei Fei is no stranger to hardship and sorrow, having lost her mother to illness as a girl and as the sole caretaker of her dementia-stricken father. Her willingness to sacrifice her personal fulfillment to protect her family emerges as she dedicates her final performance in the contest to finding her father, who recently went missing. Though the film hints at a happy ending by showing Xia's father watching her performance on the televisions in shop, his confused reaction suggests that Xia Fei Fei's challenges will continue.

Conclusion

Royston Tan's filmmaking demonstrates that the songstress figure, though less prevalent today than previously, endures as a significant narrative and cinematic trope uniquely suited for adaptations that explore local cultural politics. At the same time, this figure valuably brings into view relations between Sinophone filmmaking sites and histories that risk being obscured in an era of globalization. As much as this study spotlights the circulation and reinvention of the songstress trope, it is also concerned with strategic cinematic relations between the "small nation cinema" sites of Singapore, Taiwan, and Hong Kong. As Hjort and Petrie point out,

> Small nationhood need not be a liability nor a clear sign of sub-optimality, and the task in any analytic of small nationhood associated with film is thus a dual one: to identify those factors that are genuinely debilitating and caught up with questionable power dynamics; to pinpoint strategies that ensure access, visibility and participation; and to transform these strategies, through analysis, into cultural resources that can be appropriated in, and adapted to, other circumstances.[69]

The use of the songstress and related allusions in Royston Tan's filmmaking must also be seen as part of a strategy that aims for "visibility and participation" for Sinophone auteurs in Singapore, Taiwan, and Hong Kong. By contributing to the imagining of the Sinophone as a multiply-centered network sustained by cultural—cinematic, musical, literary—flows, as Tan's use of this figure suggests, the songstress figure critically aids in identifying a distinctive Sinophone filmmaking tradition comprised of diverse but related film histories.

Notes

An earlier version of this paper was presented at "Sinophone Meets Francophonie: Concepts and Controversies" (Humboldt-Universität zu Berlin, April 2018); I would like to thank the conference organizers as well as the participants, whose comments and questions subsequently helped me to revise the work.

1. Chris Berry and Mary Farquhar, "The National in the Transnational," in *China on Screen: Cinema and Nation* (New York: Columbia University Press, 2006), 213.
2. Jan Uhde and Yvonne Ng Uhde, *Latent Images: Film in Singapore*, 2nd ed. (Singapore: National University of Singapore Press, 2010), 129–30.
3. Quoted in Uhde and Uhde, *Latent Images*, 130.
4. Mette Hjort and Duncan J. Petrie, *The Cinema of Small Nations* (Bloomington: Indiana University Press, 2007).
5. Sam Ho, "The Songstress, the Farmer's Daughter, the Mambo Girl and the Songstress Again," in *Mandarin Films and Popular Songs: 40's–60's*, ed. Law Kar (Hong Kong: Urban Council, 1993), 59.
6. Jean Ma, *Sounding the Modern Woman: The Songstress in Chinese Cinema* (Durham: Duke University Press, 2015), 61.
7. Ho, "The Songstress, the Farmer's Daughter," 60; Law Kar, "Song of a Songstress," in *Mandarin Films and Popular Songs: 40's–60's*, 94.
8. Po-Shek Fu, *Between Shanghai and Hong Kong: The Politics of Chinese Cinemas* (Stanford: Stanford University Press, 2003); Ma, *Sounding the Modern Woman*, 24.
9. Other songstress types include: the *femme fatale*/sexy type, or in Stephen Teo's phrasing, the "sour beauty," represented by Bai Guang; and the farmer's daughter, "singing country lass" or "Little Wildcat," associated mostly with Chung Ching (Zhong Qing). Emilie Yueh-yu Yeh also identifies the "Opera Girl," exemplified by Ivy Ling Po and the "Go-Go

Girls" featured in *Xiangjiang huayue ye* (*Hong Kong Nocturne*, 1967). For more information, see Ho, "The Songstress, the Farmer's Daughter"; Stephen Teo, "Shanghai Redone: Les Sing-Song Girls in Hong Kong," in *Hong Kong Cinema: The Extra Dimensions* (London: BFI, 1997); Ma, *Sounding the Modern Woman*; Emilie Yueh-yu Yeh, "China," in *The International Film Musical*, ed. Corey K. Creekmur and Linda Y. Mokdad (Edinburgh: Edinburgh University Press, 2012); and Law Kar and Frank Bren, *Hong Kong Cinema: A Cross-Cultural View* (Lanham, MD: Scarecrow Press, 2004), 231–78.

10. Ma, *Sounding the Modern Woman*, 139.

11. Yeh, "China," 179.

12. Yeh, "China," 176.

13. Yeh, "China," 179.

14. Ma, *Sounding the Modern Woman*, 214.

15. For further analysis of Lee's and Wong's allusions to Zhou Xuan and her music, see Ma, *Sounding the Modern Woman*, 1–5, 213–18.

16. For analysis of allusions in Tsai's work, see, for example, Fran Martin, "Wild Women and Mechanical Men: A Review of *The Hole*," *Intersections: Gender, History and Culture in the Asian Context* no. 4 (September 2000), accessed January 15, 2020, http://intersections.anu.edu.au/issue4/holereview.html; Ban Wang, "Black Holes of Globalization: Critique of the New Millennium in Taiwan Cinema," *Modern Chinese Literature and Culture* 15, no. 1 (2003): 90–119; Weihong Bao, "Biomechanics of Love: Reinventing the Avant-Garde in Tsai Ming-Liang's Wayward 'Pornographic Musical'," *Journal of Chinese Cinemas* 1, no. 2 (2007): 139–60; Vivian Lee, "Pornography, Musical, Drag, and the Art Film: Performing 'Queer' in Tsai Ming-Liang's *The Wayward Cloud*," *Journal of Chinese Cinemas* 1, no. 2 (2007): 117–37; Song Hwee Lim, "Positioning Auteur Theory in Chinese Cinema Studies: Intratextuality, Intertextuality and Paratextuality in the Films of Tsai Ming-Liang," *Journal of Chinese Cinemas* 1, no. 3 (2007): 223–45; and Jean Ma, "Delayed Voices: Intertextuality, Music and Gender in *The Hole*," *Journal of Chinese Cinemas* 5, no. 2 (2011): 123–39.

17. Ma, *Sounding the Modern Woman*, vii, 21, 23.

18. Ma, *Sounding the Modern Woman*, 24.

19. Ma, *Sounding the Modern Woman*, 24.

20. Ma, *Sounding the Modern Woman*, 25–26.

21. Uhde and Uhde, *Latent Images*, 288.

22. Uhde and Uhde, *Latent Images*, 117.

23. Song Hwee Lim, "*15*: The Singapore Failure Story, 'Slanged Up'," in *Chinese Films in Focus II*, ed. Chris Berry, 2nd ed. (New York: Palgrave Macmillan [on behalf of BFI], 2008), 10.

24. Lim, "*15*," 10; James Bell, "Rushes: Singing for the Censors," *Sight & Sound* 15, no. 2 (2005): 6. In *Cinema and Television in Singapore: Resistance in One Dimension* (Leiden: Brill, 2008), Kenneth Paul Tan cites the Media Development Authority's claim that only nine cuts were required, "citing the promotion of gangster activity as the main justification for censorship" (241).

25. Lim, "*15*," 10.

26. Tan, *Cinema and Television in Singapore*, 247.

27. Tan, *Cinema and Television in Singapore*, 246–47.

28. Tan, *Cinema and Television in Singapore*, 247.

29. Lim, "*15*," 10; Tan, *Cinema and Television in Singapore*, 219; Uhde and Uhde, *Latent Images*, 288.

30. Ma, *Sounding the Modern Woman*, 3.

31. Ma, *Sounding the Modern Woman*, 215.

32. Alison M. Groppe, *Sinophone Malaysian Literature: Not Made in China* (Amherst, NY: Cambria Press, 2013), 180.

33. This film is available on YouTube at https://www.youtube.com/watch?v=PDXCNmfb ZG8 (accessed January 8, 2020).

34. Wong, Kee Chee (Huang Qizhi), *The Age of Shanghainese Pops: 1930–1970* (Hong Kong: Joint Publishing [H.K.], 2001), 144.

35. Gaik Cheng Khoo, "Where the Heart Is: Cinema and Civic Life in Singapore," in *New Suburban Stories*, ed. Martin Dines and Timotheus Vermeulen (London: Bloomsbury Publishing, 2013), 106.

36. See, for example, Emilie Yueh-yu Yeh and Darrell William Davis, "Camping Out with Tsai Ming-Liang," in *Taiwan Film Directors: A Treasure Island* (New York: Columbia University Press, 2005), 217–48.

37. Also available on YouTube at https://www.youtube.com/watch?v=6DKnqp9KVvI (accessed January 8, 2020).

38. Tsai often discusses with critics his love of Chang's music and his musical and cinematic tastes in general; two good examples are interviews with Michael Berry and Shelly Kraicer. See Michael Berry, "Tsai Ming-Liang: Trapped in the Past," in *Speaking in Images: Interviews with Contemporary Chinese Filmmakers* (New York: Columbia University Press, 2005): 362–97; and Shelly Kraicer, "Interview with Tsai Ming-liang," *positions: east asia cultures critique* 8, no. 2 (Fall 2000): 579–89.

39. *The Hole*'s influence on contemporary Sinophone filmmaking can also be seen in the Hong Kong film *Soundless Wind Chime* (*Wusheng feng ling*, dir. Hung Wing Kit, 2009), which features an older woman lip-synching to Grace Chang's "Ah choo cha-cha." See Zoran Lee Pecic, "Queer Auteurs of Hong Kong Cinema," in *New Queer Sinophone Cinema: Local Histories, Transnational Connections* (London: Palgrave Macmillan, 2016), 101–38.

40. Ma, *Sounding the Modern Woman*, 4.

41. Liew Kai Khiun and Brenda Chan, "Vestigial Pop: Hokkien Popular Music and the Cultural Fossilization of Subalternity in Singapore," *SOJOURN: Journal of Social Issues in Southeast Asia* 28, no. 2 (2013): 281.

42. Anne Ciecko, "Cinenumerology: An Interview with Royston Tan, One of Singapore's Most Versatile Filmmakers," *Jump Cut: A Review of Contemporary Media* no. 51 (Spring 2009): 1.

43. Brenda Chan, "Gender and Class in the Singaporean Film *881*," *Jump Cut: A Review of Contemporary Media* no. 51 (Spring 2009): 14.

44. Edna Lim, *Celluloid Singapore: Cinema, Performance and the National* (Edinburgh: Edinburgh University Press, 2018), 146; and Liew Kai Khiun and Brenda Chan, "Popular Music and Contemporary Singaporean Cinema," in *Singapore Cinema: New Perspectives* (New York: Routledge, 2017), 99. For more information about the Speak Mandarin campaign, see Singapore Mandarin Council, "About the Speak Mandarin

Campaign," accessed January 15, 2020, https://www.languagecouncils.sg/mandarin/en; Alison M. Groppe, "'Singlish' and the Sinophone: Nonstandard (Chinese/English) Languages in Recent Singaporean Cinema," in *Sinophone Cinemas*, ed. Audrey Yue and Olivia Khoo (London: Palgrave Macmillan, 2014), 151–54; Peter Teo, "Mandarinising Singapore: A Critical Analysis of Slogans in Singapore's 'Speak Mandarin' Campaign," *Critical Discourse Studies* 2, no. 2 (2005): 121–42; and Beng Huat Chua, "Taiwan's Future/Singapore's Past: Hokkien Films in Between," in *Life Is Not Complete without Shopping: Consumption Culture in Singapore* (Singapore: Singapore University Press, 2003), 166–73.

45. For an insightful analysis of Hokkien in Jack Neo's *Money No Enough* (*Qian bugou yong*, 1998), see Chua, "Taiwan's Future/Singapore's Past."

46. Liew and Chan, "Vestigial Pop," 279. Liew and Chan's statistical analysis also shows a decline in Chinese language proficiency despite the continuation of the Speak Mandarin campaign.

47. Ciecko, "Cinenumerology," 2.

48. It was also screened at the 12th Pusan International Film Festival—where its screening sold out and about a thousand fans attended an event with director and cast—the 44th Taipei Golden Horse Film Festival, and, in 2008, at the 37th International Film Festival Rotterdam (Chan, "Gender and Class," 2).

49. Chan, "Gender and Class," 2.

50. Chan, "Gender and Class," 15; and Liew and Chan, "Vestigial Pop," 283.

51. Liew and Chan, "Vestigial Pop," 274.

52. Ciecko, "Cinenumerology," 2.

53. Goh Chok Tong (1999 speech), quoted in Lim, *Celluloid Singapore*, 141; and Chan, "Gender and Class," 4.

54. Goh Chok Tong (1999), quoted in Lim, *Celluloid Singapore*, 140–41.

55. Goh Chok Tong (1999), quoted in Lim, *Celluloid Singapore*, 141.

56. See Kam Tan and Jeremy Fernando, "Singapore," in *The Cinema of Small Nations*, ed. Mette Hjort and Duncan J. Petrie (Bloomington: Indiana University Press, 2007), 128.

57. Edna Lim, "Singapore Cinema: Connecting the Golden Age and the Revival," in *Singapore Cinema: New Perspectives*, ed. Liew Kai Khiun and Stephen Teo (London: Routledge, 2017), 26.

58. Voiced by Royston Tan (Chan, "Gender and Class," 11).

59. Chan, "Gender and Class," 7.

60. Chan, "Gender and Class," 16.

61. Linda Chiu-han Lai, "Film and Enigmatization: Nostalgia, Nonsense, and Remembering," in *At Full Speed: Hong Kong Cinema in a Borderless World*, ed. Esther C. M. Yau (Minneapolis: University of Minnesota Press, 2001), 236.

62. Kar and Bren, *Hong Kong Cinema*, 234.

63. Law Kar, "Love Without End," in *Mandarin Films and Popular Songs: 40's–60's*, 117.

64. Lai, "Film and Enigmatization," 236 and 237.

65. Fong Fei-Fei's predilection for performing in hats gave rise to her nickname, the "Queen of Hats"; because they also wear hats, Singapore's generally female parking attendants are collectively dubbed "Fong Fei-Fei" (as well as "summon aunties").

66. Eddie C. Y. Kuo, "Multingualism and Mass Media Communications in Singapore," *Asian Survey* 18, no. 10 (1978): 1075–76; Joshua Chia Yeong Jia and Pei Ying Loh, "Rediffusion," Singapore Infopedia, accessed January 15, 2020, http://eresources.nlb. gov.sg/infopedia/articles/SIP_1198_2008-10-24.html?s=Rediffusion.

67. Jia and Loh, "Rediffusion."

68. Ah Luan's fashion choices also evoke Lady Gaga's style; Ah Luan is also referred to as "Lady Ka-ka." Singaporean hip-hop artist Shigga Shay plays the role of Ah Luan's son, Yoyo, and performs highly multilingual, Hokkien-heavy, and localized raps, harking back to Tan's use of music in *15* (2003).

69. Hjort and Petrie, *The Cinema of Small Nations*, 7.

9

Implicit Sexuality

The Representation of the Femme Fatale Figure in *Black Coal, Thin Ice*

Yushi Hou

The Chinese neo-noir *Black Coal, Thin Ice* (*Bairi yanhuo*, 2014), directed by Diao Yi'nan, won Best Picture at the 64th Berlin International Film Festival on February 15, 2014[1] and then exceeded 100 million yuan at the box office after being released in late March of 2014;[2] it was praised by a *Variety* film review as a "powerful, carefully controlled detective thriller."[3] The success of the film piqued the interest of the Chinese film administration and made film scholars take note of its stylistic noir outlook.[4] Although there is fruitful Chinese-language scholarship about this representative Chinese neo-noir as a "turning point of Chinese film industrialization" that makes a contribution to the diversity of contemporary Chinese cinema by integrating authorship into the genre system,[5] my research engages with the femme fatale figure, a social-historical archetype in Western culture, and its transnational transplantation in contemporary Chinese neo-noir. I situate this noticeable and appealing generic character in the context of global film noir, which has not yet been substantively addressed by film academia. Moreover, East Asian film noir enriches the spectacle of global noir filmmaking and raises many scholarly discussions about film industries, aesthetics, and culture; concerning the potentiality of the mainland Chinese film market, it is worthwhile to place recent Chinese mainland neo-noirs as a genre into these broad discussions, to rethink the profound linkage between national specificity and the origin of classic film noir in the social, historical, and cultural contexts of postwar America through a comparative research method.

My research focuses on the individual femme fatale in *Black Coal, Thin Ice* not only because this character is played by Taiwanese actress Kwei Lun-mei—who exemplifies a sense of alienation in the urban setting of northeast China and signifies the flows of transnational stardom—but also because the femme fatale pertains to the completeness and identifiability of this genre, since women are not often presented as murderers in mainland Chinese crime thrillers or East Asian film noirs. More typically, women are superficially alluring and passively involved in crime cases in such narratives, despite women being portrayed as law-breakers more often in Chinese crime thrillers. Thus, by comparing this film with the iconography of the seductive femme fatale in classic Hollywood, this chapter analyzes the implicit sexuality of this female character who interacts with the absence of the male's erotic gaze and reconciles with the loss of love, marriage, and family in *Black Coal, Thin Ice*. This implicit sexuality uses male impotence as a metaphor for the harsh realities of the film's post-socialist milieu. I argue that masculine anxieties in Chinese neo-noir originate from an oppressive political system and a patriarchal society rather than emanating from the fatal woman, and the typical femme fatale figure in Chinese neo-noir, with its pessimistic gender politics, refers to the destruction of domestic ideology—the disillusionment of the "Chinese Dream" slogan in the post-socialist cultural context.

The Concept of the Femme Fatale

The femme fatale, a seductive, mysterious, and deadly woman, is regarded as a film noir icon. Primarily driven by money, she entices the male protagonist with her sexuality in hopes of achieving her selfish desires. In classic Hollywood film noir, femme fatales are usually equal to male protagonists rather than subordinate to men; they cannot be restrained in any relationship nor disturbed by emotion. In terms of the femme fatale's iconography, Janey Place outlines the scope of her sexualized image as "long hair (blond or dark), make-up, jewelry, cigarette" and "long, lovely legs"; she also emphasizes that the cigarette, with its "wispy trails of smoke," is a symbol of the femme fatale's "unnatural phallic power."[6] Since smoking is generally regarded as a masculine action, the image of a sexy woman with a smoky cigarette underlines her potential power, which might threaten the patriarchal order.[7] Also, the femme fatale often shows her beautiful legs in her first appearance, and she is often the primary focus of the composition in the foreground. Corresponding to this image, Place mentions that "the original transgression of the dangerous lady of film noir is ambition expressed metaphorically in her freedom of movement and visual dominance."[8] The femme fatale visually dominates the camera movement, lighting, framing, and shooting angle, which threateningly embodies an of out-of-control sense for the male protagonist. As she is a beautiful and mysterious woman who often "gaze[s] at her own reflection in the mirror, ignoring the man she will use to achieve her goals," the camera focuses on her and moves to follow her, signaling her independence, ambition, and her "self-absorbed narcissism."[9]

The rise of the femme fatale in classic film noir is associated with socio-cultural changes in the postwar cultural contexts of the United States. Those ambitious and unsatisfied femme fatale figures reflect a burgeoning feminism in postwar society, especially as former housewives played an important role in the workplace during wartime; women's social status had soared because of their social and economic contributions, although the reintegration of men into the postwar economy yielded a tension between the new possibilities for women and the traditional gender order.

As Hanson illustrates, "seductive" means both "alluring" and "distracting," and the seductive individuality of the femme fatale transgresses traditional gender roles, producing a symptomatic anxiety in a male-centered society.[10] Due to the absence of normal families and steady marriages in film noir, these "exciting, childless whores"—in opposition to "boring, potentially childbearing sweethearts"[11]—menace traditional family structures and conservative values, and disenchant the American Dream related to family and national unity.

Simultaneously, the popularity of the femme fatale on screen evokes a set of male anxieties in the postwar period. Working women were requested to subordinate to men's career ambitions and competitiveness because "postwar retrenchment involved shifting women out of their work or back into lower paid positions."[12] Thus, the femme fatale in film noir dramatizes postwar male anxieties in the face of proficient and forceful working women not only breaking gendered stereotypes but also threatening the economic standing of men. As a result, femme fatales visualize a masculinity crisis in the postwar cultural context, and the emergence of the femme fatale in classic film noir leads to female audiences' self-awareness and self-identification, reflecting the far-reaching impacts of the postwar feminist movement.

Such gender conflicts and masculinity crisis of postwar society are expressed in the sexual tension between the antihero and the femme fatale on screen. These femme fatales are opposites, either "the phallic femme or the feminine woman,"[13] because they challenge stereotypes about ideal coupling, families, and home in the American Dream that was constructed by mainstream media. The femme fatale's sexually appealing and perverse power does not derive from male support—she dresses like a glamourous woman but thinks and acts like a cold-blooded man. These deadly women never present their expectations for romantic love and a happy marriage until the end of the film, and then they "either died, reformed, or turned out not to be a femme fatale after all."[14]

In postmodern film noir and recent neo-noirs, femme fatales are more inclined to accept advanced higher education. Lindop examines the concept of pre-millennial femme fatales in neo-noir and points out that these "intelligent, educated, self-inventive and active" femme fatales might be a metaphor about the "contradictions and tensions that are indicative of postfeminist discourse" after the second wave of feminist activism.[15] The well-educated femme fatales on screen are "perfectly at home in the corporate realm and other typically male dominated spaces," while they "kill for thrills, reject conventional relationships and boast complete mastery over their victims."[16]

It is not easy to sum up the common features of the new femme fatales within the diversity of global neo-noir—as Tasker writes, "the noir woman has become a sign of a different kind in neo-noir"[17] on screen—but the contemporary femme fatale figure is still worth exploring further. Based on the critical discourses around the femme fatale and her history, Helen Hanson states, "Fatal female figures, the ways in which they are placed within genres, narrative strategies and regimes of representation, and the ways in which they are part of an ongoing dialogue with popular incarnations of female identity in different contexts will continue to be a fertile area of debate."[18]

Implicit Sexuality

The femme fatale is a transnational character that arose in classic Hollywood but has been taken up in global neo-noir in a variety of contexts. Corresponding to film noir tropes, the heroine of Black Coal, Thin Ice, Wu Zhizhen, who seduces men and must be punished in the end, seems to be a cold-blooded femme fatale who prompts a series of deaths. However, her appearance, mannerisms, and motives in the story are not consistent with the classic Hollywood femme fatale. Her sexuality tends to be implicit rather than explicit, and she is more often presented as a victim of poverty who needs to be protected or punished in order to resuscitate the male protagonist's manhood. These generic complexities—her image, history, and con-texts—demonstrate a series of cultural conflicts in contemporary Chinese neo-noir.

The deadly woman in Black Coal, Thin Ice, exemplifies the specificity of the femme fatale in East Asian popular culture, or, more precisely, in contemporary Chinese post-socialist cultural contexts. She is placed in a more nuanced narra-tive context in which money is only one of the protagonists' impulses fueling their criminal behavior.

The film takes place in Harbin, a provincial capital city in northeast China, and starts in the summer of 1999. The hero, Zhang Zili, is a just-divorced policeman who had previously worked a grisly murder case. The victim was Liang Zhijun, a scale operator in a provincial coal mine weighing station. The murderer cut Liang's body into small pieces to destroy the evidence, and his body parts were found on coal piles across the province over the course of a single day. After five years unsuc-cessfully working the case, Zhang has been transferred to a factory to work as their security guard. He has not remarried and has become an alcoholic. One day he hears from his previous colleagues that Wu Zhizhen, the widow of Liang, has had two boyfriends after the death of her husband, and they were both murdered. Zhang begins working the case again with his former colleagues by pretending to pursue Wu romantically.

In the course of the investigation, the police suspect that Liang might still be alive and that he may be the real murderer, killing all of his wife's lovers out of jeal-ously. With Wu's cooperation, Liang is shot and killed by the police during their attempts to arrest him. The serial murder case is seemingly closed.

However, Zhang still believes that the 1999 murder is connected to Wu. During his investigation, he learns from Wu's boss at the dry-cleaning business that she had accidentally damaged an extraordinary fur coat worth RMB 28,000 in 1999 before the murders happened, and he suggests that Zhang keep investigating. The annual average wage in Heilongjiang province for urban staff and workers was just RMB 7,094 in 1999,[19] so RMB 28,000 was an enormous expense for a fur coat. Following the clue of the destroyed coat, Zhang finds that the owner of the coat runs a nightclub called Daylight Pyrotechnics. The wife of the nightclub's boss tells Zhang that her husband indeed had a similar coat, and her husband has disappeared five years ago. This wife believes her husband eloped with his mistress, but she still reported the case to the police a year later, then she was only informed that her husband had vanished.

Zhang considers Wu to be the prime suspect and invites her to wander in an old park in the evening. When they are on a Ferris wheel, Zhang asks Wu to look at the nightclub Daylight Pyrotechnics and suggests she needs to keep him happy. Wu actively kisses him, and Zhang has wild sex with her on the Ferris wheel. The next morning during breakfast together, Wu asks Zhang whether he wants to see her tonight. Zhang agrees, but still provides the clue about the coat to the police, even though he has romantic feelings for her. Wu is taken away by the police from the dry cleaner's shop, and Zhang deliberately does not show up. Wu confesses her crimes under interrogation: according to Wu, the nightclub owner sexually harassed her, using the destroyed coat as leverage to demand that she repay him with sex. Fed up with the harassment, Wu lured him to her home with the promise of sex, stabbed him to death, and asked her husband, Liang, to cut his body into pieces. Liang deeply loved his wife, so he chose to be the scapegoat and kept this secret until his death, but still murdered Wu's the other 2 boyfriends out of jealousy. In the wake of Wu's confession, Zhang is reinstated to the police force for having solved the serial cases.

Despite the sex performance on the Ferris wheel, throughout the film Wu is not represented as an alluring and seductive figure. Wu's first appearance in the film happens on a summer day when policemen inform her that husband has been killed. In the composition, she shows her bare legs behind a portière and wears shorts and a pair of slippers.

According to Laura Mulvey's notion of the "female as image, male as bearer of looking,"[20] substituting a close-up of part of a woman's body in place of her whole image is a classic strategy through which the dangerous woman is turned into a fetish object. Male audiences' voyeurism is thus satisfied by gazing at that fetish object—an anonymous woman's bare legs through a portière—before the camera moves into the room.

The next scene is a static long shot in which the heroine sits between three standing plainclothes officers in an untidy and narrow room, weeping with her face covered because of her husband's grisly murder and because she is being investigated by the police. She wears loungewear and slippers without any jewelry, and has short, black, and straight hair.

Figure 9.1: Wu Zhizhen's first appearance in *Black Coal, Thin Ice* (2013).

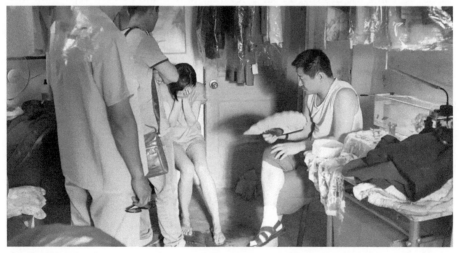

Figure 9.2: Wu Zhizhen is consoled by plainclothes police officers in *Black Coal, Thin Ice* (2013).

This appearance is quite different from the classic Hollywood femme fatale's seductive appearance, with big curls, red lipstick, high heels, and a close-fitting dress. It is a condensed sequence that portrays a woman who looks vulnerable and innocent, with an implicitly seductive feature—bare legs—when she is facing the male policemen, the typical symbol of masculine power and the state apparatus. Even though she has not yet shown her face in this scene, the setting still indicates that the young widow has to passively face up to a male-dominated society and deal with the death of her husband in the story that follows. Male policemen not only represent the powerful political system but also imply the oppression of a patriarchal society. Here the vulnerable woman is centered in the frame, surrounded and investigated by three male policemen, passively responding to their questions—with two men standing in the foreground, suggesting their dominance over her.

In the plot that follows, after the funeral Zhang Zili and his fellow policeman witness the heroine burying her husband's ashes under a tree outside the dry cleaner's shop where she works. In this static long shot from Zhang's subjective view, she wears a T-shirt and trousers and still does not show her face.

Wu's next appearance in the narrative is five years later. On a winter day, she rides a bicycle and is followed by several plainclothes policemen in a car. One policeman tells Zhang that after the death of Wu's husband she has had two boyfriends in these five years, who were both murdered in succession after they went ice skating; their bodies had been dismembered. They suspect Wu is involved. In this sequence, through the windshield, Wu is followed and gazed at by the male policemen until she enters the dry cleaner's shop. Afterward, Zhang decides to interfere in the case because he is interested in this mysterious woman and the serial murders that surround her.

The first meeting between Zhang and Wu is inside the dry cleaner's shop, twenty-five minutes into the film, and it is also the first time Wu shows her face. She is thin, wears a grey turtleneck, has short, straight, black hair, wears no make-up, and looks introverted and taciturn.

In these four scenes, the heroine is close to the center of composition and always in the male's gaze, surrounded by men or conversing with the male protagonist. It could be argued that she plays a passive role, to be gazed at by both the male protagonist and the audience; however, that gaze is often more of a curious nature than an explicitly erotic one. The heroine's face has been deliberately hidden until she has dialogue with Zhang, which might imply a neglect or a denial of her seductiveness for the male characters and audiences. Moreover, until the indoor scene in the dry cleaner's shop, Zhang and Wu never share the same space in the framing. That absence makes Wu's image look ambivalent: even though the narrative implies that she might be a deadly woman, her appearance is too ordinary and inexpressive to attract male protagonists. Such invisible seductiveness also exemplifies Wu's powerless status; she looks more like an innocent who is incapable of dominance in her own life.

Wu's lipstick, then, signals a change in her appearance and in the narrative. For her date with Zhang, she wears a red sweater and puts on lipstick in her workplace, even though her husband was killed by the police. Thus, the color red becomes a metaphor for the blood spilled on her account and refers to her status as a femme fatale. Although she looks vulnerable, innocent, mysterious, and oppressed—like a woman who was passively involved in the previous murder cases—in this scene the red lipstick implies her potential power and desire and an expectation for romance. In contrast, the only female character who looks like typical femme fatale in the film is the wife of the nightclub owner, and she is simply innocent and sorrowful when she mentions her vanished husband. Therefore, the Chinese femme fatale's potential power and desire often cannot be clearly discerned by the typical femme fatale's iconography. Instead, men can be confused by her ordinary appearance and trust that she is innocent and vulnerable.

That misrecognition might illustrate why women in Chinese neo-noir usually dress themselves to meet conservative standards: they are not allowed to deliberately show their feminine glamour and potential power. The male's erotic gaze, therefore, is also denied because the female character's sexy image is absent. In other words, the ordinary appearance of the femme fatale in most cases does not arouse the male protagonists' sexual desire. The conservative iconography of the Chinese femme fatale in neo-noir in this way reflects the male protagonists' powerlessness because the male's voyeuristic gaze is also rarely shown on screen. As a result, the Chinese femme fatale in neo-noir is portrayed as a voiceless woman who belongs to the working class and is subordinate to men in her relationships. However, she is also mysterious, dangerous, and tricky, and her oppressed status in a patriarchal society allows her crimes to seem reasonable. Thus, the femme fatale's ordinary visual image suggests her potential danger and desire in Chinese cultural contexts.

The Chinese femme fatale also often attracts downtrodden male protagonists, because she is often weaker than male protagonists in terms of social class and suffers from bullying and oppression, eliciting a protective and yet also exploitative response from them. When these male protagonists protect subordinate female characters, their sense of gender superiority is developed, boosting their self-confidence. In other words, these downtrodden male protagonists in neo-noir do not fear the tricky femme fatale, even though they know this pitiful woman is utilizing them for her own private goals. In Chinese neo-noir, the femme fatale's sexuality mostly derives from her reliance on men; the femme fatale is a psychological consolation for male protagonists, who would still love to repay the femme fatale in their own ways. However, both men's and women's sexual desire remains repressed and concealed in their relationship, and their libido is not the direct motive for their crimes in the story.

In this way, the Chinese femme fatale's implicit sexuality on screen is the crucial feature that differentiates her from the classic Hollywood femme fatale. Her seductiveness might be more psychological and reasonable in Chinese cultural contexts as a response to her low class standing and gender oppression. In mainland Chinese neo-noir, women's silhouettes are sometimes displayed but they are never deliberately naked for the purpose of arousing male desire; women's appearance is often ordinary, and their sexuality is too implicit to visually attract male protagonists. In other words, unlike the classic Hollywood femme fatale—who has a beautiful, sexy, and mysterious appearance—as a generic character, the Chinese femme fatale is mostly discerned through the storyline and her iconography, often related to black, straight hair; casual clothes and shoes; and an innocent face without makeup. In Chinese neo-noir storylines, male protagonists often dominate their relationships with the femme fatale and control these female characters because they believe these women need their protection. Briefly, although those male protagonists in Chinese neo-noir are also oppressed by authorities in a patriarchal society, female characters are still portrayed as being weaker than them and as needing their help. Women's reliance on male protection results in female characters choosing to utilize male protagonists for their personal goals. Simultaneously, psychologically disturbed male protagonists are compensated through the relationship, regardless of whether the woman is glamorous or attractive. Indeed, those psychologically disturbed male protagonists in Chinese neo-noir, like Zhang in *Black Coal, Thin Ice*, generally live in a lower social class and face masculine anxieties and crises; however, they can assuage these anxieties through their complex relationship with the femme fatale. Thus, these weak female characters and their reliance on men might boost the desire of the male protagonists when the men actively help them.

The scene on the Ferris wheel is the crucial narrative sequence in the whole film and is filled with emotional tension. On the amusement ride, Wu kisses Zhang actively and they have intense sex in a narrow space. In that intense sex scene, Zhang shows his violence and strong libido as he pushes Wu down on the seat while she passively caters to his offense. Wu's sexual pleasure is still invisible during this sequence, even though she shows some initiative at his request. Wu is completely controlled by Zhang, not only by having sex but also by revealing the crimes she committed. So, in this male-dominated sex scene, the femme fatale figure finally loses her ability to manipulate men, subordinating herself to men's erotic desire. Also, because she is a guilty, ordinary single woman who only put makeup on for the date night, the domineering sex on the Ferris wheel seems to be rationalized as a moral punishment and a compensation for these two alienated protagonists.

The next scene takes place in a small breakfast restaurant, implying that Zhang and Wu have spent the entire night together: Wu sits and inclines toward Zhang, the composition showing that they share a common psychological space, with Wu relying on Zhang. She has not yet finished her breakfast and picks up her lipstick, asking Zhang, "Want to meet up again tonight?" Her line suggests that she is beginning to rely on the man and feels satisfied with the sex last night—her repressed sexual desire has been released in their sexual relationship. Afterward, Wu is arrested by the police at the dry cleaner's shop, and Wu and Zhang never see each other again in the film. The narration demonstrates that the femme fatale's sexual pleasure has been oppressed by the patriarchal society. By contrast, Zhang not only acquires her sex and reliance but also successfully regains his position as a policeman by revealing her crimes.

Unlike the classic Hollywood femme fatale that Straayer terms "greedy, crazy and unexplainable,"[21] the Chinese femme fatale does not seem to show a soaring desire for money. In the film, a working-class couple commits a murder because they cannot afford ¥28,000 compensation for a destroyed fur coat, and the husband, Liang, could not protect his wife from harassment because they both live at the bottom of a rigid social hierarchy. The only way for them to resist is murder. On the contrary, classic Hollywood femme fatales are inclined to manipulate male protagonists to commit crimes via their sexuality, and their primary motive is money; they are never satisfied with what they already have. After the femme fatale and the man manipulated by her jointly conduct their crimes, those women often choose to break away from the man and seek money and power independently. However, in Black Coal, Thin Ice, Wu's desire is more complex, combining sex, money, safety, protection, love, and marriage. She works in a lower-paid position as a laundress, endures sexual harassment from her dry-cleaner boss, is monitored by her "dead" husband on the sly, and has to deal with other men's pursuit. Consequently, female power is absent in Black Coal, Thin Ice: the deadly woman, unlike the mysterious, gorgeous, and sexy classic femme fatales in modern cities, could not threaten masculinity. It might be said that they in fact represent the living conditions of the overwhelming majority of Chinese women, and their choice of committing crime seems reasonable in the story.

The Absence of Love and Family

The absence of romantic love and normal family life in contemporary Chinese film noir challenges assumptions around domesticity in post-socialist China. Arguably, the "Chinese Dream" could be regarded as the dominant ideology in contemporary China and has become a mainstream value in official Chinese cultural contexts. That phrase was officially used by the government after Xi Jinping was inaugurated as president of the PRC, and mirrors forecasts that the PRC will fully achieve modernization and become a developed country by 2049.[22] Thus, the Chinese Dream became a new official slogan indicating the current direction of development in the Chinese Reform era. The Chinese Dream is thus embodied in the ideological system of current Chinese film genres, as they depict a safe, wealthy, and urbanized imaginary space. In other words, the Chinese Dream generally affirms that most people will live a happy life and their conflicts can be solved appropriately by state organizations, an ideal that is constructed by the mainstream media and emphasized on screen.

According to Chris Berry's discussion of the PRC as a post-socialist country, the reappearance of love and romantic themes on screen is an important phenomenon in post-socialist, Chinese cinemas.[23] Berry argues that romantic love and the family emerged on mainland screens after the Cultural Revolution and became a common theme presenting liberalism in China during the 1980s.[24] Romantic love, free marriage, and happy families in Chinese films released in the Reform era might signify cultural developments in post-socialist contexts.

Contemporary Chinese neo-noir, however, might not only present the decline of love and family in post-socialist cultural contexts; it might also signal a challenge to the Chinese Dream. The primary characters of Chinese neo-noir—the oppressed femme fatale and downtrodden male protagonist—live in old city blocks or rural areas, suffer from bullying, work in low-paid and low-status jobs, and commit crime to alleviate the financial difficulties they face. Although the PRC government publicly states that complete urbanization will be fulfilled in China by 2035 and promises that citizens will enjoy a high standard of living as part of the larger 2049 modernization goal, contemporary neo-noir still reveals the harsh reality in which most Chinese people live, especially women, as represented by the femme fatale with her ordinary, non-glamorous appearance. Similar to classic Hollywood noir, romantic love and happy marriages on screen (suggesting a fantasy of happiness and a harmonious society) are absent in contemporary Chinese neo-noir, whose characters live in a tough, out-of-date, and threatening environment. The couples do not have children, never enjoy a happy family, and seem to lose the ability to love altogether. These unhappy couples represent a large number of common people in contemporary China who cannot bring up children or build an ideal family, not only because of financial constraints but also because of poverty's psychological toll. The crimes that occur in Chinese neo-noir may happen to everyone in every place because of these conditions, and the value of love, marriage, and family is undermined because nobody seems to live a happy life in this post-socialist cultural context. As this argument suggests, the masculinity crises of post-socialist Chinese culture are also not resolved in these neo-noirs.

Hollywood and mainland Chinese cinema, then, use different strategies to handle masculinity crises and the threat to patriarchal society posed by the femme fatale. The classic Hollywood femme fatale's sexuality is visually objectified and, simultaneously, punished by legal authorities in the end, re-establishing male dominance. In contrast, contemporary Chinese neo-noir's gender order hinges upon female dependence and the necessity of male rescue missions, so the femme fatale is undoubtedly subordinate to the male protagonist. These despondent male protagonists themselves cannot escape from the oppression of legal and political authorities, even after the criminal mysteries have been solved. The Chinese political system, as an invisible subject in Chinese neo-noir, positions itself in the film's sexual economy when the male's erotic gaze and the female's visual sexuality are double-denied on screen. Both male and female characters in contemporary Chinese neo-noir are spiritually oppressed by the alliance of a patriarchal society and the political system, which might be the reason that these couples lose the ability to love.

These helpless characters, therefore, struggle in the narrow spaces between the political system and patriarchal oppression, trying to find rare warmth from each other. They are inclined to escape from the narrow place but still must be captured and never able to leave their original lives in the end. Their struggle and rebellion prove meaningless in a world where love, marriage, and family just make trouble for people. Hence, contemporary Chinese neo-noir mirrors the cynical, nostalgic, and pessimistic mood of classic noir, this time in post-socialist cultural contexts. Specifically, the masculinity crisis in Chinese neo-noir generally relates to the male protagonists' lower social class and financial difficulties, which might imply, to some extent, that the underclasses in post-socialist cultural contexts are incapable of building a normal family and leading a happy life. As a result, Chinese neo-noir not only presents contemporary women's harsh living conditions in a patriarchal society, but also reveals the profound difficulties that the Chinese proletariat might face in post-socialist cultural contexts.

Finally, even if these Chinese neo-noirs show sympathy for women's challenging living conditions, a truly feminist discourse is still absent in these neo-noirs. According to Dai Jinhua's argument about women in contemporary Chinese film, there has been an absence of feminism in the cultural revolutions that took place after the PRC's establishment in 1949.[25] Dai illustrates that, although the PRC has enacted policies in many spheres to support the women's liberation movement after 1949—and even though the liberation of women has significantly changed Chinese society—a truly feminist cultural revolution that should have happened in Chinese culture has been postponed indefinitely. Dai argues that women's social and cultural positions have experienced a slow or at times rapid drop in post-Mao China after the Cultural Revolution, and contemporary women have gradually lost power and agency during the modernization process.[26] This underlying landscape in China today might be the primary reason that the Chinese femme fatale often takes on an ordinary appearance with a more implicit sexuality while relying on men to save her from oppressed living conditions, even while the femme fatale in Hollywood film noir has been considered a visual symbol of female power.

I believe that the Chinese femme fatale adheres to audiences' common-sense assumptions about most Chinese women's living conditions today; hence, the visual and narrative differences between the classic Hollywood femme fatale and the contemporary Chinese femme fatale derives not only from the uniqueness of post-socialist cultural contexts but also from the fact that feminism has not yet widely impacted social and cultural assumptions in China. In other words, Chinese women are still represented as a dependent, fragile, helpless figures in neo-noir, even though they occupy an important and powerful role in the narrative. In this way, the denial of their visual sexuality reflects the absence of female power in post-socialist cultural contexts. A typical femme fatale in millennial global neo-noir—a more independent, well-educated, forceful female figure—still hasn't reached the Chinese mainland.

Notes

1. "Chinese Film Wins Best Picture at Berlin Film Festival," *BBC News*, February 15, 2014, accessed June 18, 2017, http://www.bbc.co.uk/news/entertainment-arts-26211896.
2. That represents a significant box office success in mainland China. See "China's Box Office Takings Surge Since 2002," *China Daily*, June 6, 2014, accessed June 18, 2017, http://usa.chinadaily.com.cn/business/2014-06/06/content_17568703.htm.
3. Scott Foundas, "Film Review: 'Black Coal, Thin Ice,'" *Variety*, February 13, 2014, https://variety.com/2014/film/reviews/berlin-film-review-black-coal-thin-ice-1201099676/.
4. The seminar on *Black Coal, Thin Ice*, jointly organized by State Administration of Press, Radio, Film and Television of The People's Republic of China, China Film Art Research Centre, etc. on April 17, 2014. See Yao Rui, "A Summary on The Seminar of *Black Coal Thin Ice*," *Dangdai dianying*, no. 5 (2014): 4–43.
5. Yao, "A Summary on the Seminar of *Black Coal Thin Ice*," 41.
6. Janey Place, "Women in Film Noir," in *Women in Film Noir: New Edition*, ed. E. Ann Kaplan (London: BFI, 1998), 47–68.
7. Place, "Women in Film Noir," 54.
8. Place, "Women in Film Noir," 56.
9. Place, "Women in Film Noir," 57.
10. Helen Hanson, *Hollywood Heroines: Women in Film Noir and the Female Gothic Film* (London: I. B. Tauris, 2008), 216.
11. Sylvia Harvey, "Woman's Place: The Absent Family of Film Noir," in *Women in Film Noir: New Edition*, ed. E. Ann Kaplan (London: BFI, 1998), 35–46.
12. Yvonne Tasker, "Women in Film Noir," in *A Companion to Film Noir*, ed. Andrew Spicer and Helen Hanson (Chichester: Wiley-Blackwell, 2013), 356.
13. Chris Straayer, "Femme Fatale or Lesbian Femme: Bound in Sexual Différance," in *Women in Film Noir: New Edition*, ed. E. Ann Kaplan (London: BFI, 1998), 155.
14. Straayer, "Femme Fatale or Lesbian Femme," 153.
15. Samantha Lindop, *Postfeminism and the Fatale Figure in Neo-Noir Cinema* (Basingstoke: Palgrave Macmillan, 2015), 57.
16. Lindop, *Postfeminism and the Fatale Figure in Neo-Noir Cinema*, 57.
17. Tasker, "Women in Film Noir," 367.
18. Helen Hanson, "The Big Seduction: Feminist Film Criticism and the *Femme Fatale*," in *The Femme Fatale: Images, Histories, Contexts*, ed. Helen Hanson and Catherine O'Rawe (Basingstoke: Palgrave Macmillan, 2010), 225.
19. "Annual by Province: Average Wage of Employed Staff and Workers in Urban Units (yuan)," National Bureau of Statistics of China, accessed June 18, 2017, http://data.stats.gov.cn/english/easyquery.htm?cn=E0103.
20. Laura Mulvey, *Visual Pleasure and Narrative Cinema* (Basingstoke: Palgrave Macmillan, 1989), 21.
21. Straayer, "Femme Fatale or Lesbian Femme," 158.

22. Xi Jinping uses this phrase to describe "the great rejuvenation of the Chinese nation" in modern history; see Robert Lawrence Kuhn, "Xi Jinping's Chinese Dream," *The New York Times*, June 4, 2013, accessed June 18, 2017, http://www.nytimes.com/2013/06/05/opinion/global/xi-jinpings-chinese-dream.html.

23. Chris Berry, *Postsocialist Cinema in Post-Mao China* (New York: Routledge, 2008), 100.

24. Berry, *Postsocialist Cinema in Post-Mao China*, 107.

25. Dai Jinhua, "Invisible Women: Women in Contemporary Chinese Cinema and Cinema of Female," *Dangdai dianying*, no. 6 (1994): 37–45.

26. Dai Jinhua, "Invisible Women," 39.

Part IV

Film Markets and Financial Reform

10

The China Film Co., Ltd. and the Stock Market

Financialization with Chinese Characteristics

Shiying Liu

The post-Reform era (1978 to present), particularly the post–World Trade Organization (WTO) era (2001 to present), has seen China become the second-largest film market in the world by box office standards.[1] At the same time, the country's film industry has shifted from a fully state-owned studio system producing political propaganda and pedagogical films to a market-oriented, profit-driven industry with a significant, privately owned production sector. As part of this reform, the key role played by the important China Film Group Corporation (CFGC) has also been transformed. Originally founded by the government in 1951 as China Film Management (*Zhongguo Yingpian Jingli Gongsi*) to exclusively distribute films around the nation,[2] it was also exclusively responsible for importing and exporting films.[3] In 1999, it was conglomerated with seven other state-owned film studios and companies, and renamed CFGC. After the corporation failed to go public, a shareholding conglomerate, China Film Co., Ltd. (CFC), was founded in 2010—containing film production, distribution, and exhibition sections as well as most of CFGC's business and valuable properties—for release on the stock market. Since 2016, when the CFC went public, CFGC has been its biggest shareholder.

This transformation suggests a change in management style and the way in which the old state-owned corporation sought financial support, as Chinese cinema transitioned into an era of commodified globalization after China joined the WTO in 2001. The WTO is a flag-bearer of a capitalist system that is controlled by transnational corporations and financial magnates. This international institution was originally founded to regulate global finance and trade from which the State highly benefited.[4] For film industries, globalization is synonymous with Americanization, since Hollywood is the globally dominant film industry; joining the WTO meant that Chinese film industries had to compete with Hollywood not only in terms of films but also capital flow for both production and film exhibition. Scholars and industrial practitioners have long expressed their fear of foreign films and capital routing indigenous film industries. When China began to import foreign films, Chinese scholar Dai Jinhua predicted that "the wolf is coming."[5] Indeed, around 2000, Hollywood blockbusters took approximately two-thirds of the Chinese film market's revenue.[6] When China joined the WTO, it was then a case of "the wolves are here."[7]

However, with two decades of development, the Chinese film industry has expanded rapidly, especially since 2010. Recent years have witnessed China playing an increasingly influential role in global film industries due to its audience market and financial power.[8] Further, the Chinese government has boosted joint film production to decrease the cultural trade deficit.[9] Undoubtedly, consisted of audiences from the People's Republic of China (PRC) and overseas, the global Chinese market is the biggest market, comparable to Hollywood.[10] Moreover, it is the foundation for emerging Chinese media conglomerates with the potential to shake Hollywood's hegemony.[11] The central question is, therefore, how does the national film industry redeploy its creative resources and lead Chinese films to "go out" and serve the "vast and increasingly wealthy Global China market"—and further, improve the visibility of China's image among global audiences?[12]

The CFGC, a key player, changed its strategies to sustain its influence in this post-WTO era. Many scholars have shed light on the relationship between CFGC and the national film industry. Emilie Yueh-yu Yeh and Darrell William Davis's article analyses the conglomeration of CFGC as a way for the state to re-nationalize and transnationalize Chinese cinema.[13] They argue that CFGC utilizes market mechanisms to sustain its dominant power and status in the film industry, accompanied by the government's protectionist policies.[14] In support of this argument, Yi Lu suggests that by corporatizing and conglomerating CFGC, the state facilitates its status as a leading media conglomerate and monopolizes the film industry.[15] This arrangement creates a special model for Chinese film corporations, which combine the Hollywood business model and SOEs' (state-owned enterprises) reform experience. To engage with Hollywood, Wendy Su and Aynne Kokas both propose Sino-Hollywood co-relations as a form of "competitive cooperation," used by the government to transform the cultural industry and enhance China's soft power around the world.[16] All in all, while the management style and strategies of the state's corporations are changing, the logic remains unchanged. CFGC sustains its leading role in the indigenous film industries and enhances soft power by maneuvering its market power.

Following this logic, this chapter revisits the history of CFGC and considers how and why China Film Co., Ltd. (CFC) became a listed company in 2016. Further, this chapter assesses the implications of this progression for the development of the Chinese film industry. CFGC is the biggest shareholder of CFC, and CFC was founded in 2010 purposely for the intial public offering (IPO).[17] The first time Beijing Film Studio—later integrated into CFGC—attempted to go public in 1993, it failed due to a lack of government approval. Between 2004 and 2016, CFGC and CFC tried three times to go public and list itself on the stock market, finally succeeding in 2016. Such a collaboration between CFGC and CFC prompts various questions. What challenges did they have to overcome in order to become listed on the stock market? What were the main benefits and opportunities from making the company public, and what changes have been brought about by these developments? Before CFGC entered the stock market, the Huayi Brothers Media Group (2009), Enlight Media (2011), the Wanda Group (2014), and other private media corporations had already listed themselves on the stock market. Compared to their experiences, what does CFGC's listing tell us about the direction and rationale behind this state-owned corporation's financialization?

Combining CFGC's historical materials, CFC's financial reports and prospectuses, and other multimedia resources, this chapter traces the past attempts of this company to go public and explains the impact of CFC's listing on the stock market. I argue that to go public is to make the state-owned corporation part of the Party-State's endeavor to incorporate capital power, sustain domestic hegemonic control, and enhance the visibility of China's image around the world. Thus, it contributes fresh insight into scholarly understanding of the development of Chinese cinema in contemporary times when the government tried to build a stronger film industry, both competing and collaborating with Hollywood. Hollywood has been the main global force for the Chinese film industry due to its influence on both film aesthetics and production practices. Financialization in the Chinese film industry is a significant step at a time when Chinese films entered the Hollywood-dominated global film market and produced Hollywoodized blockbusters with Chinese characteristics. The next section explains the history of CFGC and the challenges it confronted during the marketization process of the film industry as the precondition of the IPO event.

China Film Group Corporation: History and Challenges

CFGC is embedded throughout the PRC era's film history. The company's name changed several times and was consolidated with other film units; however, it has served the state's interests and retained a controlling role for the whole industry from the very beginning. CFGC was founded in 1951 as China Film Management Corporation (*Zhongguo yingpian jingli gongsi*) to exclusively distribute films around the nation.[18] Consolidated with the Exhibition Circus Management Office, which was previously owned by the film bureau, the company became China Film Distribution and Exhibition Company in 1958 (*Zhongguo dianying faxing fangying gongsi*). In the planned economy, CFGC bought films produced by the state-owned studios and covered the cost of film copies and promotional items such as posters; local film companies would then submit their revenue to CFGC. The company was also responsible for importing films from socialist countries and exporting Chinese films abroad. Post market reform, this company remains the largest state-owned and

-run film company, playing a significant role in the film industry. CFGC adjusted its strategies to mediate the production sector and exhibition sector, and in 1999 it merged with seven other state-owned studios or corporations and became the media conglomerate known as China Film Group Corporation (*Zhongying jituan*).[19]

The conglomeration of CFGC was a top-down measure, since the government had to confront the serious situation of the film market becoming increasingly competitive with more private and foreign films. Hollywood films' popularity in the global film market, including China, defined the quality and standard of a blockbuster for international filmgoers.[20] The industry's structure and the market practices of Hollywood therefore became a model for the Chinese film industry to emulate, as Chinese films were targeted at both local and global audiences.[21]

With four decades of development, the industry has transformed and become more dynamic with more private capital and companies involved in. The films themselves have become more oriented toward a mass audience and profitability, with a shift toward younger middle-class filmgoers as their target audience. In years past, films tended to be educational and didactic; nowadays films are more diversified and entertaining with a broader range of genres, such as animation, sci-fi, main melody films (films that embody official ideologies), and so on. Films can offer both a joyful and entertaining experience as well as profound meaning. Many Chinese commercial films adopt Hollywood storytelling or mise-en-scène to tell Chinese stories. Even the main melody genre combines commercial and propaganda elements, since they have to attract an audience willing to pay to watch the films, instead of showing them to the public for free for educational purposes as in the planned economy era. Further, with large amounts of capital flowing into the film industry, there has been a rise in big-budget Chinese blockbusters characterized by special effects and famous actors. The changes to Chinese films are the result of the film industry's transformation, which includes the changing role of the government, the corporatization of the film companies, the emergence of new audiences growing up in a consumer culture, and the newly emerged media conglomerates in the private sector. These factors are embedded in the broader economic shift from 1978 onward, Deng Xiaoping's economic reform, and the "opening up" of China to the world economy.

Coping with market reform has been a long struggle for the Chinese film industry, which must balance the different goals of state propaganda and mass audience appeal. Failure to attract audiences has rendered the film studios barely financially sustainable under the old film-production management system. In the command economy era (the early 1950s to the early 1980s), film production was treated as a political assignment, since films were propaganda tools. Studios received government funding and were assigned certain films in accordance with their production capacity and specialties. China Film Management Corporation (later CFGC) purchased films dependent upon cost rather than film quality or their potential market value.[22] After the Cultural Revolution, sixteen state-owned studios produced 120 to 150 films according to the annual plan; CFGC then purchased the film prints from the studios for a flat fee and distributed them. In 1984, the state began to urge the studios to become financially sustainable.[23] However, given that the industrial reform only happened in the distribution and exhibition sector, studios were unable to obtain any share of the revenue. Thus, the whole industry kept losing audiences and money. The number of filmgoers dropped from 27 billion in 1979 to 14.39 billion in 1991, and many film-related enterprises were closed or converted into other businesses.[24] It was not until 1993 that reform reached the production sector, thus connecting film production with the market. For example, Policy Document No. Three, issued by the Ministry of Radio, Film and Television, allowed studios to sell their films directly to local distribution units (provincial or municipal distribution corporations) without operating via CFGC.[25]

To bring the audience back and revitalize the film industry, the Chinese government made the decision to import only ten revenue-sharing foreign films per year, starting in 1995. This regulation initiated negotiations between global and local forces. WTO regulations required China to increase its import quota from ten to twenty films, allowing for a 49 percent shareholding of cinema ownership and the audiovisual market for foreign investors.[26]

On the one hand, global forces relieved the pressure of lack of capital and essentially saved the Chinese film industry, as Hollywood films have drawn audiences back to the cinema. Over time, the Hollywood film style has influenced audiences' tastes and this formulaic Hollywood blockbuster style has become a standard for a qualified film.

On the other hand, these changes had the potential to swallow the fragile domestic industries. China had to build a strong film industry and provide films with comparable quality to imported ones. Feeding China's own market was a strategy often used to boost a certain industry, since the country's large population meant it had an equally sizeable market. Along with the emergent, younger middle-class audience and popularity of consumer culture, the Chinese film industry has boomed in the post-WTO era. With rapid marketization and commercialization of society and industries, capital from non-media sectors has flowed into the film industry and boosted its development.[27] For example, Wanda Group, a prestigious real-estate company, opened a media corporation in 2009. Beginning as an exhibition company, it grew into a media conglomerate with businesses ranging from the production to exhibition sectors. Wanda purchased the theater chain AMC Entertainment and the Hollywood studio Legendary Pictures in 2012 and 2016, respectively, suggesting that with capital flowing both in and from Hollywood, the Chinese film industry was well-integrated into the global film industry.[28]

Financialization therefore becomes more significant. With more flexible capital and talent, private media corporations had an increased share in the film market. For instance, in 2014, the net profits of Huayi Brothers Media Group and Wanda Cinemas were both over RMB 800 million.[29] However, the net profit for CFGC was only RMB 494 million,[30] and CFGC's controlling role was therefore severely undermined. To regain its dominant status, CFGC had to transform its old state-owned enterprise (SOE) management system, optimize its resources, eliminate the inevitable burdens of being a state-owned enterprise, and make big-budget films that were more visible. Going public was necessary. Financializing this large state-owned, state-run film corporation, however, was not smooth sailing.

The Path to CFC's Initial Public Offerings

CFC's very first attempt to go public can be traced to 1993, when Beijing Film Studio prepared to cooperate with private enterprise to launch itself on the Chinese stock market.[31] This event reflected the continuing decentralization of the film industry, as part of a larger trend. Deng Xiaoping gave a speech during his Southern Tour in 1992, considered a milestone, in which he proposed a notion of a "socialist market economy" and suggested that the practice of development should transcend the ideological debate about whether China is on a socialist or a capitalist route.[32] The speech emphasized the function of the market and called for bolder steps of mar-ketization.[33] Within this context, the film industry experienced a structural overhaul to tackle the conflict between the market-oriented distribution-exhibition system and the government-planned production system.[34] In January 1993, the Ministry of Radio, Film and Television issued Policy Document No. Three, which connected the production sector directly to the market by allowing studios to negotiate print prices and profit-sharing arrangements.[35]

In the same year, Beijing Film Studio signed a contract with the Ministry of Finance, promising that the studio would make a profit instead of losing money, that it would be responsible for finishing a certain number of films, and that it would improve film quality to attract audiences. As a result, the studio changed its method of financing film production from being dependent on government funding to raising capital from the private sector and foreign investment, as well as using its own funds. It was this autonomy that made Beijing Wantong Industrial Co., Ltd. visit Beijing Film Studio in 1993 and propose starting a new company funded in part by public shares.

In 1991, Feng Lun co-founded a real estate company in the Hainan Special Economic Zone with five other people, turning 30,000 yuan into 50 million by the end of 1992.[36] The next year, he withdrew from Hainan and founded Beijing Wantong Industrial Co.[37] Later, Wantong became one of the most profitable private real estate companies with a large market share. It offered Beijing Film Studio a wealth of capital to make films and promised that it would not intervene with the film production process; at the time, Wantong planned to construct a cinema chain for the studio. The director of Beijing Film Studio Cheng Zhigu took Warner Brothers Studios as an example to express the importance of owning a cinema chain, and Feng Lun and Pan Shiyi confirmed that they shared the same goal. Since they owned a real estate company, they would build cinemas in different-sized cities and aim to create their own "Eastern Hollywood."[38] This plan showed the initial idea of and potential for achieving vertical integration. There were also plans for other projects to expand their business in following three years: first, to build an international film culture center including a cinema, apartment building, office building, conference center, and hotel in the film studio; and second, to construct a film cultural business center, including a state-of-the-art building for both residential and business purposes, luxury apartments, shopping malls, theaters, and restaurants in the Xiaoxitian Temple area where CFGC was located.

These plans seemed profitable and practical; however, they were premature and ultimately not realized because of the cumbersome procedure involved in getting approval from various government branches. According to He Zengxi, the secretary of Beijing Film Studio at the time, the company had drafted four application documents for various agencies: the Feasibility Report of Beijing Film Studio's Joint-Stock System Reorganization; the Initiators Agreement of Restructuring and Establishing Beijing Film Studio Co., Ltd.; the Input and Output Analysis after Beijing Film Studio's Joint-Stock System Reorganization in Three Years; and the Application of Restructuring and Establishing the Beijing Film Studio Co., Ltd. These documents showed the motivation and potential for the studio to bring in private capital and achieve their ambitions. Two vice ministers of the Department of Radio, Film, and Television, Tian Congming and He Dongcai, visited Beijing Film Studio and discussed the IPO issue; both approved and encouraged this plan. While it was also approved by other state branches, including the national Economic Trade Committee, the plan was abandoned when a previous member of the Political Bureau of the CPC Central Committee, Li Tieying, asked them whether the Publicity Department of the Communist Party had given approval and suggested they postpone the IPO.

As a result, the first attempt to create the largest state-owned studio failed to incorporate private capital given the complicated administrative barriers at different government levels. The studio was still stuck between the old system and the market incentivized mechanism. The director Cheng Zhigu commented that this was unfortunate, since the plan was not well timed. At that time, the government was still somewhat conservative in its approach to opening the film market and strict regarding private capital entering the film production sector, particularly given films' historical function as the main apparatus for the party to maintain its political and ideological control.

The whole process of privatization and corporatization of the media industry lagged behind other strategically significant sectors like financial services, infrastructure construction, telecommunications, and energy and raw materials.[39] From 1978 to 1993, most of the SOEs were transformed into a modern corporate system, gaining increasing managerial autonomy and later separating the ownership and management of the company.[40] However, the film studios were not synchronized with this development, and the film industry's reform as a whole fell behind that of other sectors. For Beijing Film Studio, ownership and management rights were interlinked. Although the studios confronted problems like low productivity, labor redundancy, and lack of funding, they exclusively owned the official rights to produce films, since it would have been too risky to share the ownership of the studios with the private sector. Film was still considered a propaganda tool; however, its economic performance needed to be improved.

Then, private investors were introduced in to the film industry. However, like outsiders, they could only coproduce films with insiders, namely, the state-owned studios, and only if they paid more than 70 percent of the production costs.[41] Per the policy issued in 1995, they were required to pay a flat administrative fee of about RMB 300,000 if they chose to coproduce with a state-owned studio.[42] Thus, the IPO plan between Wantong and Beijing Film Studio should have been abandoned: since the ownership and the management rights were not separated, Wantong would have become one of the owners of the studio had they co-founded a company limited by shares—which would be too risky for the government to allow. It was not until the founding of CFGC in 1999 that the state figured out how to develop the old studios by incorporating into media conglomerates.

Private capital was not officially allowed to enter the film industry until 2002.[43] The Regulation on Administration of Movies, issued by the State of Council at the end of 2001, ruled that the state should encourage enterprises, public institutions, social organizations, and individuals to invest in film production.[44] The government was finally expanding market access and bringing in more market and competitive mechanisms to revive the industry.

After the integration and founding of CFGC in 1999, CFGC and the newly founded CFC tried three times to list themselves on the stock market between 2004 to 2016, with CFC finally succeeding in 2016. The first time CFGC planned to go public was in Hong Kong in 2004, with their decision driven primarily by capital imperative. However, it was not approved by the government due to the restriction on introducing foreign capital into mainland China. In 2008, for the second time, CFGC failed to list itself on the stock market due to the prevailing global financial crisis.

State policy dictated the direction for state-owned film corporations and shaped the film industry. After the State Council issued a plan to elevate the film industry as a national strategy in 2009, it issued guidance the following year on promoting film industry prosperity that provided policies to boost investment and financing.[45] One policy breakthrough was to offer solutions for financing film production and encouraging eligible state-owned corporations to go public and seek private capital,[46] signaling a broader change in the film industry, which began to extend financing channels and share the risks of film production. For example, the policy suggested that large corporations invest in film production through participation by or holding shares. Local governments could use the medium- and small-sized enterprises' investment fund to support film venture capital, thus accelerating enterprise restructuring, corporatization, and joint-stock reform for the government-affiliated film institutional units. Further, it would support a few state-owned corporations in taking the larger share of the market, boosting a range of specialized small- and medium-sized enterprises.

Following this policy, CFC was founded in 2010, with the approval of the Publicity Department of the Communist Party and the State Administration of Press, Publication, Radio, Film, and Television of the PRC. This new company comprised services in all production, distribution, and exhibition sectors, including businesses in film equipment production and sales, projection system rental, and brokerage.[47]

CFC was founded as a way of integrating the superior resources of CFGC and helping CFGC shake off its historical burden. In the planned-economy era, SOEs were responsible for job security and social protection for their staff by offering housing and health care instead of pursuing profit as a priority. SOEs were known as "iron rice bowls" (tiefanwan), as their staff would normally work for the company their whole lives. Further, SOEs provided pensions and other welfare benefits like health care and subsidies for their retired staffs. As an old SOE, CFGC still had the burden of taking care of more than 2,000 retired staff, although it had reduced the number of employees on different occasions during the market reform; the government transformed its pension scheme to release SOEs of this burden.[48]

Initially, CFC took over the rights to import and distribute revenue-sharing foreign films from CFGC, which was a clearly profitable business. However, in 2012, the Memorandum of Understanding between the People's Republic of China and the United States of America Regarding Films for Theatrical Release (MOU) added fourteen 3D and IMAX films, and increased the commission split rate from 17.5 percent to 25 percent for American production companies.[49] This change made the business less profitable and riskier for Chinese companies, since the cost of distributing films was increasing; at this time, CFGC stopped making CFC complete this job on a commission basis.

Compared to CFGC, CFC is more business-oriented. The two companies are both located geographically close to each other in Beijing; however, according to a current staff member of CFC, there are actually not that many connections between the two at a business level.[50] From the style of the buildings and their surroundings, they are quite different. CFGC is situated close to the China Film Archive, China Film Research Center, and China International Cinema, suggesting a closer connection with historical properties and the old system. In contrast, CFC is located in an enterprise center surrounded by other media companies. The CCTV-Film Channel is, however, on the other side of the CFC building, as the two have a 10-year business contract in place from 2012 to 2021, stipulating that the Film Channel purchase films produced by CFC.[51] A film-themed café with sculptures of famous film characters on the ground floor complements CFC's more business-oriented company culture.

After experiencing a series of asset appraisals and structural reforms, CFC published its prospectus in 2014, but it was rejected by the CSRC (China Securities Regulatory Commission) for insufficient information. In the same year, however, President Xi Jinping raised the issue of China's cultural soft power again in an article in the *People's Daily* entitled "Build Socialist Culture to Strengthen the Nation, Focus on Improving the Country's Cultural Soft Power."[52] He proposed efforts to "strengthen construction of international broadcasting capacity, meticulously construct external discourse, exhibit up-and-coming media activity, increase the creativity, inspiration, and accountability of external discourse, tell Chinese stories well, broadcast Chinese voices, and explain Chinese characteristics properly,"[53] thus encouraging Chinese media companies to improve production capabilities in order to enhance China's soft power.

The turning point happened for CFC in 2015 when its IPO took on a new sense of urgency as shooting began on *The Great Wall* (*Changcheng*, dir. Zhang Yimou, 2016). Produced by Legendary Pictures, Universal Pictures, Dalian Wanda, and CFC, the film was originally a Hollywood investment in China. However, after Wanda purchased Legendary Pictures during the production process in 2016, the film became a Chinese investment in Hollywood.[54] Although China has been taking advantage of its audience size and financial power to circulate the image of China around the world, that image of China is homogeneous and shaped by state policy soft-power objectives.[55] As a state-run film corporation, CFC has responsibility for presenting the image of China and the party as well as improving the quality of its films to make them popular among audiences. Thus, it registered itself on the stock market to position itself within the process of further capitalization to achieve its ambition of promoting a state-approved Chinese culture around the world.

The Great Wall was a significant attempt at Chinese cultural exportation, one made by collaborating with Hollywood studios and offering CFC a chance at an IPO. It created a new model of film production that comprised a popular Hollywood genre, Chinese cultural elements, and studio funding to achieve a Chinese propaganda purpose. Combining martial arts with science fiction, the film portrays the story of brave Chinese soldiers who collaborate with two unscrupulous Western powder traders to protect the nation on the Great Wall against alien monsters from the periphery. During the war, trust is built between the two Western traders and the Chinese soldiers, and with the power of the Chinese political leaders and their military skills, they finally overcome the alien monsters. Judging from the content, CFC had an obligation to produce this kind of Hollywood-style blockbuster.

The heads of production companies and the above-the-line creative laborers of the film had high expectations for the influence and commercial value of this collaboration, as it came with a big budget, big stars, and talent from both Hollywood and China. It was targeted not only at Chinese audiences but also global filmgoers.

Director Zhang Yimou said in an interview that he decided to direct this film is because the film tells a Chinese story with Chinese values to global audiences which is a rare chance for a director.[56] Also, if the film did well financially, there would be more films in succession.[57] Thus, this film was a chance for CFC to gain more influence and financial value, which would positively impact its stock price. In subsequent years, CFC also invested in the Disney film *Mulan* (dir. Niki Caro, 2020), which is based on a Chinese folk tale and features one of the most popular Chinese stars, Liu Yifei, and an Asian cast. Though it did not receive a successful reception in China, the film was meant to target the Chinese film market. Eventually, having experienced two generations of CEOs—from Han Sanping to La Peikang—CFC launched itself in 2016 on the Shanghai Stock Exchange, offering 467 million one Chinese yuan shares, under the short corporation stock name of China Film and the stock ticker 600977.[58]

The next section explores the relationship between China's film industry and the nation's larger picture of financialization. It then investigates the power relations behind the corporation, in terms of the constitution of shareholders and capital management. Finally, it explores the purposes of the IPO and its offering of more CFC films that target mainland audiences as evidence of the company's attempts to incorporate more financial capital to enlarge production scale and sustain its leading role.

CFC's IPO and Financialization with Chinese Characteristics

CFC's IPO was more politically driven than it would be in a solely profit-driven corporation. CFC was launched in the A-share catergory, which trades in RMB and targets investors from the mainland. This IPO event helped CFC attract a certain segment of investors, such as other state-owned corporations, and improve its social influence while reclaiming a status befitting a large state-owned film corporation. Furthermore, CFC's IPO set a model for other state-owned film companies to follow in how they might survive in today's more competitive film industry; in fact, Shanghai Film Co., Ltd. initiated its IPO after CFC.

The IPO of CFC was a part of the state-led financialization process in which "the Chinese state refashioned itself as a shareholder and institutional investor in the economy and resorted to financial means to manage its ownership, assets and public investment."[59] Broadly, fiancialization means "the increasing importance of financial markets, financial motives, financial institutions, and financial elites in the operations of the economy . . . both at the national and international levels."[60] In liberal and developed economies, it suggests that states deregulate policies and let the market play a bigger role. However, China's model tells a different story. In China's case, financialization refers to "a process in which the state increasingly relies on a set of financial means (financial market, financial indicators and financial instruments), to manage its assets and fund public investment."[61] It suggests that the government shift its management style from "administrative intervention and fiscal allocation to supervising its massive state assets according to shareholder value."[62] The shareholding state refers to the trend that "hundreds of state asset management bodies have sprung up across the nation in various organizational constellations— as state asset supervisory agencies, state holding corporations or state asset management and investment companies—to represent state ownership as well as manage and appreciate the value of state assets."[63] In this way, the government combines market power and political power: the state managenment agencies transfer their assets into equities and the government keeps the controlling role by taking the largest portion of the equities.

The composition of shareholders exposes the power relations among the corporations. As an illustration, this section compares and contrasts the formation of shareholders of CFC and Huayi Brothers. While CFGC holds the largest share of CFC at 67.36 percent, a figure that has held constant since 2016, most of the top ten shareholders of CFC are state-owned legal entities. CFC's 2018 annual report showed that five of the top ten shareholders were marked as state-owned legal entities and the other five were marked as "unknown"; however, tracing the ownership by their names shows that indeed they are also state-owned.[64]

Huayi Brothers Media Corporation was the first Chinese film company to be listed on the stock market. It chose to list on the Shenzhen Stock Exchange ChiNext Board on in 2009 and raised RMB 1.15 billion with 4,200 shares (stock ticker 300027).[65] Compared to CFC, the top ten investors of Huayi Brothers change from time to time but remain entities from the private sector. In 2018 these included four CEOs of private-sector companies, including Alibaba CEO Ma Yun (Jack Ma) and Huayi Brothers CEO Wang ZhongJun, three legal persons of domestic non-state-owned corporations, and three other companies.[66] The company's share price soared after the 2009 IPO, and it became China's largest private film conglomerate at that time. As a profit-driven, private company, which is more flexible with its ownership, capital could be more easily managed to help the development of the corporation. By increasing capital and shares, several prestigious directors and stars became shareholders, including Feng Xiaogang, Li Bingbing, and Huang Xiaoming.[67] In addition, there were 18,050,000 restricted IPO shares for its 136 staff as incentives, which fostered a reward mechanism. Thus, Huayi attracted creative talent who bonded their own interests with the company's interests. The corporation also raised private equity to foster its development, resulting, for example, in Tom Group joining Huayi in 2004, which formalized Huayi's internal management system and helped it form a legal framework. In 2007, Focus Media Information Technology Co., Ltd. joined Huayi and assisted with the IPO process. Throughout, the corporation always retained its share above 50.5 percent in order to maintain a controlling interest.[68]

In contrast, CFC was unable to apply business strategies that were similar to those of the private corporations, since it had restrictions on its ownership. The state had to retain the majority of shares and the state-owned corporations were likely allied with other state-owned corporations.

Before listing on the stock market, CFC had a strong capital reserve and total assets of RMB 14,358 million in 2016. From 2016 to 2018, assets increased slightly, to RMB 16,337 million; for them, going public was not only to attract more private money but also to gain influence. According to the prospectus, there were five purposes to its fundraising activities.[69] The first was to recoup the investment in film and television production (RMB 1,239 million). The second was the plan to invest in the construction of digital cinema (RMB 1,176 million), and the third, the popularization of digital distribution (RMB 1,433 million). The last two aims were to purchase the rights to manage advertising prior to film releases (RMB 240 million) and repay the 2007 China Film Group's principal loan and interest (RMB 531 million).[70] From this list, it's clear that film and TV production was a priority in CFC's development strategy; they sought to produce big-budget Chinese commercial films as well as mainstream cinema. As mentioned above, CFC lost the exclusive rights to distribute Hollywood films, since this business was not as profitable after the US-China MOU. CFC therefore looked for breakthroughs in the production sector. In the meantime, the corporation also tried to keep its advantage in the film exhibition sector by constructing more digital cinemas, since one of CFGC's most profitable businesses was its cinema chains. The digital distribution system helped supervise and oversee box office figures to prevent fabricated statistics. Thus, CFC continued to adopt the market mechanism to sustain its power in the new era, as did CFGC.

With more financial power, CFC put an increasing emphasis on producing Chinese blockbusters to attract domestic audiences, as the mainland film market is big enough for CFC's films to take their market share. These new CFC-produced blockbusters, including various main melody films like *Wolf Warrior 2* (*Zhan lang 2*, dir. Wu Jing, 2017), *The Wandering Earth* (*Liulang diqiu*, dir. Frant Gwo, 2019), and *Leap* (*Duoguan*, dir. Peter Chan, 2021), as well as commercial films like *Mermaid* (*Meirenyu*, dir. Stephen Chow, 2016) and *The Monkey King* series (*Xiyou xilie*, dir. Pou-soi Cheang, 2014, 2016, 2018) are based on Chinese culture and have been popular among young local filmgoers. These films also contribute to building up China's cultural confidence as stressed by President Xi.

Listing itself on the stock market also brought challenges to CFC. Its prospectus offered detailed financial data, including assets, investments, and other company payments, such as salaries of the director, supervisors, and senior executives. CFC was obliged to produce seasonal, half-year, and annual reports that updated investors on the latest changes inside the company management team and provided detailed financial data including financial indexes, expenditures, government subsidies, taxes, and so on. This transparency of company information helped inform potential investors about the company and facilitate its supervision. Thus, this state-owned company could get more involved in the market while keeping its economic strength within the state's control. However, how and to what level the state engaged with the film market deserves further investigation at a financial level.

One may also ask whether this quasi-state-public ownership could maintain itself as a strategy, and whether such entities could produce enough revenue to continue to exist in the era of the triumph of global capital. In other words, will CFC still maintain a state-approved "Chineseness"? My answer to these questions is yes. First, CFC contains many valuable resources such as studios, cinema chains, and the like, as well as the right to import foreign films, all of which contribute significantly to its revenue. CFC could then attract potentially profitable projects or projects promoting—and thus cooperating—with state-approved "Chineseness" content. Furthermore, the direction of film productions has changed from propaganda-oriented to market-driven. The previous CEO of CFC, Han Sanping, stated in an interview that "it is not difficult to make a film that political leaders are satisfied with; however, to make audiences feel satisfied, it is the making of an 'enjoyable' film that we will take as our understood goal."[71] Scholar Shuk-ting Kinnia Yau asserted that the "party-state ideology" buried in main melody films had become "the target of laughter and criticism or has been replaced or drowned out by commercial elements."[72] However, she neglects to consider that the ideology itself has been changed by the party to legitimize its authority according to different social conditions; whether the authorial ideology is undermined should have more to do with the broader picture of the industry. Commercialization of the main melody films suggests the importance of market performance. Second, cultural proximity theory should be considered, which presents that local audiences prefer films rooted in their own culture. Chinese films have become more popular among mainland filmgoers, winning more box office sales than the Hollywood blockbusters in the PRC.[73] Because of the increased market size and the increasing financial power in the film industry, there are more films that target Chinese audiences, including films produced by domestic film companies and Hollywood studios, and those coproduced between China and different countries.

Overall, to list CFC on the stock market was one significant step in its corporate development to maintain its leading role in the film industry. As a state-owned and -run enterprise, it is responsible for producing and supporting a state-approved "Chineseness," including both content and market share. Different from other film industries—especially Hollywood, which is aimed at maximizing profit and led by industrial practitioners—the Chinese film industry is led by the state and economic profit is not the end goal. Financialization and capitalization are approaches of marketization to achieve the goal of boosting the quality and quantity of domestic films and increasing the soft power of China in the global arena.[74] If this quasi-public strategy of CFC does not work, the company would find other ways to achieve its goal.

Conclusion

This chapter offers a linear history and analysis of CFC's IPO event, which can be viewed as a sign of the company's successful development in the market era. On the way to marketization, CFGC/CFC struggled between the old system and the new management style, as commercial and entertainment factors sometimes conflicted with political and national interests. According to this IPO case, CFC's unsuccessful attempts to go public suggest the difficulties this company had in adapting itself to the commercialized global era. Going public was a significant step for CFC to integrate into the market, reorganize its resources, build a positive image, and gain public funding. However, because the reforms of the state-owned corporations were generally initiated from the top, their reflection toward the market was generally slower than that of the private sector. Although as a state-run company CFC has abundant capital and advanced facilities, it still undergoes reforms to adapt itself into the laissez-faire economy and sustain its market power as one of the largest and most powerful film companies.

The assessment in this chapter is that China Film Co., Ltd.'s (CFC) going public is both a political maneuver that indicates the direction for state-owned film companies and a market behavior that helps the traditional state-owned companies engage with the overall market, helping to eradicate bad business decision-making, which inevitably leads to loss of profits; it enlarges the film production scale to attract domestic audiences, which also contributes to the growth of the Chinese film industry. Despite the drawbacks of the quasi-state-public ownership strategy, it can maintain itself to produce state-approved "Chineseness" in film content during an era of triumphant global capital as long as the domestic film market keeps increasing or maintains its large size.

Notes

1. "China Becomes World's Second-Biggest Movie Market," BBC News, March 22, 2013, https://www.bbc.co.uk/news/business-21891631.
2. Wang Zengfu, "Zhongying gongsi mingcheng gengdie ji zhineng de bianhua" [The changes of China Film Corporation's name and responsibilities], in *Zhongying wushinian* [*50 Years of China Film*], ed. Zhongguo dianying gongsi (Beijing: Zhongguo dianyin gongsi, 2001), 49–50.
3. Z. Wang, "Zhongying gongsi mingcheng gengdie ji zhineng de bianhua."
4. David Harvey, *A Brief History of Neoliberalism* (Oxford: Oxford University Press, 2005).
5. Wendy Su, *China's Encounter with Global Hollywood: Cultural Policy and the Film Industry, 1994–2003* (Lexington: The University Press of Kentucky, 2016), 27.
6. Su, *China's Encounter with Global Hollywood*, 19.
7. Su, *China's Encounter with Global Hollywood*, 27.
8. Su, *China's Encounter with Global Hollywood*, 27.

9. Aynne Kokas, "Producing Global China: *The Great Wall* and Hollywood's Cultivation of the PRC's Global Vision," *Journal of Chinese Cinemas* 13, no. 3 (2019): 215.

10. Michael Curtin, *Playing to the World's Biggest Audiences: The Globalization of Chinese Film and TV* (Berkeley: University of California Press, 2007), 1.

11. Curtin, *Playing to the World's Biggest Audiences*, 4.

12. Curtin, *Playing to the World's Biggest Audiences*, 3–4.

13. Emilie Yueh-yu Yeh and Darrell William Davis, "Re-nationalizing China's Film Industry: Case Study on the China Film Group and Film Marketization," *Journal of Chinese Cinemas* 2, no. 1 (2008): 37–51.

14. Yeh and Davis, "Re-nationalizing China's Film Industry."

15. Yi Lu, "Commercial Renaissance of Chinese Cinema Movie Industry Reforms, Chinese Blockbusters, and Film Consumption in a Global Age" (PhD diss., University of Texas at Austin, 2016).

16. Su, *China's Encounter with Global Hollywood*. See also Aynne Kokas, *Hollywood Made in China* (Berkeley: University of California Press, 2017).

17. China Film Co., Ltd. was founded by the CFGC allied with China International Television Corporation, China Broadcasting Corporation, Changying Group Co., Ltd, Jiangsu Broadcasting Co., Ltd., China Unicom, Beijing Gehua CATV Network Co., Ltd., and Hunan TV and Broadcast Intermediary Co., Ltd.

18. The resources of this paragraph all come from a book that was circulated internally at CFGC. "Zhongying gongsi mingcheng gengdie" [The changes of CFGC's names], in *Zhongying 50nian* [50 years of Chinese film], ed. China Film Corporation's editorial board (Beijing: 2001): 49–50.

19. The China Film Corporation integrated with other four state-owned film companies and three studios in 1999. The four companies were China Film Equipment Corporation (built in 1951), China Central Television Film Channel (CCTV-6; started in 1995), Beijing Film Developing and Video Technology Factory (started in 1960), and Huayun Film and Television Disc Co., Ltd. (founded in 1998). The three studios were Beijing Film Studio (began in 1949), Children's Film Studio (founded in 1981), and China Film Co-Production Corporation (started in 1979).

20. Ying Zhu, *Chinese Cinema during the Era of Reform: The Ingenuity of the System* (Westport, CT: Praeger, 2003).

21. Zhu, *Chinese Cinema during the Era of Reform*.

22. Ying Zhu and Seio Nakajima, "The Evolution of Chinese Film as an Industry," in *Art, Politics, and Commerce in Chinese Cinema*, ed. Ying Zhu and Stanley Rosen (Hong Kong: Hong Kong University Press, 2010), 24.

23. Su, *China's Encounter with Global Hollywood*, 14.

24. Su, *China's Encounter with Global Hollywood*, 14.

25. Zhu and Nakajima, "The Evolution of Chinese Film as an Industry," 27.

26. Yang Yuanying, "Zhongguo dianying rushi de huayu biaoda" [The discourse expression of China film enters the WTO], in *Zhoongguo dianying nianjian 2003* [China film year book 2003] (Beijing: Zhongguo dianying nianjianshe, 2003), 262.

27. Bingchun Meng, *The Politics of Chinese Media Consensus and Contestation* (New York: Palgrave Macmillan, 2018), 14.

28. Meng, *The Politics of Chinese Media Consensus and Contestation*, 98.

29. "Zhongying gufen IPO guohui nengfou chongzuo laoda" [Can China Film Group regain its leadership after its IPO?], *China Business News*, July 9, 2015, https://www.yicai.com/news/4643287.html.

30. "Zhongying gufen IPO guohui nengfou chongzuo laoda."

31. Cheng Zhigu, "Nanwang de beiying wunian" [Unforgettable five years in Beijing Film Studio], in *Zhongying Shiliao* [Historical materials of China Film Group Corporation], ed. Huang Shihua (Beijing: Zongguo dianying jituan gongsi, 2019), 1–22.

32. Meng, *The Politics of Chinese Media*, 14.

33. Meng, *The Politics of Chinese Media*, 66.

34. Zhu, *Chinese Cinema during the Era of Reform*, 83.

35. Zhu and Nakajima, "The Evolution of Chinese Film as an Industry," 27.

36. "Fenglun: Weida shi aochulai de" [Feng Lun: The great thing comes from persistence], *China News*, July 20, 2018, http://www.chinanews.com/cj/2018/07-20/8573520.shtml.

37. "Fenglun: Weida shi aochulai de."

38. Cheng, "Nanwang," 20.

39. Lu, "Commercial."

40. Lu, "Commercial."

41. Zhu and Nakajima, "The Evolution of Chinese Film as an Industry," 29.

42. Zhu and Nakajima, "The Evolution of Chinese Film as an Industry," 29.

43. Shen Yun, *Zhongguo dianying chanyeshi* [The history of Chinese film industry] (Beijing: Zhongguo dianying chubanshe, 2005), 225.

44. Shen Yun, *Zhongguo dianying chanyeshi*, 225.

45. Zhang Huijun and Yu Jianhong, eds., *Zhongguo dianying chanye fazhan baogao 2010–2011* [The China film industry annual report 2010–2011] (Beijing: China Film Press, 2011), 3.

46. Zhang and Yu, *Zhongguo dianying chanye fazhan baogao 2010–2011*, 3.

47. "Zhongguo dianying fufen youxian gongsi" [China Film Co., Ltd.], Baidu baike, accessed September 26, 2021, https://baike.baidu.com/item/中国电影股份有限公司/9119953.

48. This information comes from a private interview with a retired staff member of CFGC. Hanying Qiao, telephone interview, August 10, 2019.

49. Hou Guangming and Wu Manfang, eds., *Zhongguo dianying chanye fazhan baogao 2012–2013* [Reports on China film industry development 2012–2013] (Beijing: China Film Press, 2014), 118. The MOU can be found on the US Department of State's website: https://www.state.gov/wp-content/uploads/2019/02/12-425-China-Trade-Films-for-theatrical-release.pdf.

50. Yifei Jiao, personal communication through WeChat, August 2019.

51. China Film Co. Ltd., *Prospectus for Initial Public Offering of A Shares* (2016), 13.

52. Kokas, *Hollywood Made in China*, 20. The original article can be found on People's Daily website: http://cpc.people.com.cn/n/2014/0101/c64094-23995307.html.

53. Kokas, *Hollywood Made in China*, 20.

54. Kokas, "Producing," 1.

55. Kokas, "Producing," 1 and 2.

56. Xu Zhiyuan, Shisanyao Zhang Yimou: Renzouchaliang ni haixiang chaoyue shidai [Thirteen invitations Zhang Yimou: The tea cools donw as soon as the person is gone,

how can you think about transcend the times], Tencent Video, accessed September 26, 2021, https://v.qq.com/x/cover/o041nixzo23h6tm/b075186d94x.html.

57. Yimou Zhang, "Zhongguo wenhua ruhe jieru haolaiwu gongye" [How Chinese culture integrates into Hollywood], interview by Yang Liu, *People's Daily Online*, December 19, 2016, http://culture.people.com.cn/n1/2016/1219/c1013-28958418.html.

58. Baidu baike, "Zhongguo dianying fufen youxian gongsi" [China Film Co., Ltd.].

59. Yingyao Wang, "The Rise of the 'Shareholding State': Financialization of Economic Management in China," *Socio-Economic Review* 13, no.3 (September 2015): 603.

60. Gerald Epstein, "Financialization, Rentier Interests, and Central Bank Policy" (Paper presentation, PERI Conference on "Financialization of the World Economy," University of Massachusetts, Amherst, December 7–8, 2001), 3, http://peri.umass.edu/fileadmin/pdf/financial/fin_Epstein.pdf.

61. Yingyao Wang, "The Rise of the 'Shareholding State'," 604.

62. Yingyao Wang, "The Rise of the 'Shareholding State'," 621.

63. Yingyao Wang, "The Rise of the 'Shareholding State'," 621.

64. The top ten shareholders are CFGC, Social Security Transfer of State-Owned Shares Second Account (this is the national fund for social security for aging-related problems; the State Council sets out that every state-owned corporation should transfer 10 percent shares from IPO); China Securities Finance Co., Ltd.; China United Network Communications Group Co., Ltd.; China International Television Corporation; Yangguang Media Development Corporation; Changchun Film Group Corporation; Hong Kong Securities Clearing Company Ltd.; China Social Security Fund One Zero Five Assembly; and Industrial and Commercial Bank of China-Guangfa Jufeng Mixed Securities Investment Fund in 2018. China Film Co., Ltd, *Zhongguo dianying youxian gongsi 2018nian niandu baogao* [CFC 2018 Annual Report], 60. You can find this report via this link: http://file.finance.sina.com.cn/211.154.219.97:9494/MRGG/CNSESH_STOCK/2019/2019-4/2019-04-27/5310047.PDF.

65. CFI.CN, *Huayi xiongdi (300027) 2009nian niandu baogao* [Huayi Brothers Media Corporation (300027) 2009 Annual Report], last modified March 25, 2010, http://www.cfi.net.cn/p20100325000634.html.

66. Huayi Brothers Media, *Huayi xiongdi chuanmei gufen youxian gongsi 2018nian niandu baogao zhaiyao* [Huayi Brothers Media Corporation 2018 Annual Report Summary], 3–4, accessed August 10, 2019, http://www.cninfo.com.cn/new/disclosure/detail?plate=szse&stockCode=300027&announcementId=1206122830&announcementTime=2019-04-27.

67. Hou Guangming and Wu Manfang, *Zhongguo dianying chanye fazhan baogao 2012–2013*, 42.

68. Hou Guangming and Wu Manfang, *Zhongguo dianying chanye fazhan baogao 2012–2013*, 42.

69. China Film Co. Ltd., *Prospectus for Initial Public Offering of A Shares*, 37.

70. China Film Co. Ltd., *Prospectus for Initial Public Offering of A Shares*, 37.

71. Shuk-ting Kinnia Yau, "From *March of the Volunteers* to *Amazing Grace*: The Death of China's Main Melody Movie in the 21st Century," *Jump Cut: A Review of Contemporary Media* 59 (Fall 2019), accessed September 13, 2021, http://ejumpcut.org/archive/jc59.2019/KinnieYauMainMelody/index.html.

72. Yau, "From *March of the Volunteers* to *Amazing Grace.*"

73. Joseph Straubhaar, "Beyond Media Imperialism: Asymetrical Interdependence and Cultural Proximity," *Critical Studies in Media Communication* 8, no. 1 (March 1991): 39–59.

74. Darrell William Davis, "Market and Marketization in the China Film Business," *Cinema Journal* 49, no. 3 (2010): 123.

11
Big Shot's Funeral

Sino-Foreign Collaboration and Industrial Commercialization

Qi Ai

Introduction

Mainland Chinese "New Year Films," or *hesui pian*, are films made to screen around the New Year holiday season spanning from Christmas to the Chinese New Year. The idea of the genre came directly from the Hong Kong film industry; it was introduced into the mainland market in the mid-1990s, alongside revenue-sharing Hollywood films under the 1994 import quota system. The genre had been cultivated by the government initially to improve domestic films' competitiveness in general and to support the "9550 Project" (*Jiuwu wuling gongcheng*) in particular.[1] The project aimed to nurture excellent domestic (*jingpin*) films that were capable of rivaling Hollywood imports culturally and economically during the ninth Five-Year Plan period from 1996 to 2000.[2] Feng Xiaogang's New Year cinema features were once the only consistently profitable films in the genre and usually topped the annual mainland box office. His works therefore were considered the most promising products for fulfilling the project, at least from the late 1990s into the early 2000s.[3]

After China's entry to the World Trade Organization (WTO) in December 2001, the import quota doubled to twenty revenue-sharing films a year. The increase aroused a general sense of anxiety that pervaded the whole industry. For many Chinese film professionals, the previous quota system had already impeded the development of domestic commercial film, especially those attempting to emulate Hollywood filmmaking models; it in effect uprooted the possibility of cultivating a market for the imitations.[4] The new quota literally meant a greater challenge. Heated discussions proceeded among film intelligentsia, various suggestions were given, and more expectations were placed on Feng's New Year films.[5]

Big Shot's Funeral (*Dawan*, dir. Feng Xiaogang, 2001) was released in this context, several days after China became a full member of the WTO. The film revolves around a funeral-planning project, which Feng himself compared to a filmmaking process.[6] The film's production involved nearly all the newly emerging filmmaking forces of the day, including the state-owned China Film Group Corporation as well as the domestic private film investment company Huayi Brothers and its foreign partner, Columbia Pictures Asia. Bearing this in mind, one may see the funeral planning depicted in the film as a quasi-coproduction, a self-reflexive commentary on the interaction among these forces in the contexts of globalization.

The film tells the story of a freelance cinematographer, Yoyo (played by Ge You), working with his former colleague Louis Wang (Ying Da), the boss of a media company specializing in organizing live stage performances to plan a funeral for Don Tyler (Donald Sutherland), a Hollywood director who comes to China to remake Bernardo Bertolucci's The Last Emperor (1987). Yoyo has been hired on to the remaking to shoot a documentary about its creation. The director has a heart attack during the filmmaking and, before falling into a coma, asks Yoyo to give him a Chinese "comedy funeral"—but leaves no money to initiate the project. Yoyo and Wang have to raise funds by auctioning off the project's advertising spaces and seeking tie-in sponsorships. This series of activities leads the project, which should have been a solemn event, to become a farcically TV show. Tyler's revival disrupts their planning and brings them further into debt, and the two men are finally committed to an asylum for their delusion that Tyler was dying. The film ends with a sequence where Tyler works with Yoyo to turn this experience into his new Sino-American coproduction.

In both the film and the real-life film industry at this time, film professionals and their fictional equivalents assume the role of the negotiator or "cultural broker" (Yomi Braester) between the two sides of a Sino-American collaboration. Their task, as Braester suggests, "involves not only the translation of culture into capital but also the translation of one culture into another."[7] The two translations happen simultaneously, leaving the film professionals to also undertake a task of negotiating the two cultures. Allowing for the political nature of the genre, the new task is to balance industrial commercialization and cultural protection within Chinese cinema under the WTO agreements. This situation parallels the government's consistent attitude toward transnational cultural collaboration since the 1994 quota system began; for example, the government reiterated the principle of "Yi wo wei zhu, wei wo suo yong" in 2000 when facing the forthcoming grim competition from Hollywood.[8] Wendy Su interprets the principle as "China's national interest takes precedence, and imports should serve China's agenda."[9] Thus, it can be said that the main idea of the government's countermeasures is to seize the initiative in the globalization process. Film professionals who agree to participate therein obviously become the implementers of this nationalist principle.

Shujen Wang also describes the role of film professionals in this process, pointing out that the government and the film executives had prepared ahead of time through "shrewd market calculation and control in dictating whom they shall allow

in and when."[10] A common metaphor of Sino-American collaborative tension—
"wolves at the door"—may be reinterpreted as hunters (Chinese film professionals)
setting traps and waiting for the approaching pack of hungry wolves (Hollywood
enterprises). *Big Shot's Funeral*, according to her, is about such interaction between
the hunters and wolves. But why would Chinese film professionals, or Feng in this
case, be the "hunter"—or, to put it differently, how? Does the film reflect Feng's
techniques as a hunter as well? If so, how should one understand the reflexive
comments?

These questions guide this chapter and its subsequent examination of the
commercialization of Chinese filmmaking alongside a rising trend of Sino-foreign
collaboration. The chapter subscribes to the idea that, as previous scholarship
suggests, the film highlights the state of the industry during the time of crisis; its
self-reflexivity serves as a response to the new power relations between both sides
and the resulting industrial anxieties in the Chinese context.[11] Referencing Robert
Stam's analysis, similar kinds of responses are common in Hollywood, and reflexive
films take on symbolic significance, suggesting that "the film industry would once
again survive its present difficulties" (e.g., *Sunset Boulevard*, dir. Billy Wilder, 1950)
or convey individual criticism of production patterns (e.g., *Le Mépris*, dir. Jean-Luc
Godard, 1963).[12] But in the Chinese context, things become more nuanced. The film
professionals, based on the previous argument, coordinate cultural negotiations by
implementing official coping strategies in the early stages of this new transnational
collaboration. This socio-political landscape leads the cinematic reflexivity of *Big
Shot's Funeral* to function not merely as commentary on the industry but as an
annotation to the government-directed globalization process.

The film, then, can be read as a reified interpretation of the coping strategies,
namely Feng's individualized countermeasures against superimposed demands
from the government, domestic private investors, and foreign investors. It visualizes his imagination of transnational collaboration and reflects his blueprint for the
kinds of commercial practices that proved successful with his subsequent films. In
this sense, one may further argue that the practice of his reflexive commentary contributes to forming the Chinese version of commercialization within film industry.

In the film, the reflexive commentary is delivered by constructing the interaction between characters. The characters have symbolic meaning. The ones frequently discussed are Yoyo, Tyler, and the latter's Chinese American assistant, Lucy
(Rosamund Kwan). Yoyo is regarded as a personification of Chinese film professionals; Tyler as their Hollywood counterparts; and Lucy as Hollywood's agent of global
film culture, a transcultural broker bridging the two industries.[13] The transcultural
broker boosts the visibility of Chinese film professionals and their works overseas,
but it is a domestic private film company that materializes their creative abilities;
in the film, Louis Wang represents this role. My examination gives attention to this
rarely mentioned symbol and revolves around character relationships.

I consider the film in three parts: (1) Yoyo and Tyler's relationship; (2) Yoyo and Wang's collaboration; and (3) their funeral preparation, linking the text to contemporaneous cultural policies, industrial directives, and film regulations. By linking together these aspects, this chapter demonstrates the function of Feng's reflexive comments from three corresponding aspects, that is, the transformation of Sino-foreign collaboration, the resulting interaction between film professionals and domestic private film enterprises, and their new commercial practices in matters of film production.

Before carrying out this analysis, it is necessary to review the industry's situation around the year 2000 to understand its correspondence with Feng's reflexive commentary.

Industry Preparation for the Increasingly Close Transnational Collaboration

By integrating the industry's internal resources, the government set up a new framework for Sino-foreign film production at turn of the 2000s. It also opened all the sectors of the industry to non-state capital, but at different levels. The two-pronged strategy engendered a situation in which foreign film enterprises have to rely on their Chinese counterparts to produce films locally. This requirement caused changes in the form of transnational collaboration. Columbia Pictures Asia, for instance, chose to proactively collaborate with Feng and Huayi Brothers, the company to which he belonged.[14] Further, in *Big Shot's Funeral*, this reliance is portrayed through Tyler's crisis of creativity, which offers an opportunity for Yoyo and Wang's project planning. Details of this correspondence are discussed in the next section.

In early 1999, the Chinese government had begun its industry preparation for the possible impact of WTO entry on domestic filmmaking. Private capital was encouraged to return to the film sector; the government did not clearly define its legal status, but de facto allowed private media companies to become involved in film production. This ambiguous legal status rendered related filmmaking politically compliant but indeed helped to boost the industry's viability. Huayi Brothers alone invested in three projects during this period, including Chen Kaige's *The Emperor and the Assassin* (*Jingke ci qinwang*, 1998), Feng's *Sorry Baby* (*Meiwan meiliao*, 1999), and Jiang Wen's *Devils on the Doorstep* (*Guizi lai le*, 2000).

Prior to this change, the companies had briefly withdrawn investments from the film industry and moved them into more-profitable television dramas. The immediate cause was the suddenly rigid film censorship that accompanied the implementation of the 9550 Project: plenty of film professionals' works were banned and some of them were even aborted soon after filming, such as Feng's drama, *Living a Miserable Life* (*Guozhe langbei bukan de rizi*).[15] This situation reduced investors' enthusiasm, but facilitated the combination of film professionals and state-owned film enterprises. A series of commercially successful films that toed the Party line, the so-called *jingpin* film, emerged as a result. One striking example of them is Feng's New Year filmmaking, produced by the government-sponsored Forbidden City Company.

In this context, when becoming active again, private companies almost had no other choice but to adapt to politically commercial filmmaking patterns. For them, working with mainstream (officially recognized) film professionals appeared to be a promising solution. Huayi Brothers, for instance, started an enduring partnership with Feng after producing *Sorry Baby*. Thus, one may note that either constraining or encouraging private capital serves the same purpose—that is, to rebuild the market order so as to place the industry's commercialization under the government's control. It follows that a state-led framework is built, within which the government can coordinate different sectors to concentrate superior resources against the imminent challenges posed by foreign cinema.

The state-led framework was consolidated in 2000, in tandem with the government's de jure endorsement of private capital and the concurrent establishment of film conglomerates. The 2000 directive "Opinions on the Further Reform of Chinese Cinema"[16] specifies to what extent non-state capital is permitted to participate in relevant film business and how. For example, the involvement of domestic and foreign funds in film production was confined to single projects; film companies were encouraged to cooperate to found joint ventures in response to the proposed reform of shareholding system in the sector. Non-state companies were only allowed to invest in film distribution companies and theaters as shareholders, while many state-owned and joint stock conglomerates appeared at the provincial level, such as Changchun Film Group (founded in 2000) and Shanghai Film Group (2001). They, together with the centrally managed China Film Group (1999), almost monopolized the whole industry. Such market power enabled the government to flexibly decide how to open the industry and adjust its strategies circumstantially. For transnational collaboration in particular, this meant a Chinese-led pattern was taking shape by, as Ying Zhu and Seio Nakajima described, "a market-based means of managing market share and market entry."[17]

The government did not empower foreign film companies to independently engage in the filmmaking business. This legal design also weights domestic film companies and film professionals more heavily in Sino-foreign collaboration. As stated previously, *Big Shot's Funeral* represents this collaborative trend and celebrates it by redefining the partnership between Tyler and Yoyo. An interesting coincidence is that the State Council issued a law four days after the film was released to reiterate the limitations on foreign film companies and simultaneously remove several restrictions on domestic companies, especially the private ones. According to the law, "Regulations on Administration of Films,"[18] entities outside the film production sector are encouraged to participate in film production in the form of financial aid and investment; these entities include corporations, public institutions, social organizations, and individuals. The requirement is that the entities need to apply for a one-off production license in advance. These provisions explicitly endow domestic private companies with an overwhelming competitive advantage in transnational collaboration, the advantage similar to that of their state-owned counterparts. The law, in a certain sense, validates the new partnership that a film like *Big Shot's Funeral* suggests; in other words, it supports the film's depiction of the government's coping strategies.

Arguably, the government and film professionals prepared together for the increasingly foreign competition within the WTO framework or, borrowing from Wang's metaphor, the hunters aimed at the wolves hovering in the opened door. The question then becomes, how are these dynamics visualized in the film? Perhaps to be more precise, what are Feng's self-reflexive countermeasures in particular?

Local Popular Narratives and Sino-Foreign Collaboration

The challenges Tyler faces filming in China and the transition of Yoyo's role in their relationship represents the shape of Sino-foreign collaboration when China first joined the WTO. The film starts with a sequence in which Tyler is directing a child-birth scene for his remake of *The Last Emperor*. The actress works hard to play the role but Tyler is unsatisfied, as he has not yet found an appropriate way to visualize his idea. In real life, *The Last Emperor* marked the beginning of coproduction between Chinese and Western film industries, as it was the first Western feature film about China that gained the full support of the PRC government.[19] The idea to remake it suggests that the collaboration is reaching a new stage in which foreign film enterprises treat Chinese elements not merely as a background of their films as they had in the past, but also use them to make films that meet the demands of China's market in the early 2000s.

Many Chinese audiences are familiar with films like *The Last Emperor*, as they gained greater access to foreign films through governmental imports, online platforms, Video CDs, and DVDs in the 2000s. The "cannot-give-birth" sequence in *Big Shot's Funeral* manifests the dilemma that foreign film professionals were encountering in seeking new, creative ideas for making a Chinese-related film for China's market. Feng's explanation of Tyler's dissatisfaction in an interview further validates this assessment, attributing Tyler's dilemma to the repetition of using Bertolucci's narrative perspective: "[N]o matter how well Tyler shoots the film, he knows he merely imitates the emperor's emotion (since he does not understand the Chinese society and culture)."[20] Applying Feng's words to the sequence, it can be seen that the basis of the new Sino-foreign collaboration from the perspective of foreign film companies is to find a way to understand China's market.

The film uses Tyler's connection with Yoyo to represent Columbia Pictures' way of understanding China's market. Such understanding directly triggers the company's involvement in Huayi Brothers' production of Feng's New Year films. In one scene where Tyler is walking with Yoyo and Lucy, Tyler comments that Bertolucci's portrayal of the emperor as a tragic figure appeals more to Western audiences, while Chinese audiences may not accept that interpretation. In order to validate this conjecture, he allows Lucy to ask Yoyo who is filming their discussion for his understanding of the emperor. Yoyo replies that he does not think the emperor is a tragic figure, since he lives a state-subsidized life and has many wives. This opinion is different from Bertolucci's but accords with Tyler's thinking of his remake, that is, seeking local perspectives to coproduce films. Later, the same thought leads Tyler to authorize Yoyo to plan a Chinese funeral for him, and this interaction parallels the collaboration process between Feng (Huayi Brothers) and Columbia Pictures, in which the company first analyses the Chinese film industry's annual reports and then decides to invest in *Big Shot's Funeral*, placing a high value on Feng's filmmaking, which usually results in high-grossing films.[21]

Feng attributes this commercial success to his local narrative principles, namely his "affinity with ordinary people" and "the fantasy for ordinary people."[22] Therefore, it is Feng's popular local narrative that activates the collaboration; in other words, Columbia Pictures' solution for understanding China's market is to participate in its local popular film production.

This emphasis on local narrative improves the status of Chinese film professionals in the Sino-foreign collaboration and further develops a mode that relies on their filmmaking skills and insights. In the film, this development is subtly reflected in Yoyo's function and Tyler's changing attitude toward him. In the beginning, Yoyo is only allowed to sell his technical skills—"being a pair of eyeballs recording Tyler's remaking as a documentary"—and has no copyright or final-cut rights to his work.

Figure 11.1: As an outsider, YoYo has nothing to do but record Tyler and Lucy's conversation in *Big Shot's Funeral* (2001).

Tyler regards Yoyo more as an employee than a working partner, demonstrated in the first half of the walking scene where the film uses a long shot to visualize the relationship: Tyler is talking to Lucy, while Yoyo keeps a distance from them as an outsider who silently works to record.

This relationship evokes the initial phase of Sino-foreign collaboration in the 1980s, when foreign enterprises dominated filmmaking whilst the Chinese film industry assisted them by offering sets and labor resources via the China Film Co-Production Corporation (CFCC).[23] At this stage, Chinese film professionals merely worked to implement their foreign counterparts' plan. For example, Bertolucci had the final say in *The Last Emperor* while the CFCC had little influence on the coproduction. This imbalance is apparent in the domestic criticism of the film's "historical inaccuracy" and "orientalist imagination."[24] These criticisms reflect the foreign film companies' market positioning of *The Last Emperor*—it was not made for China's market, which naturally leads the film's production to rely less on Chinese film professionals.

Things changed in the early 2000s when the government systematically engaged in the industry's commercialization, establishing a state-led commercial filmmaking framework through the 9550 Project and industrial conglomeration. Under this framework, domestic filmmaking's commercial success was correlated with its political compliance, which developed into a protective mechanism alongside the industry's deepening commercialization under the WTO agreements. This context makes domestic popular narratives (and relevant filmmakers) important in Sino-foreign collaborations, especially when foreign film companies take the collaborative opportunity to localize their productions for China's market.

Correspondingly, in *Big Shot's Funeral*, only when Yoyo engages in filmmaking alongside Tyler does his status in the relationship change and their true collaboration start. As Tyler explains in the aforementioned walking sequence, either Bertolucci's narrative angle or his thinking of Chinese perspective was profit-oriented. Therefore, when Yoyo works with a local media company and uses on-the-ground knowledge to turn the funeral project into a live TV show, Tyler approves of Yoyo's idea rather than withdrawing his authorization of the funeral. For Wang's media company, this approval consolidates Yoyo's domination in their close collaboration, since they used Tyler's fame to attract investment and sponsorship; Wang's participation in turn strengthens the value of Yoyo to Tyler, because he has sufficient experience in organizing live stage performances in China. In this sense, Yoyo's role is so crucial in implementing the project that it bridges the interaction between Tyler and Wang and contributes to their collaboration.

Considering the three characters' symbolic meanings, the interaction among them figuratively represents Feng's function in Huayi Brothers' collaboration with Columbia Pictures, which accordingly suggests that Chinese film professionals begin to dominate Sino-foreign filmmaking in the early 2000s. This does not mean, however, that foreign film companies do not still have disproportionate influence in the collaboration, since they offer investment and therefore can draw the coproduction toward their intention of localization. For example, the distribution advantage allowed Columbia Pictures to set markets for release, which meant that *Big Shot's Funeral* never played in North American cinema chains.[25]

The film visualizes this influence in a mocking way by displaying how the ailing Tyler supervises Yoyo's funeral planning from his hospital bed. Admittedly, Yoyo can plan the show based on his personal preference; however, this plan's success depends on Tyler's health. Therefore, when Tyler leaves the hospital, the show's advertising sponsors all come to Yoyo for compensation. It is Tyler who pays the money for Yoyo and Wang at the expense of appropriating Yoyo's ideas into his new China-related film. Compared to Tyler's authorization, the payment more directly suggests that the foreign film companies' latent controlling influence on Sino-foreign collaboration in the early 2000s, as he represents "the real authority who pulls strings behind the puppet show," having the last word with the funeral project and its ownership.[26]

Commercial Filmmaking and Industrial Globalization

In addition to this new stage of Sino-foreign collaboration, *Big Shot's Funeral* uses Yoyo and Louis Wang's coalition and their consequent division of labor in the funeral project to visualize Chinese film production's commercialization in the context of international collaboration. In the film, after getting Tyler's authorization, Yoyo contacts Wang, his former colleague at a state-owned studio who now makes his living running live stage performances. Considering the film's setting in history, both Yoyo and Wang probably started their own businesses after the institutional restructuring of state-owned studios alongside the 1993 market-oriented reform. Their similar experiences helped cultivate Yoyo's and Wang's commercial awareness and further contribute to their collaboration. This motive for collaboration echoes the factors that triggered Feng's work with Huayi Brothers. As a private company, the latter naturally centers on commercial filmmaking and expects a high return on their investment; for Feng, he had already accepted commercial filmmaking at the beginning of his career as a director, which can be seen in his manifesto of filmmaking principles in an interview about his early works: "I'll continue to follow the path of commercial filmmaking and simultaneously bring delicate designs of art-house films into it."[27] This idea, in concert with the high box-office receipts of his New Year films, attracted Huayi Brothers' attention in the late 1990s when the company was "eagerly looking for cooperation with profitable directors in order to raise its profile and expand its market share."[28]

This combination illustrates the characteristics of Chinese film production's commercialization in the early 2000s, that is, forming a productive collection of professional producers (film production companies) and a particularly well-known or bankable director. This collaborative pattern had existed in Zhang Yimou's work with the Beijing New Picture Film Company in late 1999, although it was on a small scale and did not last long.[29] By comparison, the combination of Feng and Huayi Brothers appears relatively late but is more commercialized and influential, since their New Year films continued with strong box-office performances and attracted many other film professionals to follow their pattern. One case in point is an influx of similar partnerships that emerged after 2005, such as between Chen Kaige and China Film Group, between Ning Hao and China Film Group, and between Jiang Wen and Polybona Films.[30] In this sense, the collocation of Feng and Huayi Brothers not only conforms to the industry's commercialization process but also accelerates its progress. This collaborative pattern can be understood as an outcome of a particular division of labor, which brings specialization and efficiency to domestic filmmaking.

In *Big Shot's Funeral*, displaying Yoyo and Wang's duties in funeral planning is a perfect metaphor for how this pattern works in implementing film projects. Yoyo takes charge of designing the funeral show, leading a crew to put his ideas into practice; Wang undertakes the task of seeking sponsorships exploiting Tyler's fame, connecting technological support, and providing personnel for the show. The division of labor results in an assembly line-style mechanism, in that Wang brings advertising sponsorships to Yoyo, who then finds an appropriate way to coordinate different product placements in the show. This division accelerates the planning process so that Yoyo and Wang can complete the project during Tyler's short stay in the hospital. A similar productive efficiency is also created in the division of labor between Feng and Huayi Brothers, in which Feng concentrates on filmmaking and the company works to find investments to produce his projects. It guaranteed the output of Feng's work in the 2000s, during which time Huayi Brothers launched almost one New Year film per year, and most of them were made within only two months.

This division of labor also commercializes Chinese film production by, for example, propelling domestic film companies to introduce operational approaches that are used widely in other media areas or sophisticatedly in foreign film industries, such as product placement. In the film, one sees this when Wang makes use of his approaches from his live stage performances, such as advertising sponsorships and integrated marketing strategies, to produce and promote the funeral project. He suggests that Yoyo sell the funeral's advertising spaces for initial capital; following the sales, he brings his cooperative partners to join. He gives the funeral's broadcasting rights to his friend, who promises to pay to rent a satellite for sending over the funeral program, and asks Yoyo to leave advertising spaces on the hearse truck for a music company that has a business contact with him. Wang's friend also promises to send his popular singers to perform at the funeral for free. Thus, Wang binds the funeral project with other companies' merchandising, including his own business, covering the project's cost and spreading it out by sharing promotional resources.

This series of commercial operations metaphorically represents Huayi Brothers' approach to producing Feng's New Year films. As the company started business as an advertising agency, it introduced product placement in making Feng's New Year films in 1999 when producing *Sorry Baby* (*Meiwan meiliao*), their first collaborative film. At that stage, the advertising sponsorship already covered part of the film's cost, which brought in revenue of RMB 15 million (USD 2.2 million), nearly twice Huayi Brothers' investment of RMB 8 million (USD 1.17 million).[31] Not only does this arrangement make product placement a common approach for Huayi in producing Feng's New Year films, it also allows an integration in which Huayi Brothers combines film production with its other businesses.

This integration is a symptom of industrializing filmmaking, which suggests that Huayi Brothers had begun to regard film production as an industrial business in the early 2000s. One result is that the company sought opportunities to create a distribution subsidiary and thus established its own industrial chain after losing distribution rights during the collaboration with Columbia Pictures. It can be said that global collaboration accelerates the commercialization of Chinese film production and the industrialization of Chinese private film companies.

The film also represents this symptom with a farcical sequence in which Yoyo and Wang are sent to a mental hospital because Tyler's recovery makes them go insane. With a long take, the sequence first establishes suspense when the characters discuss China's economic prospects and industrial development, such as the market potential of making television and films, the program of developing online businesses, and predictions around housing prices. Nearly all the characters wear red robes in a place that looks like a business club. However, following the camera's movement, they start to talk to themselves and many hospital beds appear on screen: these people are actually patients. Nevertheless, their discussions are reasonable and foresighted, since these ideas were based on China's contemporaneous economic and social contexts and most of them came true several years after the film's release, such as rising house prices and booming online shopping. In this sense, the patients' ideas represent an awareness of industrialization in various fields. Unlike the other patients, however, Yoyo wears a blue robe while Wang wears red. As Yoyo is malingering, this color distinction puts Wang in the same category of the aforementioned patients. The darker the robe worn by the patients, the more serious their condition, and the stronger their awareness is of industrialization.

Considering the symbolic meaning of Wang's image, this farcical sequence figuratively indicates the growth of industrialization among domestic private film companies in China. In fact, one year after the film's release, the government proposed a policy establishing cultural industries, and since 2003 both film authorities and film professionals have generally recognized the commercial attributes of film-making, which directly triggered the wave of making big pictures such as *wuxia* films and even led to a genre shift in Feng's New Year films. After these changes, the rapid industrialization of Chinese film production engendered more international

Figure 11.2: The patients in a mental hospital discuss the economic prospects of China; YoYo, who wears a blue gown, is malingering (top left), while Wang, wearing a red gown, actually goes insane (top center) in *Big Shot's Funeral* (2001).

collaboration, propelling the industry toward commercial prosperity rather than decline or collapse, which many film professionals used to worry about after China joined the WTO.

Integrated Marketing Strategies and Product Placement

Partly due to its previous advertising business, Huayi Brothers became the first to introduce integrated marketing strategies into film production in China. Most of the strategies used by characters in *Big Shot's Funeral* also appear in the actual making of the film itself and Feng's subsequent New Year films in the 2000s. From this point of view, the fictional funeral planning was similar to how Huayi Brothers tested integrated marketing strategies, in which it rehearses various commercial approaches on a large scale without worrying about criticisms such as abusing product placement.

This strategy is first manifested in the scene where Wang holds a global, live-streamed auction selling advertising space at Tyler's funeral. During the auction, Wang and Yoyo keep making sensational statements to attract as much attention as possible, such as claiming that they are the "exclusive agency" of the event and suddenly cancelling a participant's qualification after he wins the bid in order to spread the project and gain sufficient financial support. Taking the withdrawal of the successful bid as an example, unexpected events happen immediately after Yoyo finds the bidder selling pirated films. Yoyo's dramatic reaction successfully draws media attention and causes a fierce and public debate on whether commercializing the funeral is ethical. In the film, this debate pushes the funeral into the national news, after which a large number of advertising sponsorships flood into the funeral planning. The auction in many ways is like a press conference before filming begins on a high-profile project whilst Yoyo's deeds resemble a publicity stunt suddenly occurring in the middle of the press conference setting an agenda to maintain the project's visibility and media buzz.

Correspondingly, holding a press conference and executing public stunts are Huayi Brothers' conventional approaches for promoting Feng's New Year films. Early in their collaboration in the late 1990s, holding meet-and-greet events had been frequently used in introducing Feng's films, during which he usually created topics for public discussion such as making bitter comments to defend against criticisms of his commercial filmmaking. Since *Big Shot's Funeral*, the company's promotion created sensational effects and turned accidental events into publicity stunts. For example, it held the premiere of *Big Shot's Funeral* at the Cultural Palace of Nationalities, a Beijing landmark, and made the film a fashionable must-see.[32] For their next collaborative film, *Cell Phone* (*Shouji*, 2003), the company seized on public discussion about the similarities between the film's protagonist, Yan Shouyi, and the actual famous host Cui Yongyuan, using this gossip to raise the film's visibility. When promoting *A World Without Thieves* (*Tianxie wuzei*, 2004), the company's pursuit of sensationalism was more conspicuous: it rented a train named "A World Without Thieves" to carry the cast, fans, and investors to attend the film's premiere in Hong Kong.

Comparing these examples with the sequence of Wang's auction, it is evident that the filmmaking-like funeral planning worked as an illustration of Huayi Brothers' integrated marketing strategies. Apart from creating sensational effects, the funeral planning also demonstrates the company's two widely used approaches—tie-in promotion and product placement—in producing Feng's New Year films. Tie-in promotion is a form of cross marketing, "a joint promotion of two or more products or services."[33] According to Charles Lubbers and William Adams, the tie-ins display "partnerships developed with other organizations that are designed to promote both of the organizations."[34] In film industry, partnerships are built on resource sharing between film companies and other enterprises. These enterprises incorporate film promotion into their own merchandising; thus, they "get to associate their products with films."[35]

In the funeral-planning sequence, Wang indeed combines the funeral event with his own business; as mentioned above, he organizes several tie-in promotions such as the satellite rental and free singing performances to simultaneously promote his company and the funeral project. Correspondingly, in Huayi Brothers' operation, tie-in promotion allows the company to spread Feng's New Year films efficiently but with few costs. For example, it allied with the catalog retailer Gome for promoting *Cell Phone*, playing clips from the film in Gome's stores and, in return, asking Feng and Ge You to attend the catalog-signing event held in the stores, a win-win situation for both Huayi Brothers and Gome.[36]

Compared to tie-ins, product placement is a unidirectional communication, a purchasing behavior, rather than a resource-sharing operation. It is mainly used to cover the cost of filmmaking, since there is usually no direct association between films and the products advertised therein. By portraying Yoyo's countermeasures to the advertising sponsors' requirements, *Big Shot's Funeral* visualizes Feng's principles of using product placement and Huayi Brothers' influence on forming these principles. In the film, based on Wang's suggestion, Yoyo agrees to involve product placement in Tyler's funeral but insists on introducing big brands, since they match Tyler's fame, and cultivating a strong ally will benefit their project. When inserting advertisements into the funeral, Yoyo emphasizes that product placement must fit into the funeral's setting. These two ideas—allying with big brands and integrating the product into the film's plot—continue as Feng's main principles for implementing product placement in reality. Many products that emerge in the film are actual, popular brands inserted in the funeral-planning sequence, such as SunRun Beauty Cream and Outback Steakhouse. As this sequence is about how Yoyo coordinates different product placements, Feng's insertion mixes the advertisements of the actual brands into those of the fictional ones, making the actual brands that fund *Big Shot's Funeral* also the advertising sponsors of Yoyo's funeral project, thus fulfilling the commercial mission of the film without breaking the film's narrative flow. The two principles subtly solve the conflict between film funding demands and the narrative disjuncture caused by product placement, which further develop into Feng's signature style in his subsequent New Year films.

Using story-driven product placement is one conspicuous manifestation of this signature style. Along with the increasing number of advertised products appearing in Feng's New Year films, advertising sponsors increasingly influenced his filmmaking, leading to a high-concept pattern that manifests as simple story themes, appealing visuals, and comprehensive merchandising. *Big Shot's Funeral* uses an absurd scene in which Yoyo has to make full use of every surface on a dummy representing

Figure 11.3: SunRun Beauty Cream (left) and Outback Steakhouse (right) are actual companies that sponsored *Big Shot's Funeral* (2001), appearing in the film as sponsors of the fictional funeral.

Figure 11.4: YoYo makes full use of every place on the dummy to plug in advertisements in *Big Shot's Funeral* (2001).

the deceased Tyler for product placements, reflecting the advertising sponsors' influence. Yoyo dresses the dummy with the shorts and tank top of one brand; puts a trainer on its left foot and a leather shoe on the right; and makes it wear a pair of sunglasses but takes out one lens, leaving a spot for a brand of contact lenses. He even makes the dummy hold a tea bag in its mouth and sprinkles soot over half of its hair, leaving the other half to display a shampoo's anti-dandruff effect. At this point, using product placement no longer works for collecting investment to support the funeral and instead makes the solemn ceremony become a carnival of advertisements. Advertising sponsors dominate the project's production, leading to the conditions that Mark Crispin Miller identifies as "the transfer of creative authority out of the hands of filmmaking professionals and into the purely quantitative universe of the CEOs."[37]

Yoyo's absurd experience is corroborated in Feng's subsequent New Year films, as his filmmaking relies more on advertising and sponsorship, leading many to mock *Cell Phone* as an advertisement for Motorola phones and leading some film professionals to joke that Feng is the CEO of the product placement business in the industry.[38] This heavily financial relationship has a considerable influence on his storytelling, as he mentions in an interview in 2005: "If a film's budget was over 80 million, I just don't know what the film would look like, just imagine how many advertisements I would have to find a place for."[39] One change resulting from this business model has been the theme of Feng's New Year films becoming simple and concise—a complicated theme might increase the difficulty for filmmakers in balancing product placement against narrative.

Conclusion

Big Shot's Funeral explores the negotiations between film professionals and sponsors, and is a response to Chinese film production's commercialization featuring global collaboration starting in the early 2000s. Commercial techniques (e.g., the use of integrated marketing strategies) are introduced from foreign film industries and are then widely used under foreign funding support, such as Columbia Pictures' investment in Feng's work including *Big Shot's Funeral*. Thus, these tactics accelerated Chinese filmmaking's commercialization and the industry's globalization under the WTO agreements. This commercialization explores the potential of China's market, facilitates domestic film companies in building industrial chains to compete at home and abroad, and consolidates the state-led filmmaking framework. These changes formed a new mode of Sino-foreign collaboration, which pivots on Chinese film professionals and their local popular narratives. It is worth noting that neither party of the collaboration is passive in this mode: they both seize the collaborative opportunity to explore each other's markets. Chinese film companies use foreign investment and management experience to complete conglomeration and improve international influence, whilst their foreign partners rely on Chinese film professionals to localize their production to adapt to China's market.

In *Big Shot's Funeral*, Wang and Tyler's attitudes toward Yoyo's project represent the different purposes of Chinese and foreign film companies participating in such collaborations. Tyler regards the project more as a filmmaking experiment, since he has no inspiration to make a China-related film, while Wang organizes the funeral using Tyler's global fame to expand the influence of his company. For the Chinese film industry, collaboration combines the domestic and foreign advantages of film production. For example, *Big Shot's Funeral* integrates Feng's popular narrative perspectives on ordinary Chinese people with product placements and high-concept filmmaking to tell a Chinese story, just as the film's character Yoyo uses an imported commercial approach to organize a funeral featuring Chinese culture. The advantage of this combination is to localize global collaboration in order to promote the industry's development.

This operation corresponds to many film professionals' positive opinion of the industry's development after China's entry into the WTO, such as Feng's aforementioned theory of hybridizing two industries' advantages. It indeed goes on to facilitate the industry's commercialization in the 2000s, popularizing the use of product placement, elevating the trend of coproducing big pictures related to the *wuxia* genre, and bringing a shift in genres to New Year film production. This commercial development in turn strengthens Chinese film professionals' domination in subsequent Sino-foreign collaborations. For example, collaborating with Columbia Pictures propels Huayi Brothers to build a distribution subsidiary, which leads the company to be quite influential in coproducing *A World Without Thieves* with the Hong Kong–based Media Asia Company. A further study revolving around the relationship between industrial commercialization and transnational filmmaking collaborations since the mid-2000s may indeed be worthwhile.

Notes

1. The 9550 Project is a production scheme launched by the government during the National Cinema Conference held at Changsha in 1996.
2. Regarding how to define a film as "excellent," film officials such as the then-Minister of Propaganda, Ding Guangen, defined it as one that "promoted ideological rectitude as the criteria of foremost importance"; he also stressed that such a film should enlighten, educate, and amuse people, achieving a unification of political and economic benefits. For more details, see Ding's talk at the conference. Cf. Rui Zhang, *The Cinema of Feng Xiaogang: Commercialization and Censorship in Chinese Cinema after 1989* (Hong Kong: Hong Kong University Press, 2008), 65.
3. Feng claimed that his films saved the Chinese film industry at that time. See Shuyu Kong, "Big Shot from Beijing: Feng Xiaogang's *He Sui Pian* and Contemporary Chinese Commercial Film," *Asian Cinema* 14, no. 1 (March 2003): 178.
4. Zhang Yiwu, "Zaidu xiangxiang zhongguo: quanqiuhua de tiaozhan yu xin de 'neixianghua'" [Imagining China again: The challenges of globalization to the Chinese film industry and its response], *Dianying yishu*, no. 1 (2001): 19.
5. For example, see Stanley Rosen and Jinhua Dai's discussions, respectively. Stanley Rosen, "The Wolf at the Door: Hollywood and the Film Market in China from 1994–2000," in *Chinese Cinema: Critical Concepts in Media and Cultural Studies, Volume II: Chinese Film Production and Reception*, ed. Chris Berry (Abingdon: Routledge, 2002), 87–113; Dai Jinhua, *Wu zhong fengjing: Zhuoguo dianying wenhua, 1978–1998* [Landscape in the mist: Chinese cinema and culture, 1978–1998] (Beijing: Peking University Press, 2002).
6. Yomi Braester, "Chinese Cinema in the Age of Advertisement: The Filmmaker as a Cultural Broker," *The China Quarterly* 183 (2005): 558.
7. Braester, "Chinese Cinema in the Age of Advertisement," 558.
8. According to Wendy Su, the then-director of the Film Bureau had illustrated the government's central policy of "Yi wo wei zhu" in March 1996. In 2000, the government underlined the policy as a guiding principle and stated it in the directive "Opinions on the Further Reform of Chinese Cinema" (Document No. 320). See Wendy Su, *China's Encounter with Global Hollywood: Cultural Policy and the Film Industry, 1994–2013* (Lexington: University Press of Kentucky, 2016), 20.
9. Su, *China's Encounter with Global Hollywood*, 20.
10. Shujen Wang, "*Big Shot's Funeral*: China, Sony, and the WTO," *Asian Cinema* 14, no. 2 (Fall/Winter 2003): 146.
11. Wang, "*Big Shot's Funeral*"; Braester, "Chinese Cinema in the Age of Advertisement"; and Jason McGrath, *Postsocialist Modernity: Chinese Cinema, Literature and Criticism in the Market Age* (Stanford: Stanford University Press, 2008), 90–131.
12. Robert Stam, *Reflexivity in Film and Literature: From Don Quixote to Jean-Luc Godard* (New York: Columbia University Press, 1992).
13. For the role of Lucy, see Braester, "Chinese Cinema in the Age of Advertisement" and Wang, "*Big Shot's Funeral.*"

14. In 2000, Huayi Brothers formally established the collaboration with Feng through swapping its shares for the ownership of Feng's personal studio.

15. Feng Xiaogang, *Wo ba qingchun xiangei ni* [I dedicated my youth to you] (Beijing: Changjiang wenyi, 2003).

16. The Ministry of Culture directive (in Chinese and English) can be found online. See Rogier Creemers, ed., "Some Opinions Concerning Further Deepening Film Sector Reform," *Chinese Copyright and Media* (blog), June 6, 2000, last updated June 15, 2010, https://chinacopyrightandmedia.wordpress.com/2000/06/06/some-opinions-concerning-further-deepening-film-sector-reform/.

17. Ying Zhu and Seio Nakajima, "The Evolution of Chinese Film as an Industry," in *Art, Politics, and Commerce in Chinese Cinema*, ed. Ying Zhu and Stanley Rosen (Hong Kong: Hong Kong University Press, 2010), 33.

18. State Council, "Regulations on Administration of Movies," No. 342, December 12, 2001, http://www.lawinfochina.com/display.aspx?lib=law&id=2253.

19. Whitney Crothers Dilley, *The Cinema of Ang Lee: The Other Side of the Screen* (London: Wallflower Press, 2015), 41.

20. Feng Xiaogang, Ge You, Wang Zhongjun, and Wang Zhonglei, "Dawan tan Dawan" [Chinese film big shots discussing *Big Shot's Funeral*], *Dianying yishu*, no. 2 (2002): 48.

21. Feng, Ge, Wang Zhongjun, and Wang Zhonglei, "Dawan tan Dawan," 47.

22. Chen Shangrong, "Feng Xiaogang shangye dianying de shichang guannian" [Feng Xiaogang's thinking on commercial filmmaking], *Yishu guangjiao*, no. 4 (2004): 33.

23. Lin Lili, "Sanshi nian hepai pian licheng: kaifang hezuo gongying" [Thirty-year history of Sino-foreign coproduction], *Zhongguo dianying bao*, July 27, 2010, http://www.dmcc.gov.cn/mainSite/zt/gkf30znnctcgcyxypzy/134355/496947/index.html.

24. Fatimah Rony Tobing, "*The Last Emperor*," in *Bertolucci's The Last Emperor: Multiple Takes*, ed. Bruce H. Sklarew, Bonnie S. Kaufman, Ellen Handler Spitz, and Diane Borden (Detroit: Wayne State University Press, 1988), 137–46.

25. Qiu Yuan, *Dapian shidai: Feng Xiaogang yu Huayi Xiongdi* [The blockbuster era: Feng Xiaogang and Huayi Brothers] (Guilin: Guangxi Normal University Press, 2011).

26. Yingjin Zhang, "*Big Shot's Funeral*: Performing a Post-modern Cinema of Attractions," in *Chinese Film in Focus II*, ed. Chris Berry (London: BFI, 2008), 19.

27. Yu Shaowen, "Feng Xiaogang tan dianying yishu" [Feng Xiaogang on cinema arts], *21 shiji*, no. 3 (1995): 16.

28. Li Haixia, "Feng Xiaogang dianying shichang yanjiu" [Research on marketing of Feng Xiaogang's cinema], *Contemporary Cinema* 6, no. 135 (2006): 57.

29. Lei Xiaoyu and Ding Wei, "Feng Xiaogang yu Wang Zhongjun: Shanye pian zhi wang" [Feng Xiaogang and Wang Zhongjun: The kings of Chinese commercial filmmaking], *Zhongguo qiyejia* 14 (2010): 44.

30. Qiu, *Dapian shidai*.

31. Li, "Feng Xiaogang tan dianying yishu," 57.

32. Cheng Huizhe and Zhang Junpin, "Cong *Jiafang yifang* dao *Jijie hao*: Feng Xiaogang dianying de piaofang celüe" [From *Party A, Party B* to *Assembly*: Feng Xiaogang's marketing strategies], *Yishu yanjiu*, no. 8 (2008): 58.

33. Ken Kaser, *Advertising and Sales Promotion* (Mason, OH: South-Western Cengage Learning, 2013), 304.

34. Charles A. Lubbers and William J Adams, "Merchandising in the Major Motion Picture Industry: Creating Brand Synergy and Revenue Streams," in *Handbook of Product Placement in the Mass Media: New Strategies in Marketing Theory, Practice, Trends, and Ethics*, ed. Mary-Lou Galician (New York: Routledge, 2004), 60.

35. Robert Marich, *Marketing to Moviegoers: A Handbook of Strategies and Tactics* (Carbondale: Southern Illinois University Press, 2013), 147.

36. Zhou Hui, *Shui Zhizao le zhongguo dianying de Shenhua* [Who created the myth of Chinese films] (Beijing: China Youth Publishing Group, 2006).

37. Mark Crispin Miller, "Advertising: End of Story," in *A Pantheon Guide to Popular Culture: Seeing through Movies*, ed. Mark Crispin Miller (New York: Pantheon Books, 1990), 186–246, 198.

38. Shenliang Liu, "Feng Xiaogang cheng zhiru guanggao CEO" [Feng Xiaogang, the king of product placement in film], *Beijing Youth Daily*, December 23, 2013.

39. Rui Zhang, *The Cinema of Feng Xiaogang*, 143.

12

Sticks, Not Carrots

The Discourse of Soft Power in Popular Chinese Cinema

Katherine Chu

The Chinese box office broke its all-time yearly record in 2019, with local films accounting for eight of the top ten movies, generating 64.1 percent of total box office revenue.[1] Earlier that year, China's first big-budget, outer-space, sci-fi epic, *The Wandering Earth* (*Liulang diqiu*, dir. Frant Gwo, 2019), earned a remarkable $699.8 million worldwide.[2] That record did not last long. In the summer, it was surpassed by the incredible performance of the Chinese animated film *Nezha* (*Nezha zhi motong jiangshi*, dir. Yu Yang, 2019), which earned $710 million. In the following year, the early autumn of 2020—which included a clutch of patriotic movies with releases intended to celebrate the seventieth anniversary of the People's Republic's founding—turned into the blockbuster season for the Chinese film industry. The top-grossing films were *My People, My Country* (*Wo he wo de zuguo*, dir. Ning Hao, Xu Zheng, Guan Hu, Chen Kaige, Zhang Yibai, Wen Muye, Xue Xiaolu, 2019), *The Captain* (*Zhongguo jizhang*, dir. Andrew Lau, 2019), and *The Climbers* (*Pandengzhe*, dir. Daniel Lee, 2019). In the spring of 2021—the peak season for Chinese cinema screens—*Hi, Mom* (*Ni hao, Li Huangying*, dir. Jia Ling, 2021) and *Detective Chinatown 3* (*Tangren jie tan'an 3*, dir. Chen Sicheng, 2021) both soared past the $600 million mark during their second week in theaters. From sales in just the Chinese market alone, both titles have not only become the second- and third-biggest grossers for any movie released in China behind *Wolf Warrior 2* (*Zhan lang 2*, dir. Wu Jing, 2017)—which earned $870.3 million—but have now far surpassed the world's highest-grossing film in 2020: China's *The Eight Hundred* (*Babai*, dir. Guan Hu, 2020), which earned $468 million.

Hollywood used to dominate China's film market, but since the mid-2000s, its share has decreased due to protectionist policies combined with the improved quality of Chinese blockbusters. In 2020, domestic films accounted for 83.7 percent of China's total box office revenue, with only 16.3 percent generated by foreign movies, down from 35.9 percent in 2019. Of the top ten films of 2020 at the box office, all were domestic-made films.[3] Underneath the success of high-grossing Chinese films lies a force that could affect everything from perceptions of nationality to the shape of foreign policy and transnational narratives: in his first speech as General Secretary, Xi Jinping launched a new mission; under his leadership, the Chinese Communist Party (CCP) would lead China's return as a global power. Choosing to establish a conceptual idea- rather than an economic target or policy is significant. His Chinese Dream also set the stage for elevating ideological work to a level perhaps not ever seen in Chinese history.

There has also been a remarkable shift in China's propaganda policies. Since the mid-2000s, the Party has launched a Grand External Propaganda Campaign, or Big Foreign Propaganda (*Da Wai Xuan*), by pouring billions of dollars into publicity agencies, including print media (e.g., by inserting *China Daily* into a newspaper such as the *Washington Post* for as much as $250,000 an issue), broadcasting (e.g., CGTN broadcasts in six languages), and social media (e.g., Twitter, Facebook, Instagram, and YouTube),[4] all while the film industry promotes a positive view of China and its place in global politics and culture. Strategies such as "Chinese Culture Going Global" in 2011,[5] the Chinese Dream in 2012, "Telling Chinese Stories" in 2014,[6] and "generate positive energy" in 2017[7] all aimed to enhance the appeal and influence of Chinese culture globally through multiple channels, levels, and forms. China's miraculous economic growth supported the transformation from Deng Xiaoping's low-profile and "hide-our-capacities" approach of power projection to a more assertive role at global and regional levels. China spread its footprints worldwide, but Beijing's leadership also vigorously promoted Chinese language and culture as a cultural soft-power tool. As of January 2018, it had established more than 500 Confucius Institutes worldwide since the first Confucius Institute was opened in Seoul, South Korea, in 2004. Interestingly, the official Chinese discourse on soft power began in 2007 as a political strategy mainly to simmer domestic discontent in order to safeguard, sustain, and prolong the Chinese Communist Party (CCP) regime's longevity. Nevertheless, Chinese leaders also recognized the value of soft power to provide an alternative model to the Western liberal order and ultimately reshape the entire global information environment.

With this in mind, this chapter examines the potency of China's notion of soft power and applies it to the Chinese film industry in particular. While tracing the genesis of reform within the Chinese film industry from a historical perspective, this chapter first discusses the term "soft power," coined by Joseph S. Nye in 1992. Second, the chapter investigates how the Chinese government institutionalized its film industry in dealing with domestic audiences and, to a lesser extent, its foreign audiences. In this regard, this chapter will examine a host of questions. For instance, why did the Beijing government embrace and promote soft power through the film industry? Does it work? What were the overriding reasons behind the film industry's reform as an integral component of China's soft-power diplomacy?

Central to Xi's three-hour opening speech at the 19th Party Congress in 2017 is the great rejuvenation plan he drafted for the country. Xi Jinping not only wants to modernize the military into a world-class army by 2050, but he also wants to use China's cultural products to show the world that China is not only a "strong country" or "great power," but that it will move closer to the center of the world stage.[8] However, even China's economy and the military will dominate globally; many countries do not want to emulate its political system. China's government structure remains the weakest part in its score of soft power.[9]

Theoretical Underpinnings of Soft Power in the Context of China

In the field of foreign policy, actions based on practical, self-interested principles rather than moral or ideological concerns are called "realpolitik." In his 1990 Foreign Policy essay, international relations theorist Joseph Nye argues that this type of policy has become too costly and intangible to deal with the world order after the collapse of the Soviet Union. He wrote, "[W]hen one country gets other countries to *want* what it wants [that] might be called co-optive or soft power in contrast with the hard or command power of *ordering* others to do what it wants."[10]

Nye's soft power was translated into Chinese in 1992, sparking interest and discussion among Chinese scholars.[11] It was not until 2007, at the 17th Party Congress, however—when President Hu Jintao linked China's rejuvenation with the country's ability to project soft power—that soft power became a more standard component of Chinese foreign policy.[12] At that time, Hu was hoping to explore the concept of soft power by showing the world his country's achievements in all aspects, not only the economic and military achievements but also those of its political structure and cultural heritage. One of the Chinese soft-power goals in the early days was to dilute the influence of the US's soft power in China. The Chinese government aimed at preventing the promotion of Western values, such as democracy, human rights, and freedom of speech to subvert the Communist Party's rule.

Primarily, the goals of soft power in the Chinese context relate to national security. The concept of security to China heavily emphasizes preemption. Internal security is not as simple as forcefully ending civil unrest, while external security is not limited to managing relations with the US. Instead, internal and external security entails managing the CCP and its power, protecting the CCP from delegitimization. Security, therefore, is focused on protecting the Party's position in power. In practice, managing security threats is not limited to enhancing the police force and the PLA's (People's Liberation Army) capabilities. The ideological realm is heavily influential. As such, crisis prevention is crucial for soft-power initiatives. Xi Jinping once noted: "We must put the prevention of risks in a prominent position. [We must] nip [risks] in the bud and be concerned about what has yet to come to pass."[13] Failure to effectively prevent threats could mean that the Party failed to prevent a crisis, reducing its legitimacy. Ideas do not shift into a narrative overnight; narrative control is required far in advance of a conflict to have informational superiority.

Abruptly pulling movies from Chinese cinemas without explanation is not a rare practice for the Chinese government. In February 2019, four big-budget movies were removed from Chinese cinemas, which left many moviegoers confused. *The Eight Hundred* was a war epic, and it was the first Chinese film shot entirely on IMAX cameras. *The Hidden Sword* (*Daobei cangshen*, dir. Xu Haofeng, 2017) was a long-awaited martial-arts film, and *The Last Wish* and *Better Days* both tell stories about high school. None of these films appear to touch on taboo subjects, such as Western lifestyles, homosexuality, cleavage, and time travel, which had been laid out in guidelines issued in 2016.[14]

In recent years, this type of control also extended to Hong Kong, making Hong Kong's entertainment industry move closer to "mainlandization." In 2016, *Ten Years* (*Shi nian*, dir. Kwok Zune, Fei-Pang Wong, Jevons Au, Kwun-Wai Chow, Ka-Leung Ng, 2015) won Best Picture at the Hong Kong Film Awards; the Chinese government banned the broadcast of the ceremony, calling the film "a virus of the mind" and "a fake proposition without any possibility of realization."[15] One of the *Ten Years* co-directors, Jevons Au, moved to Canada in June 2020 due to Hong Kong's new National Security Law, which may restrict his freedom of speech in making movies.[16] The Hong Kong Film Critics Society also canceled a screening of *Inside the Red Brick Wall* (*Lida weicheng*, dir. HK Documentary Filmmakers, 2020), a documentary about a Hong Kong university besieged by riot police in November 2019. *Where the Wind Blows* (*Feng zai qi shi*, dir. Philip Yung, 2021)—a film about police corruption in 1960s Hong Kong—was pulled from the Hong Kong International Film Festival three days before it opened to the public.[17] Indeed, this preemptive action could be seen as a crisis-prevention process to shape, manage, and respond to some narratives that the Party believes are risky, dangerous, or do not follow the propaganda department's line. The government has taken a set of resolute measures to nip the problems in the bud. The narrative has to be controlled in advance in order to have informational superiority and prevent a negative narrative from developing beyond the Party's capacity to control.

For many years, Beijing's soft-power approach had been aimed at its domestic audience: it was defensive and passive. This approach's most visible expression was film censorship, banning directors from filmmaking for years, and canceling films from national release indefinitely. However, since 2009, China has adopted a more sophisticated and assertive strategy, reshaping the global media system by investing massive amounts of money. Dalian Wanda bought the US's second-largest cinema chain, AMC Theaters, with a historic $2.6 billion purchase in 2012. Dalian Wanda later made the largest deal in American movie production history when it announced it would acquire production and finance company Legendary Entertainment for $3.5 billion in cash in 2016.[18] Chinese firms have also courted Hollywood's film industry by investing in productions such as *Godzilla* (dir. Gareth Edwards, 2014),

Wonder Woman (dir. Patty Jenkins, 2017), *Venom* (dir. Ruben Fleischer, 2018), *Mission Impossible—Fallout* (dir. Christopher McQuarrie, 2018), *Green Book* (dir. Peter Farrelly, 2018), *Jurassic World: Fallen Kingdom* (dir. J. A. Bayona, 2018), *Terminator: Dark Fate* (dir. Tim Miller, 2019), *Gemini Man* (dir. Ang Lee, 2019), *Godzilla: King of the Monsters* (dir. Michael Dougherty, 2019), *Top Gun: Maverick* (dir. Joseph Kosinski, 2022), *Jurassic World Dominion* (dir. Colin Trevorrow, 2022), *Godzilla vs. Kong* (dir. Adam Wingard, 2021).[19] The "mysterious" Chinese Starlight Culture Entertainment Group has launched a $100 million development fund to enlist veteran Hollywood directors, including F. Gary Gay, Roland Emmerich, and James Wan.[20] Within China, film productions are increasingly tightly controlled, but abroad, Beijing has sought to coopt Hollywood filmmakers to "tell China's story well" and attempt to use Hollywood's talents to increase Chinese power.

Xi Jinping's Soft Power: Discourse Power

In the current government, Xi Jinping has adopted Hu's effort with his own, updated version. In 2014, he announced, "We should increase China's soft power, give a good Chinese narrative, and better communicate China's message to the world."[21] He continued much of his predecessor's policies, such as supporting the Confucius Institutes, reinforcing the relationship with developing countries by creating the Belt and Road Initiative, encouraging the media to "go out," and supporting research in different China-related think tanks. Besides all these continuities, Xi Jinping's soft-power policy has renewed its concept to a more offensive nature. Besides the 500-or-so Confucius Institutes, as David Shambaugh has detailed, China has increased its investment in media production and telecommunication infrastructure.[22] Due to the lack of freedom of speech in mainland China, its ambition in the mediascape has posed a challenge to the press's freedom and freedom of expression, and can undermine and discredit the US and other Western's democratic political system. As Freedom House has warned, "[O]ver the past decade, top CCP officials have overseen a dramatic expansion in efforts to shape media content and narratives around the world, affecting every region and multiple languages."[23] In addition, Xinhua News Agency has set up at least 170 bureaus abroad worldwide and China Radio International covertly controls more than 30 radio stations in 14 countries, whose broadcasts are notable for excluding commentary unfavorable to Beijing. A report on widespread demonstrations in Hong Kong supporting universal suffrage, for example, stated that the demonstrations had "failed without the support of the people in Hong Kong."[24]

At the global level, social management is mainly about shaping the direction of international conversations, ranging from sovereignty to cyberspace security, in ways that accommodate the CCP's viewpoints. Thus, in the official Chinese conception, the role of media is to avoid discussing issues and themes the People's Republic of China (PRC) perceives as threatening while simultaneously promoting discussion that favors CCP viewpoints and eventually drowns those unfavorable to the CCP. This perception helps explain why Xi Jinping, during his well-publicized visits to the *People's Daily*, CCTV, and Xinhua, made clear that "the mission of the Party's media work is to provide guidance for the public, serve the country's overall interests, unite the general public, instill confidence and pool strength, tell right from wrong and connect China to the world."[25]

The CCP's objective is to achieve a "discourse power" (*huayu quan*) or "right to speak." The concept of a discourse power "is an extension of soft power, relating to influence and attractiveness of a country's ideology and value system."[26] One of the greatest threats the PRC perceives about protecting the Party in the ideological realm is that "hostile forces," either domestic or foreign, will attempt to subvert China through ideas. For instance, the CCP concluded that the Color Revolutions that took place throughout the "post-Soviet space" in the early 2000s were driven by "raging domestic grievances, electoral politics exploited by the opposition, and Western powers' (the US in particular) intervention for geostrategic interests."[27] While this may not be entirely true, it does not matter. Instead, it reflects the CCP's longstanding perception that hostile external actors like the US meddle in other countries' "internal affairs" and are, therefore, a threat. Thus, Chinese authorities have come to view the free flow of information as a threat—or, as "Document No. 9," promulgated in Spring 2013, puts it, Western journalism "undermine[s] our country's principle that the media should be infused with the spirit of the Party."[28] Thus, as the *Beijing Daily* explained, "The discourse power must focus on the 'discourse,'" and "throughout China's revolution, development and reform, it has persistently emphasized ethnic characteristics such as literature and art, culture, and ideology."[29]

From Soft Power to China's Sharp Power

In their National Endowment for Democracy Report, Walker and Ludwig argue that the soft power of Russia and China is not "soft" but "sharp"; it "pierces, penetrates, or perforates the political and information environments in the targeted countries."[30] Russia and China's sharp power "harness the allure of culture and values to enhance a country's strength."[31] They also argue that the result of this sharp power approach is different from their Cold War strategies.[32] With colossal capital resources, China has injected several narratives about China-related issues. The Chinese government especially wants to mute foreign critics of their increasingly totalitarian political system, human rights issues in Tibet and elsewhere, its territorial claims in the South China Sea, the pro-independence stance of Taiwan, the controversial tech giant Huawei, the 2019–2020 Hong Kong democratic protests, and Xinjiang internment camps.[33]

Over the years, China has used different tools to silence criticism. For example, denying critical journalists' and academics' visas has the effect of "cut[ting them] off from archives, libraries, fieldwork, and government officials."[34] According to the

Foreign Correspondents Club of China (FCCC), in 2020, the Chinese government expelled more than a dozen correspondents, the largest number since the Tiananmen Square massacre in 1989.[35] In March 2021, Beijing escalated its response to the EU's decision to sanction China over Uyghur abuses by putting sanctions on some research scholars.[36] Sometimes journalists or scholars have received vituperative attacks from CCP-controlled media outlets and proxies, attacks that describe them as "frivolous," having "lost their minds," or as individuals whose "obsession with this illusion has deprived them of rational and critical thinking."[37] One of Australia's most prominent publishers, Allen & Unwin, has stalled Clive Hamilton's book *Silent Invasion*.[38] Hamilton is a well-known intellectual and professor at Charles Sturt University in Australia; his book revealed that Australian journalists are being pressured to present China in a positive light. Cambridge University Press, in 2017, removed more than 300 articles related to certain issues that the Chinese government does not want subscribers inside China to be able to read.[39]

Moreover, the CCP has effectively squeezed out alternative Chinese-language voices abroad. Thirty years ago, overseas Chinese-language news media were diverse with a wide range of political perspectives. Today, *The Epoch Times*, *Apple Daily* (Taiwan), *Stand News*, *CitizenNews* and *Initium Media* are the few non-CCP media outlets offering an alternative Chinese-language news source. China's propaganda has thus dominated the narrative within its borders and can influence the world's media.

Scholars have described China's soft power as not-so-soft, but sharp and pervasive instead. China is steadily building its brand of soft power both internally and externally; it seeks to promote a positive image of the country by countering negative narratives to suppress dissent. Starting at least as early as 2009, the Chinese government has begun to use a broad range of Western social media platforms, such as Twitter, Facebook, Instagram, and YouTube, to expand its international influence. Although this strategy's effectiveness is still doubtful, its incentives to establish a social media presence in the media ecosystem are not only targeting domestic users but worldwide users. The film industry, in this regard, is one of the Chinese media outlets to spread Beijing's narrative to the world.

Chinese Films and China's Soft (Sharp) Power

How, then, do these increases in China's soft (sharp) power impact the Chinese film industry?

In August 2013, Xi Jinping asked the Central Propaganda Department (CPD) to do "propaganda work better," suggesting that it must treat online public opinion as its "highest priority."[40] Five years later, the Central Committee decided to dissolve the State Administration of Press, Publication, Radio, Film, and Television (SAPPRFT) and separated broadcast industries from the print and film industries. Under this new configuration, one of the Central Committee members heads the

National Film Bureau, making it directly under the Party's control. Xi Jinping's new structure has shown the importance of films (together with literature and the internet) for propaganda work.

Besides reading over scripts and making sure all films are within the Communist Party's ideology, the same announcement also emphasized that the Film Bureau should make sure all the films produced are playing a "special and crucial role" in "spreading propaganda."[41] The message of the reform is unmistakable and cannot be missed: the popularity of the film is not determined *only* by moviegoers; Beijing remains the center, and the Party is affirming that they are going to tighten the level of political and ideological control over the process of film censorship. Moreover, although the Party made the first law on film passed by the Standing Committee of the National People's Congress in late 2016, the law and regulation were written in a vague format so that no one could say for sure what they can do or cannot do. Some people do something without running into trouble; other people do the same thing, but do get into trouble. Making films also not just based on rules and norms but also the current political circumstances, environment, and other factors. The status of Chinese superstar Fan Bingbing, who has disappeared from public view since 2018, serves as a reminder of the Chinese film industry's opaqueness and uncertain nature.

Xi Jinping Is the "Good Narrative"

What is a "good narrative" in Chinese film? Besides Xi Jinping's trademark slogan "positive energy," what else do we know about this good narrative?

The ultimate goal of this good narrative campaign is, at its core, to shape the opinions and ideas about China and to ensure that the narrative power in films is used in a way consistent with the Party's interests. The first step is to beat back the public's skepticism about the Party's capacity to lead the country. To champion the Chinese political system's superiority, a film in China needs to reveal extraordinary economic success and make the world see China as a great power—and Xi Jinping as the crucial figure in making it one. *Amazing China* (*Lihaile, Wode guo*, dir. Wei Tie, 2018), a documentary released in March 2018 in Chinese theatres, is a good case for illustrating this "good narrative."

Amazing China is a ninety-minute film inspired by Western-style techniques; it has become the all-time, top-grossing domestic documentary in China. The film made its debut three days before China's annual Two Sessions political meeting, where delegates voted to approve the removal of presidential term limits, allowing Xi Jinping to potentially rule China for life. Xi Jinping, who appears in the movie twenty times for more than thirty minutes, is the only star in the film. He congratulates workers on engineering feats, meets peasants who have climbed out of poverty, and delivers slogans to the Communist Party faithful. The film has used multiple grandiose panoramic shots with sharp, high-definition frames to show the nation's famous high-speed rail, bridges, dams, satellites, and aircraft. This state-sponsored documentary aims not only to present the nation's achievements since Xi Jingping assumed office in 2012 but, most importantly, to boost Xi's popularity. In Xi's words, "The Chinese nation, which since modern times began had endured so much for so long, has achieved a tremendous transformation: it has stood up, grown rich, and is becoming strong; it has come to embrace the brilliant prospects of rejuvenation."[42]

Amazing China is a short version of the six-part CCTV Channel 1 miniseries titled *Brilliant China (Huihuang Zhongguo,* dir. Pan Min, 2017), aired a year earlier. Official media said that the film is based on the new development concepts of innovation, coordination, greenness, openness, and sharing to fully reflect the outstanding achievements of China's economic and social development since the 18th National Congress of the Party. The films created a gargantuan set, including hiring eight film crews who traveled to thirty-one provinces, autonomous regions, and municipalities across the country over three months. They filmed nearly 3,200 hours, included 300 hours of aerial footage, interviewed 108 people and documented numerous records.[43] Through the spectacular and shocking large-scale aerial photography scenes, *Amazing China* earned $72.5 million,[44] surpassing the 2017 film *Twenty Two* (*Er shi er,* dir. Ke Guo, 2017), a film about World War II comfort women, to become the highest-grossing documentary film in China.

The titles of the six-part of *Brilliant China* are "Dreams Come True Project" ("*Yuanmeng gongcheng*"), "Vigorous Innovations" ("*Chuangxin huoli*"), "Coordinated Development" ("*Xietiao fazhan*"), "Green Home" ("*Lüse jiayuan*"), "Sharing Prosperity" ("*Gongxiang xiaokang*"), and "Opening China" ("*Kaifang Zhongguo*").[45] Besides its economic success, the miniseries records a series of achievements China has made since 2012, demonstrating its robust technology, science, military advancement, poverty reduction, environmental stewardship, and global integration. These six episodes all fall under the rubric of Xi Jinping's Chinese Dream. Thus a "good narrative" in the film must put Xi Jinping in the center, and all other leaders (especially Deng Xiaoping) in the periphery.

My People, My Country and the 2020 world's highest-grossing film *The Eight Hundred* (2021) are two more examples showcasing what a "good narrative" is. *My People, My Country* is comprised of seven short films by seven different directors, including well-known directors Chen Kaige and Huang Jianxin. The film celebrates the seventieth anniversary of the founding of the People's Republic of China; however, there are many differences between the *My People, My Country* and other National Day celebration movies. Other National Day movies are traditional types of historical films that look at the Chinese civil war and the founding of new China, such as *The Founding of a Republic* (*Jianguo daye,* dir. Huang Jianxin and Han Sanping, 2009) and *The Birth of New China* (*Kaiguo dadian,* dir. Li Qiankuan, Xiao Guiyun, 1989); *My People, My Country* chronicles seven historical moments after the civil war. Additionally, *The Founding of a Republic's* success was an all-star movie where at least 100 A-list actors and actresses were hired to play different historical figures, while *My People, My Country*'s seven stories are about nameless, ordinary people living during historical moments. For example, the second story, "Passing By," is a love story about a girl and an atomic bomb technician. At the end, the film's narrator said:

> On the road to the modernization of our national defense, many technical developers, workers, and soldiers died young. They set a historical milestone with their incredible lives. They were nameless to the public and away from their families. Toiling selflessly, they completed thousands of experiments under challenging conditions. They are nameless heroes and the pillars supporting our nation. Time erodes rocks, but it will not wither our memories of them because being unnamed does not mean being unknown.

Moreover, these seven stories in the movie all build upon three themes: political ceremony (the first story, "The Eve," and the fourth story, "Going Home"), military technology (the second story, "Passing By"; the sixth story, "The Guiding Star"; and the seventh story, "One for All"), and competitive sports (the third story, "The Champion," and the fifth story, "Hello Beijing"). Unlike the old generation of National Day celebration movies used to express collective national sentiment, these stories are filled with personal stories and individual struggles, such as love, poverty, father-and-son relationships, work, and gender inequality.

Notably, the great political leaders are nearly absent in this new version of the celebration film. While the early National Day celebration films used to cultivate nationalistic feelings through the perfect leadership of the Communist political leaders, such as Mao Zedong in *The Birth of New China* (*Kaiguo dadian*, dir. Li Qiankuan, Xiao Guiyun, 1989), *My People, My Country* uses the seven stories to trigger national sentiments via those unknown people to enable all audiences to recognize themselves in the seventy-year history of the country. The nameless characters in *My People, My Country* cross multiple classes, ethnicities, and regions, including elites in the city, working women, poor rural farmers, jobless minorities, divorced fathers and mothers, factory workers, people from Hong Kong, minorities in autonomous regions, and Chinese who live overseas. The film's Chinese title, *Me and My Motherland*, is borrowed from a classic song originally performed by singer Li Guyi in 1985. The song was reworked by pop diva Faye Wong in 2019, and its release triggered national discussions on social media. The song's lyrics suggest an unbreakable unity between citizen and country, and the seven stories enable all audiences to relate to the country's process of development and achievement. The message "I am the country" or "the country is mine" is poured into the movie. The mass response to the song and the movie shows that cultural engineering has worked very well, not only with domestic audiences but also among the Chinese Diaspora.

The Eight Hundred was pushed away from screening in 2019 but released back into Chinese theaters in the middle of the pandemic with minimal publicity, yet through word of mouth it managed to become the highest-grossing film of 2020. The film is based on a historical incident of soldiers defending the Sihang Warehouse in Shanghai on November 1, 1937. It started with a strong cast of well-known Chinese actors and was directed by the man behind the fantastic *Mr. Six* (*Lao paoer*, 2015), Guan Hu. Compared to the Taiwanese version of *Eight Hundred Heroes* (1976), not only are the "heroes" missing in Guan Hu's version but the "eight hundred" (in history, a little over 400) soldiers are comprised of "a plucky rag-tag band of 800 soldiers."[46] Some of these soldiers are leftovers from other defeated regiments, as well as several men marked as deserters. Some are capable of fighting, some are scared of battle, and some are just young boys, while one is merely an accountant. This war movie is unashamedly patriotic, but what is refreshing about this patriotism is that it did not fall into the typical depiction of Chinese suffering in the Second World War, like the once-most-expensive Chinese movie *The Flowers of War* (*Jinling shisan chai*, dir. Zhang Yimou, 2011). This time, Guan Hu is not afraid to show soldiers being leaderless and planless in a war; they are still fighting with a spirit of unity against the Japanese or foreigners. However, some critics argue the movie failed to build a "personal connection" between the audience and its protagonists, saying "it was just a compilation of many deaths" and lacks "any sense of camaraderie among the defenders of Shang Warehouse."[47]

Heroes in the movies are not typical soldiers but ordinary people, like the girl who crosses the bridge to deliver the national flag or the man who pulls the phone line across the river. This leaderless and planless resistance shown in *The Eight Hundred* would only have happened in pre-modern China. Indeed, this criticism is precisely what Xi Jinping's "good narrative" film is: there was no hero before the founding of the People's Republic of China. Shang Warehouse's battle offered a sacrifice to the "old" China or even a "non" China; the death of the people in the film was a ritual to welcome a new China's formation. The movie's final scene is a wide shot of Sihang Warehouse; it is immediately replaced by a new, developed, modern view with numerous skyscrapers in "new" Shanghai. The film's underlying message is that a prosperous and robust China is rising to lead on the world stage.

My People, My Country, and *The Eight Hundred* shed light on those ordinary people instead of perfect political leaders, which is very different from previous generations of propaganda films. These two films also reveal one of the main goals of the "good narrative" in film: to venerate the indefinite ruler Xi Jinping, who is the most powerful leader in China since Mao Zedong—and who is now unchallengeable by the Chinese and the world.

"Good Narratives" with High Budgets

One of the most significant differences between the old propaganda films and recent propaganda is the high production value. China is not only the world's fastest-growing movie market, but it was also the world's largest market in box office revenue in

2020, and it has the largest number of viewers in the world. Many new forces (such as internet companies and real estate developers) are not only emerging, but are penetrating the entertainment industry and creating a vast media ecosystem within and across the border of China. Of the 100 most expensive non-English films, the Chinese made one-third of them.

These big-budget Chinese blockbusters are different from the previous nationalist movies that came out of the state sector. These Chinese films have large budgets to accomodate top actors, glamorous locations, and spectacular special effects. In other words, these are "Hollywood made in China," a term borrowed from Aynne Kokas,[48] but full of Chinese nationalistic sentiment and statements. Films in the 1950s and 1960s, such as *The White-Haired Girl* (*Baimao nü*, dir. Wang Bin, Shui Hua, 1950), *Battle on Shangganling Mountain* (*Shangganling*, dir. Sha Meng, Lin Shan, 1956), and *The Red Detachment of Women* (*Hongse niangzi jun*, dir. Xie Jin, 1961), were aimed at spreading a unifying message: a Communist vision to knit together a vast and divided country. The contemporary films aim to link Xi's "new era" to China's past, present, and future in a single narrative. *Amazing China* and *Brilliant China* are more sophisticated, and are no longer selling an "anti-foreign" worldview by indulging in cheap gimmicks such as those "divine anti-Japanese dramas" (*kangRi shenju*), a popular genre of Chinese TV shows that are rather decidedly pro-China.

"Good Narratives" with High Revenue

As mentioned earlier, cinema has been promoted to a higher "priority" and is directly under the Party's control. The reason behind this bureaucratic restructuring is the market value of the fast-growing Chinese film industry. Compared to the film market two decades ago, the Chinese market today is nearly 170 times as large (total gross $5.45 million in 2002 versus $9.14 billion in 2019), and the pandemic has accelerated the geographic transition of the largest movie market from North America to China. China's box office reached $1.988 billion on October 18, 2020, slightly more than North America's total of $1.937 billion.[49] Indeed, the 2020 box office for all films released in China was $3 billion compared to only $2.2 billion in the US and Canada.[50] Although China is now officially the world's top moviegoing market, its box office was down 70 percent from 2019 levels, even as it recovered more quickly from the COVID-19 pandemic than the US and much of Europe. According to the same report, the vast majority of Hollywood's big-budget films have been delayed and most were sent or sold to streaming services, leading to a 31 percent increase in the global digital home/mobile entertainment market. This leaves some uncertainty about the film market competition between the US and China, but Hollywood's dominance in China has been replaced by the country's homemade, big-budget blockbusters.

The patriotic blockbuster *Wolf Warrior 2*, which has made $875 million world-wide, not only became the highest-grossing Chinese-made film ever but also the highest-grossing non-English film of all time. It was also the first non-English film to make the list of the 100 highest-grossing films of all time. Different from the 2020 highest-grossing film *The Eight Hundred*, the core sentiment of *Wolf Warrior 2* is not anti-foreign but rather pro-China. This pro-China stance has inspired many followers, including Dante Lam's *Operation Red Sea* (*Honghai xingdong*, 2018) and the first Chinese science fiction film, *The Wandering Earth* (2019). *Wolf Warrior 2*, released in July 2017, tells the story of an unnamed African country where workers in a Chinese factory are taken hostage by mercenaries from Europe. The action hero is played by director Wu Jing, who took on the role of an ex-military man. *Operation Red Sea*, which came out in February 2018, is based in a fictional country called Yahweh, and *The Wandering Earth*, released in February 2019, takes Chinese cinema even further afield: it is a science fiction film set in space. None of these three films followed the conventional propaganda or main melody film (*zhuxuanlü dianying*) structure, focusing instead on a specific moment or event—for example, like *The Birth of New China* (*Kaiguo dadian*, dir. Li Qiankuan, Xiao Guiyun, 1989)—or on special characters, as with *Mao Zedong 1949* (*Juesheng shike*, dir. Huang Jianxin, 2019). These films' settings are semi-fictional with solid heroic figures. As Stanley Rosen has argued, this new type of propaganda film has a huge budget, but they are just like Hollywood-made patriotic films. They do not stress collectivism, which was commonly seen in the old patriotic films, and they downplay the Communist Party in favor of an individualistic personal quest.[51]

In the past, propaganda films mostly came out of the state-owned studios; reforms in 2000 saw many of those studios disappear, get consolidated, or become overtaken by private sector companies. The state sector has also learned from what the private sector has been doing: Chinese filmmakers learned how to make films with messages that the Communist Party liked but with a Hollywood system. The box office receipts has picked up where the Chinese film industry is delivering popular films that at the same time meet the requirements of the Party. Super-hit films are becoming essential for the Communist Party's media strategy.

Conclusion

This chapter began by looking at the definition of soft power in the Chinese context, then delved into different exemplifications of soft power in the Chinese film indus-try, including China's sharp power and Xi Jinping's "good narrative." Then, based on soft power manifestation in Chinese films, this chapter discussed the current changes and adaptations seen in big-budget propaganda films. Change does not happen overnight; it happens in different stages. Through consolidation of the Party's control in the film industry and related changes, the Party will continue exert discipline over the people involved in the field. However, in order to attract more audiences, more creativity in film content is required. Looking forward, greater control in the internet and digital streaming arenas will continue to be the defining features of China's soft power in Xi Jinping's New Era. State-sponsored works such as the *Wolf Warrior* sequel, *Operation Red Sea*, and similar genres will be seen more often.

Some studies have shown that China's soft power did not transport well. People in other countries appreciate China's economic transformation and benefit from the Belt and Road Initiative, but they do not "trust" China.[52] In contrast, based on film industry statistics, it has been suggested that the Chinese cultural plateau has enormous influence on its own people, particularly with regard to Chinese national identities and endorsement of the authoritarian regime. Arguably, Xi Jinping's propaganda policies and ideological work is already exerting tremendous soft power within its borders. Based on a 2008 survey, Tang and Darr found among 35 countries and regions, the Chinese have the highest level of nationalism, with a score out of 80 of 100, higher than the US, Japan, Australia, or South Korea. The US-China trade war since 2018, tensions in the South China Sea, the suppression of Hong Kong's pro-democratic movement in 2019–2020, and the Xinjiang cotton ban in 2021 all added fuel to the flames of Chinese nationalism.[53] In this environment, big-budget propaganda films have become an outlet for people to vent their anger and emotions. While the potential of *Wolf Warrior 2* or *My People, My Country* in the West remains doubtful, primarily due to its jingoistic and unrealistic vision, its favorable reception in the Chinese market signifies a victory for Chinese domestic policy and future soft-power potential. Although people may argue that using film to promote Chinese soft power to foreigners is less critical than influencing foreign governments' behaviors, Beijing and its ambitious entertainment conglomerates are running an extensive and sophisticated long-term policy to reshape the global film industry landscape with a China-friendly global narrative.[54] Through different acquisitions, large-scale film studio ventures, and the fastest-growing film market, China is increasing its footprint in the global film industry; and Beijing, in turn, is moving from building censorship control over domestic content toward greater influence over the content of overseas creations and productions. Moreover, through various coproductions, Beijing is cultivating a cadre of Party supporters (such as Andrew Lau, Dante Lam and Tsui Hark, among others)[55] to outsource its influence to individual industrial talents. To this end, Beijing is leveraging global filmmakers and workers to serve its goal: telling stories about China and spreading China's voice. Overall, Beijing's principal objective is boosting its influence overseas in a way that aligns with its policy priorities, particularly in gaining favorable depictions and deflecting attention from its repressive regime and poor human-rights records. Thus, the Chinese film industry may not be Beijing's priority or the most effective tool in promoting its soft power, but once it controls the industrial landscape's nodes (market, finance, and talent), it can use them as it wants.

Notes

1. Patrick Frater, "China's Box Office Total Breaks All-Time Record," *Variety*, December 18, 2019, https://variety.com/2019/film/asia/china-box-office-breaks-all-time-record-cinema-ne-zha-wandering-earth-1203447147/.

2. Box Office Mojo by IMDbPro, "The Wandering Earth," accessed March 27, 2021, https://www.boxofficemojo.com/movies/?id=thewanderingearth.htm.

3. CGTN, "Domestic Films Open Record-Breaking New Year Box Office," *China Daily*, January 13, 2021, https://www.chinadaily.com.cn/a/202101/13/WS5ffe7743a31024ad0baa2569.html.

4. Mareike Ohlberg, "Propaganda beyond the Great Firewall," Mercator Institute for China Studies, December 5, 2019, https://merics.org/en/short-analysis/propaganda-beyond-great-firewall.

5. During the Sixth Plenary Session of the 17th CPC Central Committee in 2011, China's national strategy of "Chinese Culture Going Global" was first put forward.

6. On October 15, 2014, Xi Jinping pointed out at the Symposium on Literary and Artistic Work that while developing China's economy, the cultural voice should not lag. China should make more robust a large number of cultural aircraft carriers with Chinese characteristics and carry out the global dissemination of "Chinese Stories" in order to strengthen the voice of China, which is the essential cultural mission of Chinese people at present, which is also the responsibility of Chinese people to realize Chinese Dream.

7. Xi Jinping, "Full Text of Xi Jinping's Report at 19th CPC National Congress," *China Daily*, October 18, 2017, https://www.chinadaily.com.cn/china/19thcpcnationalcongress/2017-11/04/content_34115212.htm.

8. Xi, "Full Text of Xi Jinping's Report at 19th CPC National Congress."

9. Vijay Gokhale, "China Is Gnawing at Democracy's Roots Worldwide," *Foreign Policy*, December 18, 2020, https://foreignpolicy.com/2020/12/18/china-democracy-ideology-communist-party/.

10. Joseph S. Nye, Jr., "Soft Power," *Foreign Policy*, no. 80 (Autumn 1990): 166, https://doi-org/10.2307/1148580.

11. Barthelemy Courmont, "Soft Power Debates in China," *Academic Foresights*, no. 13 (January–June 2015), http://www.academic-foresights.com/Soft_Power_Debates_in_China.html; Shaun Breslin, "The Soft Notion of China's 'Soft Power'" (Asia Programme Paper: ASP PP 2011/03), Chatham House, February 2011, https://www.chathamhouse.org/sites/default/files/public/Research/Asia/0211pp_breslin.pdf; Erica Orange, Jared Weiner, and Eshanthi Ranasinghe, "China Ascendant: 'Soft Power' in an Open Global Order," *Medium* (Omidyar Network blog, March 4, 2019), https://medium.com/omidyar-network/china-ascendant-soft-power-in-an-open-global-order-b3f447a48021.

12. "Hu Calls for Enhancing 'Soft Power' of Chinese Culture," *Xinhua News Agency*, October 15, 2007, http://www.china.org.cn/english/congress/228142.htm.

13. "Zhidao xin shidai guojia anquan gongzuo de qiangda sixiang wuqi" [A powerful ideological weapon to guide national security work in the new era], *People's Daily*, May 4, 2018, http://dangjian.people.com.cn/n1/2018/0504/c117092-29964484.html.

14. James Griffiths, "Banned on Chinese TV: 'Western Lifestyles,' Cleavage and Time Travel," CNN, August 31, 2016, https://www.cnn.com/2016/08/31/asia/china-banned-on-tv-censorship/index.html.

15. Matthew Carney, "Hong Kong Film *Ten Years* Pulled from Cinemas by China," ABC News, April 3, 2016, https://www.abc.net.au/news/2016-04-03/hong-kong-film-ten-years-pulled-from-cinemas-by-china/7295420.

16. Heidi Hsia, "*Ten Years* Co-Director 'Runs Away' to Canada," Yahoo! Style, July 30, 2020, https://sg.style.yahoo.com/style/ten-years-co-director-runs-031600794.html.

17. Patrick Frater, "Hong Kong Film Festival Cancels Opening Movie, Citing Unspecified Technical Reasons," *Variety*, March 29, 2021, https://variety.com/2021/film/asia/hong-kong-festival-cancels-opening-film-where-the-wind-blows-1234939989/.

18. Brooks Barnes, "Dalian Wanda of China Offers a Carrot to Hollywood," *The New York Times*, October 17, 2016, https://www.nytimes.com/2016/10/18/business/media/dalian-wanda-goes-on-an-entertainment-shopping-spree.html.

19. Ben Fritz and Laurie Burkitt, "China's Dalian Wanda Buys Legendary Entertainment for $3.5 Billion," *The Wall Street Journal*, January 12, 2016, https://www.wsj.com/articles/chinas-dalian-wanda-buys-legendary-entertainment-for-3-5-billion-1452567251.

20. Patrick Brzeski, "Chinese Film Fund Bets $100M on Hollywood Directors amid Fraught US Relations," *The Hollywood Reporter*, August 28, 2017, https://www.hollywoodreporter.com/news/chinese-film-fund-bets-100m-hollywood-directors-fraught-us-relations-1032938.

21. "Xi Eyes More Enabling Int'l Environment for China's Peaceful Development," *Xinhua*, November 30, 2014.

22. David L. Shambaugh, "China's Soft-Power Push," *Foreign Affairs*, July/August 2015, https://www.foreignaffairs.com/articles/china/2015-06-16/chinas-soft-power-push.

23. Sarah Cook, *Beijing's Global Megaphone: The Expansion of Chinese Communist Party Media Influence since 2017*, January 2020, p. 1, https://freedomhouse.org/sites/default/files/2020-02/01152020_SR_China_Global_Megaphone_with_Recommendations_PDF.pdf.

24. Gui Qing Koh and John Shiffman, "Exposed: China's Covert Global Radio Network," *Reuters*, November 2, 2015, https://www.reuters.com/investigates/special-report/china-radio/.

25. "News Organizations Should Better Serve the People: Xinhua President," *Xinhua*, February 19, 2018, http://www.xinhuanet.com/english/2018-02/19/c_136985413.htm.

26. Peter Mattis, "An American Lens on China's Interference and Influence-Building Abroad," The Asan Forum, April 30, 2018, http://www.theasanforum.org/an-american-lens-on-chinas-interference-and-influence-building-abroad/. See also Peter Mattis, "In a Fortnight: China's International Right to Speak," *China Brief: A Journal of Analysis and Information* 12, no. 20 (October 19, 2012): 1–3, https://jamestown.org/wp-content/uploads/2012/10/cb_10_19.pdf?x69464.

27. Titus C. Chen, "China's Reaction to the Color Revolutions: Adaptive Authoritarianism in Full Swing," *Asian Perspective* 34, no. 2 (2010): 6.

28. "Document 9: A ChinaFile Translation. How Much Is a Hardline Party Directive Shaping China's Current Political Climate?," *China File*, November 8, 2013, https://www.chinafile.com/document-9-chinafile-translation.

29. Tao Wenzhao, "'Qiong' yu 'da': Zhongguo huayuquan di bianzhengfa" [Being "poor" and "well-off": A dialectic on Chinese discourse power], *Beijing Daily*, January 9, 2017, http://www.xinhuanet.com/politics/2017-01/09/c_1120270739.htm.

30. Christopher Walker and Jessica Ludwig, "From 'Soft Power' to 'Sharp Power': Rising Authoritarian Influence in the Democratic World," in *Sharp Power: Rising Authoritarian Influence*, ed. Juan Pablo Cardenal, Jacek Kucharczyk, Grigorij Mesežnikov, and Gabriela Pleschová, National Endowment for Democracy and International Forum for Democratic Studies, December 5, 2017, 6, https://www.ned.org/wp-content/uploads/2017/12/Sharp-Power-Rising-Authoritarian-Influence-Full-Report.pdf.

31. Joseph S. Nye, Jr. "Soft Power: the evolution of a concept." *Journal of Political Power*, February 2021, https://doi.org/10.1080/2158379X.2021.1879572, p. 8.

32. Christopher Walker and Jessica Ludwig, "From 'Soft Power' to 'Sharp Power': Rising Authoritarian Influence in the Democratic World," in *Sharp Power: Rising Authoritarian Influence*, ed. Juan Pablo Cardenal, Jacek Kucharczyk, Grigorij Mesežnikov, and Gabriela Pleschová, National Endowment for Democracy and International Forum for Democratic Studies, December 5, 2017, 6, https://www.ned.org/wp-content/uploads/2017/12/Sharp-Power-Rising-Authoritarian-Influence-Full-Report.pdf.

33. "How China's 'Sharp Power' Is Muting Criticism Abroad," *The Economist*, December 14, 2017, https://www.economist.com/briefing/2017/12/14/how-chinas-sharp-power-is-muting-criticism-abroad.

34. Orville Schell and Larry Diamond, "China Gets Its Message to Americans but Doesn't Want to Reciprocate," *The Wall Street Journal*, December 21, 2018, https://www.wsj.com/articles/china-gets-its-message-to-americans-but-doesnt-want-to-reciprocate-11545407490.

35. "Foreign Journalists in China See 'Rapid Decline in Media Freedom': Survey," *Reuters*, February 28, 2021, https://www.reuters.com/article/us-china-media/foreign-journalists-in-china-see-rapid-decline-in-media-freedom-survey-idUSKCN2AT182.

36. Ministry of Foreign Affairs of the People's Republic of China, "Foreign Ministry Spokesperson Announces Sanctions on Relevant EU Entities and Personnel," March 22, 2021, https://www.fmprc.gov.cn/mfa_eng/xwfw_665399/s2510_665401/2535_665405/t1863106.shtml.

37. Ilan Berman, *Digital Dictators: Media, Authoritarianism, and America's New Challenge* (Lanham, MD: Rowman & Littlefield, 2018), 36.

38. Jacqueline Williams, "Australian Furor over Chinese Influence Follows Book's Delay," *The New York Times*, November 20, 2017, https://www.nytimes.com/2017/11/20/world/australia/china-australia-book-influence.html.

39. Ian Johnson, "Cambridge University Press Removes Academic Articles on Chinese Site," *The New York Times*, August 18, 2017, https://www.nytimes.com/2017/08/18/world/asia/cambridge-university-press-academic-freedom.html.

40. "Xue xi Guanche Xi Jinping Zai Zhongguo Xuanchuan sixiang gongzhuo huiyi Shang Zhongyao Jianhua Jingshen" [Study and implement the spirit of Xi Jinping's speech at the National Propaganda and Ideological Work Conference], Xinhua Net, accessed March 27, 2021, http://www.xinhuanet.com/politics/szxzt/qgxcsxgzhy/index.htm.

41. "Zhonggong Zhongyang Yinfa 'Shenhua Dang He Guojia Jigou Gaige Fanan'" [The Central Commiittee of the Chinese Communist Party issued the "Deeping Party and

State Institutional Reform Plan"], Xinhua Net, March 21, 2018, http://www.xinhuanet. com/politics/2018-03/21/c_1122570517_3.htm.

42. "Full Text of Xi Jinping's Report at 19th CPC National Congress," *China Daily*, November 4, 2017, https://www.chinadaily.com.cn/china/19thcpcnationalcongress/2017-11/04/ content_34115212.htm.

43. "The Six-Episode TV Documentary 'Brilliant China' Panorama Shows the Achievements of Economic and Social Development since the 18th National Congress of the Communist Party," *Xinhua*, September 16, 2017, http://jingji.cctv.com/2017/09/16/ ARTIzj65QqlLKgzrN2KXMjlG170916.shtml.

44. Box Office Mojo by IMDbPro, "*Amazing China*," accessed March 29, 2021, https://www. boxofficemojo.com/release/rl147489793/weekend/.

45. *Huihuang Zhongguo* [Brilliant China], CCTV, September 2017, http://jingji.cctv.com/ special/hhzg/index.shtml.

46. Ian Freer, "*The Eight Hundred* Review," *Empire Online*, September 18, 2020, https:// www.empireonline.com/movies/reviews/the-eight-hundred/.

47. Richard Yu, "Review: 'The Eight Hundred' Shows Valiant Chinese Heroes, But Falls Short of a Good War Movie," *Cinema Escapist*, September 7, 2020, https://www.cin-emaescapist.com/2020/09/review-the-eight-hundred/.

48. Aynne Kokas, *Hollywood Made in China* (Oakland: University of California Press, 2017).

49. Patrick Brzeski, "It's Official: China Overtakes North America as World's Biggest Box Office in 2020," *The Hollywood Reporter*, October 19, 2020, https://www.hollywoo-dreporter.com/news/general-news/its-official-china-overtakes-north-america-as-worlds-biggest-box-office-in-2020-4078850/.

50. *2020 THEME Report*, Motion Picture Association, March 18, 2021, https://www. motionpictures.org/wp-content/uploads/2021/03/MPA-2020-THEME-Report.pdf.

51. Chris Buckley, "In China, an Action Hero Beats Box Office Records (and Arrogant Westerners)," *The New York Times*, August 16, 2017, https://www.nytimes.com/2017/ 08/16/world/asia/china-wolf-warrior-2-film.html.

52. Jonathan McClory, *The Soft Power 30: A Global Ranking of Soft Power 2019*, Portland and USC Center on Public Diplomacy, https://softpower30.com/wp-content/uploads/ 2019/10/The-Soft-Power-30-Report-2019-1.pdf.

53. Yanan Wang and Sam McNeil, "China Voices Strength, Pushes Nationalism around Trade War," *AP News*, May 15, 2019, https://apnews.com/article/f887e7219a6d 4269989e5f527ccb971b.

54. Many scholars have explored this topic, besides the NED's *Sharp Power: Rising Authoritarian Influence*, discussed briefly in this chapter. See, for example, Clive Hamilton and Alex Joske, *The Silent Invasion: China's Influence in Australia* (Richmond: Hardie Grant Books, 2018); Jonathan Manthorpe, *Claws of the Panda: Beijing's Campaign of Influence and Intimidation in Canada* (Toronto: Cormorant Books, 2019); Robert Spalding and Seth Kaufman, *Stealth War: How China Took Over while America's Elite Slept* (New York: Penguin, 2019); Chinese academic-in-exile He Qinglian's *Hongse shentou: Zhongguo meiti quanqiu kuozhang de zhenxiang* [Red infiltration: Global expan-sion of Chinese media] (Taipei: Ba Qi Wen Hua, 2019); Taiwanese scholar Wu Jiemin's edited volume *Diaodeng li de Ju Mang: Zhongguo ensure zuoyongli yu fanzuoyongli*

[The anaconda in chandelier: Mechanisms of influence and resistance in the "China Factor"] (Taipei: Zuo An Wenhua Chuban, 2017); and most recently, Clive Hamilton and Mareike Ohlberg's *Hidden Hand: Exposing How the Chinese Communist Party Is Reshaping the World* (London: Oneworld Publications, 2020).

55. Hong Kong filmmaker Andrew Lau directed and produced two National Day Celebration movies in 2019: *The Captain* and *The Bravest*; Hong Kong director Dante Lam directed two commercial nationalistic blockbusters, *Operation Mekong* (2016) and *Operation Red Sea* (2018); and Oxide Pang directed a not-so-well-received Korean War film, *My War* (2016). Tsui Hark and Dante Lam (and co-directed with mainland Chinese director Chen Kaige) made a National Day Celebration movie called *The Battle at Lake Changjin* (2021), which has became one of the most successful films in 2021. Finally, Hong Kong–born Peter Chan, one of the few directors to win the top prizes of China, Taiwan, and Hong Kong, has directed a biographical sports film, *Leap* (2020), that won him the best feature film in the Chinese government-backed Golden Rooster Awards in November 2020. That film is also China's entry to the Academy Awards' Best International Feature Film category in 2021. For more, read Karen Chu and Patrick Brzeski, "Why Hong Kong's Top Filmmakers Are Making China Propaganda Films," *The Hollywood Reporter*, February 13, 2018, https://www.hollywoodreporter.com/news/why-hong-kongs-top-filmmakers-are-making-china-propaganda-films-1004572.

Epilogue

Po-Shek Fu and Stanley Rosen

We were privileged to give keynote presentations at the conference organized at the University of Idaho in 2018 by Jeff Kyong-McClain, Russell Meeuf, and Jing Jing Chang. It was a rich and memorably engaging conference that covered many important aspects of Chinese and Sinophone cinemas that have been hotly debated in the fields. With amazing speed Jeff, Russell, and Jing Jing have put most of the papers into a book and asked us to write an epilogue for it. In the introduction, the editors explain that they have organized the book along the four themes of politics and dissent, transnational reception, cultural identity, and film markets and financial reform. With that in mind, we choose instead to focus our discussion on two major questions touched on by many of the chapters. First, we discuss the complexity of identity politics. Second, we examine China's attempt to use film as a medium to expand its global impact, primarily through coproductions with foreign partners, in an effort to "tell China's story well," and thereby increase the country's soft power.

I

The ambiguities of identities in China and the Sinophonic world are a big theme to come out of this book. This is no surprise. There has been so much scholarship in recent years devoted to the complex question of Chineseness and global cultural production. As a medium of sound and images, appealing to a mass audience across territorial borders, film is indeed one of the most potent sites for the struggles to construct, circulate, and contest the meanings of who we are. This fight for the power to define our imagined communities, as many contributors to this book demonstrate, permeated Chinese-language cinemas across the globe: from China to Hong Kong to Singapore and to France and the United States.

These films give voices to the weak and marginal. Just as the Cantonese-speaking British colonial businessman Alan in the China–Hong Kong coproduced drama *Shanghai Fever* (*Gu feng*, dir. Lee Kwok-lap, 1994) realizes that—in spite of his knowledge of global finances and his partnership with Chinese investor Fan Li—he is just a "second class citizen" in the country he calls "homeland," their struggle to reimagine who they are is thus to resist the hegemonic discourse of such homogenizing nationalism. As Joseph Tse-Hei Lee points out in his timely Chapter 2, the antigovernment protests that have been roiling postcolonial Hong Kong since the "Umbrella Movement" of 2014 are inspired by the fearful frustration over the "disappearance of local ways of life" (which included limited independence and a cosmopolitan lifestyle) in the face of mounting "mainlandization." These frustrations gave rise to the "indigenous turn" in electoral politics and grassroots movement, and at the same time to a new wave of films of social engagements. These small-budget films, which include the award-winning *Ten Years* (*Shi nian*, dir. Kwok Zune, Fei-Pang Wong, Jevons Au, Kwun-Wai Chow, Ka-Leung Ng, 2015) and *Lost in the Fumes* (*Dihou tiangao*, dir. Nora Lam, 2017), a documentary biography of Edward Leung who calls for local self-determination and democratic representation, give voice to the "collective vulnerability" and loss of faith, especially among the young generations in the former British colony. However, underneath the frustrations and disillusionments, Lee's chapter shows that these films seem to be ambivalent about what constitutes the collective identity of the city beyond a shared indignation against the degeneration from the promised "One Country, Two Systems" to the so-called "One Country, Two Societies." Ambivalent or not, the collective indignation would continue to bring protesters to the streets in the days ahead.

While artists and activists in Hong Kong turn mainly "local" (in connection with global values) in the search for identity, some filmmakers look beyond national boundaries for self-understanding and collective engagement. In Chapter 3, Man-Fung Yip brings to our attention the stunning experimental documentary film *Behemoth* (*Beixi moshou*, 2015) made by Zhao Liang, a media artist from Dandong, China. An independent filmmaker, he sees himself as part of a global force fighting to save the world from ecological and climatic crisis. *Behemoth* focuses on China—the environmental crisis and human suffering as a result of the illusory nature of China's "economic miracle"—but its vision and ambition is global. Funded by French sources and aimed for audiences at international film festivals, the filmmaker structures his work as a dialogue with classical Western texts (especially Dante's *Divine Comedy*) and major trends of contemporary cinema and multimedia arts. And he urges all his compatriots around the globe to consider: "As some of us are enjoying a more and more luxurious lifestyle, shouldn't we reflect on that way of life? We all are consumers of natural resources, so we are all accomplices of that evil that's hurting the environment. All of us are part of the monster."

Several chapters in this book further suggest that the complexity of identity is deeply intertwined with the politics of language. Following the Nanjing regime's (mostly inconsistent) language policy of using *Guoyu* as an instrument of national unity, Beijing suppressed local dialects as threats to unifying nationalism. Except for a spate of opera films produced in the early 1950s and '60s for the purpose of cultural diplomacy and export (especially to Hong Kong and Southeast Asia), dialects were largely absent from the silver screen. When China began to open up to the capitalist world in the 1980s, a coproduced film attracted attention for its mélange of dialects, including Shanghainese, Cantonese, and several Wu-area dialects. It was *Shanghai Fever* (1994). The use of Shanghainese, as Lin Feng argues in Chapter 7, expressed post-Mao Shanghai's re-emerged "local pride" as the former "Paris of Asia." The film represented its desires to take advantage of the Reform to "re-modernize and "re-globalize." It was popular among the audiences, and a new version was quickly released but was now dubbed into *Putonghua*. Moreover, its sequel, *Four Chefs and a Feast* (*Chunfeng deyi meilongzhen*, dir. Lee Kwok-lap, 1998), also featuring Shanghai–Hong Kong connections, speaks *Putonghua* with different regional accents. The loss of dialect on the big screen suggested the suppression of Shanghai's reemerging identity and emphasis instead of its role as the "national" model of economic modernization. This suppression of local dialect can become a "linguistic genocide" as dramatized in the third part of *Ten Years*, directed by Jevons Au. Here speaking Cantonese, which is a constitutive part of the Hong Kong identity, means no future.

When *Putonghua* becomes *Hanyu* in Southeast Asia, it takes on an ambivalent role in the web of identity politics. As Alison M. Groppe reveals, in Chapter 8, in her study of songstress trope in Sinophone cinemas, Royston Tan's acclaimed films such as *881* (2007) and *12 Lotus* (*Shi'er lianhua*, 2008) bring to light the complexity of Singapore's linguistic hierarchy. While the Singaporean government privileges English over all ethnic languages as the official language of business, since at least the "Speak Mandarin Campaign" in 1979 *Hanyu* has been designated the official language for the Singaporean Chinese community. All dialects, notably Hokkien, Teochow, and Cantonese, were banned from school curricula as well as from mass media. This brings to mind critic Trinh T. Minh-ha's notion of marginal in the center and center in the margin in discussing the ambiguity of identity politics.[1] In spite of the enormous linguistic heterogeneity in Singapore, moreover, the government has tried to give credit to the English-speaking and bilingual (also *Hanyu*) "cosmopolitans" for the city-state's economic prosperity and global success, at the expense of the poor, inward-looking ethnic language-speaking "heartlanders." So in celebrating Hokkien in his films, Royston Tan invites his audiences to join together in challenging the state's efforts to promote a homogenizing nationalism.

II

China's use of film to tell the world its story has a long history. As early as 1935, the pro-Nationalist United China studio released *The Song of China* (*Tianlun*, dir. Luo Mingyou and Fei Mu, 1935), a big-budget film celebrating the Chinese tradition of filial piety, to the global market. However, it is not known whether it was publicly shown in the US or any major European cities. In 1954, Premier Zhou Enlai took the newly made opera film *Butterfly Lovers* (*Liang Shanbo yu Zhu Yingtai*, dir. Sang Hu, 1954) to the Geneva Conference as an example to the Western world of China's desire for peace. The film was shown afterward around the Soviet Bloc countries. Chinese soft power increased its global reach after the 2000s.

The issue of Chinese soft power is addressed most directly by Katherine Chu in her discussion of the *Wolf Warrior 2* (*Zhan lang 2*, dir. Wu Jing, 2017), *Amazing China* (*Lihaile, Wode guo*, dir. Wei Tie, 2018), *My People, My Country* (*Wo he wo de zuguo*, dir. Ning Hao, Xu Zheng, Guan Hu, Chen Kaige, Zhang Yibai, Wen Muye, Xue Xiaolu, 2019) films in Chapter 12, noting their great box-office success in the Chinese market and, while acknowledging that such propaganda-heavy films will have difficulty generating positive attention abroad, nevertheless concludes that their positive reception in the Chinese market signifies a victory for Chinese foreign policy and demonstrates China's future soft-power potential. However, one could easily argue the opposite, that these films not only will not promote Chinese soft power but, going further, that using film to promote Chinese soft power internationally is far from the country's highest priority for its film industry. These films are made almost exclusively for the domestic market, with little expectation that they will have appeal beyond China—except for the Chinese Diaspora, particularly Chinese students abroad. For example, according to Box Office Mojo, *Amazing China* made all of its box office of $72.5 million inside China;[2] moreover, the reviews outside China suggested that the domestic box office was based on the requirement that audiences were forced to see it.[3] *My People, My Country* made 99.1 percent of its $450 million box office inside China.[4] If one were to make a soft-power argument, it would therefore be more persuasive to suggest that the primary focus of Chinese soft power is on its domestic audience, since the hierarchy of values promoted by the Chinese Communist Party places political and social stability, patriotism, and the defense of China's core interests at the top. Getting foreigners to *like* China is much less important than *influencing the behavior* of foreign governments so they will not take any measures opposed to Chinese interests. In this sense, film has not been a successful weapon in promoting Chinese soft power abroad. Virtually all Chinese films make over 90 percent of their box office within the China market, most often over 95 percent.[5]

The basic problem China faces in its attempt to use film to promote its soft power is that Chinese film policies are inherently contradictory. Film is expected to be multifunctional, but these functions can at times be mutually exclusive. To take an obvious example, in March 2019 *Variety* reported on Wang Xiaohui, executive deputy director of the Central Propaganda Department and director of the National Film Bureau, at the first nationwide film industry symposium under the new administrative structure:

The Chinese government has exhorted filmmakers to turn the country into a "strong film power" like the U.S. by 2035 and called for the production of 100 movies a year that each earn more than RMB100 million ($15 million) as part of a push to increase China's soft power.... They should take "the Chinese dream of the great rejuvenation of the Chinese nation" as their theme and have "patriotic plots." Filmmakers "must have a clear ideological bottom line and cannot challenge the political system."[6]

Similar comments have come from other top leaders, adding that Chinese films should emphasize "socialist core values."[7] Wang also suggested that the international influence of Chinese film has a long way to go, noting that American films in 2018 took in $2.8 billion in the China market, while Chinese films in the US market made only a few tens of millions.[8] However, it is difficult to envision films that promote the China Dream and socialist core values performing well on the international market.

If films made almost exclusively for a Chinese audience are not likely to promote Chinese soft power, the medium of coproductions has far more potential in this regard. Indeed, for many years the large majority of the top ten Chinese films in overseas markets were coproductions, although most of them were coproductions with Hong Kong. Fortuitously, Qi Ai's Chapter 11 on Feng Xiaogang's *Big Shot's Funeral* (*Dawan*, 2001) as a Sino-American coproduction and Chapter 6 by Wendy Su on *Wolf Totem* (*Lang tuteng*, dir. Jean-Jacques Annaud, 2015) as a transnational coproduction with a leading French director can be taken together as reasonably good examples of an unsuccessful and a relatively successful coproduction. As an early example of a coproduction with a major Hollywood studio and a Western star (Donald Sutherland), *Big Shot's Funeral* was influential, particularly with its emphasis on commercialization and the use of product placement, but the influence was primarily felt within China, where it made virtually all of its $51 million; the box office in North America was limited to $820 since it was released in only two theaters for six days.[9] On the other hand, it did pave the way for other high profile Chinese films to seek overseas markets through the use of Hollywood stars, as Zhang Yimou did with *The Flowers of War* (*Jinling shisan chai*, dir. Zhang Yimou, 2011), starring Christian Bale in a major role, and as Feng Xiaogang did with *Back to 1942* (*Yi jiu si er*, dir. Feng Xiaogang, 2012), using Tim Robbins and Adrien Brody in relatively minor roles. As with *Big Shot's Funeral*, neither of these films had international success, which is not surprising since both films are period pieces about wartime events in China that are unfamiliar to foreign audiences. As the China market has risen to become the largest market outside North America, Hollywood has employed a similar strategy, inserting Chinese actors into major productions, for example placing Donnie Yen and Jiang Wen in relatively important roles in *Rogue One: A Star Wars Story* (dir. Gareth Edwards, 2016), again with very limited returns. While *Rogue One: A Star Wars Story* made over a billion dollars worldwide, only 6.5 percent of that total came from China.[10]

By these standards, *Wolf Totem* can be viewed as a coproduction success, but the results also showed the limitations of the coproduction model. As Su persuasively argues, most coproductions are unsuccessful, but *Wolf Totem* had some very important advantages that distinguished it from other, less successful efforts. It was based on a very popular Chinese novel with a story about sent-down youth in Mongolia during the Cultural Revolution, giving it deep roots in recent Chinese history and culture, but in addition to the historical and cultural specificity, it was also attractive because of its focus on ecological consciousness and environmental protection, themes with a universal appeal. The Chinese authorities chose a world-renowned director known for his work with animals, provided him with major resources, and allowed him to have control over the final cut, highly unusual for any state-supported Chinese film. The film also altered the novel in significant ways to make it more appealing to an international audience. The result was a film that made over $125 million, albeit 88 percent of the box office came from screenings in China, with France the second largest market at $8.8 million, and generating only about $210,000 in North America, the world's largest market and the focus of Chinese efforts to compete with Hollywood.[11] One could reasonably argue that regardless of the box-office results outside China, *Wolf Totem* could be considered a success because it was helpful in promoting China's overseas image and its soft power, and demonstrated that China could work successfully with its foreign partners and produce quality work. All that said, the film was released in 2015 and much has changed since then, including the increased emphasis on film as propaganda, the spectacular growth of the domestic film market—making the need for overseas success much less important—and the increasing challenges to globalization and transnational cinema in a world where the rise of nationalism has made such cooperation much more difficult. The level of Chinese government tolerance and flexibility that made this coproduction possible may be difficult to achieve under current conditions.

Notes

1. Trinh T. Minh-ha, *Woman, Native, Other: Writing Postcoloniality and Feminism* (Bloomington: Indiana University Press, 1989).
2. Box Office Mojo by IMDbPro, "*Amazing China*," accessed September 16, 2021, https://www.boxofficemojo.com/title/tt8081062/.
3. "Xi Jinping Propaganda Film Breaks Box Office Records in China—Because Citizens Have to Watch It," *The Telegraph* (UK), March 17, 2018, accessed September 28, 2021, https://web.archive.org/web/20180319100926/https://www.telegraph.co.uk/news/2018/03/17/xi-jinping-propaganda-film-breaks-box-office-records-china/.
4. Box Office Mojo by IMDbPro, "*My People, My Country*," accessed September 16, 2021, https://www.boxofficemojo.com/title/tt10147382/.
5. Box Office Mojo by IMDbPro, multiple dates.

6. Rebecca Davis, "China Aims to Become 'Strong Film Power' Like U.S. by 2035, Calls for More Patriotic Films," *Variety*, March 3, 2019, https://variety.com/2019/film/news/china-strong-film-power-by-2035-wants-more-patriotic-films-1203153901/.

7. Hannah Beech, "China Morality Censors Take Aim at the Country's Film Industry," *Time*, August 30, 2016, accessed on September 28, 2021, https://time.com/4472084/china-film-industry-censorship/.

8. Rebecca Davis, *Variety*, see footnote 6.

9. Box Office Mojo by IMDbPro, "*Big Shot's Funeral*," accessed September 28, 2021, https://www.boxofficemojo.com/title/tt0287934/?ref_=bo_se_r_1.

10. Box Office Mojo by IMDbPro, "*Rogue One: A Star Wars Story*," accessed September 28, 2021, https://www.boxofficemojo.com/title/tt3748528/?ref_=bo_se_r_1.

11. Box Office Mojo by IMDbPro, "*Wolf Totem*," accessed September 16, 2021, https://www.boxofficemojo.com/title/ tt2909116/.

Contributors

(In alphabetical order)

Qi Ai is a postdoctoral fellow in the Department of Media and Communication Studies at Shandong University, China, where he is also the associate director of the Research Center for Culture, Art and Communication of Film and Teleplay (CACFT). He is a member of the Shandong Film Association. He holds a PhD in film and television studies from the University of Nottingham, UK. His research interests primarily include genre studies, film industries and regulation, and Chinese contemporary commercial cinema.

Jing Jing Chang is an associate professor of film studies at Wilfrid Laurier University, Canada. She is the author of *Screening Communities: Negotiating Narratives of Empire, Nation, and the Cold War in Hong Kong Cinema* (2019). Her current research explores the sexual politics of Hong Kong cinema since the 1970s.

Katherine Chu is an adjunct faculty at California State University, Dominguez Hills. Her research focuses on using comparative methods to gain insight into the relationship between films and politics. She is particularly interested in understanding the shared patterns and potential cultural and social characteristics in the evolution of discourse power in authoritarian regimes. Recently, her work is focused on unraveling the origin and evolution of soft-power discourse in China's film industry.

Lin Feng is an associate professor in the Department of Film Studies and the director of studies of history of art and film at the University of Leicester. She is a senior fellow of the UK Higher Education Academy. Her research interests include Chinese cinemas, East Asian film history, and transnational popular screen cultures. She is the author of *Chow Yun-fat and Territories of Hong Kong Stardom* (2017) and co-editor of *Renegotiating Film Genres in East Asian Cinemas and Beyond* (2020).

Po-Shek Fu is a professor of history at the University of Illinois at Urbana-Champaign. His current research focuses on film history, Cold War cultural history, and the interaction between war and culture. He has received several national fellowships, including from the Institute for Advanced Study in Princeton and the

Fulbright Scholar Program. His recent English publications are *The Cold War and Asian Cinemas* (2019), *China Forever: Shaw Brothers and Diasporic Cinema* (2008), and *Between Shanghai and Hong Kong: The Politics of Chinese Cinemas* (2003).

Alison M. Groppe teaches modern Chinese literature, film, and popular culture at the University of Oregon. She specializes in literary and cinematic representations of identity, Sinophone and Chinese literature and film, and world literature. Her recent publications include *Sinophone Malaysian Literature: Not Made in China* (2013) and chapters in *A Companion to World Literature* (2020), *A New Literary History of China* (2017), and *Sinophone Cinemas* (2014).

Belinda Q. He is an assistant professor of East Asian and cinema and media studies at the University of Maryland. Previously, she was a lecturer in film and media studies at the University of Oklahoma and a CCS postdoctoral fellow at UC Berkeley. She received her PhD in cinema and media studies from the University of Washington. Dr. He's research engages the role of film, photography, and video in policing, shaming, and punishing in Global Asian and especially socialist contexts. Her in-progress project has been supported by the Andrew Mellon Foundation, the Library of Congress, and the Asia Art Archive. Her work appears in the *Journal of Chinese Cinemas* and *The Child in World Cinema*, among others.

Yushi Hou is a PhD student in the Film Department at the University of Southampton. Her research interests include Chinese cinema, film noir, genre studies, and cinematic space. She is currently working on a book on urban space in contemporary Chinese neo-noir.

Jeff Kyong-McClain is a historian and director of the Idaho Asia Institute at the University of Idaho. His research focuses on the history of Sino-American educational cooperation, academic disciplines in modern China, and Christianity in Sichuan, and has appeared, among other places, in *Twentieth-Century China*, *Social Sciences and Missions* and *Chinese America: History and Perspectives*. He is co-editor of *Chinese History in Geographical Perspective* (with Yongtao Du, 2013).

Joseph Tse-Hei Lee is a professor of history and the director of the Global Asia Institute at Pace University, New York. His research focuses on Christianity in modern China. He is the editor of *Hong Kong and Bollywood: Globalization of Asian Cinemas* (with Satish Kolluri, 2016), and the author of *The Bible and the Gun: Christianity in South China, 1860–1900* (2003) and *Context and Vision: Visualizing Chinese-Western Cultural Encounters in Chaoshan* (with Christie Chui-Shan Chow, 2017).

Shiying Liu is a PhD candidate in the Department of Culture, Media and Visual Studies at the University of Nottingham. Her PhD is funded by the China Scholarship Council (CSC). Her thesis analyzes the development of the China Film Co., Ltd., and films it produced in the 2010s. She holds an MA degree in film studies from the

University College London where she developed her research interests in Chinese film industries, political cinema, and global cinema.

Xi W. Liu is a PhD candidate in the School of East Asian Studies at the University of Sheffield. Her current research project focuses on Chinese film aesthetics, *yijing* theory, and affect theory, conducting a dialogue between Deleuzian philosophy and Chinese film studies. Xi's research is highly interdisciplinary and draws on a variety of fields including Chinese cinema, Buddhism, affect studies, and critical theory.

Russell Meeuf is a professor in the School of Journalism and Mass Media at the University of Idaho, where he also directs the Film and Television program. His research often explores the transnational dynamics of cinema and popular culture. Among other work on film and celebrity culture, he is the co-editor of *Transnational Stardom: International Celebrity in Film and Popular Culture* (with Raphael Raphael, 2013) and *Projecting the World: Representing the "Foreign" in Classical Hollywood* (with Anna Cooper, 2017).

Kenny Kwok Kwan Ng is an associate professor at the Academy of Film, Hong Kong Baptist University. His published books include *The Lost Geopoetic Horizon of Li Jieren: The Crisis of Writing Chengdu in Revolutionary China* (2015); *Indiescape Hong Kong: Interviews and Essays* (with Enoch Tam and Vivian Lee, 2018) [Chinese]; *Yesterday, Today, Tomorrow: Hong Kong Cinema with Sino-links in Politics, Art, and Tradition* (2021) [Chinese]. His ongoing book projects concern censorship and visual cultural politics in Cold War Hong Kong and Asia, the politics of Cantonese cinema, and left-wing cosmopolitanism.

Stanley Rosen is a professor of political science and international relations at the University of Southern California. He is the co-editor of *Soft Power with Chinese Characteristics: China's Campaign for Hearts and Minds* (2020) and is currently co-editing *Chinese Politics: The Xi Jinping Difference*. He is the co-editor of the journal *Chinese Education and Society* and an associate editor of the journal *Global Media and China*.

Wendy Su is an associate professor in the Department of Media and Cultural Studies at University of California Riverside. She is the author of *China's Encounter with Global Hollywood: Cultural Policy and the Film Industry, 1994–2013* (2016), and co-editor of *Asia-Pacific Film Co-productions: Theory, Industry and Aesthetics* (2019).

Man-Fung Yip is an associate professor of Film and Media Studies at the University of Oklahoma. He is the author of *Martial Arts Cinema and Hong Kong Modernity: Aesthetics, Representation, Circulation* (2017) and co-editor of *American and Chinese-Language Cinemas: Examining Cultural Flows* (2015) and *The Cold War and Asian Cinemas* (2020). His work has also appeared in *Cinema Journal* (now *Journal of Cinema and Media Studies*) and numerous edited volumes.

Index